The Mountaineer
New York, Ontario & Western Railway

To The Mountains by Rail

To The Mountains by Rail

Manville B. Wakefield

Foreword by Irwin Richman

PURPLE MOUNTAIN PRESS
Fleischmanns, New York

people, events and tragedies...
the New York, Ontario and Western Railway and the famous Sullivan County resorts

> **DUST JACKET**
>
> The Mountaineer, an oil painting by the author, features the last "name" train operated by the New York, Ontario and Western Railway in 1938. The setting, near Livingston Manor, shows a typical 1920 stucco-covered, "Mission-era" resort hotel with its crescented falsefront decoration and the omnipresent handball court.

Copyright © 1970 Manville B. Wakefield

First published by Wakefair Press 1970

Second edition by Wakefair Press 1976

Third edition by Purple Mountain Press 1989

Library of Congress Catalog Card Number
76-120749

All rights reserved. No part of this publication may be reproduced or transmitted in any form without permission in writing from the publisher, except by a reviewer who wishes to quote brief passages in connection with a review written for inclusion in a magazine, newspaper or broadcast.

Purple Mountain Press, Ltd.
Main Street, P.O. Box E-3
Fleischmanns, New York 12430
914-254-4062

ISBN: 0-935796-13-4

Printed in the United States of America

To
My Grandsons
Anthony and Andrew

Hotel signs that once hung under platform roof.   *Courtesy O. & W. Station Tavern*

Acknowledgments

It was a cold winter's night by the hearthside in the cozy home of Vincent and Marge Roy, high atop the Shawangunks at Cragsmoor, that the first seeds of this book were sown. "Vince's" all-persuasive enthusiam and eternal optimism set the course that friendly night seemingly so long ago.

Vince is gone now but others emerged to demonstrate enthusiasm and encouragement. Dr. Irwin Richman of the History Department of the Pennsylvania State University for content work on the manuscript; Inez G. Gridley, Historian, Town of Neversink; Professors Shirley and Owen Davis and Professor Richard Tobey, Sullivan County Community College, all for endless hours of editing and consultation.

From the technical standpoint, the photo-copy work of my good friend, the late Fred Lewis; my esteemed colleague, L. Jack Agnew, whose long hours in the darkroom manifests itself in the exceptional historic photographic content and Thomas Ambrosino whose graphic technical acumen always stood ready to advise (and did) during the critical dummy preparation phase. Also the darkroom assistance of author-historian and crack railroad photographer, Jim Shaughnessy, and the general assistance of Mr. and Mrs. Bruce Denman, Jr. and Mr. and Mrs. Paul DeWire.

In the early phases of research I am indebted to Mr. Herbert Finch, Curator and Archivist of the Collection of Regional History and University Archives at the Olin Research Library, Cornell University, Ithaca, N.Y., Miss. Barbara Shepherd and other cooperative staff members.

To Oscar O. Bennett of Hancock, a retired O. and W. engineer whose constant readiness to assist and clear recall of operating experiences brings those bygone days clearly into focus; to Miss Laura Clements, Mrs. David Clements and Mr. and Mrs. Paul Allen for their nostalgic reminiscences of the early boardinghouse days. To Alan and Monte Steingart, of Steingart Associates, for access to their irreplaceable hotel photographic files and their father, the late Nat Steingart, who contributed much anecdotal commentary to the graphic record. Also sincere appreciation to Supreme Court Justice Lawrence H. Cooke and noted O. and W. photographer, John P. Ahrens.

To Mr. and Mrs. L. Komitzky of Hurleyville for copies from the rare Howard Wood negative collection of boardinghouse and O. and W. subjects. John Allen and the late Eli Atwell of Mountaindale and W. Ray Elmore, James Garvin and Mrs. E.T. Bradford for access to their respective collections of "Summer Homes." To Dewey Borden for his colorful 'firemanic' recollections and Liberty's Ontario Hose Company No. 3 for access to their comprehensive fire photo collection. Also the Monticello Fire Department and Walter Smith for reference to their unique fire photo collection.

Rev. Robert Houghtaling, Historian, Town of Fallsburg; Miss Martha Schidell, Historian, Town of Callicoon; Mrs. Alberta Tyler, Historian, Town of Cochecton; the late Gladys Durland, Historian, Town of Thompson; Herbert Mussman, Historian, Town of Rockland;

Arthur N. Meyers, Historian, Town of Tusten and James Burbank, Jack Stellwagen, and Muriel VanOrden whose collections deposited in the archives of the Sullivan County Historical Museum have been of inestimable value.

Access to the 'classic' photo and memorabilia collection of Gerald M. Best of Beverly Hills, California. To Miss Katherine "K.T." Terwilliger, Historian, Village of Ellenville and Mrs. Marion Dumond, Librarian and the Trustees of the Ellenville Public Library and Museum for reference to their historical archives. To Charles King, Publisher, Middletown *Times Herald-RECORD* for statistical O. and W. data.

To the multifarious assistance of Alice C. Muller, Wilfred F. Smith, William Capach, Mrs. Benjamin Bertholf, Mrs. Bruce Denman, Sr., Mrs. James Cusator, Joshua Gerow, Jr., the late George B. Smith, John Pevese, Harold Maas, Del VanEtten, Mrs. Leonard Sherwood, Mrs. Medwin Benton, Mrs. Fanny Edwards, John Joyner, Eugene Hanofee, Paul Gerry, Harold Schue, George Yaeger, the late Herbert Sprague, Dick Rosenbaum, Editor, Liberty *Register*, Rev. John Carter, Tom Masterson, Louise Stengel, Chester P. "Phip" Stanton, Kenneth Godfrey, Supervisor, Town of Mamakating, Joseph Lloyd, Mrs. Anne Lasher, Supervisor and Mrs. Joseph Raffa, Town of Neversink, the late John Knight, Bruce Fuller, Kitty and John McKenna, Joe Rider, Eli Kagen, and Mr. and Mrs. 'Perk' Jacobson.

Also Elsie Winterberger, Arlene LaPinsky, Harold Harris, Leslie C. Wood, Editor, The *Evening News,* Milton Kutsher, the late Miss Nellie White, Daniel Scribner, Abe Jacobs, Abe Goldstein, Don Battey, Editor, Livingston Manor *Times,* Paul Denman, Mrs. Maida Black and Joel Pettingill, Curator, The Harry Resnick Motor Museum. To Bob Rosch and Bill Weston of the O. and W. Station Tavern.

Particular appreciation to Gilbert O. Schmidt, Director, Sullivan County Tax Map Department, for access to June, 1964 aerial views of Sullivan County.

For complete cooperation and understanding during production, a sincere thank you to Jerry McCreary, Wally Boltz, Hal Batsch, Terry Fackler and Charles Dilsner.

But most certainly to my wife Barbara whose complete understanding and assistance with details also permitted the process of research, manuscript writing and delineation of maps and illustrative art to invade the carefree atmosphere of three successive summer vacations; a most humble and sincere, *Thank You.*

Manville B. Wakefield

Wakefair
Grahamsville, New York

May, 1970

Contents

Maps.. XIII

Aerial Views.. XIII

Foreword, *Irwin Richman* XV

1. INTRODUCTION...1

2. TO THE MOUNTAINS by RAIL, Weehawken to Bloomingburg......19

3. HIGH VIEW, Bloomingburg...29

4. HIGH VIEW TUNNEL...45

5. MAMAKATING, Wurtsboro...51

6. SUMMITVILLE..63

7. MOUNTAINDALE, Sandburg......................................75

8. CENTERVILLE, Woodridge..87

9. FALLSBURGH, South Fallsburgh.................................97

10. KIAMESHA LAKE, Pleasant Lake................................111

11. MONTICELLO..119

12. FALLSBURGH, Old Falls..139

13. WOODBOURNE..147

14. GRAHAMSVILLE 153

15. LUZON, Hurleyville 161

16. LOCH SHELDRAKE 179

17. FERNDALE, Liberty Falls. 193

18. LIBERTY, The Era of the Great Hotels. 213

19. LIBERTY, The Great 1913 Fire and After. 249

20. WHITE SULPHUR SPRINGS, Robertsonville 261

21. JEFFERSONVILLE 269

22. WHITE LAKE. 277

23. SWAN LAKE, Stevensville 289

24. NEVERSINK 295

25. PARKSVILLE 301

26. LIVINGSTON MANOR 319

27. ROSCOE, Rockland 335

28. ROSCOE WEST 345

29. EPILOGUE 377

Notes 393

Bibliography 405

Index 411

MAPS

Bloomingburg to Summitville 30

Summitville to Woodridge 64

Woodridge to Hurleyville 88

Hurleyville to Young's Gap 162

Young's Gap to Hazel 302

Hazel to Butternut Grove (Delaware Co.) 336

Butternut Grove to Hancock 346-347

Official O & W Maps (Circa 1908)

    System-wide map 390
    Sullivan County 391
    Delaware County 392
    Ulster County 410

AERIAL VIEWS
County survey flown, June 1964

High View - Bloomingburg 31

High View Tunnel 46

Wurtsboro 52

Summitville 65

Mountaindale 77

Woodridge 89

Neversink Crossing — Fallsburgh Tunnel 94

South Fallsburgh 98

Kiamesha Lake 113

Monticello 120

Hurleyville 163

Ferndale 194

Liberty 214

White Lake 281

Parksville 303

Livingston Manor 321

Roscoe 337

Graphs, by Tom Ambrosino 308-309

All line work and maps by author. Photographs without credits by or from author's personal collection.

Foreword

Vicariously or experientially, I have lived through much of the development of the resort industry of Sullivan County. My grandfather, Abraham Richman, began coming to Sullivan County, "the Mountains," in the summers just two years after he arrived in America from Russia. Many of his tales ranging back over sixty odd years are family folklore. His stories of low prices and huge meals and of hotels that no longer exist are the stuff of which nostalgia is made. He is also full of anecdotes — about the time two lady hotel proprietors (both of whose hotels still exist) had a feud on a village street, punctuating their loud, colorful remarks with barrages of eggs.

My earliest memories of the hotels go back to accompanying my grandfather from place to place when he, as President of Congregation B'nai Israel of Woodbourne, made his annual solicitation of funds on behalf of the synagogue. My maternal grandmother used to go to hotels for her vacations. I used to visit her there, and often stayed for lunch or dinner. As a teenager I remember the thrill of sneaking into the casino of some hotel to see the show on a Friday or Saturday night.

But hotels have always been tangential to my resort experience. I spent my summers in the midst of a small bungalow colony. My grandfather got tired of hotels, boarding houses, and roominghouses. About a year before I was born he decided on a place of his own for him and his family. As a result he built a house then added a few bungalows. My mother still operates the place today. I grew up knowing many people in the bungalow business and I know the annual anguish of "Will we rent before the season?"

I witnessed firsthand the great changes in the resort industry during the 1950's and 1960's. I saw the rise of the swimming pool as an essential (in the 1940's only the biggest hotels had them), the evolution of the hotel nightclub with shows every night, the appearance of the bungalow colony day camp (I worked at them for many summers), and more importantly the decline of the small hotel and the small bungalow colony — their ghosts haunt every hill.

When Wake told me he was writing a book about the resort industry and the O. and W., I was delighted because of the prospect of learning more about the railroad. Manville B. Wakefield is a rail buff par excellence. Few memories of the O. and W. came to me through the family. While they all made trips on the line, they were motor car people, and could recall the routine 7 and 8 hour (and the 12 hour "special") trips up. Reading about the O. and W. has given me a new insight into the development of the resort industry of Sullivan County and provided the answer to the question, why here? Wake takes you over the O. and W. stop by stop and anecdote by anecdote.

Sullivan County is unique, and even though I no longer can spend my entire summers there, it still draws me back for weekends. It is a land of tinsel and *chutzpa*. The O. and W's ancestor never knew what it was starting when it issued its first edition of *Summer Homes in the Mountains* in 1878.

Irwin Richman

Capitol Campus
The Pennsylvania State University
Middletown, Pennsylvania

Fort Delaware, a faithful reconstruction of an early Delaware valley fort originally built by the Connecticut Company pioneers who settled the valley in 1754. The brainchild of James Burbank, Sullivan County's first historian, the fort is a prime tourist attraction in the Delaware valley. *Photograph by L. Jack Agnew*

Introduction

Remains of the Snyder & Bushnell Tannery in Claryville.

In the summer of 1754 the shadowy stillness of the vast hemlock forests of the upper Delaware Valley was broken by the movements of two men from Preston, Connecticut – Joseph Skinner and Moses Thomas. These two pioneers, both future proprietors of the Delaware Company, were staking out what was to become the Cushetunk[1] Settlement – the first recorded community established by the white man in the upper Delaware valley. The contemporary map spelling of Cushetunk, "Cochecton," is applied to a tiny hamlet that was settled by white men before the French and Indian War (1754-1763) ended and became the heart of the territory settled by the intrepid adventurers who followed the trail blazed by Skinner and Thomas. These ambitious Yankees from Connecticut under provisions of the Delaware Company Charter are largely responsible for the settlement and development of the County of Sullivan.

The Mamakating region near present-day Wurtsboro was settled for the most part by Dutchmen and the religious and political freedom-seeking Huguenots; while the Cushetunk region was settled by energetic Yankees who had already earned and established their religious freedom but were then organized for the purpose of expanding their mother colony. The hearty Cushetunk pioneers entered the Delaware valley by a trail from Kingston, up the Rondout Creek through Chestnut Woods (Grahamsville), Blue Mountain (Liberty) and thence down to the valley of the Delaware. Just what date the first migration of settlers took place is not known, but records kept by the Skinner family indicate that several men, together with their wives, children and household effects, were on the land by 1757.

The route followed by the Connecticut Company settlers up the Rondout followed the pioneer American "Road" – the near legendary trail called the Old Mine Road. About 1650 an adventurous band of Dutchmen built the road for the carting of copper ore mined at Pahquarry-on-the-Delaware, just above the Delaware Water Gap, up the Mamakating valley to Esopus (Kingston) for shipment to Holland for refining. Just north of Wurtsboro along this old road is found the grave of the father of the first white man to settle in Sullivan County, Emanuel Gonsalus, who died while visiting his son, Emanuel Gonsalus, Jr., in 1752. The log house which nestled in this verdant valley was a stopping place for travelers and

1

drovers along the Old Mine Road.

Not only did the paths of the pioneer Connecticut Company and the copper-bearing Dutchmen overlap at the northern end of the Rondout valley, but also brushed again in the Delaware valley below Mackhackemeck (Port Jervis).

The first significant development period in the county began in 1764 when Daniel Skinner took the first raft of logs down the Delaware River to Philadelphia. As soon as raftsmen became numerous enough to gain a reputation, Daniel Skinner was constituted "Lord High Admiral" over all the rafting navigation on the Delaware and it was adopted as "law" that no one was free to go on a raft without his sanction. This could be obtained only by treating Skinner with a bottle of wine on two occasions: the first time they went on a raft to Philadelphia as a forehand and another bottle the first time they steered. When this was complied with they were authorized to navigate a raft on the waters of the Delaware in any channel except at Betch. If they ran this, they forfeited another bottle.

The Delaware valley and rafting also stimulated the moving of bluestone. This natural product of the Sullivan hills was used extensively for sidewalks and curbing in New York City. Also known as flagstone, its ability to withstand the abuse of steel-tired horsedrawn vehicles helped to prolong quarrying operations long after concrete had largely replaced the use of stone. Even this terminal use of "flag" was to pass with the import of the more durable granite from the South. Folk songs like "The Bluestone Quarry" recall this phase of the county's heritage.

One of the largest quarrying operations and one of the last to survive was Manny and Ross. Located at Hankins, the firm was started by the partnership of Anthony Manny of Jeffersonville and a man named Ross at Hankins whose fate remains obscure. Later Manny sold out to the Kenny Brothers – Edward, Patrick and John – who came to Long Eddy in 1889. The records indicate that during their management over $3,000,000 worth of bluestone went to market. The largest flagstone ever quarried in the valley was cut at Pond Eddy, floated to Philadelphia, then shipped by boat to New York City to be placed in front of City Hall.

In 1801 the Newburgh-Cochecton Turnpike was chartered by businessmen from Sullivan and Orange counties. Its completion in 1809 connected central Sullivan to the Hudson River port of

Rafting down the Delaware on a relatively calm day - a dramatic contrast to the jam that occurred in the spring of 1876. "On Thursday morning last," the contemporary press reported, "the lumbermen along the Delaware were rejoiced at the coming of the looked-for freshet. Rafting had been going on with activity for weeks and every eddy from the head of the river down was filled with rafts, ready to pull out. Thursday, these all started on their journey and the river was so crowded that many rafts wrecked on bridge piers, islands and shoals. Many rafts went to pieces and thousands of dollars damage was done. Rafts piled on top of one another and dove beneath, thundered and crashed beyond description. Below, the river was filled with detached lumber of all kinds which kept boats and shore watchers busy securing." *Sullivan County Museum Archives*

A rare photograph of raft building activities on the Delaware at Narrowsburg in 1890 just after the ice has moved out leaving the shore lined with chunks stranded by the high water of spring freshets. The smallest rafts built were started on small streams as "cribs," five cribs coupled together as the stream increased in size formed a "colt," two colts a "raft" and two rafts a "fleet." *Courtesy, John Pavese, Century Hotel*

Newburgh. More settlers and the products of the land now began to move across the East-West route. This pioneer turnpike which connected on the West with the Cochecton and Great Bend Turnpike in Pennsylvania soon became the major artery of Sullivan County commerce.

The pike was also instrumental in the building of the first covered bridge in New York State at Bridgeville. This 160-foot crossing of the Neversink River was built in 1807 by an Orange County farmer, Major Salmon Wheat, and miraculously withstood the elements for 116 years. It was demolished in 1923 after being replaced by an iron bridge. Major Wheat also built the covered bridge crossing the Delaware at Cochecton where the pike connected with the Cochecton and Great Bend Turnpike. His 1819 one-pier effort at this point met with disaster when it collapsed of its own weight after standing only a few months. His second span stood successfully until the great spring flood of 1846 when the western pier was undermined and fell, together with the Pennsylvania and middle spans. Whatever his later failures, Wheat's historical reputation rests on his triumph at Bridgeville for the Newburgh-Cochecton Turnpike Company. His accomplishment was commemorated in 1966 when the Sullivan County Historical Society adopted a drawing of the bridge as the central motif of its official emblem and later had the site marked with an historical marker sign.

The sixty mile Newburgh-Cochecton Turnpike, capitalized at $126,000, was built in the days when there was not enough public capital to expend on highways or the machinery available to implement the project. There was, however, an abundance of human labor, vast stands of forests, and the inefficient up-and-down sawmills which stood on every stream of any size and made planks readily available for any route desired. The turnpike twisted and turned to avoid the heavier grades and swamps; but where the obstacles were not too difficult, the road's survey was almost arrow-straight. Huge hand-made freight wagons carried tanbark, hand split hemlock shingles, charcoal, potash, butter firkins, barrel staves and hoops, grain scoops and shovels laboriously fashioned from hardwood by hand. When the teams lumbered westward, the merchandise on board was

A typical flagstone yard showing the kingpin derrick for lifting the ponderous slabs. By the 1880's the flagstone industry was fast supplementing and in many cases outgrowing the lumber interests on the Delaware. Rough roads for quite some time stagnated the stone business rendering it impossible to market the output of the quarries. Harry Keyes, operator of the gang saws (standing just under the angled boom) could cut about 10 inches an hour in bluestone and 16 inches an hour in limestone. *Courtesy, Mrs. Alberta Tyler*

Ice cutting on the Delaware downstream from the Narrowsburg covered bridge. The structure, originally chartered in 1830, was built in 1832 and collapsed in 1836, a victim of high flood waters. Promptly rebuilt, the 250 foot long - 32 foot wide structure (shown here) was flood-proofed by increasing its height to 35 feet above the low-water mark. Built by Eliphalet S. Rose, the timbers 40 to 60 feet long were hewn with an ax and taken from the upper end of Swamp Mill Pond. They were then floated down to the lower end of the pond, and loaded upon wagons to be hauled by a four-horse team, which made only two trips a day. The bridge was demolished intentionally to make way for an iron bridge of greater capacity. *Photograph by E. H. Decker, Narrowsburg; Sullivan County Museum Archives*

The Cochecton covered bridge crossing of the Delaware, the key link between the western end of the Newburgh-Cochecton Turnpike and the Cochecton and Great Bend Turnpike in Pennsylvania. The flood of 1902 took out the bridge leaving only the abutment and piers, left. This was the location of two covered bridge failures by Major Salmon Wheat, designer of the first covered bridge in New York State at Bridgeville. Top, *Sullivan County Museum Archives.*

gathered from the nation and world markets — spices, sugar, coffee, tea, hardware, molasses, woodmen's tools, farm tools and implements, nails, blasting powder, iron pots, and kettles as well as tinware, barrels of coal oil and whiskey — everything for the growing communities in Sullivan County.

The year 1827 saw the opening of the Delaware and Hudson Canal with its coal-laden boats floating under the Newburgh-Cochecton Turnpike at Rome. This classically named town was later to be christened Wurtsboro in honor of Maurice Wurts, one of the planners and builders of the waterway.

The juncture of canal and turnpike made possible the rise of Sullivan County's first real basic industry — tanning.

To assure the seventeen-mile lock-free Summit Level a sufficient water supply during the early fall boating season when normal feeders were generally low, the canal company built four large reservoirs which were named McKee's Pond, Yankee Lake, Wolf Pond, and Lords Pond. The last of these was very close to the Newburgh-Cochecton Pike and it was here at the pond's spillway that a Mr. Lord built the first Sullivan County tannery.

The tanning industry grew rapidly, enjoying a stature challenged by few other counties in the state or nation. This growth was obviously due to the seemingly inexhaustible hemlock forest, but location also played its role. The tanning and transportation costs were so minimal that it was economically feasible to send hides to Sullivan County from as far away as Argentina. The coming

A light boat waiting to enter Lock 71 on its three lock approach to the Delaware Adueduct from the New York side. Lock 72 may be seen in the distance. Note the deck hand at the bilge pump and the bowler topped dandy at the tiller who is, without a doubt, a son of Erin. *From* Coal Boats to Tidewater, *The story of the Delaware and Hudson Canal, Manville B. Wakefield*

of the tanneries launched what one sage described as the "tanbark slaughter." Bark-peelers with their spuds passed through the forests, not unlike the army worm through a cornfield. How wasteful the method was is suggested by a sight in the Town of Callicoon 70 years ago: An area of some 20 acres was strewn with the decaying hemlocks 70 and 80 feet long which lay where they had been dropped perhaps 40 years before. The outer layers had fallen away so that the knots projected several inches. Men armed with single-bitted axes went among the prostrate giants and knocked the knots loose for use in the kitchen range and under the sap pan.

The industry peaked during the Civil War years when over 80 per cent of the boots and leather goods worn by the Union forces were treated in Sullivan County vats. Following the war, with the development of synthetic tannic acid and the inevitable exhaustion of the hemlock stand, the industry declined and the stench of the leaching vats faded away.

During the prime years other tannery-motivated turnpikes were built across the county at various points: the Jeffersonville and Monticello Turnpike, the Mount Hope & Lumberland Turnpike, and the Callicoon Depot & Rockland Turnpike. The lengthy Ulster & Orange Branch Turnpike ran from Morsston, near Livingston Manor, through Parksville, Liberty, Fallsburgh, and Summitville into Orange County.

The natural water level gateway of the Delaware was an obvious access route for the first rail penetration of Sullivan County, and in 1847 the New York and Erie Railway entered Sullivan County at Tusten Depot. The railroad was the miracle worker of 19th Century America and Sullivan County needed its help. It was the railroad

The Bridgeville Covered Bridge crossing of the Neversink River on the route of the Newburgh-Cochecton Turnpike claimed the distinction of being the first covered bridge built in New York State and a reputation for longevity that carried it from 1807 to 1923. The bridge was adopted in 1966, as the theme motif of the Sullivan County Historical Society, based on a design by the author.

This statuesque steamer, left, of the Gould era, agleam with newness, straight out of the erecting shops stands ready for the run up the Delaware River valley, to Sullivan County points and the west. The Roebling Suspension Bridge Aqueduct built in 1848 by John August Roebling for the Delaware and Hudson Canal Co. to speed up the movement of its coal-laden boats from Pennsylvania (background) to New York State and tidewater at Kingston, N.Y. This view shows Lackawaxen across the river and the canal (abandoned) swinging to the right across the river where it passed under the main line of the Erie, just out of the picture, right. The old tow path shows in the foreground paralleling the river beside Otter Eddy. *Left, from* Brass Buttons and Leather Boots, *The Story of Sullivan County and the Civil War; below, from* Coal Boats To Tidewater, *The Story of the Delaware and Hudson Canal, Manville B. Wakefield*

February, 1888, witnessed the demise of all the structures, left to right, up to and including the large Everard House in the worst fire in Callicoons' history. "The fire broke out about one o'clock in the store of A. A. Eichoff, and was soon beyond control, and despite the efforts of the citizens of the village, spread to the large hotel known as the Everard House and kept by E. Everard and from there to the store of O. F. Traynor and to other buildings and before the flames were fully under control, Dycker's house and store, in which the Post Office was kept, Rupert's saloon and house, C. Metzgar's house and the house of S. Mitchell, were destroyed." Middletown *Argus*

At the time of the photograph the Erie tracks were still wide gauge, as dramatically illustrated by the scale of the child standing between the wide spaced rails (center). *Courtesy, Mr. Fred Starck*

The fashionable Erie Hotel at Cochecton, remodeled in 1897 and shown here in 1915, with the motorized livery of hotels at Lake Huntington as well as resorts in Pennsylvania. In its early years the hotel catered to the roustabout raftsmen on their way down the Delaware to Trenton and Philadelphia. The durable old structure burned to the ground in December, 1968. *Courtesy, Mrs. Alberta Tyler*

The spanking new facades of buildings along the main street give the effect of a western movie set. The Everard House has been replaced by the Delaware House and the Erie tracks have been narrowed to the same gauge as the rest of the rapidly spreading rail network of a growing America. *Courtesy, Mr. Fred Starck.*

and its first few station stops[2] which brought the county its first visitors.

A target for many of the adventurous was the area around Lake Huntington. The first innkeepers, of German extraction, arrived in the early 1890's developing the lake into a Teutonic summer paradise. In the ten year period after 1908, the Irish arrived on the scene with the Jews arriving about 1920.

The town's first boarding house, the "Lake Huntington Pond Hotel," owned by Peter Fahrenz, was located on the northern end of the lake and it catered primarily to German boarders. Ownership later passed to Valentine Dittmar. Kraack's Hotel, operated by Charles Kraack on the southern edge of the lake, along the road to Cochecton, was typical of the moderately large boarding houses where wholesome country food was served and where guests from New York, Brooklyn, and New Jersey would spend the entire summer.

But it remained for the spirited John Littlejohn in 1865 to include the "railroad starved" central Sullivan County in his planning for the proposed New York and Oswego Midland Rail Road. After many noisy and frustrating regional meetings the rail project got underway with the last spike driven at a place called "Hell Hole," just east of Westfield Flats (Roscoe), on July 9, 1873.

The years 1871 and 1873 are significant for events that marked the Alpha and the Omega of two great chapters of Sullivan County history. James Quinlan published his classic history in 1873 marking the end of one expansionist period of economic growth, while at the same time passenger trains of the New York and Oswego Midland Rail Road were rolling through the new tunnel opened in 1871 under the Shawangunk Mountains, thus opening the heart of Sullivan County for direct rail service to New York City.

Consummating this opening did not come easily. Bids were let, and the contract for the 3,857 foot tunnel was awarded on October 1, 1868, to Stephens, Bennett & Co. of Oneida. The job was not simple in those early days because a huge hole had to be blasted and dug through Shawangunk grit, Hudson shale, and a troublesome pocket of clay 340 feet below the top of the mountain. The drilling and blasting far from sunlight, went ahead

INTRODUCTION

George B. Mass' Nutshell, a Lake Huntington landmark, when the casino addition had been completed and the horseless carriage was starting to take over from old dobbin. Mrs. George Mass is seated in the rear seat of the car at left along with her daughter, Clara, dressed in white. Standing on railing of porch, center, is musician Lionel Farney, while singers Jack Kelly and Miss Anna May Tunney (sister of fight champ Gene Tunney) stand below the porch railing, left. *Courtesy, Mr. Harold Maas*

The band that played at the Thursday night summertime dances at Kraack's first outdoor dance pavillion (shown in the background). Left to right are Will Kraack, waiter; Charles Kraack, owner; George Merkenschlager, viola; Jacob Keim, first fiddle and caller; and Mike Busch, second fiddle. *Courtesy, Miss Nellie White*

A typical vacation group at Lake Huntington's White House, about 1910. The man with the banjo was the popular Regatta Day strummer, Phil Bresloff. Miss Nellie White, owner-operator standing at the extreme right, recalls, "I made all the upstairs beds sometimes with my brothers' help. I also waited on tables and did all the washing on a washboard and kept the kerosene lamps filled. Later I helped mother with the cooking and baking and eventually took over that chore. It was a lot of work since we always had 30 to 35 boarders at a time." *Courtesy, Miss Nellie White*

Charles Kraack's second hotel at Lake Huntington in 1912 showing the dance hall and the hotel wagon, left, that met the Erie trains at Cochecton. The Piel Brothers beer, advertised on the sign, arrived at the hotel in 400 pound barrels. *Courtesy, Miss Nellie White*

The Cochecton installation of the Standard Oil Company Pipeline, the first long-distance pipeline in America, was built in 1880 and was one of the larger facilities on the rod-wide right-of-way running between the oil fields of Olean, N.Y. and the storage fields at Bayonne, N.J. The Cochecton unit consisted of a pump house, boiler house, shop, an oil tank with a capacity of 35,000 barrels and a coal storage that held 3,000 tons and a smokestack 108 feet tall.

Today only ruins remain - the sturdy stack being demolished in 1936 by removing key bricks from the corners and inserting wedges soaked in oil and set on fire. A charge of dynamite was set off and the whole stack just leaned and then completely crumpled.

In this nostalgic picture the loggers of a simpler time are shown spiking logs down from the river road (today Rt 97) for loading onto Erie railroad gondola cars. *Courtesy, Mrs. Alberta Tyler*

The Temperance Hotel threatened by the flood of January 28, 1887, in Cochecton. In a later flood (March 6, 1902) the hotel was moved 14 feet on one side and 6 feet on the other from its foundation. Most of the men pictured here are old-time raftsmen, among them, George Buck and Nicholas Conklin. This flood, one of the most disastrous in history, resulted from an ice gorge extending from an island below Milanville to Rock Run, inundating the villages of Damascus and Cochecton. *Courtesy, Mrs. Alberta Tyler*

The Century at Narrowsburg, built in 1841 by Abraham Cuddeback and first known as the Narrowsburg Hotel, became a favorite stopping place for all those who traveled the Mount Hope and Lumberland Turnpike. During the years between the Civil War and 1896, while under the proprietorship of John Engelmann, the hotel became a favorite of the raftsmen along the Delaware--so much so that for awhile it was named the Raftsmen Hotel. During the years 1918-29 it was known as the Wayside Inn, named thusly by Harry Sulzbach who leased it from owner Michael Clark. If was officially and publicly renamed Century Hotel by Charles Goeltz who succeeded Tony Werneke. *Courtesy, John Pavese, Century Hotel*

High water on the Delaware threatens the old Pond Eddy suspension bridge on October 9, 1903. Bridge in foreground crosses the abandoned Delaware and Hudson Canal - boat No. 1107 commanded by Capt. Hensberger carrying the last load of coal out of Honesdale, Pennsylvania on November 5, 1898.

Ice on the flats at Cochecton deposited from the flood of March 1, 1902. This view from the hill in back of the Erie depot shows the residence of J. B. Reilly and the site of the Presbyterian Church (X mark) in the upper right distance. Town of Cochecton Historian, Alberta Tyler, recalled the doleful sound of the "steeple bell which tolled erratically as the structure moved off its foundation and broke-up downstream." The bell never was found and very little of the six homes that once stood on the flats. *Courtesy, Mrs. Alberta Tyler*

The great flood of March 6, 1899, at Callicoon showing the flour, feed, apples and potato store of John Kaute on the edge of destruction, while cows and pigs look on unconcernedly. In the background an eastbound Erie freight feels its way out on the threatened Callicoon Creek trestle. *Photograph by J. G. Stenger; Courtesy, Mr. Fred Starck*

The Riverside Hotel at Pond Eddy on the tow path of the Delaware and Hudson Canal during the flood of October 9, 1903. Household effects have been moved out of the threatened hostelry while flood waters inundate the garden--marked by the protruding bean poles.

relentlessly. Month after month stretched into years while the project dragged on and at times almost came to a standstill.

The final breaking through of the last barricade of Hudson shale was marked by mischief as both sides became excited by the sounds of the other's approaching drill. The crew on the west heading, determined to have the 11 foot, 32 pound final drill, perpetrated a hoax which was recalled by J.V. Morrison, one of the conspirators: "...about the middle of September, 1871, the operatives in the west end, knowing by the sound produced by the drill on the other side that the perforation must soon be made, ceased operations, or made little headway with their own drills."

In a little while the rock was started by the eastern drill, and one or two more blows sent it through five or six inches. "It was instantly seized by the men on the west side, who pulled it through a few more inches and by putting a pickaxe beneath it, held it so firmly that the men on the east side could not withdraw it, although they tried for a long time to do so. After they had ceased their efforts and left the work the men on the west side pulled the drill through and buried it beneath

INTRODUCTION 15

three or four tons of rock; they then placed another drill on the floor of the tunnel in front of the hole."

The next morning the eastern crew arrived and picked up what they thought was their drill and proceeded to have it cut up for souvenirs. Meanwhile the buried drill was spirited away to Morrison's house where the next day, with tongue in cheek, it "... was formally presented to him." The plot leaked out and the cutting up of the phony drill was abandoned. The "last drill" was supposedly sent to Albany for exhibition by Mr. Morrison. Judge Henry R. Low, lawyer of Monticello, was the first man to walk through the tunnel and Mrs. James V. Morrison was the first lady to perform the same feat. The first regularly scheduled passenger train passed through on February 1, 1872.

Quinlan's opus wrote finis to one great chapter on the use of the natural resources of the county, while the holing through of the Shawangunk barrier opened the door to the exploitation of still another of Sullivan's great natural resources — its clean mountain air, scenic beauty and its corporate creation, "Summer Homes."

And so the people came.

A few affluent Protestants, more German and Irish Catholic immigrants, and then the waves of Jews who have given the county its distinctive flavor.

They came to the mountains.

To the mountains by rail.

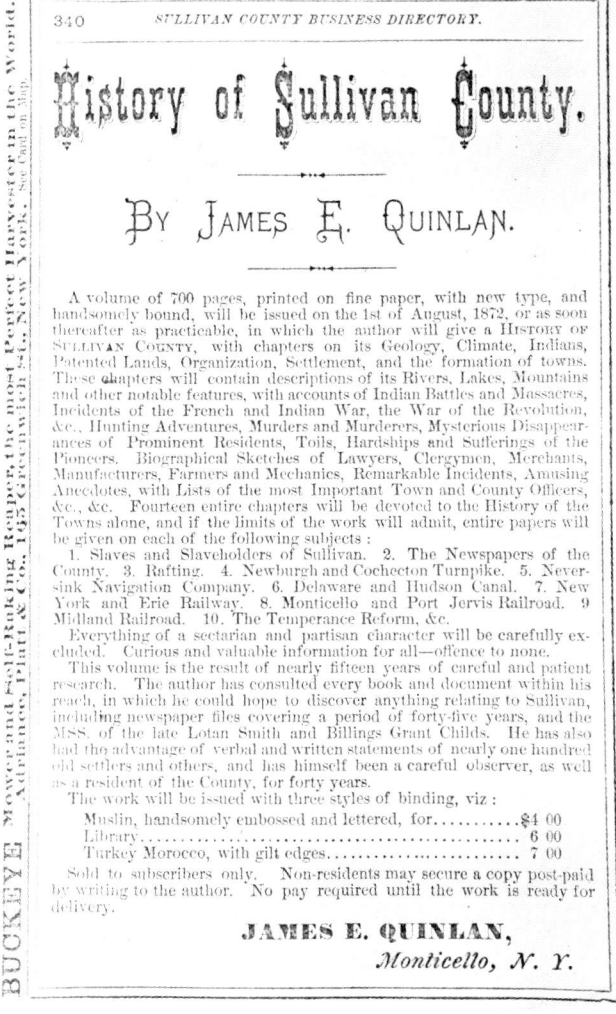

Just before James Eldridge Quinlan's history of Sullivan County was published, this advertisement appeared in the 1872-73 Sullivan County Gazetteer and Business Directory, noting as one of the chapters, the then aborning Midland Railroad.

SUMMER BOARDING.

NOTICE TO PROPRIETORS
—OF—
SUMMER HOTELS
AND
BOARDING HOUSES

Along or near the line of the Middle Division and Branches of the
MIDLAND RAILROAD.

It is proposed to issue about May 1st, 1878, for distribution in New York, Brooklyn and vicinity, a Pamphlet entitled

SUMMER HOMES ON THE MIDLAND

The object of this publication is to offer the thousands who annually look for Summer homes in the country, detailed information concerning the accommodations and facilities offered along the line of the MIDLAND Division and Branches of the MIDLAND RAILROAD.

In order to render the forthcoming Pamphlet a complete directory of information on this subject, there will be given, under the name of each Station, a general description of the advantages of the locality, followed by a statement showing the names and post-office address of all persons in the vicinity who offer accommodations for Summer visitors, their distance from the Station, the number that can be accommodated by each, terms per week for adults and for children, and any facts which may be of interest to those seeking Summer board.

☞ Station Agents will, (until April 25th, but not later,) receive the names of any wishing to register themselves as having accommodations to offer, and will forward them for publication in the forthcoming Pamphlet on payment of $2.00

☞ A limited amount of space will be reserved for Hotels, or Summer Boarding Houses, whose Proprietors wish to pay for inserting displayed advertisements.

WM. H. WEED,
General Passenger Agent.
145 Broadway, New York.

The advertisement, left, first appeared in the Liberty *Register* of April 19, 1878, the first public manifestation of a railroad promotional piece that was to transform a region in three decades. The first issue, above, from the collection of W. Ray Elmore, measures 6 7/8 by 4 3/4.

The Sullivan County Express poised at Weehawken for its varnish run to the mountains. The proud crew includes, at left, the near-legendary engineer, DeForest Diver. The Sullivan County Limited (1895 calling) was composed of Vestibuled Pullman Drawing-Room Cars and Vestibuled Day Coaches and made but two stops south of Mountaindale; "north of Mountaindale it makes all the stops." The 1895 "Summer Homes" devoted a full page to its virtues, summing up: "The train is intended to afford a quick and luxurious journey from and to Sullivan County stations." *D. Diver Collection, Cornell University*

To The Mountains by Rail

Weehawken to Bloomingburg

Sunday mornings in July were often muggy in the Weehawken, New Jersey, depot of the New York, Ontario and Western Railway. Bundles of newspapers were stacked on coach seats around Pete Reilly, a fortyish "newsboy" for the New York Sun. Settling himself for the early morning newspaper run to the boardinghouse and hotel laden resort communities of Sullivan County, he griped at the 2:15 p.m. departure time.

Train No. 29, the Express Freight, was pulled by "the powerful anthracite coal-burning engine with no cinders or dust" — as promised in the 1886 "Summer Homes among the Mountains."[1]

The success of "Summer Homes," an O. and W. sponsored promotional booklet, was great. By the time that the 1886 edition came out, the number of farmhouse, boardinghouse and small hotel operators had grown to such numbers and affluence as to be able to effectively demand the Sunday papers before noontime. Hence, the Sun newsboy and his towering bundle of papers.

However, there were other newspaper boys representing other papers — each of which would claim in print the following week that No. 29 was run expressly to deliver their particular Sunday edition.

A thirteen car weekend special, carrying over 700 passengers, pausing at the Havastraw depot on its way to the Sullivan County resort region. The 140 was the star performer on June 12, 1893, when it highballed a special train to the Hotel Wawonda at Liberty to commemorate the inaugural run of the new Class "T" locomotives into fast passenger service on the all-vestibule Sullivan County Limited.
Sullivan County Museum Archives

The 110 foot high, 1800 foot long Orrs Mills trestle near Cornwall. The newness of the concrete strengthened abutments would indicate the picture taken shortly after double-tracking.

NEW YORK
AND
Thousand Island
LINE
BETWEEN
NEW YORK AND ALEXANDRIA BAY
VIA THE
New York, Ontario & Western Railway
AND
DAILY LINE OF STEAMERS
—FROM—OSWEGO—TOUCHING
AT KINGSTON (ONTARIO), CLAYTON, ALEXANDRIA BAY;
AND ALL THE LANDINGS OF
The Thousand Islands

NEW, FIRST-CLASS, STANCH PALACE STEAMER LEAVING OSWEGO
On arrival of Night Express from New York.
PULLMAN PALACE BUFFET SLEEPING CARS ON THIS TRAIN.

SUPERB DAYLIGHT RIDE OF SIXTY MILES
Across the blue waters of Lake Ontario, and down
THROUGH THE ENTIRE LENGTH OF THE THOUSAND ISLANDS.

Steamer leaves Oswego every morning, including Sunday, on arrival of train, touching at Kingston (Canada), Clayton and Alexandria Bay.

Night Express leaves New York at 7.00 P.M.; arrives in Oswego, 7.45 A. M.
Day Express leaves New York at 8.30 A.M.; arrives in Oswego, 9.55 P.M.
Meals on the boat.

See description of Thousand Island Route on page 75.

☞ Time Tables, Tickets and full information furnished at all the Company's offices in New York, Brooklyn and Jersey City.

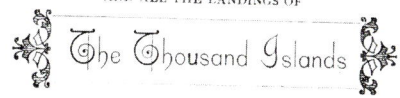

The boys with bundles of papers teeteringly perched on freight wagons, converged on the two New York, Ontario and Western ferry slips in Manhattan, at the foot of West 42nd Street or at the end of Jay Street.

Also aboard No. 29 that morning was what the Liberty Register sneeringly called a "four cent reporter" to prepare an account of the activities of the Sun representative on the high speed run through Sullivan County.

The route of the O. and W. trains was described eloquently in "Summer Homes" of 1886 as passing "modern palatial residences and quaint old Dutch houses built with bricks brought from Holland centuries ago ... The peaceful and fertile slopes of the valleys through which we pass ... have echoed and re-echoed the bugles of conflicting armies." But it was of little concern to Pete Reilly that hot, dark Sunday morning that he was passing "almost

At the time of Pete Reilly's ride to Sullivan County, feature ads were appearing in the "Summer Homes" publication promoting travel to such vacation spa's as Niagara Falls and the Thousand Islands. *Sullivan County Museum Archives*

Train No. 1 leaving Middletown on June 24, 1937, under the capable command of engineer DeForest Diver, shown in the high cab of Brooks-built No. 228. *Collection, Gerald M. Best*

The upbound Saturday afternoon Mountain Express behind Y-class 404 preparing to depart the Gilbert-designed **Middletown station.** *By M.B. Cooke, Collection, Gerald M. Best*

Train No. 1 heading for the Sullivan County resorts behind double header No. 227 and No. 226 with a typical mixed consist of milk cars, baggage, mail and half-empty coaches. *By Steve Maguire, Collection, Gerald M. Best*

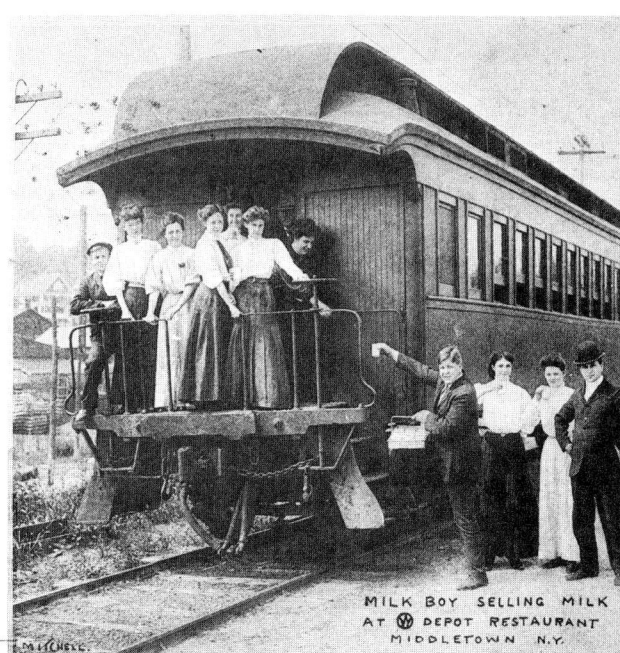

The milk-boy, a legendary fixture at the sprawling Middletown Depot/ Restaurant.

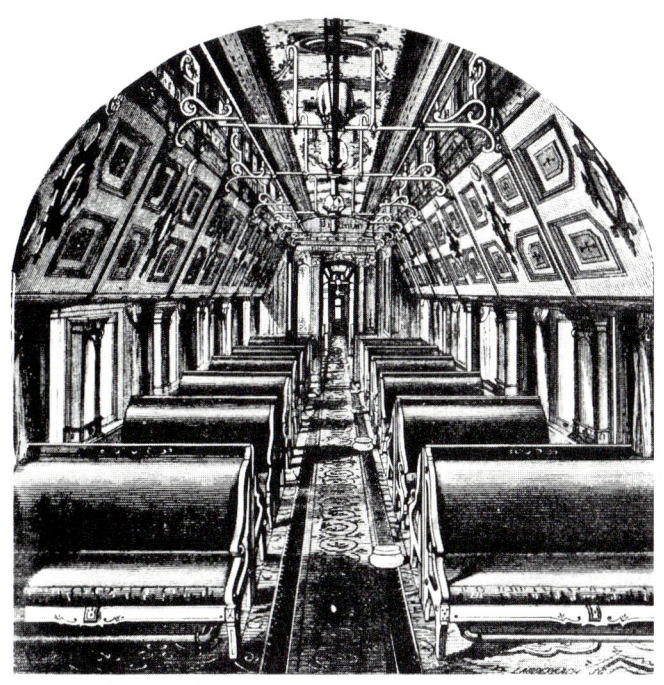 

The interiors of O. and W. equipment as illustrated in the 1886 "Summer Homes." On the left, the sleeping car facility liberally supplied with shiny spittoons. Right, the opulence of a Pullman drawing room car is quite apparent.

Late 19th Century Ontario and Western vestibule chair car replete with the craftsmenship of the "finelining artist" very much in evidence. *D. Diver Collection, Cornell University*

A 62-passenger, 58-foot long Pullman Company car, top, built in 1883 and typical of the older coaches used well into the 20th century to facilitate the increased summer passenger load.
Below, at one time there were 200 of these coaches, the backbone of the summer passenger business. The **77-passenger, 72-foot long cars built by Harlan and Hillingsworth in 1905 were used until the 1940's.** *Sullivan County Museum Archives*

over the spot where Alexander Hamilton and Aaron Burr fought their famous duel" or at Tappan that the "road skirts the base of the low hill upon the summit of which, in 1870, Major Andre was executed as a spy."

The oppressive roar in Pete's ears told him the train was passing through the Haverstraw Tunnel. Leaving the north portal, "Summer Homes" enthused "... one is greeted with a magnificent view, the broad Tappan Zee spread below dotted here and there with the white sails of river craft" and beyond stretching "the blue hills of Westchester County."

Just past Stony Point, No. 29 entered the Hudson Highlands which "... of its praises, poets have sung and historians have written. Justly celebrated has it been from the time when Hendrick Hudson ... gazed upon its shores from the deck of the 'Half Moon'."

Passing the United States Military Academy at West Point, the paper laden train skirted around the base of Storm King Mountain to Cornwall where it eased off the tracks of the New York, West Shore and Buffalo[2] onto its own right-of-way and at which point, in the parlance of the O. and W. publicists, "we turned our faces toward the mountains before us."

Perhaps Pete was asleep when, four miles west of Cornwall, the train eased across Moodna Trestle, a 1,100 foot long iron bridge, 105 feet above the waters of what was once known as Murderers Creek. After passing through Orrs Mills, the train, on a constantly ascending grade, passed through the little hamlets of Meadow Brook, Denniston's, Little Britian, Rock Tavern and Burnside.

Sixty-nine miles from New York, Pete knew he was nearing Middletown. He felt the pace of the engine ease off as the train approached the

Seeholzer's famous O. and W. restaurant, described in its day as "one of the finest depot restaurants on any railway system in the United States," was ravaged by fire in the early morning hours of October 23, 1919. Two restaurant employes, who occupied a room directly over the kitchens, were the first to smell the smoke of the $20,000 blaze. Before they had time to dress, flames broke through the floor and they were forced to jump out of the second-story window. Huyler's chocolates, the sponsors of this post card, were prominently featured in most of the O. and W. depots.
Sullivan County Museum Archives

The original station at Middletown, first floor built in 1874 and the second floor in 1886, was moved across the street in 1892 to make way for construction of the new $50,000 Hudson River brick structure designed by Bradford Lee Gilbert. *Collection, Gerald M. Best*

Engine No. 161, with Fred Wagner riding the right side, decided to take an alternate route in December (3), 1908, when its following engine, No. 131, blew up near Winterton. *Collection, Gerald M. Best*

Engine No. 131 after it blew up at Milepost No. 84 with engineer John Dougherty and fireman E. O. Tompkins miraculously escaping death. *Collection, Gerald M. Best*

The first O. and W. grade crossing in Sullivan County at Winterton. The siding at left was the setting for the discovery of a boxcar of illegal hooch during the dry prohibition era. *Sullivan County Museum Archives*

Campbell Hall junction with the Wallkill Valley Railroad.³ Alerted, he was ready and waiting at an open door as the train "whizzed through Middletown at 4:15 o'clock" and he proceeded to drop "bundles along a half mile of track as a corn planter drops seeds in a long furrow."

Pete probably wished the train would have stopped, at least long enough for a cup of coffee at the famous Wickham Avenue Station dining room, as most trains did. The restaurant, operated by W.H. Somers, later achieved almost national fame under the direction of William Seeholzer; and the "ten minute stop" at Seeholzer's allowed enough time for previously ordered meals to be put aboard for parlor car patrons.

Miss Laura Clements in 1968 recalled her many trips back from Teachers' College at Columbia in 1910 when the parlor car porter, a lifelong friend, would come through the cars and take orders for dinner to be put on at Middletown.

"We always had lamb chops, potato salad, mashed potatoes and rolls served on little tables set up at our seats, by the porter."

Pete knew when he crossed into Sullivan County by the ominous rumble of the Shawangunk Kill trestle and the brief blur of lights, Winterton depot.

On this dark Sunday morning in 1886 only three resorts were listed under Winterton in "Summer Homes"; two farmhouses, J.C. Lockwood's and Miss L. Dick's, and Mrs. W.W. Winter as a private residence, located near the depot. Winterton's prime importance was as a milk depot for the rich dairy farms that dotted the green foothills of the Shawangunks – the mountain ridge gateway to Sullivan County.

High View, N.Y., Bloomingburg (note station sign) was the first major stop in Sullivan County. Feldman's Hotel, left, featured ice cream sodas, which made it popular with hot and thirsty passengers detraining at this mountainside resort. The structure in the center distance was the Joe Rogers' banjo head factory. The heads, made from hides of unborn calves, were considered the best in the business and were shipped out in quantity on the O. and W. The shed at right, for baggage carts, has been usurped by the stationmaster's car. *Courtesy, Anne Lasher*

High View

Bloomingburg

As No. 29 eased into the depot at Bloomingburg, people from the "Christian only" boardinghouses clustered trackside "to lay in a supply of the Sunday Sun." Pete leaped to the platform amidst a cascade of papers to distribute as many copies as possible before the 'all aboard.'

In 1890 the number of Jews "going to the mountains" was increasing to such an extent that many of the boardinghouse operators were beginning to show signs of alarm, and vocal resistance to this movement was noted when in 1892 "Summer Homes" editors permitted the insertion of 'no Hebrews,' 'no Jews taken,' and 'guests taken to church free of charge,' into resort descriptions.

The flood-gates of anti-semitism in resort regions were opened in 1877 when Joseph Seligman[1] became the *cause celebre* when refused accommodations at the sprawling Grand Union Hotel in Saratoga Springs.

The Seligman affair simply brought out into the open anti-semitism in America and made convenient the inclusion of racially restricting copy in resort promotional publications.

In the Bloomingburg section the Leander Crawford farmhouse, the A.T. McEwan farmhouse, the Mrs. E. Gaudineer boardinghouse, the Overlook Place, the High View House and the Mount Pleasant House all indicated their preferences in keeping their establishments Christian.[2] Spirited complaints were made to the Ontario and Western management, and, when the second printing of the 1892 issue cleared the presses, all overtly anti-Semetic references were deleted. More subtle phrases were resorted to.

As late as the 1935 issue, resorts in Neversink, White Sulphur Springs, High View,[3] Ellenville and other communities were noted 'Christian House,' or had 'Gentile management, Catholic and Protestant Churches nearby.'

By the same token, Jewish houses were identified by their listings: 'Dietary Laws observed,' 'Jewish cooking,' 'Kosher cooking.' That Sunday morning, when Pete momentarily detrained at Bloomingburg, there were fifteen boarding and farmhouses listed in "Summer Homes"; fourteen more than in the first thirty-six page issue which

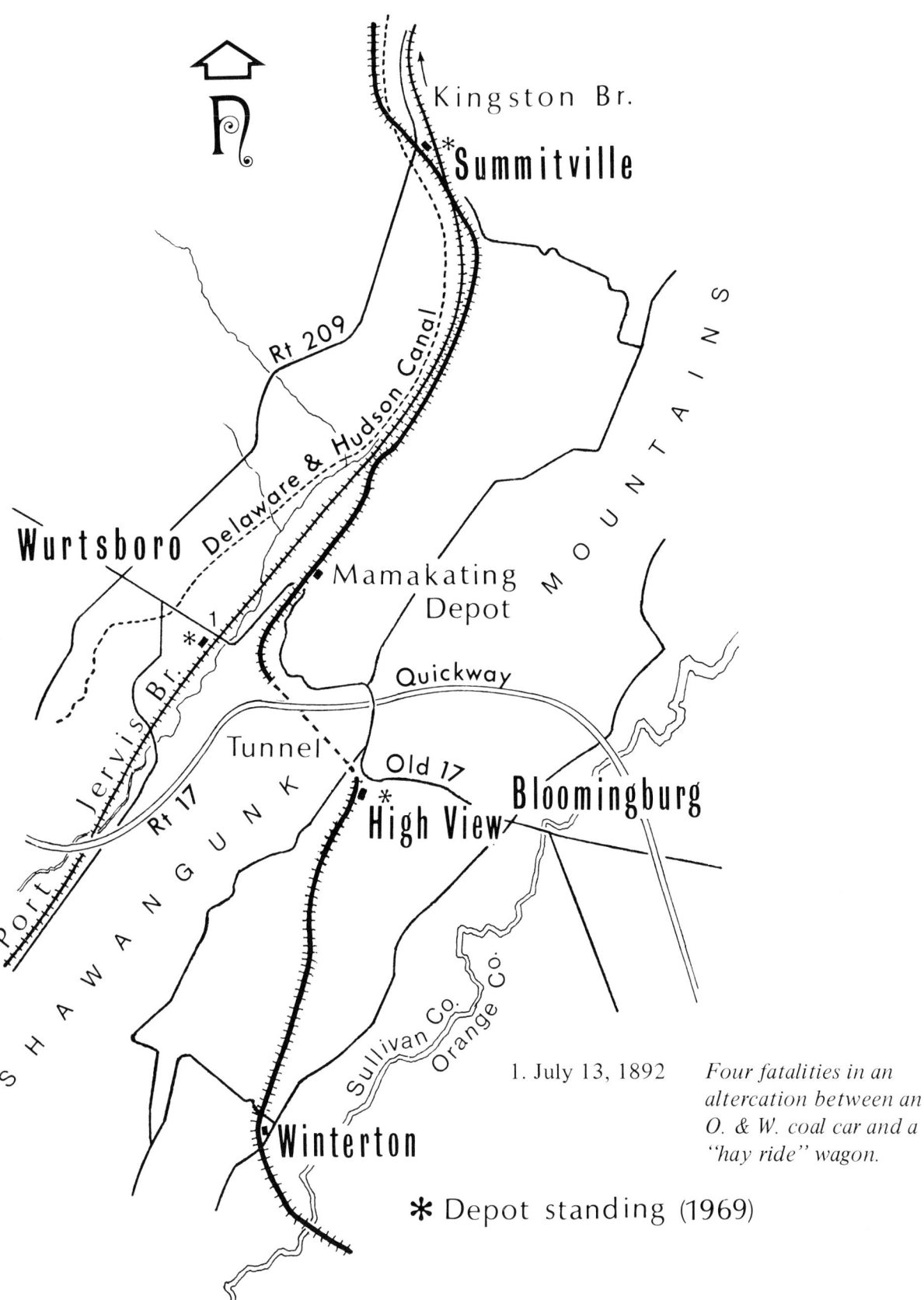

1. July 13, 1892 — *Four fatalities in an altercation between an O. & W. coal car and a "hay ride" wagon.*

* Depot standing (1969)

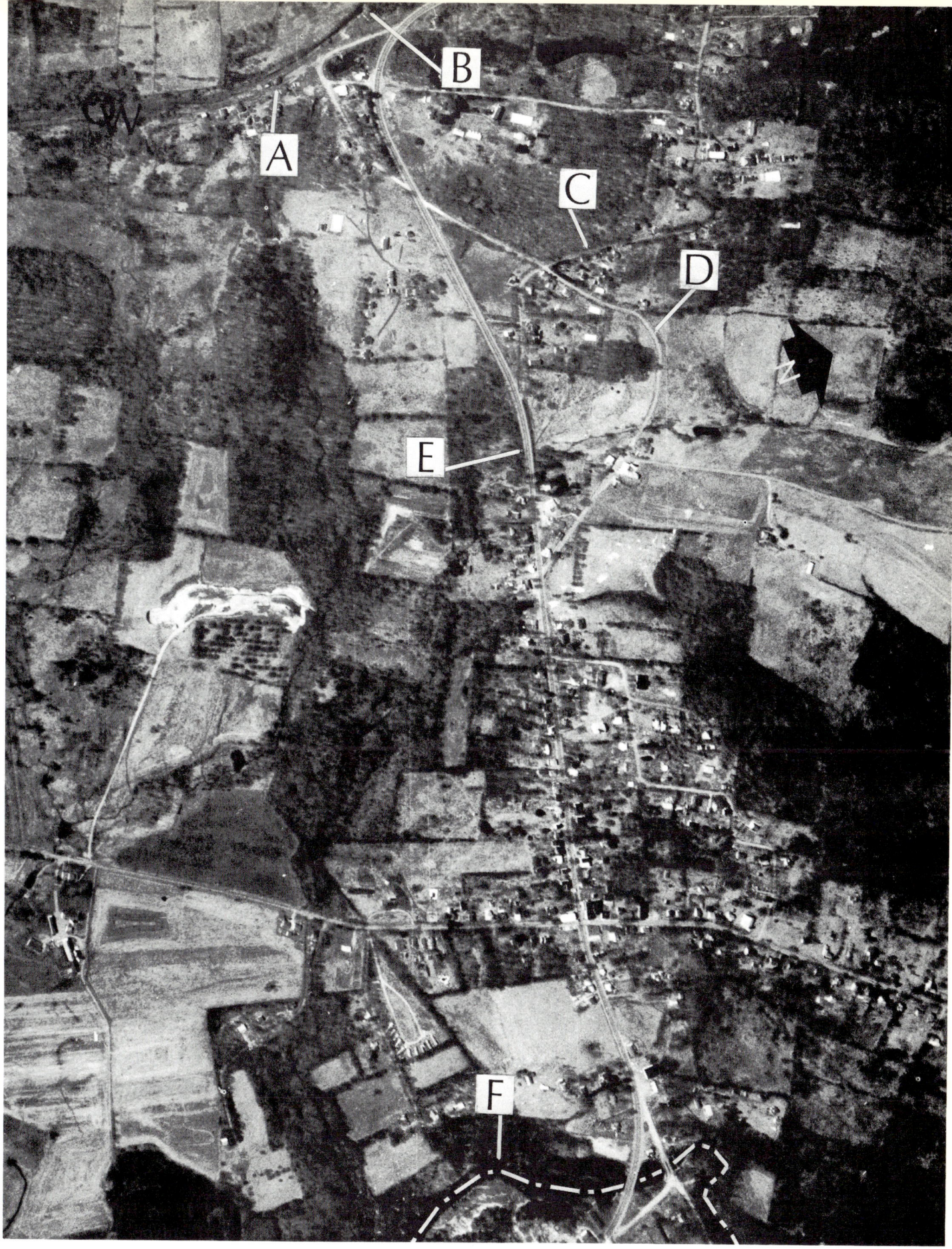

A. High View–Bloomingburg depot, B. South(east) portal, High View tunnel, C. Original route over mountain of the pioneer Newburgh-Cochecton Turnpike, D. State Route 4, Liberty Highway, developed to connect with O. and W. depot, E. Route 17 right-of-way, F. Shawangunk Kill, county line, Sullivan and Orange

HIGH VIEW. Bloomingburg

noted that "the summer guests (would) find at the Godfrey House — on the Shawangunk slope, only three rods from the station — excellent accommodations for the season. His terms are $1 per day, and he has room for eight boarders."

By June of 1893 business at Bloomingburg had improved to such an extent that the railroad was enlarging the platform with covered archways so that passengers would be protected from inclement weather while passing from trains to carriages, wagons and stages. The local press in March, 1897, reported plans of the O. and W. management to build an entirely new depot "due to the attractions of Bloomingburg as a summer resort as there are about 500 guests accommodated here in summer."

Out of the myriad boardinghouses and farmhouses there emerged a few large, substantial hotels. One of the first was the three story, 30-room Overlook Hotel built about 1890 by Charles Godfrey. Passing through six owners, it finally burned to the ground on October 22, 1925. The fire, which started near an old chimney, was similar to many which destroyed a number of the old frame hotels. Another hotel, the Shawangunk Mountain House was built to accommodate 100. The 1910 "Summer Homes" rhapsodized: "2000 feet of piazza,[4] 1,000 foot elevation, overlooking 1500 square miles of grand and varied scenery, bath and all rooms lighted by acetylene gas." Not to take any unnecessary risks, the management added "no obnoxious guests entertained."

The very artistic 1892 "Summer Homes" contained within its covers the first manifestations of anti-semitism in the railroad publication. The Overlook Place, right, operated by D. G. Carpenter was one of three resorts at High View-Bloomingburg that noted "no Hebrews" or "no Jews taken" in the 1892 "Summer Homes." *Top, collection, Gerald M. Best*

Hotel Lawrence,

L. W. LAWRENCE,
PROPRIETOR.

Loch Sheldrake, Sullivan County, N.Y.

ACCOMMODATE 100. TWENTY MINUTES FROM R. R. STATION. HIGH GROUNDS OVERLOOKING THE LAKE. OWN LIVERY. LONG DISTANCE TELEPHONE. TWO MAILS DAILY. SPECIAL RATES JUNE AND SEPTEMBER.

NO BAR. NO CONSUMPTIVES OR HEBREWS.

Typical examples of anti-semitic advertising that appeared around the resort region as more and more Jews arrived in the mountains to engage rooms for the "season."

Evergreen Farm,

Ulsterville, Ulster Co., N.Y.

Evergreen Farm is situated two miles west of Pine Bush, on a breezy elevation, with a fine outlook to the Shawangunk mountains. The house is two story, convenient to post office, Church etc.

There is a romantic brook flowing through the farm, with fishing and boating. The large lawn in well shaded, being cool and delightful. A bountiful table is provided with fresh milk, eggs, vegetables, berries and fruit, raised on the farm.

Guests and baggage conveyed to and from the depot free of charge. There are pleasant drives to Lake Minnewaska, Sam's Point, Lake Mohonk etc., at reasonable prices.

Pine Bush is eighty miles from New York, at the terminus of the Crawford branch of the Erie R. R.

Good laundry work at moderate rates.

HOUSE OPEN JUNE 1st, 189 .

ADULTS, $5.00 TO $6.00 PER WEEK. CHILDREN UNDER TEN YEARS, $3.00   UNEXCEPTIONAL REFERENCES GIVEN.

NO JEWS TAKEN.

Geo. H. Upright, Proprietor.

◁ THE HALL HOUSE ▷

J. C. HALL, Proprietor.

THE HALL HOUSE is situated on an eminence. in the village, in the midst of well shaded and well drained grounds. It contains large, airy, pleasant rooms, is finely finished and furnished, Modern in structure and conveniences. Sanitary plumbing, Baths, Hot and Cold Water, Electric Lights, etc. The proprietor intends that it shall not be excelled by any other house of its class in this country. Terms: For one in a room, $8.00 to $12.00, two in a room, $16 00 to $20.00. **NO HEBREWS OR CONSUMPTIVES TAKEN.** New York references on application to the Proprietor, LIBERTY, N. Y.

HIGH VIEW.   Bloomingburg

Line drawing of the Bloomingburg (High View) area that appeared in the 1891 "Summer Homes", showing the original depot, center, and Fallon's Hotel, left, later known as Feldman's.

Early print view of depot area at High View before completion of the Shawangunk Tunnel. The up-train has just arrived, disgorging passengers for the bumpy ride over the mountain to the west railhead. The community of Bloomingburg shows in the distance marked by the commanding steeple of the Reformed Church. *Courtesy, Kenneth Godfrey*

The hulking original Sha-wan-ga Lodge that burned to the ground in November, 1926. The hotel, with a capacity of 125 guests, issued a pictoral brochure, ten years before its demise, which noted single rooms at $10 to $15 per week and double rooms $26 to $30. "Refined Christian House" was also delicately inserted in the promotional text to help maintain house policies.

On May 1, 1895, the Sha-wan-ga Lodge, the "grand" hotel of High View opened its doors. Built for D.G. Carpenter, the resort with sleeping accommodations for seventy was perched atop the Shawangunks overlooking "the counties of Orange and Ulster, with the Catskills and Highlands in the distance."

A full page ad in the 1895 "Summer Homes" described it as being "tastefully designed and surrounded by broad piazzas aggregating 3,000 square feet. The first floor is divided into large and small parlors with open fireplaces, a gentlemen's hall twenty feet square, an office and dining-room."

When the Sha-wan-ga Lodge burned on November 22, 1926, at a loss of $150,000, it was termed Sullivan County's worst fire since the destruction of the Shindler Prairie House in February. The flames were first noticed coming from the upper floor at about the center of the hotel very close to the chimney. "My mother," recalls Ray Dunn,[5] "upon spotting the fire, while preparing lunch, raced upstairs and scooped me out of my bed and dashed back downstairs, my folks being the housekeepers at the time. Most of the furnishings on the first floor were saved by firemen and workers about the place. Ironically, a large lake near the hotel had been drained about two weeks previously to permit the planking of the bottom thus removing the only source of water in the vicinity."

The most recent owners, Dan and Coopersmith, had bought the Lodge about two years before from Solomon Hector, who in turn had secured it from its original owner D.G. Carpenter about 1901 for $55,000. Following the fire Sha-wan-ga was rebuilt and has been in successful operation down through the years.

Bloomingburg (High View), the community with which the "Lodge" is intimately identified, was from the earliest years a center of county political life and culture. Officially named around 1812, until the completion of the Delaware and Hudson Canal in 1827, it was a minor commercial center, especially active in the lumber business as a result of its location on the newly completed Newburgh-Cochecton Turnpike. It was the site of the first printing-office[6] in Sullivan County and of the first academy.

In the 20th Century, fate has not treated it kindly. Two generations of motorists cursed it as a bottleneck on the way to the mountains, and finally the route 17 by-pass eliminated it from most people's consciousness.

Wet road conditions in the 20's led to this altercation to a Capitol Coach Lines of Brooklyn bus somewhere on Rt. 17. *Courtesy, L. Komitzky.*

The trip over the Shawangunks, whether in buckboard or stage coach or horseless carriage, was frequently an adventure. In the earliest days of the New York and Oswego Midland, before the Shawangunk Tunnel was holed through, passengers had to detrain and cross the rocky ridge of the mountain by stage to connect with the completed section on the other side. Contemporary accounts mention frequent upsettings of horsedrawn vehicles by high winds in storms and squalls. The dependability of the driver was often assessed by his ability to judge weather and wind conditions atop the ridge.

The hazards of crossing the mountain were even present in the "modern" age of the gasoline engine when we take note of the plight in January, 1927, of twelve passengers snowbound for seven hours in a Middletown-Monticello bus.

"The bus gave its last chug as it neared Mount Prosper, atop the Wurtsboro Mountain at 7:40 P.M. ... at 2:45 A.M. on Sunday morning, Fred Little of Mount Prosper and Charles Kadlee of Yankee Lake succeeded in reaching the stalled bus and led the twelve passengers to the home of H.B. Tompson. During the trip three of the party collapsed and were carried the rest of the way to the farmhouse, reaching there just before 4 A.M."[7]

The bus war raged on into the early thirties resulting in large advertisements of this nature which appeared in August, 1932.

2^{00} Mohawk Stages

BUSES TO
Bronx - New York - Brooklyn

LIBERTY DEPOT—75 South Main Street, Next to Walt's Diner.
NEW YORK DEPOT—Palace Hotel, 132 West 45th St., East of Broadway.
BRONX DEPOT—Bob's Bus Terminal, 170th Street and Jerome Avenue.
WASHINGTON HEIGHTS—Bus Terminal, 505 West 181st Street.

SCHEDULE
Leave Liberty — 8:30, 11 A.M. — 2, 5, 7:30 P.M.
Leave Palace Hotel, N.Y.— 9:15, 11:30 A.M.— 1:30, 3, 6 P.M.

Dependable and Safe Transportation

Travel via Purple Swan De-Luxe Coaches

TRAVEL to and from intermediate points on the "Liberty Highway" in a *Purple Swan Motor Coach* will prove to be a revelation to both the experienced tourist and the occasional passenger as to the wondrous possibilities of this modern method of transportation.

Purple Swan Coaches are as far ahead of rail travel as that was an advance over its predecessor, the stagecoach; providing expeditious yet safe conveyance with absolute freedom from the smoke and kindred annoyances so common to steam transit lines.

No item that would add to comfort or convenience of passengers has been overlooked — whether it be air cushion seats or electric fans. Coaches are not only adequately ventilated, heated and lighted but are even equipped with lavatories and water coolers. And even card tables for bridge are available!

The Purple Swan bus timetable featured a photograph which showed the railroad observation car-like rear styling so popular during the 1920's.
Sullivan County Museum Archives

Purple Swan Terminals

NEW YORK
ASTOR BUS TERMINAL
45th St. & Broadway,   Tel. CHickering 7730

LIVINGSTON MANOR
POLEY'S UNITED CIGAR STORE

PARKSVILLE
KAMENETSKY'S DRUG STORE
Phone Liberty 673 or 287

LIBERTY
PURPLE SWAN TERMINAL
Below Post Office   Tel. Liberty 624

LOCH SHELDRAKE   **WOODBOURNE**
Gardner's Store   Mel's Garage
Hurleyville 36   Fallsburg 216-M

FALLSBURGH
Post Office   Tel. Fallsburg 153 M

SO. FALLSBURG
ELEFANT BLDG.
Tel. Fallsburg 152 J

KIAMESHA
Schlagler Dairy Store   Phone 158 F 12

MONTICELLO
231 BROADWAY
Next to Post Office   Telephones 591-201

ROCK HILL
William's Store   Tel. Monticello 513-F-2

WURTSBORO
Arthur's Garage   Telephone 125-F-6

MIDDLETOWN
50 JAMES ST.
Opposite Erie Depot   Telephone 836

TIME TABLE
Busses Operate on Daylight Saving Time.

Purple Swan Motor Coach Co., Inc.

THROUGH MOTOR COACH SERVICE TO AND FROM
ASTOR BUS TERMINAL
45TH STREET AND BROADWAY
TIMES SQUARE, NEW YORK

FOR SAFETY, CONVENIENCE AND DEPENDABLE SERVICE

Travel Via
Purple Swan De-Luxe Coaches
Transportation Service of Distinction

HIGH VIEW.   Bloomingburg

With the development of State Route 4, later Route 17, the road was widened somewhat, but by necessity had to narrow for the hairpin curve under the O. and W. tracks on the west flank of the mountain. As the number of automobiles multiplied on Rt. 17, the narrow railroad underpass and the traffic light in Bloomingburg became a big slowdown factor on Sunday afternoons when the Sullivan County resort crowds headed back to the city.

By the early 30's, as more and more vehicles clogged the highway, the congestion between Bloomingburg and Wurtsboro increased proportionately. Between these two points "... eight hundred and four cars were counted in the scant four miles of highway between Bloomingburg and Wurtsboro. The bulk of the cars stood in two and three-lane formation from High View to the O. and W. underpass on the Wurtsboro side of the mountain awaiting their turn to enter the single lane of traffic through High View and Bloomingburg."[8]

Three years later double lines of pleasure cars, busses and trucks would extend all the way from

BX Tower controlled train movements through the single track Shawangunk Tunnel from the Bloomingburg side. The well maintained High View depot, in distance. Today, top, it broods hauntingly over a field-like thicket, a vandalized shell, nothing more than a shelter for a flock of chickens. *Lower photograph by Koontz*

Rock Hill to Bloomingburg, a distance of about 10 miles, moving at a snail's pace through Wurtsboro and the O. and W. underpass.

In May of 1919, seeds were planted to further congest matters when an auto bus line, making three trips daily, was established between Bloomingburg and Middletown. Within four years, traffic volume and fast, reckless driving by both autos and busses had reached such serious proportions in the Bloomingburg area that highway enforcement took on new dimensions in August, 1923, with the delegation of six men to patrol Rt. 17; James Hawkins, Thomas Budd and Fred Owen assigned to patrol the highway from the Shawangunk Kill bridge to the corporation line above "the Virgil Godfrey house" and Thomas Flaherty, Abraham Felman and Joseph Rogers to give "their undivided attention" to the High View Mountain.

In the first week $822 in fines was taken in, but by the second week the driving public was evidently catching on—only $371 collected. It was estimated that in that first weekend, from Friday to Monday, 15,000 cars passed through the village and in a given hour on Saturday afternoon 1,200 cars passed by the traffic light.

The traffic net caught "a larger fish last Saturday than is usual" when Deputy Sheriff Abe Felman arrested Adolph L. Simons, State Republican Committeeman from the 17th District for reckless driving and contempt of court.

Despite the deputies' fervent diligence, auto traffic altercations were continuing to increase along with the proliferation of resort bus lines, causing much concern to the driving public as well as the O. and W. management.

The railroad was well aware of the threat to their business in January of 1921, when they brought suit against Morton C. Griffin to restrain him from operating an "auto-bus" line between Middletown and Liberty. The railroad asked that Griffin be "perpetually enjoined from operating and also such other relief as the court may deem just and proper."

Mr. Griffin had been granted a franchise to operate a bus line over the streets of Middletown and was running a bus line from the Erie Railroad station to Monticello and ending at N.S. Beringer's garage. Because Griffin was operating his busses on the streets of Liberty without either the consent of, or a franchise from, the Board of Trustees of Liberty, the O. and W. believed that the bus line was operating illegally and that it could be killed. The railway's adversary, however, was not ready for a funeral.

On July 26, 1921, Griffin applied to the Public Service Commission for a certificate of public convenience and necessity. The O. and W. sent representatives to oppose the application at the public hearing held on October 11, 1921. They were unsuccessful and the certificate was granted on November 23.

But before the decision was made public, the Board of Trustees of Liberty, generally friendly toward the O. and W., passed a resolution stating that Section 26 of the Transportation Corporation's Law should apply to Liberty. This required the consent of the trustees for the use of local streets.

The litigation ground on until March, 1923, when the courts contended that "inasmuch as the City of Middletown did not object to Mr. Griffin's bus line or to the consent granted, the court held that the objections by the railroad to its operation could not be sustained." The O. and W. still claimed the right to maintain the action because of the interference of the bus with its passenger traffic business. Finally, in June of 1923, the Ontario and Western capitulated. At a public hearing the decline of public interest was apparent when only 13 spectators attended as contrasted with the 50 or 60 at the previous meeting.

Consent to use the streets of Liberty for bus operation was also granted to the many more applicants who had come to the fore during the protracted litigation. Bus lines that were permitted to congest the streets of Liberty were the Mountain Bus Company (Liberty to Ellenville, Liberty to Monticello via Ferndale and Liberty to Monticello via White Lake), Jeffersonville Transportation Company (Liberty to Jeffersonville), Charles Bellinger's route (line from Liberty to Livingston Manor), and Meola & Meola of Middletown (line from Liberty to White Lake, by way of Stevensville and Liberty to Callicoon). Almost as one, the bus operators intoned, "we intend to honeycomb the two counties (Sullivan and Orange) with bus lines." After the settlement of the O. and W.-Griffin litigation, the two parties decided that cooperation was the better course. Griffin inaugurated a bus line between Monticello and the railroad at Mamakating.

The railroad-bus dispute though was not at all near death just because this case was settled. The Liberty Town Board once again had to stand and be counted in June, 1925, when the Midland Transit Corporation asked permission to use town roads in the operation of a bus line between Liberty and Hancock. The request was denied with the stated reason being that while the O. and W. paid substantial taxes to the town, the bus lines provided comparatively little revenue. It is probable, however, that upstate Delhi's unhappy

HIGH VIEW.   Bloomingburg

Coaching day parades in Bloomingburg were gala occasions as witness these two separate events - the above cluttered scene in front of Evans General Store was taken in 1897 and, right, the opposite side of the street photographed in 1901. *Courtesy, Anne Lasher*

The heat soon ignited the cornice of the now enlarged Evans Department store across the street, opposite page, and shattered the extensive plate glass facade. *Courtesy, Anne Lasher, Courtesy, Joseph Lloyd*

The above tree-framed joyous scenes were wiped out on February 24, 1922, when wind driven flames roared through Collin's General Store, now sporting a gas pump and sign, taking with it the homes of William Oliver and Al Hultslander, right below.

The Bennett Hotel, long a Sullivan County landmark, came to a blazing end in February, 1922. *Sullivan County Museum Archives*

The Lakeside Hotel, right, was at one time known curiously as the "lower dock." The garage and its lone pump were a welcome stopping place for the weary motorist in the years before its flaming demise in the 30's. *Courtesy, Anne Lasher*

experience with a bus line helped influence the Liberty board's action.[9] The O. and W. was fighting a losing battle. Bus competition inexorably made its inroads on passenger revenue, whether delayed by Town Board action or not.

The reckless driving habits of the bus drivers, passing on curves, passing on the brow of a hill, and passing long lines of traffic at excessive speeds, led to accidents. One incident especially raised tempers when two children of the Henry Winokur family were killed in an auto accident with a Capitol Coach Lines bus just east of Bloomingburg in August, 1931.

Winokur's account of the accident, of course, conflicted with that of the bus driver's; but one thing was certain — citizen and official concern over reckless driving was aroused.

Orange County launched an all-out clamp-down on speeding "motorcoaches" resulting in resolutions seeking legislative control of motorcoaches and vans. The resolution would limit busses to a forty-mile speed maximum and also ask the Board of Supervisors to petition the State Legislature to enact laws to minimize traffic hazards created by motor busses and large trucks.

The legal action and upswing of arrests of bus drivers in Orange County prompted an editorial by the Liberty *Register* on August 13 which denounced "traffic abuses indulged by busses," raised the hope that "it may be expected that violations of this sort will be fewer in that county in the future," and concluded "Sullivan County may well follow Orange's example."

Whether the editorial was the motivating factor or not is not clear, but the following week's press reported a meeting between District Attorney Gardner LeRoy, Liberty Sheriff, Ben R. Gerow, and state police officials to discuss the "speed and alleged recklessness with which the busses are driven over the highways of Sullivan County." The popular sheriff commented that "notice of intended action will be sent to the bus lines." Tighter controls of bus operators were instituted in both counties with an ensuing lowering of the accident rate.

In 1922 there were fourteen boarding and farmhouses listed in "Summer Homes" under Bloomingburg; and there was hardly one that did not feel the effects, the following resort season, of the fire that destroyed most of the little com-

It was a warm September 10, 1953, when Edward H. Weber fortuitously rode the O. and W. train to Roscoe, camera in hand, and photographed all the passing depots- High View included. It was the last passenger run to Sullivan County for that season and as events on the line worsened, it became the last scheduled run for all time.

munity on February 24 of that year. The holocaust was discovered at 2:30 P.M. in the little barber shop run by Philip Greco. The blaze quickly spread to the Collins block occupied by the D.F. Collins general store, bowling alleys, pool hall and ice cream store. When the blaze was at its height, a gust of wind "hoisted the flames across the street" igniting the cornice and roof of Evan's store. The exterior of the store had been thoroughly soaked by water, but the heat and flame quickly overwhelmed the structure to sweep on to the former Bennett Hotel, then owned by the Wolinsky family.

Less than a year before (May, 1921) John F. Bennett (who had owned it for 40 years) had sold his hotel to Marcus Corin of New York City. The famous old hostelry had been built in 1866 by Elias Terwilliger and for many years was known as the Terwilliger House. At one time the gathering place for Sullivan and Orange County notables, it was famous for its flamboyant dinners and dances.

It was at least four hours before the Bloomingburg fire could be controlled. When it was over, the loss was estimated at $120,000. Fifty persons were left homeless and eleven buildings were in smoldering ruins.

Brooks-built No. 71 heeling to the super-elevation at the east portal of the Bloomingburg tunnel. The box-like framework to the right of the coaches was scaffolding used by the tunnel crews for the maintenance of the lining and loose rock. *Sullivan County Museum Archives*

High View Tunnel

North (west) portal.

For Pete Reilly the 1922 fire disaster was in the unforeseen future, the one immediate sensation was the rumbling in his ears as the Mogul worked the slight upgrade inside the Shawangunk Tunnel. Fortunately, Pete didn't know the operational hazards posed by the passage he was making through the ridge of the Shawangunks.

The tunnel was originally jerry-built[1] with little regard to safety and geological faults were not bolstered. Decaying shale rock could not support a mass of clay and minor cave-ins were frequent, resulting in operational delays that were becoming increasingly uneconomical. The company finally installed a tunnel liner in 1878. This was a kind of tunnel-within-a-tunnel made of brick masonry which literally sealed off the cavernous area of falling rock and clay.

For all of the improvements to the physical tunnel, little was done by the railway company to alleviate the stifling conditions created by the blasts of smoke and steam as Class X and Y-2's[2] walked their loads of anthracite into the west portal.

A concentration of gas overcame brakeman Marvin Tripp of Livingston Manor in August of 1919 when southbound freight No. 32 halted in the tunnel. He had been working outside the train when members of the crew found him unconscious and carried him out. They placed him aboard a way-freight caboose and he was taken to Thrall Hospital in Middletown.

John Kirk of Wurtsboro and James Mulligan of Bloomingburg employed as watchmen in the tunnel almost lost their lives when walking through after a train passed. As the Liberty *Herald* of August 11, 1904, reported it "...they had quit work and were about to leave for home, when Kirk fell into a ditch. As he did not get up, Mulligan went to him and found him unconscious. He could not arouse the man and it dawned on him that Kirk had been overcome by gas in the tunnel. Mulligan worked over his companion for a time and then started for the mouth of the tunnel to summon help. He had not gone far when he too began to feel the effects of the deadly fumes, and it was with difficulty that he reached the opening.

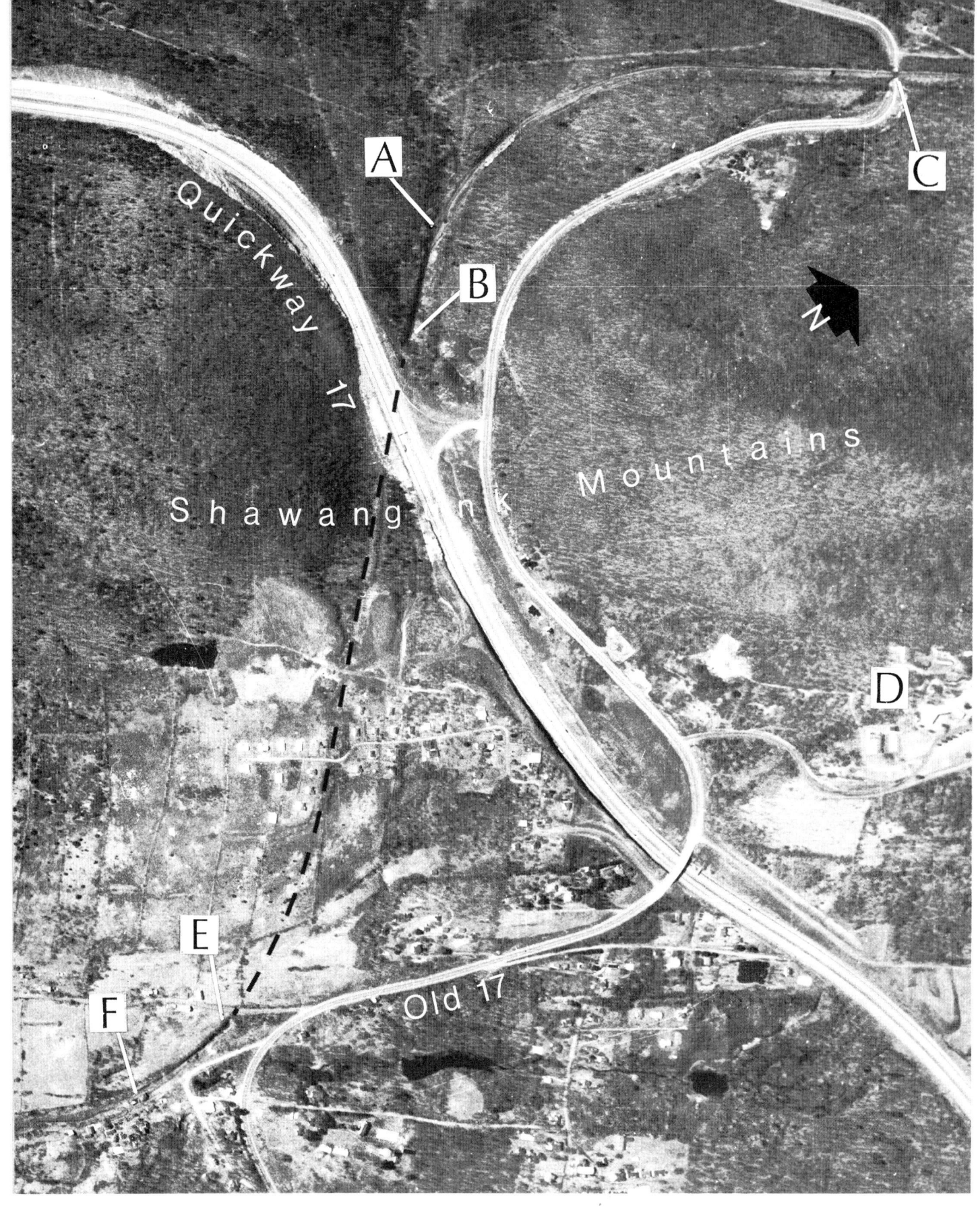

A. Site of "WX" Tower, B. West(north) portal, C. Site of hazardous Rt. 17 overpass, D. Sha-wan-ga Lodge, E. East(south) portal, F. High View (Bloomingburg) depot.

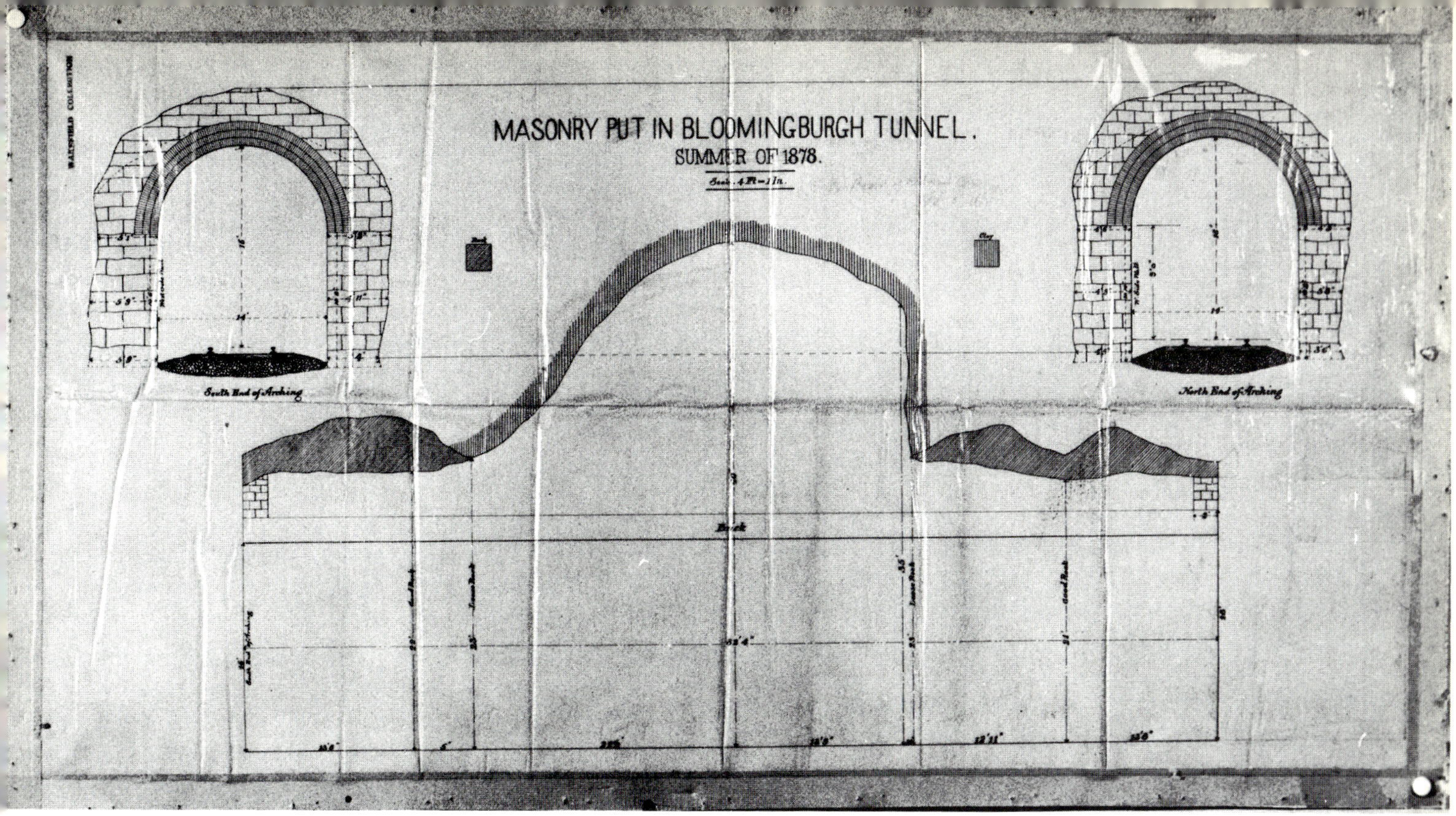

Engineering department drawing showing details of a tunnel within a tunnel built to protect trains from persistent roof rock falls. The August 30, 1878, Liberty *Register* reported "the Midland is doing a good job in the tunnel, laying a solid brick arch which will make it safe for all trains to come." *Sullivan County Museum Archives*

After he revived somewhat he secured assistance and returned to rescue his companion." By a strange coincidence Kirk's father, who was also employed as a watchman in the tunnel, was overcome by gas in 1894 and killed by a passing train.

More trouble occurred in July of 1897 when the O. and W. put a large force of men to work under J.L. Matzinger for the purpose of further arching of the tunnel. The local press reported the gas and smoke almost unbearable for the workmen. While the arching was underway, Oley Banks of Wurtsboro, the day watchman in the tunnel, was overcome by fumes and was struck by train No. 1. He died after being rushed to Thrall Hospital in Middletown for treatment.

Operating crews also experienced death from the tunnel, too often a victim of carelessness with the hazards of the craggy passageway. "When the train reached Summitville, Brakeman Benjamin Cross's prostrated form was found lying on top of a box car by a member of the train crew." The press of November, 1901, went on to graphically note that "... blood was oozing from the nose and mouth and it was evident that his head had come in contact with something while the train was in motion." Indeed it had! While acting as brakeman

Inside the east portal in September 1953, the water running out the bore just as it was in 1870 when an Orange County *Press* reporter noted "water continued to pour from the ceiling and it ran from both ends..." *Photograph by Edward H. Weber*

on No. 33, it was surmised that he stood upright on the car while passing through the tunnel and was struck on the head by a low, hanging rock. Cross was last seen alive at Bloomingburg when he boarded the engine as it was pulling out of the station, and climbed atop the first box car where his body was later found.

It seemed as if trainmen got careless, particularly when running on northbound train 33 as noted in an article three years later. "Soon after train No. 33 emerged from the Bloomingburg tunnel on its way north, Hawley was found on the tank of the engine with his head crushed in."[3] The sudden demise of Simon E. Hawley of Fishs Eddy, head trainman, resulted when he decided to walk back over the train as it entered the north portal of the tunnel. A low projecting rock did the rest.

Some of this same roof stone collapsed on the night of October 17, 1903, but not because of the lack of maintenance. "Flagman Reilly Bullis was in the caboose of the first section (train 22) when he heard the second section come thundering along in the tunnel." Fortunately, Bullis had time to get out and run down the side of the train which had stopped at the Bloomingburg depot to receive orders. The rear of the first section was extending about two hundred feet back into the tunnel.

Although the second section, with engineer F.B. Case at the throttle of engine 128, was proceeding slowly, the caboose was shattered, upsetting the stove and setting the splintered wood on fire. The caboose and one car on the first section and the first two cars on the second section were immediately aflame along with the woodwork on engine 128.

The crews could do nothing to contain the fire and finally Middletown was telegraphed for its hand engine. The stream at the tunnel entrance was dammed and water pumped on the fire from five a.m. until four p.m. The intense heat in the bore soon brought down large quantities of rock aggregating one hundred tons, which threatened to completely close the tunnel.

Emergency maintenance-of-way crews were brought in and the line was cleared by seven o'clock Sunday night in time for the "Night Line," the crack northbound night express.

A highly romanticised linecut of the west portal that appeared in the 1885 "Summer Homes." *Sullivan County Museum Archives*

"WX" tower controlled eastbound trains through the tunnel; levers in the tower and pipe linkage activating the semaphore, thereby indicating conditions ahead in the tunnel. *Sullivan County Museum Archives*

The year 1937 saw the maiden run of the new streamliner "Mountaineer" shown here emerging from the west portal with "WX" tower standing guard at the beginning of the long downgrade to Summitville. *Painting by Manville B. Wakefield*

Probably the most bizarre accident at the tunnel occurred at four o'clock Sunday morning May 23, 1926, when John Fox, O. and W. tower watchman at High View, heard an unusual noise coming from the direction of the south portal. Upon investigation he was astounded to discover a Hudson sedan resting on the rails at the very mouth of the tunnel. The car was resting on the right-of-way with its wheels lodged securely between the tracks.

When Fox reached the scene, none of the occupants of the car were to be found; but it was thought the car was going at a high rate of speed when it left the highway. Since a train was due momentarily, Fox set the signals against it and notified a garage to come and remove the car.

Upon investigation it was discovered that the car was leased to eight men going to Kiamesha Lake.

"The tunnel passed, the railway descends toward the Mamakating Valley," read the 1886 "Summer Homes," an understatement of classic proportions in a publication in which overstatement was generally the rule.

For Pete, as No. 29 eased out of the tunnel and into the bend for the descent to the floor of the Mamakating Valley, the unfolding panorama was one that never ceased to amaze him. Nor did the conglomeration of buckboards, freight wagons and stages that were always waiting at the grade crossing of the Newburgh-Cochecton Turnpike near the Mamakating depot, ever become commonplace for the newsboy.

For Pete and the thousands of summer sojourners it was indeed a dramatic curtain raiser. The heartland of the Sullivan County resort regions lay in the valley below and just over the horizon.

The Delaware and Hudson Canal at Wurtsboro with a light boat running south to Pennsylvania for a load of coal. The bridge in the background is the crossing of the Newburgh-Cochecton Turnpike. To the right of the bridge is the Seaside Supply Store, which still stands (1969) as a private home. Across the turnpike from the supply store stood the Harding House, a favorite with the canalmen and turnpike drovers. *From* Coal Boats to Tidewater, *The Story of the Delaware and Hudson Canal, by Manville B. Wakefield*

Mamakating

Wurtsboro

Mamakating was geographically related to Wurtsboro in somewhat the same way that High View was to Bloomingburg, with the exception that Wurtsboro had a depot on the valley line between Summitville and Port Jervis while one facility served both Bloomingburg and High View. However, even with the convenience of a valley depot, passengers still insisted on detraining at the mountainside depot at Mamakating.

Three years after Pete rolled through on the paper train the following item appeared in the *Register* for June 7, 1889. "The Wurtsboro station[1] on the O. and W. will be discontinued and all the freight and passenger business will be done from the station on the new road, which being in the village will do away with the heavy trucking up the mountain."

The station on the mountain may have been closed down for a short while; but by May 29, 1903, it was obviously in business again as evidenced by a newspaper demand "...why don't the O. and W. erect a shed at its Mamakating station? Nearly a mile from any human habitation, horses waiting for trains have to stand in the heat, cold or rain without shelter. It seems up to the enterprising O. and W. to build sheds – nobody else's business half as much."

Whether or not the excursionists from the New York-based realty venture, called the Sullivan County Club, detrained at Mamakating or down in the valley at Wurtsboro is not recorded; but it is more than likely the club's venture on the mountain above Wurtsboro far outweighed any momentary concern over a much needed shed. Over two hundred members of the one-year old club arrived on a pleasant June 10, 1893, and rode up to inspect their vast mountain holdings which they planned to develop. When the organization was formed, the building lots were priced at $100 but demand soon advanced the price to $125. As of June sixteenth, 359 lots had been sold and the club was talking of building a cable railroad along the brook from the site at Masten Lake to Wurtsboro. In September of 1893 a very lively rumor was making the rounds that Mountaindale people were planning to build an electric railroad from that place to the park. It is fortunate that it proved a rumor since a good team out of Wurtsboro could be at the park by the time the train got to Mountaindale.

As more cottages went up, the park's proponents boasted it would outdo Tuxedo Park[2] in a short while, which for opulence's sake, it never did. It did, however, open up the natural beauties of

51

A. General location of Yaugh House Springs, popular stopping place along the Old Mine Road, B. Remains of abandoned Delaware and Hudson Canal, C. Wurtsboro depot, D. O. and W. branch to Port Jervis and Monticello, E. Newburgh-Cochecton Turnpike, F. Pioneer 'Old Mine Road', G. Treacherous 'Wurtsboro Turns' of D. and H. Canal.

The Mamakating depot on the main line originally served Wurtsboro in the valley. The old board and batten structure burned to the ground on March 20, 1914, at 7:00 in the evening. Ernest B. Lyons was station agent at the time.

the mountain vastness west of the Mamakating Valley to the rapidly growing influx of summer visitors.

The Mamakating Valley, continuing an earlier trend, was laced and criss-crossed by the epochal development of Sullivan County transport in the 19th Century. Running on a northeast – southwest axis through the valley was the pioneer Old Mine Road.[3] It intersected in the valley at Wurtsboro[4] with the Newburgh-Cochecton Turnpike. Later, in 1825 the Delaware and Hudson Canal was built; followed in 1872 by the New York and Oswego Midland (O. and W.). Wurtsboro sat astride these lines of commerce and business in the great development years of Sullivan County; but, to a considerable extent, it remained aloof from the resort fever that overtook many parts of the county.

Mamakating (Wurtsboro) did serve as the de-training point of many guests for the resorts in the Rock Hill area — the Glenwood with accommodations for 150,[5] the Six Lake House and the Maple Lawn Villa.

The village of Wurtsboro itself had a number of hotels which, being located on avenues of commerce, could be classified more as drummers' (traveling salesmen) establishments than resorts; although they very early grasped at the opportunity of a listing in "Summer Homes."[6]

The 1878 first issue of "Summer Homes" noted for Wurtsboro that "there are several [boardinghouses] in the place, but this season Mr. Fred Harding is the only citizen who publicly invites city guests to visit the place. He is nicely located one mile from the depot and offers the best of accommodations to 12 boarders (adults preferred) at the low price of $5 a week." Across the Newburgh-Cochecton Turnpike from the canalside Harding House was the older Seaside Place (first listed in 1892), which had been a supply store during the heyday of the Delaware and Hudson Canal. Occupying a hill at the west end of the village stood the Wayside Inn, erected in 1910, while down in the village Frank McCune's Dorrance House was rapidly becoming a favorite with sportsmen.

All of these resorts sounded much better on paper than they were in reality. The more than slight distortions of truth brought about occasional blasts from the editorial press and once in a great while a closer look at the copy by the "Summer Homes" editors.

Harding House was recommended in the 1886 "Summer Homes" for "parties in search of a quiet and healthy resort with rowing in a stream 30 feet from the door." It may have been healthy but quietness is doubtful since the stream 30 feet (actually less) from the door was the bustling Delaware and Hudson Canal and until 1898 a

Lake Wood House, S. Burtis proprietor, was one of many hotels that dotted the area around Rock Hill. *Sullivan County Museum Archives*

Because of the "restricted" nature of the Sullivan County Club, the Glenwood was built further west at Rock Hill in direct competition to the private club. The large frame structure, under the proprietorship of Herman Krienke, overlooked Foulwood Lake and boasted "large windows, reception rooms" (shown here) "ladies parlors and men's smoking rooms." *Courtesy, Elsy Grant*

One share of stock in the exclusive and "restricted" Sullivan County Club. The 4,600 acre tract embraced virtually all of the 4,000 foor long Masten Lake, and featured a main club house, pictured on the stock, which generally opened on June 15th with special excursion trains operating over the O. and W. to Mamakating depot for $2.22, and a livery charge of .75 for adults from the depot to the park. Livery arrangements were under the direction of Frank McCune, the holder of this share of stock and proprietor of the Dorrance House in Wurtsboro. *Courtesy, Chester P. Stanton*

haven for the roustabout "canawllers."[7] The door noted was probably the one that opened on the towpath for ease of access to the barroom. As far as rowing in the stream was concerned, the D. and H. Canal operators took a dim view of this type of activity.

By 1891 some boarding house advertising had become so distorted it flushed out the editorial wrath of Charles Barnum, publisher of the Monticello *Republican Watchman*. In his July 31 column, "In Our Rocker," he stated, "We are sorry to have to say so, but several city people have complained that some advertisements about boardinghouses are 'way off' from the truth. So don't advertise large airy rooms if yours are an eight foot cube and you put five in a room.[8]

"Don't advertise first-class livery if your only horse is a plug old enough to vote for Cleveland next fall. Don't promise more than you can fulfill, for the worst that can happen is to have a guest who feels that he has been 'taken in' badly...often, when printing cards and circulars for boardinghouse keepers have we warned them of the folly of setting forth the advantages of their resorts in too poetic and imaginative a strain." J.C. Anderson, General Passenger Agent of the O. and W., agreed with Barnum. In a letter to the editor appearing in the *Watchman*, August 14, 1891, he took a swipe at the boardinghouse operator out to "skin the city visitor." Humorlessly he did not consider the much protested railroad rates to fall into the skinning category. He proceeded to cite a "...certain farmer in Sullivan County...who advertised in the most glowing terms the beauty and attractions of his farm, that he would further transport his guests free from and to the station, that his rooms were large and airy, that fresh vegetables were served at every meal, and that a trout pond was at his door." Reality did not match. Anderson continued to describe the plight of a New York familyman attracted by the glowing copy who "...was met at the station, driven to the farm, and to his astonishment found the rooms small, the lake a hog-wallow, and the only meal which he had was anything but first-class. He left in disgust, and was charged one dollar per head for dinner, and ten dollars for driving back to the station, a distance of one mile. That city man is today a walking advertisement against Sullivan County."

Publisher Barnum in his original editorial plugged for the establishment of a Boardinghouse Keepers' Association which would meet each "...fall and let each of those who take boarders subscribe something towards a fund for having this county properly boomed, either in some of the big dailies or by means of pamphlets." Anderson

Frank McCune's Dorrance House was popular with the sporting set, as witness the deer-laden vehicle about to return triumphantly to the city. The Dorrance House, when not entertaining hunters, was essentially a business hotel.

emphatically seconded the suggestion for an organization which in retrospect may very well be the first public pronouncement for the organization that eventually evolved into the Sullivan County Hotelman's Association. But this was still many years in the future, and each hotelman was, as he essentially remains today, a promoter unto himself.

One amusement that was a consistent favorite with the summer season visitor was the hay ride, or straw ride as it was also known at the turn of the century.

Picnickers and hay ride devotees from Bloomingburg often made the small resorts around Wurtsboro their destination on moonlight nights. One such outing — a dance at the Shady Side Grove two miles south of Wurtsboro — resulted in one of the worst disasters in the history of the O. and W. on July 13, 1892. Michael Denneen, driver of the leading three-seater wagon in a four or five vehicle caravan that approached the O. and W. tracks at the east end of Wurtsboro's Sullivan Street (Newburgh-Cochecton Turnpike) at 2:30 a.m., recalled later that "it was impossible to discern objects at a distance of more than ten feet, the darkness of the night rendered the fog even more impenetrable." He was, however, able to discern coal train No. 33 approaching from the south and halted accordingly. What he did not know, however, was that the crew was switching "on the fly."[9] After the engine and the first two or three coal cars had

The cupola topped Olcott House dominated the intersection of the Old Mine Road and the Newburgh-Cochecton Turnpike and boasted a sobering exhibit of live rattlesnakes in the barroom. The house, like all hostelries in the year 1873, found it good business to advertise, right, in Hamilton Child's Gazetteer and Business Directory of Sullivan County. *Sullivan County Museum Archives*

crossed, he gave the horse the whip. Half way across the tracks he spotted more coal cars not ten feet to his right looming out of the gloom moving at what he figured to be 20 to 30 miles an hour, but which train hands say was not greater than six miles an hour.

When the loaded coal cars crunched into his wagon, hitting Denneen's right shoulder, he held onto the reins "...and the quick jump of the horses pulled him away from further danger." As he fell he caught a Miss Case, on the seat next to him, and thus rescued her from the wheels of the car. The horses continued on a frantic dash up and over the Shawangunks to be finally corralled in High View.

The ill-fated coal car and train continued down the track for 250 feet until the doomed wagon derailed the forward truck of the car. The carrier then ran over the ties for seventy-five feet, bringing the train to a standstill 300 feet from the scene of the impact. The first of four bodies, that of a Miss McCoy, was, in the parlance of the 1890's press, "...found with her head cut open and brains strewn along the track for several rods. Twenty-five feet further down the track Mr. Frank was found...with his left arm and one foot...cut off, one hand crushed to a pulp and body more or less mutilated." The other two victims were also horribly maimed.

On July 22, 1892, two law suits were initiated against the O. and W., one by driver Frank Denneen of the livery firm of Denneen & Murphy and the other by Miss Frances Brown, one of the survivors. The speed of the train was an issue during the proceedings, but the bigger question

The first intrusion of the horseless carriage into the buckboard and rail-dominated pages of "Summer Homes" occurred in 1903 with a sepia-wash illustration of a chicken-chasing runabout.

"When the whispering whirr of the wheels will kiss
The ear, like a silent caress."
— H. W. PRYNNE.

Ye Clarendon Inn was originally owned and operated for several generations by Samuel Gumaer and was appropriately known as the Gumaer House. Chauncey B. Newkirk bought the hostelry and named it Ye Clarendon Inn and operated the Inn for summer boarders — without the necessity of a barroom. Today the grand old landmark still carries on as Ye Olde Inn, managed by John and Betty Couchon. *Courtesy of John and Betty Couchon*

The movement of White Motor cars and trucks from Cleveland to New York City over State Route 4 inspired the management to name the route the "Liberty Highway" which caught the fancy of newspaper editors across the length of the southern tier. *Courtesy, The Liberty Register*

The enthusiasm of the goggle and duster set was occasionally dampened, however briefly, by an upsetting mishap such as this turn-over in 1916 of a Locomobile. *Sullivan County Museum Archives*

The deadly curve and O. and W. underpass of state Rt. 4 (Rt. 17) near the Mamakating depot was a catastrophe to the contractor, Henry McNamee, who went bankrupt excavating the uphill cut and developing the massive fill below the underpass. *From a rotogravure print*

concerned the practice of fly-switching. In the early 1890's there were no laws on the statute books regulating the practice at grade crossings.

At the other end of Sullivan Street, away from the scene of the frightful accident, at the busy intersection of the Old Mine Road and the Newburgh-Cochecton Turnpike stood two classic *fin de siecle* hotels, the Olcott House and the Clarendon Inn (formerly the Gumaer House) which is still standing (1968) on the northeast corner of the intersection.

The Olcott House, one of the oldest and probably best known hostelries in Eastern Sullivan County, had been run for about 30 years by George H. Olcott. After his death in April, 1897, his daughter, Adelaide Olcott, assumed ownership of the landmark, one of whose unique features was a third floor museum room which exhibited local Indian relics. On display in the barroom was a glass case housing several very much alive rattlesnakes, a curiosity for the guests.

The museum was destroyed early in the morning of September 29, 1903, when at 12:30 the wagon house and horse sheds adjoining and connected with the hotel were discovered all ablaze, the fire having started in the hay loft of the wagon house. Despite the efforts of the firemen to prevent the spread of flames, the west side of the hotel was soon a mass of flames. "After three hours' battle, the fire was extinguished, the street frontages up to the third floor remaining, as well as the first and second floors being intact, though badly damaged." Fortunately there was no loss of life; a peddler from Kingston, a guest at the hotel was the only loser, having lost his wagon and horse.

The hotel was rebuilt to accommodate twenty less guests than the original fifty. The museum was never replaced. In 1920 the Olcott family sold the hotel; and three years later, on March 9, 1923, as the Hotel Butler, it burned to the ground. It was never rebuilt.

As the years passed, the Newburgh-Cochecton Turnpike declined in importance as a through route from the Hudson River to the Delaware

The climax of agitation for a bypass of Wurtsboro came on a hot Sunday afternoon in July (8), 1951, when a brakeless tractor trailer plunged into a string of cars at the Rt. 209 stoplight. The Wurtsboro Fire Department immediately responded under the direction of C.P. Stanton and fearless department members such as Fred Leinpinsel, shown here, right.
Sullivan County Museum Archives

River. It was replaced by what was eventually to become Route 17 — the main trunk line connecting Metropolitan New York with the Sullivan County resort regions and continuing westward to Binghamton. As the horseless carriage multiplied in the decade 1900-1910, it became increasingly apparent that some state action was necessary to establish an all-weather highway across the southern tier of New York, particularly between New York and Binghamton. Matters came to a head in the middle of May, 1911, when a delegation from Middletown and Monticello[10] called on Gov. John A. Dix at Albany to urge his approval of Assemblyman Evans' bill appropriating $1,200,000 for the construction of State Route 4 from Middletown, west. The delegates were successful, and the Governor supported the bill which the Legislature subsequently passed.

One of the more difficult engineering problems to be solved in constructing State Route 4 was on the side of the Shawangunks where the O. and W. grade crossing at Mamakating depot was eliminated. The solution, the construction of an underpass, was widely praised at the time; but in ensuing years it was evident that a monstrous bottleneck had been created — especially after the highway was widened from 2 to 3 lanes. But in 1916 the deep cut on one side of the concrete underpass and an equally high fill on the outside curve was a sight to marvel at in the infancy of highway engineering. By August of 1915 the $75,000 railroad overpass was about half completed.[11]

In April, 1917, teams, wagons and machinery had arrived to begin work on the unfinished seven mile section of the road in the Town of Mamakating under the direction of the Rockwell Contracting Co. Rockwell had about 10 teams and a well organized force of 75 men who worked like a piece of well oiled machinery.

Although construction of Route 4 had begun around Mamakating in 1916, work on other sections had begun earlier. Surveys for the road were commenced in 1910 by State Surveyor Philip Haas and a corps of six assistants who surveyed the route of a proposed highway between Liberty and Monticello in November of that year. The State Highway Commission announced its intention that the route should follow "...as nearly as practicable, the old Newburgh-Cochecton Turnpike." The road would go from Middletown to join the Newburgh-Cochecton Turnpike at Bloomingburg, thence westward through Wurtsboro to Bridgeville and Monticello.

The surveyors and engineers swarmed out across the route through 1911. All the surveys were completed by early winter thereby permitting the letting of contracts the following spring, with the Liberty to Delaware County line contract let in March of 1912 and the section from Monticello to Bloomingburg in April of the same year. All sections of State Route 4 in Sullivan County were begun in 1912, except for the section between Liberty and Monticello which the press reported as "indefinitely held up."

By fall of 1913 the editorial pens were busy at work taking pop-shots at the contractors on the various sections under construction. "The Merritt Construction Company has been working about two years on the state road between Liberty and Livingston Manor, a distance of some nine miles, and judging from present conditions it is altogether probable that for some time to come the road will not be completed and ready for travel."

Then there was Hallock and Angle, contractors who would begin work "...at a certain point only to...abandon it and start up...at another part of the route thus needlessly tying up traffic over the entire route and seldom leaving a portion of the highway completed and fit for use." Despite all delays and criticism by the press, State Route 4 between Monticello and Middletown was officially opened on Thursday November 1, 1917, by an assemblage of the Middletown Chamber of Commerce who motored from Orange County to Monticello and Liberty.

The following April (1918), State Route 4 acquired a nickname when R.H. Johnston, President of the White Company, a motorcar manufacturer of New York proclaimed in a speech: "owing partly to the spirit of the times and partly to the fact that the tourist setting out from New York over the new route makes his way toward Liberty, N.Y., it seems to me that the new route should be known as the 'Liberty Highway' and I so designate it."

Mr. Johnston's new cars and trucks were soon driving the 'Liberty Highway' enroute from Cleveland to New York, and barely a month later Harry J. DeBear, manager of the New York Maxwell Motor branch, laid out a route from Buffalo to New York for Maxwell drivers which included Route 4. The following July the Buick and Hudson people fell into line.

To further publicize 'Liberty Highway' Johnston announced that the "...White Company has completed arrangements to send an expert moving picture operator over the highway to take several thousand feet of film." The camera crews were received with great enthusiasm by the Business Men's Association of Liberty and Monticello and by the public in general, and more than six hundred feet of film out of the several thousand feet taken across the entire southern tier were shot in Liberty. The completed film, greeted with appropriate parades and hoopla, was shown to enthusiastic Sullivan County audiences.

To further boost the new traffic artery, the Liberty Highway Association[12] was launched. Typical of its promotions was a 1927 proposal to erect "...large de luxe billboards measuring 45 feet by 12 feet" and to interest chambers of commerce, hotel proprietors and businessmen of every town and city in their program and to enroll them into the association. The Sullivan County Chamber of Commerce was not caught sleeping. That same year it erected two signs "...30 feet long on the most traveled highways leading out of New York City, on the Jersey side of the Hudson River," and arranged with New York City papers – the *Evening Graphic,* the *American* and the *Herald-Tribune* – to run pictures and stories about Sullivan County. The chamber printed a booklet listing the county's boardinghouses and points of interest.

It was now apparent that the role of Sullivan County promoter was passing from the O. and W. to organizations formed and given impetus by the newly completed "Liberty Highway." The automobile was starting to pressure the passenger train out of the Sullivan transport scene. It is not known whether the New York, Ontario and Western Railway endorsed automobile sponsored resort promotion, but the implications were obvious.

The new highway carried a constantly increasing traffic load over the next decade and inevitably a proposal was made in 1928 to add another lane to the two-lane road. The suggestion came none too soon. A 12-hour auto count on Saturday, August 13, 1932, recorded 88,370 cars on the renumbered Route 17. Old State Route 4 had become the three-laned jugular vein of Sullivan County carrying the life-blood of the resort industry back and forth each summer-season weekend. But even three lanes proved too few. Each vacation season the inadequacies of the highway became more and more apparent, and a tragic Sunday in 1951 knocked the road's shortcomings into naked focus, when at about 12:15 P.M. a runaway tractor-trailer roared brakeless down the mile-long grade of Route 17 just north of Wurtsboro and bowled into a line of cars and taxis waiting for the traffic signal at Route 209. Fifteen automobiles were knocked helter-skelter by the huge trailer that tragic July 8 – four of them in flaming ruins when gas tanks exploded. Four people died in the flaming wreckage and a fifth, Mrs. Celia Weinberg, died later.

A resolution was immediately passed by the Sullivan County Board of Supervisors calling for the reinforcing of the State Police on duty in the southern part of the county and again decrying the fact that Route 17 was "narrow and congested and during the summer months is inadequate to take care of the increased traffic." Events on that flaming Sunday afternoon dramatically pointed out the desperate need for a new Rt. 17 bypass of Wurtsboro and no doubt brought the day of that improvement closer.

Class "E" locomotive 227 pausing on the Kingston branch trackage at Summitville, summer of 1939. The depot, left, is shown before platform extensions were installed. *Photograph by M.B. Cooke, from* Minisink Valley Express, *courtesy, Gerald M. Best, author*

Summitville

Pete dozed off as Train No. 29 eased down the mountain into Summitville. He knew that he could catch a few additional winks of sleep before the South Fallsburgh stop. The consist[1] creaked to a halt in front of the Summitville depot, an important junction point on the O. and W. for the unloading of express and a few passengers for the Ellenville branch.

Summitville was a busy railroad town but not a resort center. The 1886 "Summer Homes" listed only two farmhouses and one boardinghouse. Its role as a junction soon took on new status when a line was built southeastward down the Mamakating Valley to Valley Junction, switching point for the branch to Monticello.

The O. and W.'s northern branch to Ellenville was virtually as old as the main line. It operated its first train on January 16, 1871, a dark rainy Monday; but the event was brightened by the presence of the famed Liberty Coronet Band and a large crowd from the neighboring towns of Bloomingburg, Wurstboro, Phillipsport, Sandburg [later Mountaindale], Fallsburgh, Woodbourne and Liberty.

"At 2:30 in the afternoon an expectant throng gathered at the depot to see the cars come in. The passenger coach was crowded, inside and out, and a box car attached was also filled with passengers."[2]

In 1878 the first of a series of unusual special trains were run over the Ellenville branch, 'huckleberry trains', for the accommodation of berry pickers. It was an interesting concept, but a short lived one. A year later an announcement appeared in the local press of August 8, 1879, advising that the extra train for the huckleberry season would be taken off. These trains were brought into existence because of the popularity of berry picking among the summer visitors and commercial picking by migrant workers. The average daily shipments soon fell to less than 50 bushels per day. The potential of the Ellenville branch beyond huckleberry trains was not fully realized until extension to Kingston in 1902.

The first hearing granted to the Rondout Valley Railway Co. (later O. and W.) by the State Railroad Commissioners to explore the proposal of building a railroad from Ellenville to Kingston was held in January of 1898. Through 1899 and 1900

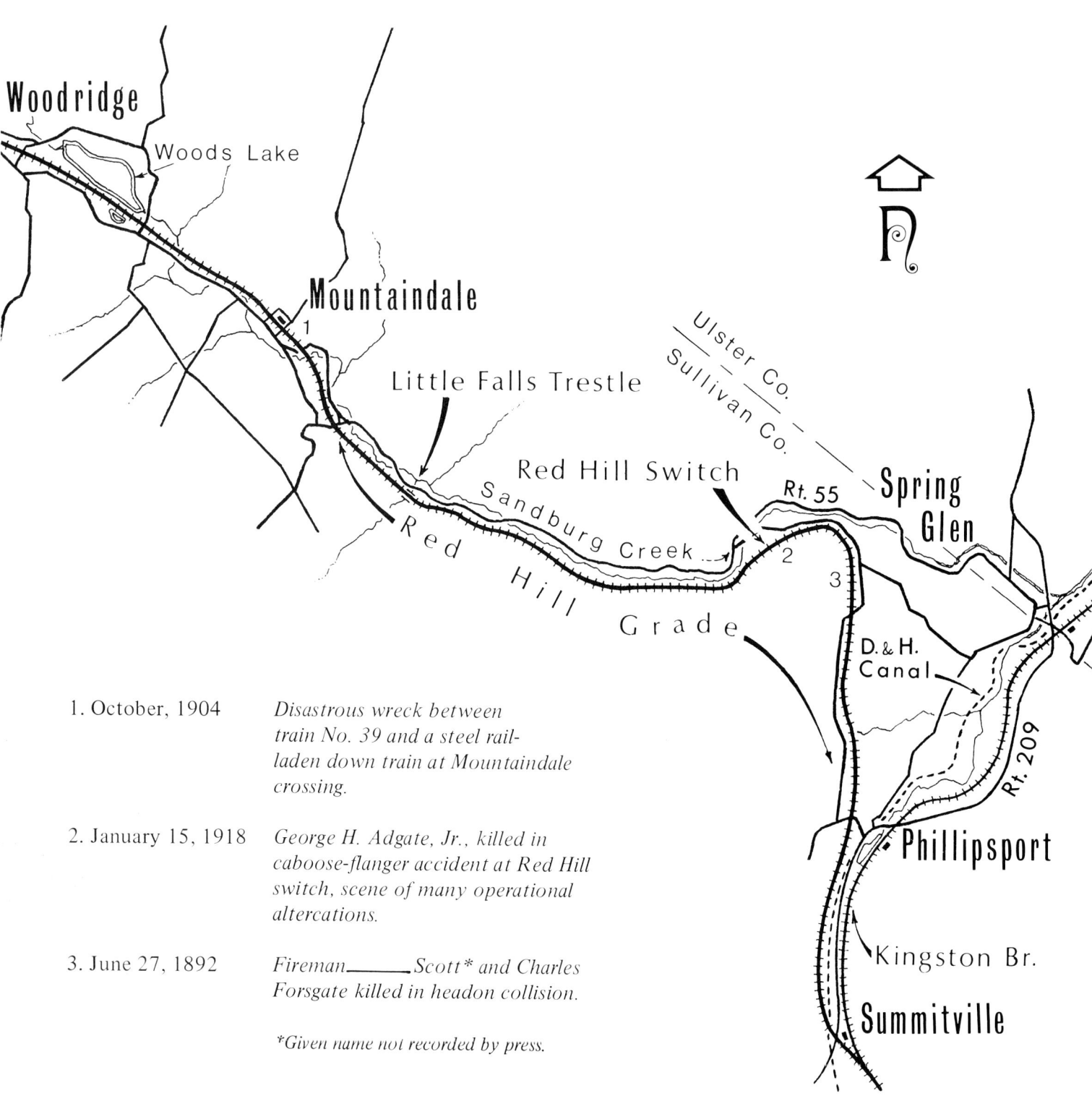

1. October, 1904 — *Disastrous wreck between train No. 39 and a steel rail-laden down train at Mountaindale crossing.*

2. January 15, 1918 — *George H. Adgate, Jr., killed in caboose-flanger accident at Red Hill switch, scene of many operational altercations.*

3. June 27, 1892 — *Fireman _____ Scott* and Charles Forsgate killed in headon collision.*

*Given name not recorded by press.

the O. and W. prepared specifications and was "making other arrangements" for letting contracts for the extension. At the same time independent coal operators and the Coal Trust were conducting hearings before the State Railroad Commissioners on the application of the Delaware Valley and Kingston Railway Company for permission to construct a road from Lackawaxen to Tidewater at Kingston along the bed of the Delaware and Hudson Canal.

Part of the Ellenville planning involved crossing the old Delaware and Hudson Canal, parts of which had been abandoned in 1898. Resistance to this idea developed almost instantly and as a result the canal was described as looking "like a Boer War entrenchment." The Coykendall people[3] flooded the ditch and drew up artillery — two old smooth bore cannon that had heretofore only seen duty on July 4th. "Watchmen day and night are kept on duty with instructions to blow to smithereens

A. Remains of the Delaware and Hudson Canal, abandoned in 1898, B. Summitville depot, C. Ellenville – Kingston branch.

anyone who attempts to throw a bridge across the canal."[4] By June 7, 1901, the Ontario and Western had purchased from the Cornell Steamboat Company that part of the Delaware and Hudson Canal lying between Summitville and Alligerville (twenty-five miles in length) and proceeded at once to extend its road to Kingston under the name of the Ellenville and Kingston Railroad.

The road was surveyed to follow the canal from Ellenville to Alligerville, thence along a line already run through Stone Ridge to Kingston. The Coykendall people were allowed sixty days to remove freight on the line of the canal after which time it was entirely abandoned west of High Falls.

On June 28, 1901, the contract for building the line to Kingston was let to J.M. Jackson and Co.

Roscoe-bound passenger train approaches Summitville behind locomotive No. 225 on a warm August day in 1939. *Photograph by John P. Ahrens*

Summer special leaving Summitville, eastbound, behind Y-class locomotive No. 409. Camp specials constituted a large percentage of the extra train movements. Train on trackage, extreme left edge, is moving into depot area from Port Jervis/Monticello branch. *Photograph by M.B. Cooke, Collection, Gerald M. Best*

Construction progressed through the fall and winter with "45 men employed on the work which will be continued for 10 miles to a rock cut which must first be blasted out before operations can proceed beyond."

The honor of running the first construction train over the new line, nicknamed the "Dago Flyer" and "Guinea Express,"[5] was credited to engineer "Val" Powell and conductor Dan Herlihy. They arrived from Hurley in Kingston at 5:30 on Friday afternoon, October 24, 1902, in a train consisting of a locomotive and seven cars. The press noted "... at 2:35 o'clock Friday afternoon the last rail was laid making the connection complete between Kingston and Ellenville, and at 5:23 o'clock Friday afternoon the last spike was driven."[6]

The new line not only served Kingston; it was also the impetus for opening up a whole new region to the summer boarder, as evinced by additions to "Summer Homes." In 1898 the O. and W. publication credited the Ellenville branch with resorts listed in Phillipsport, Spring Glen and Ellenville — the last mentioned having 35. North of Ellenville only one community was noted, Napanoch, which was accessible "... over a splendid road winding through the valley past broad and fertile well-kept farms." Ellenville in the pre-Ellenville and Kingston Railroad branch days was also the detraining point for Cragsmoor and Sams Point, as well as Kerhonkson, Ulster Heights, Greenfield, Montela and Lackawack.

Lackawack got its place in the sun through the efforts of the well-known hotelman, John Shiels. On a site now covered by a massive 180-foot high earthen embankment, Merriman Dam of the New York City Board of Water Supply, once stood the famous Lackawack House — a politician's retreat in the days of leisurely living.

A rare post card scene of three passenger trains at the junction simultaneously. The picture, taken about 1908, shows the train down from the Monticello branch, left, the mainline southbound from Liberty pausing at the water plug and, at right, as Henry Kortright wrote, "old No. 3 that ran on the Kingston job for years." *Courtesy, Henry Kortright*

Summitville in the peaceable time before Pearl Harbor was not without minor aggravations to the railroad management. The time was July 30, 1940, with trains No. 4 and 419 occupying most of the thru trackage. The photographer is not a summer visitor but railroad claims agent F.H. Hoffman photographing the car steps for evidence in an accident case. *Photograph by Stephen D. Maguire*

This altercation to locomotive No. 240 in July, 1933, took engineer Seth Jackson to glory and seriously bruised fireman Casey Scales. *Sullivan County Museum Archives*

For years it was commonplace to see Alfred E. Smith, John J. Delaney, Congressman William E. Cleary and other prominent Tammany Hall leaders dining in the main dining room or out on the wide verandas surrounding the famous resort.

In the 1885 "Summer Homes," it was still listed as a "hotel and boardinghouse" featuring 14 rooms and accommodations for 25, with adult rates ranging from $5 to $8 and a "liberal table supplied with chickens, eggs, milk, butter and farm products." Over the next 15 years dramatic changes took place. In the 1910 "Summer Homes" listing, the restyled Lackawack House took 12 lines of copy (as compared to five in the 1885 issue), to note accommodations for 250 guests and adult rates ranging from $7 to $15.

Features advertised ranged from "hot and cold water on every floor" to "sanitary plumbing, gas and electric lights." Especially highlighting the resort's new character was the reference to seven reservation offices located in New York City. Probably the most important of these was the one at 416 West 149th Street, the residence of Thomas Shiels, "Tammany Hall" alderman brother of the proprietor. When Tom wasn't busy delivering the votes, he was delivering the Tammany crowd to his brother as guests at the hotel.

The first real gala celebrated at the enlarged hotel was its formal opening in August, 1899. "All day Friday and most of Saturday barouches and open carriages clattered up the road from the Ontario and Western at Ellenville bringing gentlemen with checkered waistcoats and anchor link watch chains and smartly turned out women who could step between the tires of the carriage holding their ruffled petticoats and skirts in one hand and a parasol in the other, without getting a single fleck of dirt on their brocaded silks and taffetas or showing one inch more than the proper ankle."[7]

A dozen teamsters with stout drays cantered up and down the pike to get guests' trunks to the hotel in time for them to don their evening raiment. James D. Shiels recalled in 1938 that it was the "biggest party that ever happened in the valley. You should have seen the grand march. I can't describe it. And when they sat down to table, they filled the main dining room, the small one and the whole veranda. There were oysters from the Chesapeake and quail from Georgia, English mutton chops and partridge from right here in the Catskills. You couldn't name a wine or a whisky that couldn't be found in our cellar."

It all vanished in smoke in 1917. George B. Smith[8] recalled his carrying chairs out of the threatened dining room that wild night. "We heard shouting and as we came out the front door with the last chairs, the fire roared in over our heads. The stairs went up right inside the front door and when they opened the second floor windows to let out the smoke, the draft swept the fire upstairs. The entire hotel became a raging inferno in less than five minutes."

Activity at Summitville grew apace as business increased on the branches to Kingston and down the valley to Port Jervis and Monticello. Increased volume led to some bizarre happenings.

In July, 1933, a passenger locomotive struck a truck which apparently stalled on the track. The engine was turned entirely around and fell on its side against a passenger coach. The truck's motor was torn from its mounting. Fireman Casey Scaley was thrown from the top of the tender and badly bruised; while engineer Seth Jackson, drenched by live steam and scalding water, crawled through the top of the cab only to succumb later from severe burns.

The main line approaching Summitville, being on a stiff grade from both directions, always presented a challenge to throttle artists. When they erred, a "cornfield meet" resulted.[9] One occurring on January 16, 1901, involved northbound train No. 31 standing quietly at the Summitville tank and southbound train No. 32 moving briskly down the hill with 29 loaded cars. Although not a particularly heavy train, No. 32 did come into the curve at "a good rate of speed" — a bit more than the air brakes could handle. The crew on 32 remained at their posts just as long as it was safe, putting up brakes reducing the speed to five or six miles an hour before they "joined the birds".[10]

The original depot at Ellenville when the branch from Summitville terminated in a series of deadend sidings. *Courtesy, Ellenville Public Library and Museum*

Their frantic efforts were not enough as both engines poked their noses in the air and then toppled over on their sides down the embankment. Engineer Henry Herman of train 32 was later held to be responsible for the crash.

About 7:00 a.m. on January 1, 1904, northbound extra 205 in charge of conductor William Wolf and engineer John Dunham, and southbound train 35 in charge of conductor Judson Billings and engineer Thomas B. Miller had another "cornfield meet" just north of the station. Engine 161 was derailed. Engineer Dunham saw the southbound train approaching and had reversed his engine and was backing up when the crash came. Considerable damage was done to both engines and the tracks were blocked for seven hours delaying all trains. Investigation revealed that the accident was due to a freeze-up of the airlines on No. 161.

If Summitville was a challenge to the freight engineer, connections for the coach passengers were an ordeal that brought forth the editorial wrath of the Liberty *Register* on March 26, 1920. "For the last year or more the connections at that junction point have been the bane of every traveler's life." The editorial went on to illustrate how "... train #4 arrives in Summitville at 11 A.M. and the weary traveler must loaf around the station for thirty-two minutes until #1 arrives to go north on the main line. The afternoon connection is the best example of all. Train #2 arrives from Kingston at 5 P.M. missing connections with a through train – No. 3 – and the traveler cools his heels until the "SCOOT", No. 7, running as far as Roscoe only, comes along at 6:45 P.M. He is happy, for he has had to wait only one hour and forty-three minutes." The editorial droned on describing one poorly coordinated connection after another.

It is not known whether the frustrating connections at the Junction were responsible for the bizarre murder on March 24, 1916, but for a few

The new Ellenville depot was the scene of considerable carriage activity when the afternoon train was due from Summitville. The elegant Mt. Meenahga House was located atop the brooding Shawangunk Mountains, just out of picture, right. *Courtesy, Ellenville Public Library and Museum*

The commanding Terwilliger House and its gracious host and hostess was the cultural center of Ellenville society. It came to an end February 18, 1904, when it disappeared in a fire of considerable proportions. *Courtesy, Ellenville Public Library and Museum*

In 1881, U.E. Terwilliger bought one hundred acres, 1200 feet above Ellenville out of which grew the classic Mount Meenahga House destined to become the favorite of the "carriage trade" of the 1890's. Meenahga, the Indian word for huckleberry, was honored in 1887 when the O. and W. named a parlor car for the famed resort. One of the first golf courses in the area was laid out by the hotel in 1898 and later featured in the hotels advertising in the New York *Evening Post* for June 1, 1901. After forty years of Terwilliger ownership it changed hands. The genteel opulence gradually faded until its flaming curtain call in 1963 consigned it to the memories of generations of summer guests. *Courtesy, Katherine Terwilliger*

"**MOUNT MEENAHGA**," AN IDEAL JUNE RESORT.

Laurel, Sweet Brier, and Wild Flowers in Profusion.
Miles of Walks and Drives.
A home-like House with all modern conveniences.

GOLF.   **FIVE COTTAGES.**

For special June rates and illustrated circular, address the Proprietor,

U. E. TERWILLIGER, - Ellenville, N. Y.

The Wayside Inn was erected in 1907-08 on lands partially occupied by the fire-ravaged Terwilliger House. The Inn, costing over $200,000, was opened on September 24, 1908, with a sumptuous banquet honoring Mr. and Mrs. Oscar Krause and attended by 300 guests. Of Old English style, it boasted 12-foot porches along street exposures supported by pillars and porte cochere of Shawangunk grit. After passing through a number of ownerships, including the very successful managership of A.H. Fayer from 1940 to 1951, it was gutted by fire on October 25, 1967. *Courtesy, Katherine Terwilliger*

Guests at the Tammany Hall-dominated Lackawack House endured the bumpy ride up Honk Falls road past the storied Yama Farms. The steeple-topped pile burned to the ground in 1917.

SUMMITVILLE 71

The NEVELE Hotel and Country Club

On the Shawangunk Mountain Trail, Ellenville, New York

THE YEAR-ROUND VACATION RESORT

The Nevele Hotel started in 1901 as the Nevele Falls Farm House and grew into the imposing structure shown here as it appeared in the 1938 "Summer Homes." Today its velvet-smooth golf course fairways are guarded by a landmark multi-storied round tower, the trademark of the mid-20th century Nevele.

hours events stirred the village of Summitville to its depths and kept things in a furor.

Mrs. Harry Newkirk, estranged from her husband, boarded an O. and W. train for Summitville without knowing Harry was also on it. Less than half an hour after they were seen leaving the train in a heated argument at Summitville, her body, its throat slashed ear to ear with a razor, was found at the foot of a steep embankment by fireman William Hauser. Hauser had seen a shadowy figure throw something down the embankment a while before. Immediately several men began a search for the man Hauser had seen.

Shortly after 8 o'clock Ben Royce and Howard Smith were returning to Summitville along the tracks from Mamakating and came upon the mangled body of a man beside the main line tracks. An Erie pass made out to 'H. Newkirk' confirmed their suspicions of the corpse's identification. Presumably in an attempt to escape from the scene of his crime, he had attempted to board a passing train and was ground to pieces beneath the wheels of the locomotive — or perhaps in remorse, he had committed suicide.

Violence occasionally invaded the cars of the O. and W. In November, 1918, one Joseph Torri, an overly zealous smoker, on train No. 7 was asked by conductor Elmer "Shorty" Vaughn to put out a cigarette. Upon returning to the coach Vaughn discovered Torri still smoking and when again directed to throw the cigarette away, Torri drew a knife and stabbed the persistent conductor. Amid all the confusion at Middletown's Wickham Ave. station, Torri, a railroad construction worker, left the train and soon after was sent out with a wrecking crew to Ferndale where a troop train had been derailed. He was located and placed under arrest at that point.

A northbound abbreviated freight eases past a now seldom used Summitville depot in the fall of 1956. By the fall of 1969, the depot stood gaunt and lonely, the tracks and ties are gone, replaced by thistle, golden rod and the ghosts of grumbling passengers and their endless transfers from the mainline varnish to the Monticello and Kingston branch trains. *Photograph top by Jim Shaughnessy*

Minton Flurer, son of Dr. W.F. Flurer, held up at the grade crossing at Mountaindale by crossing guard flagman, Thomas Arr. The 1906 scene was the location of the whistle tooting freight train wreck in October, 1904, which terrorized patrons at the bar of the Hotel Rosen, background. The Flurer-owned Pope-Hartford was one of the first autos in the area.   *Courtesy, Eli Atwell*

Mountaindale

Sandburg

The labored exhaust of the steamer, as it moved train No. 29 up the Red Hill grade, no doubt sunk to lullaby proportions for slumbering Pete as he and the Sunday papers were lifted about 420 feet to Mountaindale from Summitville in the valley below.

Red Hill and its infamous switch and siding was so fraught with tragedy and near-tragic events that it was often called 'bad luck hill' by operating crews.

One classic newspaper account graphically described the wreck of "Andy" O'Neill on Red Hill grade. "Engineer Andy O'Neill,[1] one of the most popular on the O. and W., in charge of engine 127, Sunday night (June 27, 1892), drawing a milk train, came tearing down Red Hill about 6:30 p.m. without a thought of danger. If there was anything coming north it would be lying in the switch at Summitville. He had no orders, and hence only his own train to look out for.

"Suddenly around the curve, only fifteen car lengths away, came an engine and caboose. It was also running fast. A collision was inevitable. On the pilot of the engine sat two brakemen. The sight almost held the milk train's engine crew spellbound. Engineer O'Neill reversed his engine and jumped, as he saw the two others jump from the pilot, but fireman Scott stood as if in a trance. He crouched ready to spring, his hands in the air, his eyes starting from his head.

"Too late! The crash came. He was caught in his crouching position and life squeezed out of him. He was found thus by the excited trainmen who escaped injury.

"Engineer Wheeler's fireman, Charles Forsgate, like his brother fireman, remained in the engine and when they searched for him his lifeless body was found beside the wreck.

"Wheeler owned up at once. He forgot all about the milk train. He had orders to pass an extra at

On October 14, 1904, during blasting operations for double tracking of Red Hill Grade, a huge rock was dislodged and rolled onto the tracks. The up-grade flagman had not gone far enough to prevent engine 169 from impacting the rock. The late Eli Atwell recalled "the engineers name was Eckert and he sat right in the cab and rode it down the hill."

The Little Falls Trestle and the Red Hill grade, below (from 1897 "Summer Homes"), about mid-way up the valley of the Sandburg, was the setting for the following report that appeared in an August, 1900 issue of the Ellenville *Press.*

"An O. and W. train was fifteen minutes late in leaving Liberty, and as the track is down grade Engineer Ryan decided to make up time. The usual running time to Summitville is thirty-eight minutes, and the run was made in twenty-five, at a speed of a mile a minute. The swaying of the rear car around the many sharp curves in the road frightened the women passengers. Six of them fainted, and men rushed about the car in confusion. The bell rope was pulled several times, but as it was not connected to the locomotive, Engineer Ryan continued his fast run, unaware of the excitement and fear among the passengers. *Top, courtesy, Robert F. Harding*

Mountaindale, and it diverted his mind from the regular trains.

"He forgot it and ran into it."[2]

At the infamous Red Hill switch Andrew J. Riley, secretary for C.A. Draper, paymaster of the O. and W., was injured in a head on collision between the paymaster's car and train No. 29. Asleep in his berth in the paymaster's car, he was thrown to the floor sustaining a severe scalp wound. This mishap, occurring at dawn on November 23, 1901, was due to a simple "misunderstanding of orders."[3]

Suicidal tendencies also manifested themselves on the "hill." In May, 1912, a Jersey City woman leaped from the window of the lavatory in a passenger coach on O. and W. train No. 2 and was instantly killed.

Whether or not Red Hill or its namesake switch cast an evil spell on the mentally unbalanced is not known, but Oscar O. Bennett, a former O. and W. engineer of Hancock, might have had reason to believe it did.

A. Site of Mountaindale depot.

"Henry Osborne was my fireman that night we eased out of Summitville with a tonnage train after taking water for the run up Red Hill. About half way up the hill I noticed the steam was twenty pounds off and the stoker was not feeding coal fast enough so I yelled over to Osborne to run the stoker faster and his reply was that it was good enough.

"I walked across the deck to open the stoker steam valve more and Osborne picked up the stoker poker and said 'If you touch that valve I will kill ya.'

"Stopping at Fallsburg for water I realized that Osborne was far from sane. At Cadosia we took on coal, water and sand and had lunch and coffee. At Carbondale he asked me to have breakfast with him. As he was so surly and unlike himself I did. We had pancakes and eggs and when we had the second cup of coffee the waiter said something to him. He immediately whipped out his pocket knife and stabbed the waiter to death."

As Oscar later reflected, "It is well I decided not to mess with the stoker steam valve that night on Red Hill."

With the onset of winter the hazards were compounded. On a cold afternoon, January 15, 1918, trainman George H. Adgate, Jr., was killed at Red Hill switch, crushed beneath the caboose attached to a flanger. He had been standing on the steps of the caboose signaling the engineer while the flanger was struggling with the tightly packed snow drifts.

It was not only winter snow that caused trouble but occasionally a switch carelessly left open. No one closed the switch at Mountaindale on November 14, 1890, and the southbound mail train express entered the switch dashing into a standing freight train.

Charles Davis, the express engineer, jumped a second too late and was buried in the debris and badly cut and injured. Several passengers were scarred for life by the broken glass and flying seats. The freight was badly damaged with several of the express cars telescoped and both engines were candidates for the back shops.

Had Pete Reilly known of all the misadventures on Red Hill and at Mountaindale his sleep might not have been so sound. In any event, the paper train breezed right on through Mountaindale without incident. What Pete could not know was that the region hereabouts would develop so extraordinarily that by 1898 the paragraph blurb in "Summer Homes" would announce: "To supply the summer residents, the railroad agent at Mountaindale will sell from July 1st to October 1st all New York and Brooklyn daily papers."

"Summer Homes", Number 1, 1878, listed the settlement at the top of Red Hill grade under Summitville and described it as " ... The romantic village of Sandburg ... in the midst of trout streams and wild scenery, and commanding charming views of far-reaching landscape, lie among the hills cool and inviting."

Advertisement in the 1873 *Gazetteer and Directory of Sullivan County* when Mountaindale was still known as Sandburg.

The local name of Sandburg[4] did not last long, for on December 24, 1880, it was announced " ... the name of the Post Office at Sandburg, Sullivan County has been officially changed to Mountain Dale."[5] In the year Pete rode through, there were six 'Christian' resorts listed in the Mountain Dale area and by 1898[6] they had multiplied to 22 farmhouses including the first emerging hotels. The copy for some of the resorts was reaching for hyperbole, going far beyond the "free transportation to and from the depot" and "abundance of milk, cream, eggs, fresh fruits and vegetables" of a simpler era. The Monte-Valle House had "window screens" and was "surrounded by spacious piazzas" and their "shrubs and herbaceous plants [were cared for] under the direction of a competent landscape architect." The Mountain Dale Hotel boasted "every floor lighted by electricity, with electric bells and hall boy service." The Idlewile noted "sleeping rooms are high, with a transome (sic) over every bedroom door." Virtually every entry gave an accurate reading of the elevation above sea level and the assurance that "no malaria was lurking about." The size of the piazzas was as important here as at High View except they went one better with a number of resorts boasting "double piazzas."

The first Jewish resort listing in Mountaindale appeared in the 1899 "Summer Homes" and simply noted "Paul P. VanBarriger – Hebrews taken only, Circulars on application."[7] By 1910 four out of the six Mountaindale listings stressed "strictly Kosher," "Kosher board," "Kosher table," and "Hungarian and strictly Kosher." Today, in the 1960's, Mountaindale is a summer center of many Hasidic Jews, the ultra orthodox

The Mountaindale depot as it appeared about 1890 on the occasion of what appears to be a wedding or confirmation party. The depot, lower, after the addition of platforms. This scene depicts the era of the all-season vacationer as witnessed by the pileup of steamer-sized trunks. The box car, right rear, rests on the "house track" used on frequent occasions by the private palace car of George M. Pullman when the founder of the Palace Car Company visited his brother-in-law, Dr. William F. Flurer. *Courtesy, Eli Atwell*

MOUNTAINDALE. Sandburg

sect whose men wear captans and sidecurls.

The late Eli Atwell of Mountaindale recalled that the first Jew to settle in Glen Wild, a settlement near Mountaindale, was John Gerson "... somewhere around 1895 or 1896. He bought the George Adams farm and the Ben Howes place adjoining it. He erected a large boardinghouse which eventually accommodated 100 guests of his own class of people." Although VanBarriger's place in Mountaindale led the way with his brief notation regarding Jewish clientele, it remained for John Gerson to insert the first complete Jewish resort listing in "Summer Homes" — the year was 1899.

CENTERVILLE STATION – *Glen Wild Post Office*

J. GERSON — Rock Hill Jewish Boarding House. *5 miles; accommodate 40; adults $6, children $3, transients $1; discount to season guests; transportation free; new house, newly furnished; prepare our own meats; raise our own vegetables; scenery unsurpassed. Jewish faith and customs throughout; ¼ mile from Post Office; good road to station; fine shade; good airy rooms.*

The local press of March, 1901, reported that during 1900[8] "...the Edmond H. Conklin farm near Centerville was sold to I. Sussman and his son, Russians, and of the ancient faith of Iserael [sic.]. The place consists of about 175 acres, and they propose to erect thereon a large boardinghouse to entertain their own people. Further on, towards Glen Wild, the place formerly occupied by Herman Gillett, has been bought by Ben Gold and another of his nationality. The George M. Gillett place was recently sold to Jacob Gold and Rosa Skywinsky."

The Royal House in Mountaindale was developed by a Mr. Schlosberg who came to the mountains in 1905 and purchased a farm. In 1920 a dining room was added and the exterior covered with stucco–the architectural craze of the early 20's. *Courtesy, Steingart Associates*

An indication of the prosperity of the Forman Brother's, New Prospect House, may be traced in the pages of "Summer Homes." In 1929 the house listed accommodations for 350, and by the depression year 1938 their accommodations potential had dwindled to 200. *Courtesy, Steingart Associates*

The stately Monte-Valle House, unlike many farmhouses, expanded to boardinghouse proportions; this three-story resort facility was built expressly for summer boarders. *Sullivan County Museum Archives*

About this same period the Nathan Goldstein family occupied a farm on the Greenfield Road near Mountaindale. Goldstein's two sons, Jake and Barney, took to peddling, earned enough money and went off to school and became real estate agents selling farms and property to their brethren in the Sullivan County area. The Goldstein brothers operated the Greenfield House which in 1906 advertised "All modern improvements; raise own vegetables; good fishing; first-class livery; large, airy rooms; good board, strictly Kosher; best accommodations for Hebrews. Terms and reference on application."

The usage of the word Hebrews as just noted was the subject of a letter to the editor on January 13, 1893, which was doubtlessly prompted by the frequent use of the word Hebrew in the press. The item in the Liberty *Register* asked that Jews be called Jews, not Hebrews, "...the word Hebrew now has but one meaning, and that is a dead language. We are Jews because we are adherents of the Jewish Religion.

"There is an impression in the minds of many non-Jews and even some Jews that it is a courtesy to call us Hebrews thus implying there is some stigma attached to the name of Jew.

"We are Jews, not Hebrews or Israelites."

This plea from the then small number of Jewish summer boarders, must have fallen on deaf ears since it continued to crop up in the local press down through the years.[9]

"Hebrews have turned their attention towards Woodbourne and are buying up the purchasable farms in that section."[10] Many of the older Christian residents of the area resented the influx of Jews and did whatever they could to harass them. "These Jewish-Christian tensions still exist in Sullivan County where year round residents have formed themselves into 3 distinct societies: all Jewish, all Christian, and a mixture of the two. This last category is generally the one in which the leaders of the county's business and political power tend to be centered."[11]

On August 31, 1906, the Hurleyville *Sentinel* reported, "A Hebrew hired a horse and carriage of Durland's livery, Hurleyville, recently to go to Loch Sheldrake. On the way he took in five more passengers and when the horse did not travel as fast as they desired they lashed him with the whip. A friend of Mr. Durland's seeing the transaction, telephoned him, and he immediately went to Loch Sheldrake and had the Hebrew arrested for cruelty to animals. He was fined $18 and costs, which served him right."

Headline in the June 19, 1914, Liberty *Register* read: "Train Crew and Hebrews Fight." Other headlines read "Hebrews buy Smith Farm: Pay Thirty-Six thousand."[12] In this instance the release did not even give the name of the party. The press for January 14, 1921, under Ferndale noted "Hebrew Parties Launch Empire Hotel Corporation with $30,000 Capital."

By the 1920's most all of the real estate purchases made were by Jewish parties. The use of the word Hebrew persisted though, even in the extensive release announcing the disposal of the Shawanga Lodge by D.G. Carpenter for $55,000 in January of 1920 to Solomon Hector. "There has been considerable activity in the real estate market at Bloomingburg and High View for several weeks, and there are several other large houses which New York City parties have under consideration...All the recent buyers have been Hebrews."

Seven years before this transaction, on July 18, 1913, Attorney General Carmody directed attention to the fact that circulars are being issued by some health resorts in which announcement is made that their places are not open to certain races. He pointed out that under an amendment[13] to the Civil Rights Law by the Legislature such notices will be prohibited after September 1,1931.

Out of the farm-type boardinghouses around Mountaindale emerged a resort of consequence, the Park House, which commanded almost a full page in the 1895 "Summer Homes." "Directly in front of the hotel is a charming and picturesque waterfall, while the lake affords boating and fresh water bathing...a shady island, trout brook...a casino containing a large dancing hall, cafe, billiard room and bowling alley, is situated 200 yards from the hotel and cottages." Whether or not the Park House had double piazzas is not recorded, but the resort was important enough to have a wire cut in by Western Union with an operator on duty during the summer months. The "house" also laid claim to having the first electric lights in the county; the creek being dammed just below the house with a dynamo installed "guaranteeing lights all night long."

By 1910 it had been entirely renovated and could accommodate 300, with the expanded casino termed "magnificent" by the publicists who were by now emphasizing the "strictly Kosher table." Of course the rates went up in proportion, making it increasingly more difficult for the breadwinner to keep the family in the mountains all summer.

For the many people who could not afford, or did not want the hotels, other facilities were developed: the bungalow colonies and the *Kuchalanes*.[14] At many of these latter places a family rented a sleeping room and a space in a large communal kitchen.

Mountaindale saw some of the first such "do it yourself" kitchens which were soon springing up all over with sinks, ice boxes, stoves and no food. You arrived with food, pots and pans (with your name inscribed thereon) and the inevitable flit gun for the flies that always infested the cooking areas. Fights over choice locations on the top shelf in an ice box or a spot at the "better" sink or the desirable table at the one window that looked out on absolutely nothing, were almost daily occurrences. There was also keen competition among the women as to who was the cleanest. They engaged in endless arguments if someone was sloppy and if nobody was sloppy it was complaints against the landlord and the quantity of the toilet tissue in the community bathroom or the rough quality stocked.

The great days of the kuchalanes were also the halcyon years of the bungalow colony operators which peaked out roughly between 1945 and 1952 when the servicemen returning home to tight housing conditions in New York City, entered matrimony, and were forced to live with mama and papa. Summer afforded them the opportunity to engage a bungalow in the mountains and break away, the result being that every chicken coop and barn was pressed into service as a "summer home." When the housing market opened up later in the 50's the new homemaker had his own home, a new car and air conditioning to keep him away from the "colonies." The jet age and the proliferation of childrens' camps opened new vacation possibilities. Increasingly, people "kenneled" their children and flew off for 3 weeks in Europe. The colonies didn't easily give up. They began offering more than mere walls – Broadway shows, indoor swimming pools and night clubs soon became costly necessities for a successful "season." Although a few large colonies could compete successfully for the dwindling market, the colony owners were fighting a losing battle against a national trend, namely the obsolescence of old resorts, whose major offerings were proximity and fresh air.

In 1890 the distant horizons were unattainable except by the adventuresome few. John Allen[15] thought it an adventure when, at a very young age, he clambered down the coach steps at the old depot at Sandburg,[16] a matter of a few years before the new Mountaindale depot was built around 1890. John Allen started working at the Mountaindale depot in 1902 on a twelve-hour shift. He was joined in 1907 by Eli Atwell who

One of the casualties of the October, 1904, altercation at Mountaindale involved the shattering of a cattle car and the killing and maiming of many of the beeves. A number of the killed may be seen scattered in front of the wreckage, photograph above. The steam of the stuck whistle is shown drifting toward the Hotel Rosen, whose proprietor had a few bad moments as chunks of debris piled up outside the hotel. To the right of engine No. 33 below, may be seen the narrowly missed Mountaindale depot. *Courtesy, Robert F. Harding*

The summer home of noted brain surgeon, Dr. William F. Flurer. Located in the valley of the Sandburg, just below Mountaindale, it was a favorite relaxing point for Chicago-based, Pullman Palace Car Company founder, George M. Pullman, when on business trips in the east. *Sullivan County Museum Archives*

started as a summer helper on the baggage and passenger-laden platforms. Eli recalled how 120 to 130 trunks would go in the baggage car of No. 8, a typical middle-of-the-week train. "Me and this one-handed man would pick up the baggage just as fast as they were rolled to us, and throw them in the car where they had two or three men packing them back."

Being on the platform a good part of the time, Eli was privileged to witness some most unusual events. One day after unloading baggage from No. 1, the noon train, Eli noticed, unbelievingly, as the brakeman of a sidetracked freight anxiously threw the switch over before the last passenger car of No. 1 had cleared the points.

Eli recalled, "... the rear trucks on the last coach took the switch track, then the car went up the line, the front trucks on the main line and the rear on the switch track. Well, this guy saw what he had done and he threw the switch back and got away from there and nobody ever knew what happened." The engineer and fireman on the engine of the way freight saw it coming toward them and jumped a moment or two before the empty coach hit the engine and snapped the coupler. By coincidence the "snooper,"[17] a man Atwell remembers only as Coburn, was on board No. 1 and got off to attempt to find out what had happened but nobody knew a thing. "Coburn tried to tell my uncle, who was the section foreman, that there was something wrong with the tracks at the switch causing the trucks to jump the frog."[18]

The depot crossing was the scene of a spectacular wreck in October, 1904, when train No. 39 came around the curve north of the depot with 12-carloads of steel rail in tow. 'In the hole'[19] on the Mountaindale siding was a freight whose caboose and a few cars still fouled the main line. The weight of the steel rails carried the locomotive into the exposed cars littering the grade crossing with a splintered caboose and dead and partly dead beeves, one of the cars being a cattle car. To make the moment more dramatic the whistle on the wrecked locomotive stuck for over an hour alerting the entire countryside to the disaster.

Sunday afternoons after the emergence of the Jewish resorts were recalled by John Allen as simply 'hectic.' "On Sunday afternoons we had three passenger trains to the city and one in the evening, all heavily patronized by the rabbis. They rode on a reduced rate ticket, as did all clergy, and they had a special coupon book so when one man was selling straight tickets we would go through the line, pick out the rabbis and process their tickets at a half door arrangement we built to speed things up.

"When the money drawer got full we had a paper bag fastened to the side of the money drawer and we'd reach in the money drawer and throw it into the paper bag." The last train out at 7:40 on

The Red Hill Grade commences in earnest just past the grade crossing, right, and the former Hotel Rosen, center. The abbreviated depot is all that was required in the waning years of passenger traffic following the devastating fire of September, 1931. In this 1953 view, the volume of passenger traffic can best be measured by the lone baggage cart. *Photograph by Edward H. Weber*

Sunday evening had a special express messenger on board so that all stations could remit all monies taken in except a small amount retained for change.

An event of consequence in the community was the arrival on the 'house track' (siding in back of the station) of George M. Pullman's[20] private car. The rail tycoon came to the village to visit his sister, Emma,[21] wife of the noted brain surgeon, Dr. William F. Flurer,[22] whose summer home was just down the valley of the Sandburg below Mountaindale.

Resort life in its post-Labor Day leisure and the rhythm of the O. and W. telegraph key at the Mountaindale depot came to a smouldering halt during the early morning hours of Saturday, September 26, 1931, when a $300,000 fire, starting at about 1 a.m. in Aaron Anderman's store spread out on both sides to engulf 14 other buildings in the business district. The Meyer Levine building vanished as did the Meyerson feed store when the flames swept down to the railroad tracks to involve the O. and W. depot and freight house.

Fire Chief Mortimer Michaels[23] and his aides, summoned by men from a restaurant who were alerted by a cry of "Fire" from someone on the street, saw the severity of the blaze and promptly put in the call for men and apparatus from Monticello, Liberty, South Fallsburg, Loch Sheldrake, Hurleyville, Woodbourne and Woodridge. The mutual aid and a persistent falling rain and lack of wind all combined to save the village from complete destruction.

Mountaindale started to rebuild again just as it did after an earlier fire in October, 1912, when $35,000 worth of property was destroyed. The O. and W. suffered only a two or three hour loss of the telegraph circuit; a minor consequence compared to the loss in 1931 of the old depot. The O. and W. used an old passenger coach for the care of passengers and a freight car for express office use. It was reported in the press of October 15, 1931, that the construction of a new railroad station would not be started until the following spring. However, the depression had hit, passenger business had declined, and a full-scale station was never built.

An abbreviated facility was constructed which served Mountaindale until it was abandoned by the O. and W. in 1957.

Mother Hubbard-type locomotive No. 248 eases into the pre-platformed "Centreville" (spelling, circa, 1907) depot as passengers drift out to board the down train to the city. In the background is the Centerville House, dominant structure in a section of the business district then known as the 'Bowery'. *Courtesy, Mrs. Bruce Denman, Sr.*

Centerville
Woodridge

As the paper train highballed through Centerville[1] in 1886, there were actually more 'guest receiving' farm houses in the area than the seven listed in the "Summer Homes" — apparently many of them did not bother to seek inclusion. Centerville now had its own depot, completed in late summer of 1882. Up until then the lack of depot facilities deterred most vacationers from seeking out the few resorts located in the area. The new depot opened new horizons for the farmers. One farmhouse elevated itself to boardinghouse status. Following virtually every resort listing were two to five references with New York City addresses. Bank officials, doctors or people with a Wall Street address were frequently cited as well as the plentiful supply of Civil War colonels and majors, whose names lent a certain tone to the resorts they graced.

Sportsmen were attracted to the Mountaindale-Centerville area by trout fishing, particularly in the early years. The 1878 "Summer Homes" noted that Centerville was nestled "in the midst of trout streams and wild scenery." Even in the 1960's Sullivan County attracts fishermen and its principal river, the Neversink, although not as pristine as it once was, is a trout stream which is regularly stocked by the New York State Conservation Department.

Disgruntled fishermen are a wild lot. The fishing around Centerville on June 19, 1914, just wasn't what it should be, at least for a man named Brown, an employee of the O. and W. shops in Middletown. As the contemporary press recorded it, "Brown had come from Middletown to a stream near Centerville to fish for trout; but, his luck being poor, he patronized one of the saloons conducted by a Hebrew." An altercation developed with the proprietor and a few near knock-out blows were dealt. Soon a crowd congregated; and, as Brown could see no friendly faces, he beat a hasty retreat to the O. and W. station. "After he had gotten in the building, the mob, fighting mad, pursued and attacked him. He was being unmercifully pounded, when the way freight, extra No. 138, conductor Sam Sprague in charge, pulled into the station. The train crew, seeing what was going on, rushed to the aid of their Christian brother." A free-for-all fight developed that was far "from a pink tea affair" and several people, including Brown, were badly beaten, as an O. and W. train

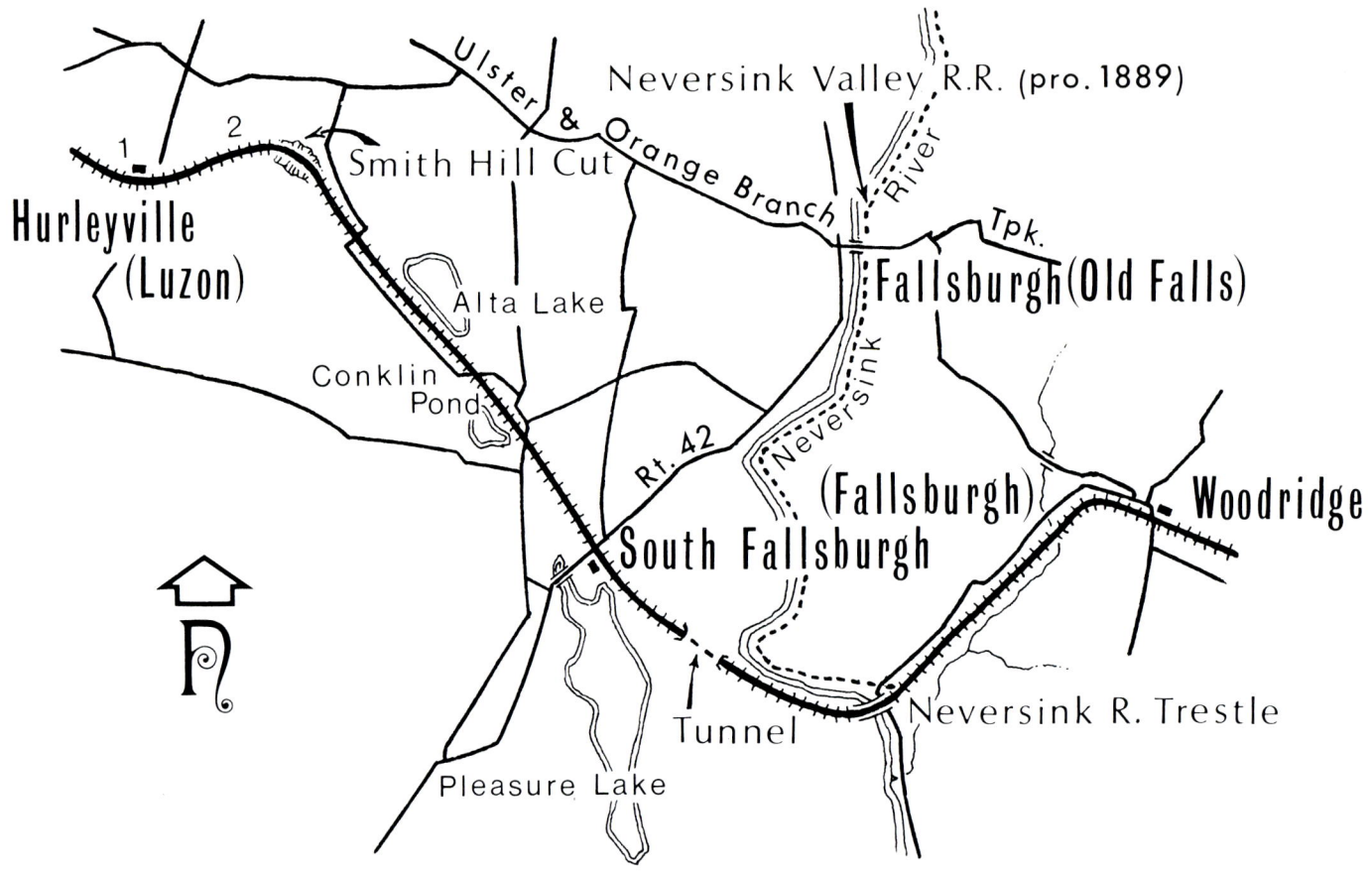

1. February 1901 — Rear-end accident between flanger, second No. 9 and passenger train, first No. 9.

2. February 13, 1907 — Explosion of engine No. 70, killing trainmen Martin Mullen, J.D. Valquette and William Gadwood.

crew "in such instances is sure to make sort of a lion's attack."

Conductor Sprague was placed under arrest and the way freight delayed an hour. The last paragraph of the story contained the understatement of the year: "There had been some ill feeling brewing for some time between the people of Centerville and the O. and W. men."

Mechanical violence also took its toll around the Centerville depot. In late January, 1904, Jesse York and Andrew Wilson were returning home by sleigh when their horse started running away. They reached the depot crossing just as the southbound second section of train No. 30 approached. The cutter upset and "...the men were thrown to either side of the track, with their heads in opposite directions. Engineer [Charles] Boyce saw the men as they were dumped out upon the track, but too late to prevent striking them." York was dead when Boyce and Engineer Charles Kent reached the victims. Wilson was badly injured.

Some railroad accidents fortunately were less serious. Oscar O. Bennett related an incident involving engine No. 410, fresh from a complete overhaul at the Middletown shops and just nicely broken in for three days as the 'Summitville pusher.' "The 410 was in perfect condition, rode like a pullman and real snappy. I had 14 empty gons [coal cars] and I was making around 60 miles per hour as I wanted to get the tunnel block ahead of No. 2 at Fallsburgh."

What Oscar did not know was that the station agent at Woodridge had placed two express trucks, each containing thirty crates of eggs, out for No. 2 on the northbound tracks. "These I hit at 60 miles per hour and you should have seen the shiny new 410; she looked as if she had yellow jaundice." Oscar was called on the carpet but the station agent admitted that he had not bothered to find out if any northbound trains were due.

Centerville depot itself was almost destroyed when an abandoned three-story coal and feed

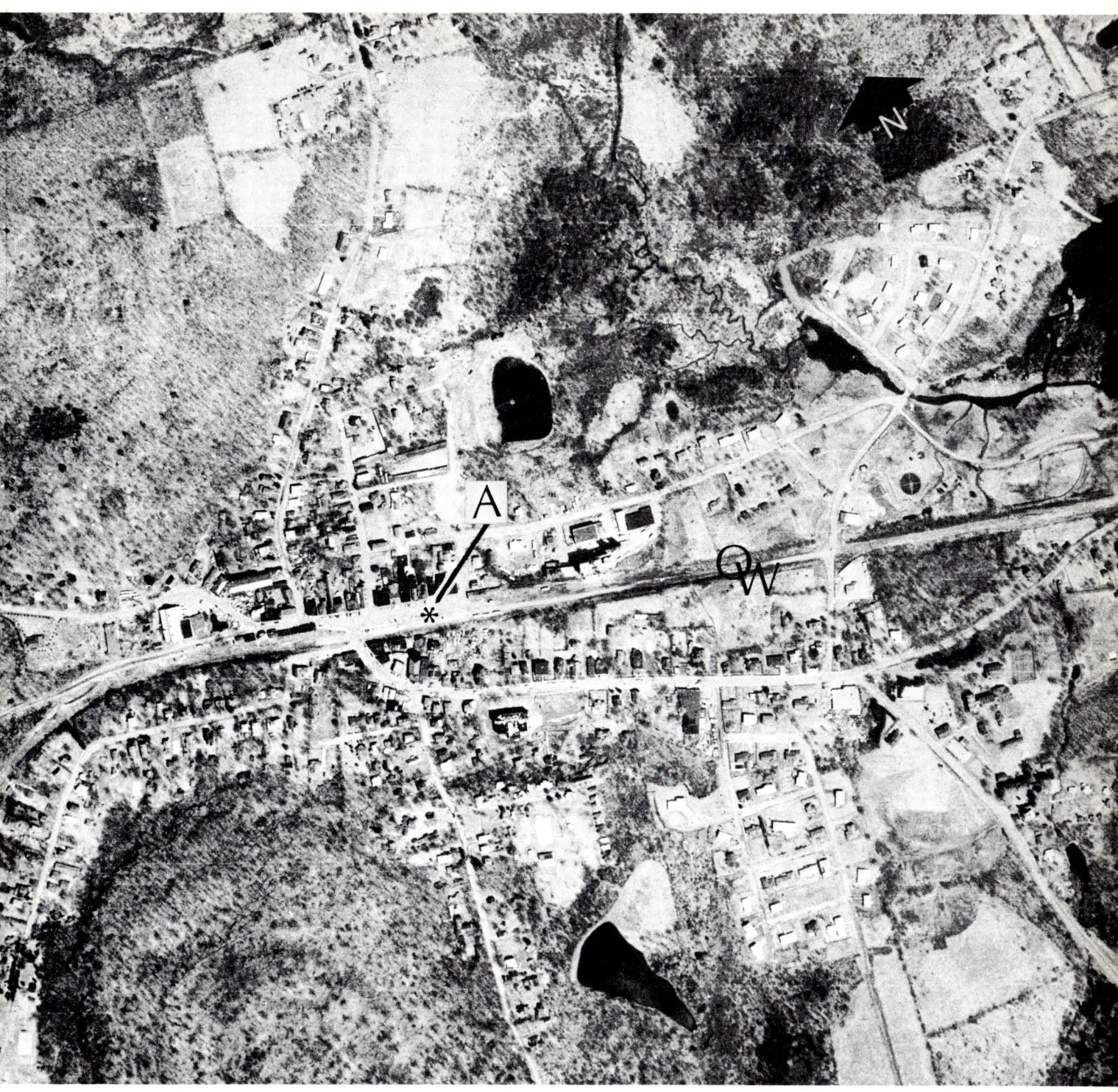

A. Site of Centerville (Woodridge) depot.

warehouse, once used as the headquarters of the Pony Express Bus line, erupted in flames during Fire Prevention Week. The blaze, which started shortly after midnight in October, 1932, swept rapidly through the building. Fanned by a strong wind, it leaped across the railroad tracks for some 30 feet to the O. and W. station. Firemen from half a dozen towns fought the blaze, many of them in the dress uniforms they wore when marching in the Fireman's Day parade in Jeffersonville earlier in the day. Damage to the railroad station reached $20,000. In addition, two box cars on the siding near the feed mill were lost.

If the conductor hadn't shaken Pete Reilly alerting him to the imminent arrival in South Fallsburgh (Fallsburgh depot) as they slipped through Centerville, then surely the rumble of the iron bridge crossing the Neversink River or the

This rare photograph from the collection of the late Eli Atwell shows the original Centerville depot with the "house track" in the background occupied by a box car. The structures, right, constitute part of the lower section of the 'Bowery' business block.

reverberating roar of the train as it passed through the short, smokey Fallsburgh Tunnel would have done the job.

The following Tuesday (July 27, 1886) the "Sullivan County Express" made a high speed run to Livingston Manor. A reporter noted that "...engineer Clark was rapidly converting the Fallsburgh tunnel into a pop-gun, whereby the train entered one end of it and the watchman was thrown 60 feet out the other end — bad luck to the man who faces a tunnel when Clark holds the throttle."

The editors of the 1878 "Summer Homes" noted the "pop-gun" tunnel and how "...another obtruding mountain was pierced by the engineers constructing the Midland, and for an eighth of a mile the fine scenic panorama is obscured from the tourist, only to burst upon the gaze again with new beauties."

As idyllic and romantic as all this sounds, the tunnel was fraught with hazards, as the late Bill Brock? well knew. Brock related that when he was on duty at the Fallsburgh depot he had to walk to the north portal of the tunnel to retrieve the body

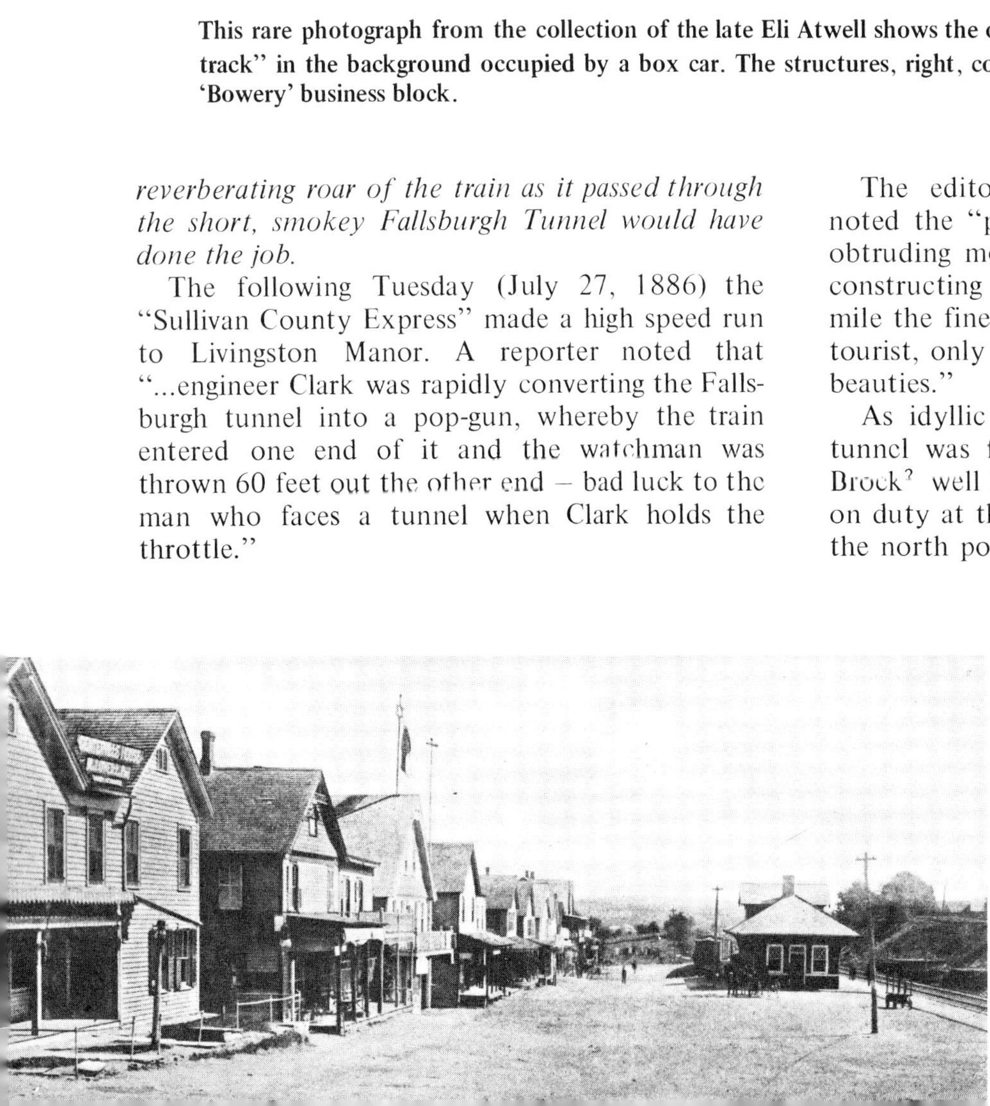

The 'Bowery' the main business section of Centerville, became a beehive of activity when the vacationist-laden up-trains pulled in from the city. Centerville House, extreme left. *Sullivan County Museum Archives*

In 1953 the depot, whose signboard now read Woodridge, slumbered peaceably in the unhurried twilight of its going. The structure was subsequently moved to Rock Hill to be converted into a restaurant known as My Father's Place. *Photograph by Edward H. Weber*

For the traveling salesman (drummer), there was but one hotel in town — the Centerville House. Operated by the congenial M.J.O'Neill, and conveniently located almost opposite the depot; the hotel acted as a "point of departure" for summer people searching out just the right kind of farmhouse or boardinghouse for their summer vacation. *Courtesy, Eli Atwell*

Typical of the large 'Bowery' business structures that provided shelter for a polyglot of enterprises that included the Post Office; Klein, the Councellor at Law; an upstairs pool room and a general store of considerable dimension. *Courtesy, Eli Atwell*

CENTERVILLE. Woodridge

Southbound freight skirting Wood's Lake just south of Woodridge. The head end power, Y-class, No. 402, out of Schnectady in May, 1922, was later sold to Lauria Brothers in August, 1948. Before going she had the distinction of being the last operating steam locomotive on the road. *Courtesy, Ellenville Public Library and Museum*

The derailment of 16 cars of the 71-car NE-6 hotshot freight blocked the line south of Woodridge on April 12, 1947. A sheared wheel axle was blamed for the badly scrambled cargo of butter, eggs and beef.

The Hotel Biltmore, typical of the spate of stucco-covered hotels built in the beginning years of the depression, in what Michael Strauss, New York *Times*, Sullivan County Correspondent, (1960's) called the "Golden Era." They are easily identifiable by the false front roof decorations that have been dubbed 'Sullivan County Mission', due in part to their similarity to roof details of the Spanish mission architecture of southern California.

of a baby who fell out of an open window of a northbound train. "The lady had placed her baby on a suitcase near an open window and as the train made its exit from the tunnel it swung to the northbound rails throwing the baby out of the window." Bill had little enthusiasm for what he expected to be a gruesome task, but near the portal he found the child "...about half buried in a carload of coal screenings which had been dumped near the track and was having a good time throwing the coal in all directions." Another experience Bill related did not end so happily. He called it his "night of horror." "On the night of July 3, 1901, a hobo came along and shook me awake while I dozed about 2:00 in the morning. 'Get up quick, the tunnel watchman wants you to come down there at once — a man is all cut to pieces.' "

Bill was a bit leery because he had a lot of money on hand. In those days station agents carried a considerable sum of money overnight on account of remitting by train[3] instead of banking as they did later on. The hobo stayed on while Brock closed the windows and put out the lights in anticipation of an attack by the stranger's cohorts. It did not come. "At daybreak [Bill recalled] I went to the hotel where I boarded and the proprietor came over to watch the station while I checked the tunnel. On arriving I found one of the local young men lying between the rails about fifty feet from the tunnel portal with both hands and both feet cut off. There were no other marks so he evidently bled to death."

Later Brock learned the hobo accompanied the watchman through the tunnel, and because of smoke coming through the arch, they had both stumbled over the corpse together. "The watchman was white as a ghost when I arrived and too weak to talk or help me get the body off the tracks. I remember he resigned that day and never came back to work on the railroad."

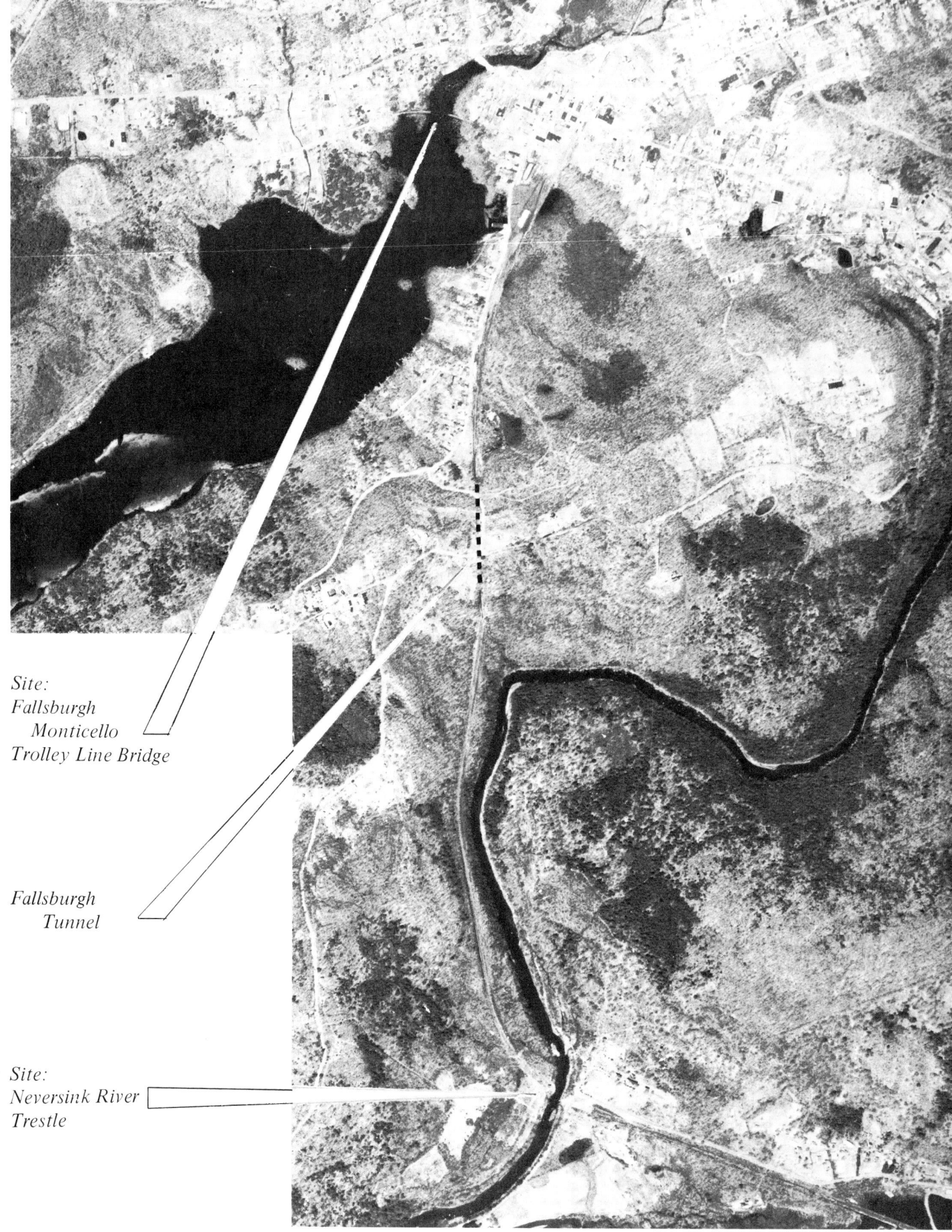

Site:
Fallsburgh
 Monticello
Trolley Line Bridge

Fallsburgh
 Tunnel

Site:
Neversink River
Trestle

The curving single track Neversink River trestle about midway between Woodridge and Fallsburgh.
Sullivan County Museum Archives

The north portal of the Fallsburgh Tunnel through Tunnel Hill. This comparatively short tunnel saw the first train, a construction consist, chug slowly through on December 2, 1871.

There were times when the tunnel was an extreme hazard to operating crews as well as watchmen and drifters. In January, 1922, "engineer Fred G. McMullen, peering ahead into the darkness of the tunnel, heard a screech of agony above the echoes of the speeding train." Looking back he saw the figure of his fireman William Scanlon of Norwich groping through the inky blackness "...outlined in fire." A rare occurrence — a backfire[4] had sprayed red hot coals from the firebox as Scanlon opened the door to spread another shovelful of coal upon the fire.

Engineer McMullen, once a fireman, instantly knew what had happened and abandoned his throttle and "...with his hands undertook to beat out the flames which soon would have claimed the life of his companion, Scanlon's face and neck were badly burned, where the coals had struck him as the great engine gulped and filled the cab with gas and flaming cinders." Engineer McMullen then demonstrated the pluck and fortitude of so many of the O. and W. operating forces. After having first aid applied to his painful burns at Woodridge, he took charge of his engine "...and brought the train into the Middletown station."

Class "U" camelback with an up train at an unusually quiet Fallsburgh depot. This high-stepping passenger hog was built in 1905 by Cooke Locomotive Works and served faithfully until the scrappers' torch cut her up in 1937. *Courtesy, Rev. John W. Carter*

Fallsburgh

South Fallsburgh

Pete Reilly was wide awake at 7:30 when No. 29 came to a halt at Fallsburgh[1] depot. He spotted his old friend, J.J. Mahoney, on the platform waiting for the bundle of papers which he delivered to farmhouses and boardinghouses. Once in the station Pete busied himself selling forty more newspapers, and he absent-mindedly watched passengers and baggage being unloaded. A Sun reporter, observing the same phenomena, noted, tongue-in-cheek, that city people wasted "... valuable time in alighting and four minutes more [was] consumed in letting their trunks down on feather beds by means of tackles."

The 1886 "Summer Homes" puffed unconvincingly that "here there are no mosquitoes, no danger of malarial diseases or hay fever," and even made the astounding observation that from the top of one hill "...a section of country ten thousand miles in extent can be seen."[2] But despite all this, South Fallsburgh was the emerging focal point of a fast-growing farm and boardinghouse resort area, the arrival and departure point on the main line for a whole string of satellite resorts including Woodbourne, Thompsonville, Grahamsville, Neversink[3] and even the busy county seat, Monticello. While the latter had its own depot at the dead-end stub of the Monticello, Port Jervis and New York Railway, most people preferred getting off at South Fallsburgh and tolerating the rough stage-ride to Monticello — rather than subjecting themselves to the inconveniences of transferring to the Monticello line.

On April 6, 1883, O. and W. officials announced plans for the inauguration of fast stage service between South Fallsburgh and Monticello to connect with both mail trains as soon as the road between the two communities [now route 42] was completed, but it wasn't until May of 1889 that the Monticello and Fallsburgh Turnpike was opened and smooth operations were underway.

A. Sullivan County Community College, (temporary campus), B. Fallsburgh depot, (Town Hall). C. Fallsburgh tunnel, west(north) portal.
NOTE: Pleasure Lake was created by the Delaware and Hudson Canal Co. in the 1820's to serve as a feeder reservoir for the 17-mile Summit Level. Later it became a private boating preserve restricted to Gentiles only.

The Fallsburgh and Monticello stage about to depart the Russell House for the county seat. This hotel landmark, long popular with drummers, was located just north of the O. and W. tracks.

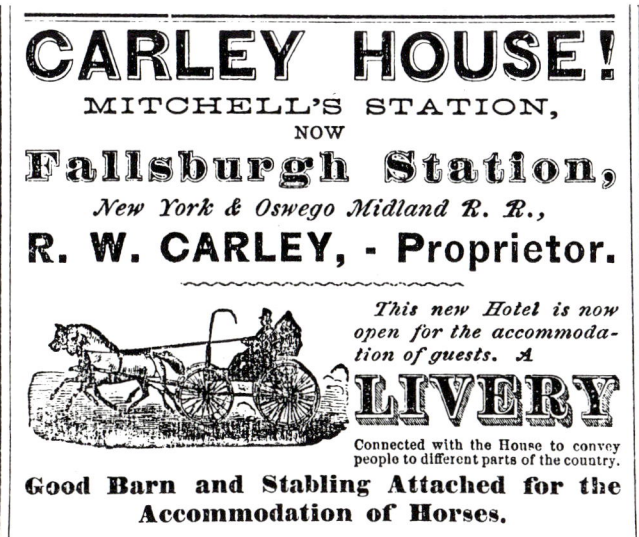

The Sullivan County Gazetteer and Business Directory of 1873 listed the pioneer Carley House when Fallsburgh's early calling of Mitchell's Station still had common usage.

Most contemporary press releases which announced the opening concluded with the aside that "...good roads are something which Sullivan County is in need of." Three years later, on June 15, 1892, the Monticello and Fallsburgh Tally-Ho Stage Line began operations. The line, under the proprietorship of Charles Stanton, maintained ticket and stage offices in the Rockwell building in Monticello. Their vehicles met all O. and W. passenger trains except the 'night line' [trains 5 and 6], and the company also offered a livery rental service.

Most people arriving at the depot had their two-month resort already picked out when they detrained in the South Fallsburgh area. In the "Summer Homes" book the satellite resort listings — Thompsonville, Grahamsville and others — were followed by Fallsburgh Station as the detraining point.[4]

In 1886 there were 12 farm and boarding houses listed under Fallsburgh proper, some of which were in the Neversink Falls area later known unofficially (and still today) as "Old Falls." In the first "Summer Homes" issue of 1878, three places had been listed under "Fallsburgh depot:" Mrs. R.G.

Carley's, South Fallsburgh, L.G. Thompson's, Thompsonville and John Waldorf's Woodbourne House in Woodbourne. By 1910 there were only 10 resorts listed, two less than the year Pete had sold his 40 papers. In the eight or ten years before World War I, there was a very gradual phasing out of the pure farmhouse operator. Farmers saw less profit in a few boarders, especially as the city folks continually demanded extras — all of which cost more.

The resort business had largely shifted into the establishment of acknowledged boarding house operators[5] — often women. These proprietors had generally begun in the business as farmers' wives, but had branched out. But even the boarding business was to phase out, and before World War I the new trends were evident — hotels and the bungalow colony, the summer cottage and the "kuchalane" were to be dominant in the resort landscape. A host of people who used to "board" during the vacation period now owned "little shacks and cottages" or rented them. The local press was beginning to point out that more than a few vacationers were renting cabins or cottages while others, in a prophetic warning of things to come, "...are tearing around on dusty motor tours."

South Fallsburgh prospered in the new era. The town's first depot, a makeshift affair originally called Mitchell's Station, was built during the

The Hotel LeRoy, managed by Matthew M. Ryan, as it appeared at the turn of the century conveniently adjacent to the tracks and depot. Later, in 1912 when known as Ryan's Hotel, it lost most of the upper porch railing to a community-damaging tornado.

Twenty-eight shares of the Monticello and Fallsburgh Turnpike Road Co. as issued to Monticello *Watchman* publisher, George M. Beebe in 1891. *Courtesy, Abe Goldstein*

The McCormack House, overlooking Echo Lake near South Fallsburgh, was a classic example of how a farmhouse grew by "tail-wagging" additions into the boardinghouse category. The O. and W. tracks ran between the house and the lake from which the railroad cut ice for use in online restaurants and cooling milk train cars. *Photograph by Howard Wood, Courtesy, L. Komitzky*

Hoffman's Mountain View House, built between 1900 and 1910, was a favorite of comedian Eddie Cantor. *Courtesy, Steingart Associates*

earliest years of construction. A more substantial station was built in 1903 on a site directly south of the old one. The 140' by 28' brick and stone structure was begun the last week of February under the direction of foundation sub-contractor J. L. Matzinger of Liberty, N.Y. Completed in 1904, the depot was used until March, 1957, when it was abandoned. Later sold to the Town of Fallsburgh, it was renovated and now serves as a civic building.

The completed depot witnessed its share of excitement. In August 1911, five young fellows got off the train and boisterously threatened what they would do "to the Jews of Fallsburgh," immediately pouncing on "...Mr. M. Roth, a local fruit dealer who was at the station to pick up tickets." Joe Mintz, working at the nearby Harden House, rushed to help Roth and was struck down along with a fellow workman from the Flagler House. Next, a bunch of young Jewish fellows rushed to protect their friends and a free-for-all was on.

"The station agent, J.J. Mahoney, drew a gun and threatened to shoot if it were not stopped. He called constable Joe Hanlon, who, after a heroic effort, arrested them." Joe Cathcart, one of the troublemakers, raced out while the hearing was going on; and, when hurriedly boarding a New York-bound train, was overheard to say "never again – in Fallsburgh."

Fallsburgh depot in September, 1903, was the scene of a bizarre one-car derailment. The accident had its origin in the Liberty yards when a carload of coal broke loose and began a frightening 80-mile an hour runaway dash across the county.[6] The telegraphed alert to South Fallsburgh was none too soon since the long milk,[7] fortunately running late, was just coming into the Fallsburgh depot as the loaded car hit the cinders.

The grade crossing at South Fallsburgh was always a subject of controversy. The first conflict came in September, 1896, when Town of Fallsburgh authorities applied to the Public Service Commission for an order requiring the O. and W. to maintain gates at five crossings in the town, including one just west of the depot. No action was taken on the request and it lay dormant through the years as traffic density at the crossing continued to increase. Proceedings were again opened and promptly closed in October of 1926, because of objections to a proposed overhead crossing. The solution was calculated to be the most economical, but was objected to strenuously by the business community because of excessive damage to commercial property. Again in July, 1929, the grade crossing controversy came up with J.H. Nuelle, General Manager of the O. and W., among others, representing the New York, Ontario and Western. This time the hearing was held before the Public Service Commission. The dilemma was rapidly turning into a three-way tug-of-war The State submitted a plan to eliminate the crossing that would have cost an estimated $1,250,000 to carry through.[8] The railroad submitted a much less costly plan which didn't seem to impress anyone; and, lastly, the citizens of the village, by now opposed to any plan for changing the crossing, claimed that any alteration would ruin too many businesses in the village.

In September, 1929, at a hearing held at the Sullivan County Court House, General Manager Nuelle along with Attorney Oakes stated that "...the O. and W. opposed the elimination of the grade crossing as unnecessary, claiming that it would deprive the company access to the station, necessitate relocation of switches, and increase operating costs." The high cost plus the estimated $130,000 damages from abutting property owners was just too much for an overhead crossing. Fifteen months later at a hearing in Middletown both the O. and W. and business community of South Fallsburgh stood as one in opposition to the overpass proposal.

Between January 1 and October 1, 1931, flashing signals were put in with the announcement made that the services of a watchman would be discontinued. The Chamber of Commerce objected, contending it was contrary to an order of the Public Service Commission. Next came an alternate plan for automatic stop gates, which was shortly thereafter changed to signal lights plus a watchman. The lights were put in – then the vacillating railroad said "no watchman."

Seven months after the tempest over the watchman, the first fatal grade crossing accident occurred at South Fallsburgh. It was a busy Sunday evening, April 24, 1932, with automobiles stopped on each side of the crossing – a Willy's Roadster approaching at high speed, passing the stopped cars, crossed the southbound tracks and impacted the tender on the left side just in back of the locomotive. The train crew, conductor H. Madison and engineer Edward A. Stoessel, brought the special to a stop an eighth of a mile from the crossing. Riding on the special was President J.H. Nuelle who prudently remained in his compartment. Witnesses said the blinker warning signals at the crossing were working and that the locomotive whistle had sounded. Three teen-age boys died, two instantly and the third was D.O.A. at the hospital.[9]

In December, 1941, tragedy again struck fatally at the crossing when an O. and W. thirty-car milk train running five minutes late collided with a 1934 sedan carrying Mrs. Lorraine Howath and her son Albert.[10] The car, left side torn away, was shoved ahead 105 feet before being deposited on a bank alongside the tracks. Both occupants were instantly killed.

A curious settlement was made as a result of an accident that occurred at the crossing in May of 1932. Suit was filed to collect for damages to a locomotive, which was struck by a truck owned by a poultry and meat company. The jury returned a verdict in favor of the O. and W. The suit was one of the first ever brought by a railroad company for damages to one of its trains as the result of a collision with a vehicle.

As with most of the major communities of Sullivan County, South Fallsburgh experienced a conflagration or two. The first was a $30,000 affair in November, 1911, that went through nine build-

The Welworth, formerly the Wadler, a product of the stucco and Sullivan County mission era, stood gaunt and deserted until one fateful rainy day in May, 1969, when the Hasselblad lens of professional photographer/educator L. Jack Agnew recorded its spectacular demise. (In the late 30's there was a Wellworth Hotel, [2 L's,] operating in the Hurleyville area.)

ings. It was only by the most strenuous of efforts that several other buildings were saved, because South Fallsburgh was without a fire department as well as a village water system. In March, 1921, five buildings containing seven stores and the brand new post office were consumed in a $100,000 holocaust.[11]

It seemed that when calamity struck in South Fallsburgh it would set its sights on the post office facilities. A severe windstorm, described as a cyclone by the local press, occurred about 4:30 o'clock Sunday afternoon, April 7, 1912. The first indication of the disturbance was seen a little south of the village, "...it having the appearance of a black cloud nearly spherical in shape and as it passed over the lake the water was thrown thirty to forty feet into the air."[12] Witnesses claim it had a whirling motion and seemed to be twenty to thirty feet in diameter.[13] As it passed up the main street of the village it stripped Ryan's Hotel of several pairs of blinds and a portion of an upper porch railing. The whirling funnel was diverted at this point; and, bearing a little to the north, tore the roof from an O. and W. box car standing on the siding, along with part of the roof from Hatch's feed store. After taking the chimney from Edd Ost's Hotel, it smacked the post office building two doors north, completely demolishing it. The second floor was used as living apartments and was occupied by Mr. and Mrs. Charles Denniston and Chester E. Couch.

FALLSBURGH. South Fallsburgh

The Brickman House, about 1935 and showing a touch of the mission influence, was founded at the turn of the century by one of the pioneer farm resort developers, Jehiel Brickman. Joe and Ben Posner have carried on the tradition following Jehiel's death in an automobile accident in June, 1928. Murray Posner, a third-generation hotelkeeper, remembers sleeping in the hayloft as a child when the family hotel was full. And when guests demanded baseball, "We just cleared a field and made base paths." *Courtesy, Steingart Associates*

The Pines Hotel in 1945, the year its name was changed from Monika Lodge. A $100,000 fire at the Monika Lodge in July, 1930, resulted in the disappearance of a large number of guests who slipped away without paying hotel bills totaling more than $1,000. A suit against the non-paying guests was subsequently instituted by the Hotelmen's Association. *Courtesy, Mrs. P. Schweid*

There were ten people in the apartment that Sunday afternoon and it was claimed afterwards by experts that it was "...nothing short of a miracle that some of them did not receive fatal injuries." Minor tornados have not been at all rare in the Sullivan County area, but they are an attraction not generally played up by the resort-promotion people.

In January, 1896, the people of Monticello initiated a movement for the building of a "...road [railroad] to Fallsburgh to be completed by spring. Whether it will be a steam or a trolly (sic) line has not yet been settled."[14]

What the civic leaders of Monticello were actually thinking about was an interurban line — a form of intercity transportation that burst on the transport scene in the late 1880's. The fast, convenient form of mobility filled a travel need to replace or supplement the slow and sometimes grimy local steam-passenger service as well as filling in the rural regions with a rail network that heretofore was pretty well restricted to old dobbin and the three-seater.

It was one year later [January 15, 1897] that the "Fallsburgh and Monticello Railroad Company" was finally incorporated "...to operate a surface railroad by electricity or other motive power, excepting steam, five miles long over the Monticello and Fallsburgh turnpike road on the company's land from Fallsburgh to Monticello. The capital is $75,000."

Wheels were put into motion the first week of February when the president of the new railroad company, Mr. B. Van Steenberg, arrived in Monticello with C.W. Arnold, the company's attorney, for the purpose of "...securing consent of property owners on Liberty Street to the laying of rails on that street." Van Steenberg claimed, with an over-abundance of optimism, that "the road will be built and ready for business by June 1 and that an arrangement has been made with the O. and W. to sell through tickets from New York to Monticello."

One of the first stumbling blocks to the fledgling company was a Baptist preacher from New York City, Rev. Samuel Colcord, the owner of a large portion of land at Pleasant Lake (later Kiamesha Lake) who refused to yield the required right-of-way.

On April 15, 1897, the Railroad Commissioner granted the privilege to the company to construct the road with the proviso that the road be extended to the Monticello, Port Jervis and New York depot in Monticello. On June 1 the "Fallsburgh and Monticello Electric Railroad Company" filed amended articles changing the route of the road so as to run over the turnpike from South Fallsburgh to Monticello — an obvious concession to the objections of Mr. Colcord. Two months later permission was granted by the Railroad Commission to construct an "electric road" from the station at South Fallsburgh to the Monticello, Port Jervis and New York depot in Monticello. Nothing much was accomplished for the balance of the year, and in April, 1898, the railroad transferred its assets to the Continental Trust Company of New York City as trustee.

Five years before all this trolley agitation started, an article appeared in an October, 1891, issue of the Orange County *Farmer* urging that the Monticello, Port Jervis & New York Railway be "extended to White Lake in Sullivan County or even further." Because "...an important dairy and summer boarder region is...found around White Lake, Bethel, Jeffersonville, etc. [and] only needs a railroad to develop it." This excerpt from an out-of-county paper resulted in a retort from the Liberty *Register* exclaiming that "...sundry attempts have long ago been made to secure the railroad and building railroads now is a very different kind of thing from what it was in days of yore." This comment in 1891 was in reference to the time when promoters could bond and saddle an enormous debt on unborn generations. At that time it was "cash now or no railroad."

Another idea came through for an extension of the "Monticello" Railroad when the Hon. M.A. Smith of Fremont in April of 1892 discussed the project of constructing a railroad from Callicoon Depot to Jeffersonville, thence to Stevensville and Monticello. Smith, another starry-eyed optimist, claimed that the hauling of milk alone would more than pay the cost of construction.

An indication of the depression years (1933) and the gradually declining promotional impact of "Summer Homes" was this cost-saving full page of South Fallsburgh orientated resorts. Formerly, most of these resorts had individual advertising space.

The Windsor Hotel grew out of a farmhouse operation at the turn of the century. Since this aerial view of the 1940's, the Sussman family operation has expanded, considerably changing the configuration shown here. One pioneer farmhouse keeper commented that one way of measuring a successful summer was the number of times the outhouse had to be moved. *Courtesy, Steingart Associates*

The Hotel Nemerson shown after the stucco treatment in the 20's also sporting a "widow's walk" of modest proportions. This period photograph, is from the commercial advertising files of Steingart Associates, an early advertising agency dedicated to the promotion of Sullivan County resort hotels.

Schenk's Paramount Hotel, about 1925, a classic example of the take-over of stucco as an economy move as well as an image changer. *Courtesy, Steingart Associates*

The original Ratner House, above, established in 1902 by Harry Ratner, was later called the Winter House when the new Ratner Hotel emerged, left, stucco covered, as part of the great 1930 hotel expansion era. Now known as the Raleigh, the hotel has expanded into a year-round operation. *Courtesy, Steingart Associates*

In March, 1896, the Middletown *Argus* commented "...if the rights-of-way are given and a suitable grade can be obtained, the Monticello Railroad will be extended to White Lake," and further added that surveys were currently underway by Irving Righter of Port Jervis. There can be no doubt that this oft talked of extension to White Lake was also in the minds of the "Fallsburgh & Monticello" promoters.

On September 12, 1898, a gang of 30 laborers finally began work on the grade between South Fallsburgh and Monticello. The force was increased to 82 by the end of the month. In August of 1901 engineer Righter finished his survey of the 13-mile power line from Honk Falls powerhouse to South Fallsburgh, over which power would be furnished to propel the electric cars. Earlier in the year (March) the extension to White Lake was clearly in the sights of the promoters and the route survey had been virtually completed.

The promoters of the road, however, were running into trouble. The June 20, 1902, Liberty *Register* noted that "...a controlling interest in the Monticello, Fallsburgh and White Lake trolley has been sold by DuBois and Keiling to a group of New York capitalists and a new contract has been entered into by the new owners to complete the road by August 15th. The price, $30,000." One month later ground was officially broken on '16'[15] for the newly formed Monticello, Fallsburgh and White Lake Trolley line, at which time there were 160 men already at work. The contractors, Hanfield and Rutherford, indicated a speedy connection between Monticello and Fallsburgh, and this to be followed by the extension to White Lake.[16]

By the Fall of 1902 the fat was in the fire for the White Lake trolley promoters when the Monticello, Fallsburgh and White Lake Railroad Co. requested the deeds for the remaining White Lake rights-of-way on or before the 15th day of Octo-

The hoopla created at the turn of the century by the Fallsburgh and Monticello Electric Railroad Company carried well into the new century resulting in this stake-setting scene for the Monticello and Middletown Railroad on February 18, 1915. The ceremony for the doomed project was attended by, left to right, Charles Martin, Walter Smith, Louis Guiomond, not identified, project mover-Blake Mapledoram, Walter Prince, Arch Carey, not identified, Fred Sprague, not identified, Russell Ross, next two not identified, Fred Stratton, ———— Kovenbach, and John Heath. *Photograph by Howard P. Thompson, Courtesy, Monticello Fire Dept.*

The slash through the woods on hill "16" at its intersection with Rt. 42 is one of the few places where the projected Fallsburgh and Monticello trolley line grade is discernible. (See aerial view of Kiamesha Lake area.)

ber, 1902. Whether they all came in was not reported, but the grading did move doggedly along for a distance of two miles west of Monticello by the end of the year.

"The trolley line is ablaze with work and business all along the line. At the station near the depot [Monticello] Mr. Michael Jannuzz is in charge of thirty-five men who are blasting and removing the rock preparatory for laying the foundation for the new passenger and freight depot."[17] Other press sources revealed grading progressing "...towards the western terminus...and work on the bridge over the Sheldrake Creek just outside of Fallsburgh station has been completed."[18]

Even with the optimistic fact of 235 men at work all along the line in the Spring of 1903, an ominous 'column filler' almost went unnoticed in the Liberty *Register* of May 29, 1903, which noted that Italian workmen "...have quit work because they have received no money for their work in about two months."

The Fallsburgh depot in the early autumn of 1953, looking toward Tunnel Hill and its single track tunnel, out of photograph, left. The Fallsburgh-Monticello trolley line was projected to start at the plaza, right, and proceed southward to a curved trestle crossing of Pleasure Lake, thence to hill "16." *Photograph by Edward H. Weber*

The handwriting was on the wall.

By December 9, 1904, the law firm of Brown and Weatherborn of New York City commenced action to foreclose a lien against the Monticello trolley road for $2500 held by the firm of Fox Brothers for materials furnished. There were other claims, mostly by local Monticello people.

"It is probable that out of this difficulty will come a trolley road. A syndicate, it is understood is being interested in the project, and if satisfactory terms can be arranged will build the road."[19] The syndicate was never formed, money was not to be found and the project, after seemingly endless birthpains, died.

White Lake, ever since the construction of the Liberty and White Lake Turnpike in 1885-86, had been a lure for railroad speculators, much as the flame lures the moth. As late as March 24, 1916, the Erie Railroad was considering a line to White Lake to run through Forestine, Bethel, Eldred and Barryville for special summertime schedules. Monticello was the focal point of a potpourri of grandiose railroad schemes during the great railroad expansion period. Rumors were rampant during the winter of 1912-1913 that the Grand Trunk Railroad was about to build a new line from some point in Canada to New York City and Philidelphia and that it would run, quite naturally, directly through the Village of Monticello. But it remained for Monticello's own Blake Mapledoram, a civil engineer of note, to come up with a proposed traction line to Middletown, one spectacular engineering feature of which would be a towering trestle across the Mamakating valley south of Wurtsboro that would bring the right-of-way grade half way up the west flank of the Shawangunks.

The company was to be known as the Monticello-Middletown Traction Company and would schedule a car of internal combustion type that would leave Monticello at 5:30 A.M., connect with the Erie in Middletown at 6:30 and arrive in New York at 23rd Street about 8:45. The return could be made leaving New York at 5:30 P.M. and arriving in Monticello at 8:30.

For all the hoopla stirred up (even to ground breaking), it never seemed to get off the ground. Monticello was destined to be forever tethered at the dead end of an unprofitable branch line operation.

The Kiamesha Lake Casino and boating enthusiasts in the year 1906. A matter of but six years later, because of the increase in drowning suicides, their presence would be of concern to authorities and hotel owners. *Sullivan County Museum Archives*

Kiamesha Lake

Pleasant Lake

If Pete Reilly had browsed through a copy of the 1886 "Summer Homes," he would not have found a listing for Kiamesha Lake. Pleasant Lake was its local name, with but one listing [under Monticello] for a resort in that area: J.J. Trowbridge's Mountain View Summer Home with 30 accommodations "near Pleasant Lake." The introductory paragraph for Monticello describes "Pleasant Lake, a beautiful sheet of water, midway between Monticello and Fallsburgh."[1]

In July of 1896 a number of residents of Pleasant Lake began a formal drive to change their community's name to Kiamesha Lake. Some people resisted, favoring the retention of "Pleasant Lake."[2] By 1898, Pleasant Lake was fast becoming a developed summer resort with a number of private cottages of well-to-do professional New York people. "Kiamesha Lake," as the O. and W. called it, was first given top billing in "Summer Homes" by having its name in the same bold type face as Monticello. In 1898 there were 14 places listed under "Monticello – Kiamesha Lake" followed in small type by "Monticello Post Office" and of the 14, eight used "Kiamesha" or "Kiamesha Lake" in reference to their resort. It seemed the establishment of a post office there by that name was inevitable; but, when it came on June 20, 1899, it was Kiamesha without the Lake.

As the resort grew and became famous in the mid-thirties, the hotel owners circulated and sent a petition to the Postmaster General requesting the name 'Kiamesha Lake,' on the grounds the present name "... Kiamesha had created a condition of confusion which was harmful to their business interests." On December 1, 1938, the change was made.

Kiamesha made the headlines in July, 1921, when the Ideal House was sacked by five gunmen. One operative walked into the hotel to ask directions to Monticello. Noticing "that some money was changing hands between a number of guests grouped about a table in the dining room," he immediately departed to return a few moments later with his four companions, guns on the ready. When they left, they had relieved the guests of between $600 and $700 worth of jewelry and money. Sheriff George D. Pelton was notified of the caper and was advised that a big black touring

KIAMESHA LAKE, Sullivan Co., N.Y.

113 MILES FROM NEW YORK.
FARE, $2.70;
EXCURSION, $4.75.

This beautiful sheet of water, formerly called Pleasant Lake, now called by its original Indian name as above, meaning "clear water," is two and a half miles from Fallsburgh Station. It is 1600 feet above the sea, and nestles at the foot of "Old Round Top" Mountain, from the summit of which a grand view is obtained. The lake is one mile long by three-quarters wide, of pure spring water, clear as crystal. It is well stocked with black bass, and the fishing is excellent. The east side of the lake is heavily timbered, and the shores edged with white and pink laurel. Splendid Macadam roads afford delightful driving and bicycling.

About the lake are some fine hotels, boarding houses and private cottages.

IN EFFECT JUNE 25, 1899.

From NEW YORK.	No. 1	No. 3	No. 7	Sat. only No. 17
	a.m. †	a.m. †	p.m. †	p.m. †
Lv. Franklin St.	7 40	9 00	3 00	12 45
" West 42d St.	7 55	9 15	3 15	1 00
" Weehawken	8 10	9 30	3 30	1 20
Ar. Fallsburgh	12 05	1 10	7 06	5 05
" Lake Kiamesha	12 30	1 40	7 30	5 30
	p.m.	p.m.	p.m.	p.m.

To NEW YORK	No. 8 †	No. 4 †	No. 2 *	Sun. only No. 18
	a.m.	p.m.	p.m.	p.m.
Lv. Lake Kiamesha	6 45	2 25	2 45	6 00
" Fallsburgh	7 16	2 52	3 14	6 37
Ar. Weehawken	10 30	6 20	7 00	10 20
" West 42d St.	10 40	6 30	7 10	10 30
" Franklin St.	10 55	6 50	7 25	10 45
	a.m.	p.m.	p.m.	p.m.

Drawing-room Cars on all Trains.
†Daily except Sunday.   *Daily.

The Kiamesha Mansion, top, with its rather precariously balanced portico and the appropriately named Gluck's Hillside Hotel, above; landmarks now vanished from the Kiamesha Lake scene. In 1899 a special timetable, left, was issued that also expounded the area surrounding the "beautiful sheet of water." *Courtesy, Steingart Associates*

A. Graded route of South Fallsburgh-Monticello trolley line skirting Hill 16, B. Concord Hotel.

car was headed toward Monticello. Eyewitness descriptions were so conflicting that little hope was held out for capturing the thieves. Incidents such as this are relatively rare in Sullivan County. Much more common are holdups of hotel business offices which, as in any resort region, are generally hushed up.

The lake itself figured prominently in and greatly affected the prosperity of the community. It was the scene of spectacular Regatta Days; one, in August, 1913, under the personal direction of Samuel Colcord, a leader in the community of Kiamesha, attracted more than 1500 spectators. "Nearly every property owner at Kiamesha Lake was represented in the regatta by some sort of decorated craft. The afternoon parade, while unusually fine, was greatly exceeded by the parade in the evening when the boats and floats were made to look very picturesque by myriads of colored lights."[3]

As time passed, however, the waters of the lake created a number of bizarre situations. During the

The Kiamesha Country Club, with its bedstead filligree showing at virtually every window, topped off with two precariously perched widow's walks.   *Courtesy, Steingart Associates*

period of 1912 to 1919 there was an abnormally high number of unusual suicides in the county. Some local paper headlines read – "Hung Herself to Bed Post with a Machine Strap," "Ends Life by Using Dynamite," "Drowns Self in Well" – but it was the increasing number of suicidal drownings in Kiamesha Lake that was creating alarm over the public image at the lake.

Concern reached a crescendo in June, 1915, when a 25-year old Brooklyn public school teacher stepped out of a row boat. For the next five days the incident put Kiamesha Lake on the front page of every county paper as the search wore on. All of this brought a Letter-to-the-Editor of the Monticello *Republican,* which ran it on the front page under the banner:

HEY, YOU WOULD BE SUICIDES,
LOOK HERE!

WHATEVER YOU DO, STAY AWAY
FROM KIAMESHA LAKE – ITS
CITIZENS SOUND WARNING.[4]

How effective the warning was, was eclipsed by the furor over the right to bathe in the lake, which came to a head in March of 1918. The case started to build up five years before, in 1913, when Samuel Colcord, who had acquired the Kiamesha Inn and considerable real estate holdings around the lake, swam in the waters to exercise his riparian rights. The dunk caused quite a stir because about 1898 the Village of Monticello had installed a pump house at the lake for the distribution of water to the citizens of the County Seat.[5] Colcord's swim led to a law suit with the village, " ... which disliked the waters of Kiamesha Lake after Colcord had bathed in it." After protracted litigation, Judge Alden Chester handed down a decision sustaining the village's contention that it was entitled to the exclusive control of the waters of Kiamesha Lake and had an absolute right to protect it from pollution by bathers and fishermen. The decision upset the boarding house keepers who contended that the number of boarders had been decreasing year by year ever since Monticello acquired the lake as a water supply. In spite of their assertions, new houses were built and the Kiamesha Inn, once owned by Colcord, was enlarged until it contained nearly five hundred rooms.

Business wasn't really as bad as Colcord would make out, since one year later, in the summer of 1919, the operators of the Kiamesha Inn refused a $100,000 offer and the famed Overlook House turned down $80,000. Bookings were good and getting better. It had been long known that board rates were higher in Kiamesha than at other resorts in Sullivan County.

Bathing did persist surreptitiously at the lake forcing the appointment of Lou Smith in July, 1925, as a special deputy sheriff "to prevent bathing, wading or spitting in Kiamesha Lake." Then in November, 1927, a very lengthy letter to the editor of the Monticello *Watchman* from Harris Goldberg, President, Kiamesha Property Owners,

The New Concord
KIAMESHA LAKE • NEW YORK

View of one of the many wings of the New Concord

Shortly after Russian emigrant, Arthur Winarick, bought the Kiamesha Ideal Hotel, the Concord Plaza started to materialize on the hillside overlooking Kiamesha Lake, above, shown under construction and left, completed. Later alterations changed its facade as noted in the "Summer Homes" advertisement, left. The Concord Plaza first started advertising in "Summer Homes" in 1937 with accommodations for 500 guests. By 1941 they were advertising as the Concord with facilities for 800 guests; and in 1946, as the *New* Concord, the expanded hotel was preeminent in the railroad publication with a four-page spread. *Courtesy, Steingart Associates*

LARGEST AND MOST MODERN HOTEL IN SULLIVAN COUNTY

From all over the East, vacationists throng to this mountain paradise in the heart of the beautiful Catskills, on the shores of Kiamesha Lake. Nestled midst acres and acres of rolling hills and verdant meadows, the New Concord happily combines the thrilling pleasures of outdoor life and activity with the most luxurious appointments of modern living . . . spacious terraces and gardens . . . a lounge and cocktail bar . . . cabaret and night club with professional entertainment on the premises. The sunlit, smartly furnished rooms are equipped with private phone to facilitate room service.

The New Concord is the one place you always come back to. That's why every visit to this happy vacationland becomes a rendezvous with old friends, a meeting with new ones.

The Kiamesha Post Office, (before the 'Lake' was officially tacked on), also sported the inevitable Huyler's Bonbon and Chocolate sign.

By 1942, the main building had been enlarged from its original facade, left, with an architectural treatment, above, with a social/athletic director conducting a rather disorganized calisthenics class — or is it perhaps Simon Sez — a la Abe Sharkey of Grossinger's, its originator. *Both, Courtesy, Steingart Associates.*

Too often many of the small hotels of the "Golden Era" are permitted to decay into landmarks of a less desirable nature such as the old Savoy near Kiamesha Lake. In September, 1967, its providential demise, left, was captured on film by newsman-photographer Charlie Crist. *Photograph above, by Paul Gerry*

was published pointing out "... with the lake open to the public it could well become a winter resort center as well as summer." That same winter the hotel keepers tried to induce the Village of Monticello to bore an artesian well on the Thompsonville flats and abandon Kiamesha Lake, to the extent of offering $40,000 to cover the expense, all to no avail.

Despite itself, Kiamesha Lake did become known as a winter resort with the development of the Concord Hotel by Arthur Winarick. Winarick, who made a fortune with Jeris Hair Tonic, started coming to a small boarding house on the present site of the Concord in the early 30's for his summer vacations. Five years later he acquired the old Kiamesha Ideal Hotel. Next came the Concord Plaza, then the sprawling complex gradually evolved that is the Concord Hotel of today, a summer *and* winter resort, despite the bathing and spitting restrictions down at the lake.

The Concord, one of the largest resort hotels in the world, exemplifies the independence of a modern resort to its site. The lake makes little difference to the hotel, which boasts lake-, or at least pond-sized outdoor and indoor swimming pools. To entice winter sportsmen, the resort also offers indoor ice skating and snowmaking machines to augment nature's supply on the ski slopes. Driving to Kiamesha from Monticello, you pass the lake; and across from route 42, crowning a hill, is the Concord with its main building designed by Miami's Morris Lapidus, a hotel which many consider the Acropolis of Sullivan County.

117

World War I restrictions had little effect on the summer vacation traffic as witness this flurry of activity at the Monticello depot. The 1914 scene, recorded by noted Monticello photographer Howard Pryer Thompson, is proof positive of the popularity of the Ford touring car and a rare photographic record of the early vintage taxis, background, known county-wide as "hacks." *Courtesy, Monticello Fire Department*

Monticello

The original 1871 Monticello depot, replaced when the line became a part of the New York, Ontario and Western system.

Monticello missed having the main line of the New York and Oswego Midland within its corporate limits, so the story goes, because its people didn't want the soot and smoke dirtying up their neighborhood. The surveyors responded by moving their lines to the north. Shortly thereafter businessmen in the county seat saw the error of their ways and made overtures to Port Jervis interests to build a line which would connect their two communities with the Erie in the south.

"Thursday morning, June 24, 1869, between nine and ten o'clock, ground was broken at the terminus of the Monticello and Port Jervis road in Monticello. Messrs. Ludington, Benedict and Niven of the railroad company as well as Mr. Crowley, one of the contractors, participated in the breaking of ground to the cheers of the men and waving of handkerchiefs by the ladies. Mr. Crowley in his remarks noted that there were at work on the right-of-way of the road over 400 men and enthusiastically assured those present that this force would be increased by the 1st of July, to at least 600. Construction moved ahead with the formal opening taking place on January 23, 1871.

The little road's career was cyclical. Its corporate name was changed from the Port Jervis and Monticello R.R. to the Port Jervis, Monticello and New York R.R. and in early 1903 to New York, Ontario and Western, when the larger system acquired control of the short branch. As the highway networks of the county grew and the autos multiplied the Monticello Branch was the first to feel the effects. At first the O. and W. tried to meet the competition by improving service. Accordingly, the company bought a set of gas-propelled cars from the J.G. Brill Company, the first of which was delivered in January, 1926. The sixty foot long, fifty seat unit, powered by a 250 horsepower gasoline electric engine was immediately tested and shortly thereafter placed on a regular schedule between Summitville and Monticello. The tide, however, was against the railroad.

In April of the same year (1926) the Post Office Department decided to forward mail to Monticello and branch points (Oakland Valley, Hartwood, St. Joseph's and Monticello) by highway bus via Middletown. This move was made by the postal authorities in view of the contemplated abandon-

119

A. Sullivan County Court House, B. Monticello Depot, C. Monticello Branch abandoned right-of-way.

ment of passenger service on the Valley Junction – Monticello branch of the O. and W. With the change to Daylight Saving time on April 28, the schedules noted abandonment of the one passenger train to Monticello: the number of trains having been gradually reduced until only one train a day was operated. The company had made efforts to compete with motor bus rates, but this failed in the public's preference to motor car travel.

Protest over the discontinuance of service was voiced by the Town Board of the Town of Thompson who demanded a public hearing. At the hearing it was noted that passenger revenues had continued to drop. In June, 1930, President J.H. Nuelle announced losses amounting to as high as $50,000 per year. He related that "the motor vehicles have so greatly become the accepted means of transportation that in one instance a certain Sunday train brought in a total revenue of $5.46 for one month." One key factor to this drop was the fact that the distance from Monticello to Middletown was some 10 miles shorter by bus than by train, and it was further revealed that the O. and W. had suffered a loss of $392,000 for the first four months of 1930. Despite the case presented by Nuelle, the road was ordered in August by the Public Service Commission to run trains over the Summitville – Monticello branch from May 15 to September 15 of each year, one round trip passenger train daily.

As things went from bad to worse, the O. and W. petitioned the P.S.C. to rescind the 1930 order. The request was granted, terminating trains No. 413 and No. 414 which ran one round trip on weekdays and No. 438 which ran one way on Sundays only. And so ended regularly scheduled passenger service on the old "Monticello," an event that prompted an editorial in the Sullivan County *Republican* for May 31, 1935, which noted that "...the Monticello branch now definitely abandoned for passengers died because of its indirect and roundabout route."

The Monticello branch was generally treated with a bit of uncertainty in the "Summer Homes" listings. In the 1878 "Summer Homes on the Midland" Monticello got brief mention with "...Monticello, five miles from Fallsburgh depot."

In 1886 Monticello was listed as a main line Fallsburgh stop with Royce's stages making the connections for the 9 listed resort facilities. The year 1890 saw a "Port Jervis, Monticello and New York" sub-heading which noted "at Summitville connection is made in 'Union Station' with the trains of this road. During the season of summer travel, through day coaches and drawing-room cars will run from Weehawken to Monticello. This will obviate any changing of cars at Summitville, and passengers boarding the cars at Weehawken will go through without change to destination."

A curious thing developed in 1898 which pointed up the emerging importance of Kiamesha Lake, (or the desire for Kiamesha Lake's importance by the management of the O. and W.) when Monticello received nothing more than a six line paragraph noting "...a drive of five miles from Fallsburgh station over the turnpike road," with the Kiamesha Lake sub-heading featuring all the Monticello listings.

The Exchange Hotel burned down one year after this advertisement appeared in the 1873 Sullivan County Gazetteer and Business Directory. The fire of April 26, 1874, was discovered in the attached barn and stable and soon consumed the hotel as well as George Hindley's saloon, Kent's Barber Shop, the Republican Watchman printing plant, Billing's Flour and Feed Store and Curley's Hotel.

The arrival of the Monticello and Kiamesha stage at the Hotel Rockwell, the Monticello terminus of the stage line. *Courtesy, Mrs. Bruce Denman, Sr.*

It was down the single track Monticello Branch, past the Hartwood depot, right, that a special O. & W. emergency run was operated on the cold snowy night of December 17, 1916. Two workers from Dr. J. Takamine's estate (Merriewold), LaRue Kinne and Charles Dill, both suffering severe burns from an acetylene gas explosion, were rushed in a single coach hauled by a Mother Hubbard-type locomotive through Summitville to Thrall Hospital in Middletown. Kinne subsequently succumbed from his injuries. *Courtesy, Elsie Winterberger*

Port Jervis and Monticello No. 3, above, highballing a string of rented Erie varnish in 1882 over the recently standard gauged right-of-way. On March 16, 1941, the last passenger special moved north up the line, pausing briefly at the Mountain Spring water tank near Oakland. *D. Diver Collection, Cornell University; lower, Photograph by Stephen D. Maguire*

The great blizzard of 1914 virtually paralized the "Monticello" as well as the main line of the O. and W. Here the O. and W. snowplow is seen arriving in Monticello after two days of bucking mountainous snow drifts on the line from Port Jervis. *Courtesy, Mrs. Benjamin Bertholf*

The great conflagration of 1909 started in the electric plant at the rear of the Palatine Hotel, shown here at the corner of Broadway and Landfield Ave. Two gaunt smokestacks etched against the sky and a jumble of scorched machinery, below, are all that is left of Murray's electric plant. Debris immediately in back of the spectators are the charred remains of the Palatine Hotel. *Courtesy, Mrs. Bruce Denman, Sr., and Elsie Winterberger, below*

Stark ruins of the National Union Bank, organized on December 11, 1850, on the corner of Bank Street opposite Court House park. During reconstruction, business was conducted at Lamont Mitchell's furniture store at the corner of Broadway and Prince Street. Looking east, on the north side of Broadway, below, toward the ruins of the National Union Bank and the trees of Court House park. *Photograph by Koonz, courtesy, Elsie Winterberger; below, Monticello Fire Department*

The same year noted a Port Jervis, Monticello and New York major heading with just two listings: Huguenot and Westbrookville. In 1902 Monticello went back under the P.J., M. and N.Y. listing which by 1910[1] was broken up into two separate major headings: "Through the Mamakating Valley" and "Through the Neversink Valley."

It seemed as though the O. and W. just could not make up its corporate mind as to how they wanted to place Monticello in their guidebook.

One thing under Monticello they were certain of in 1910 was their reference to a fire the year before, [August 10, 1909] "...last summer it was partly destroyed by fire, but the burnt section is being rebuilt with the utmost speed, and the town is to be congratulated on its splendid effort toward rehabilitation."

By the turn of the century Monticello was just beginning to acclimate itself to the wonders of the age of the telephone and electricity. In 1896 there were "43 wires" on the Monticello switchboard to service 33 phones but the demand for electricity was something else. It had grown so rapidly by 1904 that a new electric plant was under construction to supply power to all those who wanted it. The plant, being built by Peter Murray, the genial proprietor of the Palatine Hotel, would be capable

The wide angle lens of G.M. Gardner captured Monticello's Broadway about 1903 and the landmark Hotel Rockwell, center; post office, left; National Union Bank and monument-dominated Court House park, right.

Photo, right, the smouldering ruins of the once proud Hotel Rockwell. *Photograph, top right, Courtesy, Mrs. Bruce Denman, Sr.*

of servicing an unheard of 4000 lights. Mr. Murray, not to overlook any fringe benefits, adapted the plant's exhaust steam in winter to heat his hotel and the popular Palatine Casino.[2] It was this virtually new power installation that caused proprietor Murray and most of Monticello so much grief.

As prompt as the department was on that fateful night, it was no match for the "stiff wind blowing from the northwest." The fire, discovered about 8:30 Tuesday night in the powerhouse, was quickly out of control. Before the fire bell had made the "necessary strokes locating the fire section," the building was totally involved. As the local press lamented, "the flames spread and in an hour the entire village seemed to be doomed."[3]

The fire quickly ignited the Palatine "Casino" and "in less time than it takes to chronicle it, that place of masquerade, frolic and fun was in a mass of flames." The connecting Palatine Hotel became a fire-brand that put the torch to the village.

Seventy-four places of business, including the Hotel Rockwell and many residences, vanished in the resort community that awesome August night — an aggregate loss in excess of $1,000,000. Temporary shack-like structures immediately sprang up, with the Village President Joseph Engelmann dispatching an aide to New York to purchase 72 street lamps. The replacement of electric lamps along Broadway took place within a few days but the one gracious main street adornment admired by all, the magnificent shade trees, would not return so quickly, if at all. "They stand stripped of their foliage, charred and dead. It will be many many years before the fire stricken district will again be in the shade."[4]

Ironically, five years before, on March 16, 1904, a fire had broken out in a large barn and boarding stable in the rear of the Palatine Hotel that had nearly engulfed the first electric light plant erected by Murray. Quick response by the 'fire laddies' saved the day — but luck had been on their side.

In 1919 Monticello saw fit to jump the Fourth-of-July celebration by having a $200,000 conflagration. Discovered at 5:30 p.m. in the Arcade Theatre, it rapidly spread in the space of two hours

The lens of pioneer Monticello photographer, W. Milliken (1896), captures the unhurried atmosphere of the tree-lined, pre-1909, view of Broadway, left, from the extensive porches of the Hotel Rockwell. *Courtesy, Monticello Fire Department*

The archives of Sullivan County would have been far richer were it not for this fire on December 13, 1942. Lost were $25,000 worth of halftone cuts, 116 years of Republican Watchman files* burned along with the completed manuscript and carbon of Adelbert M. Scriber's "Fifty Years A Country Editor." Ironically, the manuscript was due to be sent to the publishers, Bobbs Merrill, the next day. *Courtesy, Monticello Fire Department*

* In the 1909 fire the files were removed from the doomed printing plant in the Masonic Building and stacked in Court House park.

to many structures including five large store buildings, four residences, blacksmith shop, liveries, the old Palm Hotel and the historic Monticello House.

By an ironic twist the holocaust of 1909 stopped the eastward progress of the June 30, 1919, fire when the flames reached the brick building put up by Fred Carlisle after the "great fire." The most historic hostelry in Monticello, the Monticello Inn, was again saved, as it was in 1909, by the alert fire bucket brigades that festooned every ridge line and dormer for the critical two hour period while sparks rained down.

There were, of course, fires of lesser magnitude — one of which robbed the county of its graphic and historical heritage, and the other, a fire that threatened a unique industry of the area.

The former, a $200,000 fire that leveled the Republican Watchman building on December 13, 1942, and took along with it the irreplaceable

The north side of Broadway, (photo left), from Bank Street, right, looking west. All the structures shown were consumed in the 1909 holocaust. As noted in the photo opposite, top, the only identifiable structure left standing is the National Union Bank and its Grecian-like portico.
By 1912, the dirt street was covered by pavement and the burned-out area completely rebuilt, opposite lower. Two buildings to the left of the last standing man are the frame structures, starting with the historic Monticello House, that vanished seven years later in the 1919 burn. *Photograph by Gardner, courtesy, Monticello Fire Department; both photographs opposite, courtesy, Monticello Fire Department*

photographic negative files of the Thompson photo studios. Also lost were the offices of the Sullivan County Democratic Committee, Red Cross rooms, offices of the U.S. Employment Service and Green's Hotel Supply Store, as well as the equipment of the Republican Watchman valued at $40,000. The loss to Adelbert M. Scriber, owner of the building and plant, transcended the physical plant loss. With it went valuable newspaper files and historic records, also a new history of Sullivan County in the final phases of completion.[5]

The other fire of unique proportions leveled the Synfleur Scientific Laboratories with a loss of $100,000. The facility, owned and operated by Mrs. M. Upshur von Isakovics and managed by Luis deHoyos, which concerned itself with the solution of all types of odor and flavor formulas and the development of flavoring materials, was discovered ablaze at midnight on Friday, April 20, 1928. The plant, located at the corner of Bedford and Oakley Avenues, erupted in the multicolored bright flames of perfumery chemicals and soon required the mutual aid assistance of Liberty, South Fallsburgh and Hurleyville. It is fortunate the fire did not occur the day before — on that day the village was swept by an all-day gale with winds touching the 100 mph mark. The plant was immediately rebuilt and continues to make its unique contribution to the economic stability of Monticello.

Another Monticello industry, the local tannery, also added a distinctive smell to the community. Established by Ephraim Lyon Burnham and later owned by Strong, Starr & Co., it was owned in 1888 by George W. Garner of New York City and managed by Robert McNickle. It produced the finest bookbinding leather — the sheep skins processed imported from England, Morocco and Germany. The hemlock bark [tanbark], the principal tanning agent, was obtained in Sullivan

County. Added to it were 65 barrels of naptha and about 70 tons of sumac imported from Sicily for tanning colored leathers. The survival of this tannery into the late 1880's was unusual because by 1888 the vast majority of Sullivan County's tanneries had closed up or moved because of the depletion of the hemlock stand and the appearance of synthetic substitutes for tannic acid. The Monticello tannery survived because of its specialization in high grade leathers for the bookbinding industry.

In 1870 Sullivan County had a population of 34,550 and in 1880 it had dropped to 32,491, a direct result of the change in the tanning industry which led to its phasing out as the key economic base of the county.

The New York *World* for January 28, 1881, noted, "So rapid was the destruction of the hemlock forests that in the decade between 1870 and 1880 twenty-five tanneries were compelled to suspend operations for the want of bark."

While the tanning industry was fading out, the hotel-resort industry was gradually emerging, stimulated by the promotional efforts of the New York and Oswego Midland management.

The beginnings of the June 30, 1919, blaze, recorded by alert 'Thompson the photographer,' shows the comic-like but desperate evacuation activities of the merchants whose businesses are threatened. The fire started in the arcade, center, and soon erupted between the buildings, left. Out of the picture, left, was the doomed Palm Hotel and, right, the shortly-to-vanish Rudolph Block.

The fire was stopped by the brick Carlisle building, below, right, erected after the 1909 blaze. One wall of the Monticello House has just fallen away from the brick structure.   *Both photographs by Howard P. Thompson*

The tannery once located on Spring Street was established by Ephraim Lyon Burnham and later owned by Strong, Starr and Company. The structure burned to the ground in 1924. *Courtesy, Mrs. Bruce Denman, Sr.*

Some of the classic pioneer business hotels of the county stood in Monticello with only a few making a successful transition into the resort era. The old Exchange Hotel, the meeting place of men of prominence with many a noisy political argument taking place within its meeting rooms, burned in 1874. There was also the pioneer Monticello House which succumbed in the 1919 holocaust. It was the resting place for drovers on their way with cattle from the western regions of the county to Newburgh on the Hudson. As related in Edward F. Curley's *Old Monticello,* "there was ample accommodations for the cattle at this inn."

The one old hostelry that has carried the tradition through to the resort era is the Monticello Inn, formerly the Mansion House. It did suffer one temporary setback in August of 1871 when it caught fire from the burning of the neighboring hay-filled barn of Solomon Royce. As E.F. Curley noted when the house was threatened, "...every room from cellar to garret was entered and what could be removed was with speed carried beyond the reach of the fire. Beds and bedding were thrown from the windows, carpets were ripped up and flung into the streets below, and the work went on until the shouts were heard far and wide...the Mansion House is on fire!"

The landmark was gone. It was rebuilt and again assumed its stature, the headquarters for men of prominence and the meeting place of many influential politicans and lawyers. It was also the authorized polling place for what was known in those days as town meetings; in fact it was in its time the only polling place for the Town of Thompson.[6] By 1906 its dominance in the resort scheme-of-things was such that it was lead-off resort hotel in the "Summer Homes" of that year. Within its 27 lines of copy under Monticello it was noted that "...the mattresses, pillows, sheets, blankets and all the bedding and table appointments are new." One line that should have been comforting to its guests noted the "construction of the house is such that there can be no possible danger of fire." Although no longer the only polling place in town, it still stands, converted into a motel, confirming the 1906 fireproofing installation, its cocktail bar and dining room still a sometimes meeting and relaxing retreat for county politicos.

Just down Broadway on the corner of Mill Street (St. John St.) facing the court house park stood the imposing Hotel Rockwell, formerly the Halran House, until its demise in the 1909 burn. It, too, garnered, or paid for, a substantial amount of copy in the O. and W. opus in which a "commodious sun-parlor, 75 x 25 feet with southern exposure" was advertised along with the plumbing, which "is thoroughly done and carefully looked after," and the sanitary conditions were announced as being "exceptionable." The management did promote a rather unique service to "parties in search of summer homes or cottages," as they always stood "ready and willing to furnish cheerfully all possible information."

Its fame and acceptance were almost instantaneous after George Rockwell purchased in 1889 the hotel described in a New York City paper in November, 1890, claiming it as "...second to none of the houses of the same class...visited in the larger cities of this and neighboring states." It was soon crowded with summer guests as well as "popular with the traveling boys."

MONTICELLO 131

The original Mansion House was built by David Hamilton in 1810, one year after Sullivan County was organized by Act of Legislature on March 27, 1809. Subsequent owners of the house were Stephen Hamilton, John C. Halley, William Crandall and Salomon W. Royce.

The Mansion House survived this third floor incineration on May 8, 1909, to become the Monticello Inn. Mrs. Gussie Machson began operation of the hotel in June, 1909, and because of the hostelries clientele, became known as the "actors hotel." The hotel register attests to some of the famous who stayed and ate there: Gov. Thomas E. Dewey, Presidents Franklin D. Roosevelt and Herbert Hoover, Mayor Fiorello LaGuardia, Jack Dempsey, Louis Armstrong, Jim Braddock and hundreds of others. *Top, courtesy, Mrs. Mildred Smith; below, courtesy Monticello Fire Department*

The Frank Leslie originally started out as the Sullivan County Institute and later developed into the Monticello Academy, established by Henry R. Low. Situated at the head of Bank Street, the popular summer hotel has since been demolished to provide parking space for county legislators. *Courtesy, John Joyner*

The Frank Leslie "...located on the highest ground in the beautiful village of Monticello," held tennis and croquet tournaments during the season which were set up with other hotels scattered about the village such as the Hotel Victoria, Hoffman House, Joseph Engelmann's Hotel Palm,[7] and the Albert House.[8]

Following the annual influx of summer season people came the establishment of entertainment places, this before the advent of the large self-contained hotel complex.

Especially important was the motion picture house. The year 1922 saw the end of one house of entertainment and the peaking out of another. The "Lyceum" was built about 1910 by L.F. Guimond and had a seating capacity of 1200 – on occasions it held as many as 2500 persons. It served as a theatre (largest in the county), a place for bazaar, basketball games, church fairs and lastly and most importantly, movies. Underneath the hall were bowling alleys and a pool room. On Wednesday evening January 25, 1922 it played its swan song when the play "Earthbound" was performed before the footlights by the players of St. John's Church. Its demise was brought on by the erection of the Rialto Theatre by Miller and Washington who leased it to A. Rosenthal, a New York theatrical man. The movie-goers soon deserted the Lyceum[9] for the new showplace. The "Rialto" became an entertainment and gathering center for the village and as such was instrumental in the selection of the Milliken Building directly across Broadway as an in-town ticket office by the O. and W. management in April of 1927. An ominous portent of things to come was the railroad's sharing of the facility with the Mountain Bus Company.

Offering the locals fun was a county fair. The first fair was held in the village park, but its popularity soon demanded the purchase of 12 acres of land from the Osterhout Farm holdings. In 1905 the Sullivan County Agriculture Society (1855-1931) traded its property with the Driving Park Association located south of Monticello.

The year 1922 was considered by many to have been one of the most successful seasons for the Sullivan County Fair. It generally opened on a Tuesday and closed on a Friday featuring a trotting race as well as a running race and the generally accepted displays of canned goods, flowers, Home Bureau exhibits, Grange displays, many makes of cars on show " ... including everything from a huge White Company bus that looked like a trolley car to a Ford runabout ... and an exceptionally fine showing of Durants." The Liberty *Register* when recording it as a big and successful show, emphasized the winner of the county spelling contest, Herman Seresky, a student at the Liberty High School.

Attendance at the fair seemed to slip after that and by 1927 the fair opened one month earlier to permit the summer visitor to attend. The previous opening date, the Labor Day weekend, was considered by many promoters as ill-timed since many vacationers were concerned with their return trip to the city.

The 1927 production marked the 52nd year for the event and was highlighted by a show of fancy riding and horsemanship by members of Troop C, New York State Police, a special "Poultrymen's Day" in charge of Farm Bureau Manager Paul H. Allen and additional auto racing events first introduced the previous year. By October, 1928, the

Kutsher's Country Club, which started operations in 1907, had the unique distinction of picking up its guests at both the Luzon and Monticello depots. This aerial view was taken in the early 40's just before the hostelry's transition, in 1948, into a facility noted for its athletic facilities and professional clientele. *Courtesy, Milton Kutsher*

The Hotel Belmore at Sackett Lake in happier days. It has since burned down leaving its elevator shaft as a monument to its passing. The Laurels on Sackett Lake, below, south of Monticello, as it appeared about 1945. *Both photographs, courtesy, Steingart Associates*

The Esther Manor started out on April 4, 1904, as the Beauty Maple House, the first Jewish boardinghouse in the Monticello area. Phillip Goldstein and Morris Kaplowitz bought the property from John Hill and son, Arthur. In the fall, Goldstein bought out Morris Kaplowitz. In 1928 the resort was named Esther Manor, in honor of Esther Goldstein, sister of Monticello businessman Abe Goldstein.

Sullivan County Fair was fast passing from the resort scene. Its adherence to "old fashioned methods without sufficient publicity and without the novelty attractions to attract visitors" plus the decrease in farming activity was blamed for its ultimate end in 1931.

June 22, 1929, saw the old Monticello Amusement Park reopened, and sparkling with "... the colors of blue, yellow and white paint, with here and there a black streak ... brightening up the buildings as well as the entrance to the grounds."[10] The first couple of days were good; then it rained coaxing the sightseers in out of the *heavy mist* to dance to the melodies of a seven piece orchestra. The June 29 press release, optimistic as it was with "the hum of the machinery, the rattle of the breath invigorating roller coaster, the merry-go-round and the music by the band all harmonize to make it a real amusement park," ended wistfully on a note of nostalgia that " ... it sounds like it did in the days when thousands of folks flocked there every day." They saw, but weren't quite ready to admit that the days of the amusement park were numbered. On August 16, 1932, the Amusement Park Dance Hall and other attractions burned to the ground.

One of the most amusing series of legal battles in the county was the battle of the hemline. The village fathers of Monticello, prompted by the receipt of several anonymous letters to Mayor Emil Motl which criticized the apparel of summer visitors, called the Board of Trustees into a hot session from which they emerged with a decree "that blouses must be higher and shorts not so high on the streets." Specifically, shorts were to reach the knees to be acceptable, while skirts, blouses or bathing suit tops worn with them must cover the shoulders. Legal minds immediately expressed doubt if it could be enforced.

Before Labor Day of 1931 Monticello was having its troubles with the ordinance, while several attorneys and justices expressed the opinion that the ordinance was illegal. It was enforced by the police with some difficulty with several young women arrested, fined $2.75 each, protesting indignantly. Merchants were peeved since the ordinance had cut into sales and were insisting that it be extended to apply also to Boy Scout executives and Scouts too. About the only delighted people were South Fallsburg merchants. The ordinance was sending more shoppers into their shops.

This nonsense about proper attire and "coverage" on the street had at one time or another penetrated every corner of the county. In July, 1925, the Board of Trade of the Village of North White Lake announced that no more promenades along the state road by bathers in the conventional bathing attire would be permitted. Notices were posted prohibiting appearance on the streets" ... in bathing suits made of but little cloth, under penalty of arrest and appearance before the stern court of the local magistrate."

In August, 1928, the Women's Christian Temperance Union of Liberty made such an effort to control summer street wear that it provoked a pointed feature story in the Newark *News* by columnist Jean Newton. In the sharply worded

The entrance to the Monticello Amusement Park, left below, was the magic gateway to a $500,000 investment once located at the northwest end of Wheeler Street. The popular fun spot, above, burned during the height of the 1932 summer season. *Both photographs by Howard P. Thompson, courtesy, Monticello Fire Department*

The Hammond and Cooke building was formerly owned by Giles Benedict and A.M. Fulton. The well-known clothing store was founded in 1904 by John and Joseph Cooke and Andrew Hammond.

The Monticello Post Office (1905) on the corner of St. John's Street opposite the Hotel Rockwell, now the location of the County Trust Company. Fast work by the fire laddies in 1909 saved the building from the menacing flames of the Hotel Rockwell and further spread of the holocaust. *Photograph by Howard P. Thompson*

The proliferation of automobiles and the brooding gasoline signs along Broadway bore ominous portent to the O. and W. management of a changing attitude in the minds of the traveling public.

commentary Miss Newton noted that "... what the women of Liberty are thinking of probably is protecting the eyes of their men from too much roving." In any event, in July, 1931, Mayor Edward Hallenback and the Liberty Village Board of Trustees decided that "men and women vacationists garbed in vacation wear which leaves the major portion of the body exposed ... must be dealt with firmly." Police Officers were instructed to chase all such visitors out of town or under cover.

The little village of Bloomingburg, as late as July 6, 1945, posted a copy of an ordinance in the Post Office declaring that "one and all must be covered below the shoulders and above the knees." From time to time a bruhaha would develop in the various Sullivan County resort centers over attire but few ever followed it up with ordinances such as those at Monticello and Bloomingburg. How many made them stick is a moot question.

The tannery dam at Old Falls, as seen from the old stone arch bridge. The impounded water fed into an old grist mill as well as the Palen Tannery, which consumed 4,000 cords of tanbark and 700 cords of hardwood each year. Its vats could accommodate 25,000 sides (hides) at a time.
The passage of time has taken its toll at the falls with the demolition of the graceful stone arch bridge, the virtual disappearance of the dam and, more recently, the unfortunate defacing of the cataract's picturesque rocks and outcroppings.   *Sullivan County Museum Archives*

Fallsburgh

Old Falls

The turnpike running from South Fallsburgh to Woodbourne (Rt. 42) intersects the old Orange and East Branch Turnpike at Fallsburg or as it is more commonly known — Old Falls, where the Neversink River abruptly drops over a series of rocky outcroppings. Neversink Falls, for generations, has scenically identified the busy intersection. The Orange and East Branch Turnpike passing the intersection was widely known for its handsome stone arch bridge built in 1819 and unfortunately demolished in 1952.

Just below the bridge stood the pioneer Sullivan County tannery erected by Rufus Palen and Matt Adams which relied on the falls as a power source and water for hide treatment. The scenery, but hardly the smell, also attracted summer visitors who stayed in a cluster of farm boarding houses within a short walking distance of the falls.

Just as at Kiamesha Lake, each "Summer Homes" Old Falls (Fallsburgh) boarding house noted, with more or less candor, how far or how many minutes walk it was to the Neversink Falls. For example, an 1886 listing read:

WILLIAM JOHNSON — *Boarding house; 2 miles; accommodates 40; 18 rooms; terms on application; transient, $1.25; free transportation; house few minutes walk from Neversink Falls; ample shade; pure spring water; excellent fishing and boating; boats free to guests; post-office Fallsburgh. Refers to Dr. McCready, 43 East 23rd St. N.Y.C.*

Johnson's Boarding House was typical of the thousands that dotted the Sullivan County landscape before the turn of the century. Notes from an anonymous though romantic diarist floridly recorded impressions of the Johnson house over the 1889 Labor Day weekend:[1]

"The house is filled with New York and Brooklyn people who have seen a new effect set up every weekend for the enjoyment of all. For this particular weekend (Labor Day) a floral arch superstructure of evergreens formed the gateway and the piazza (sic) and grounds were a garden of flowers brilliantly illuminating the grounds. Inside, the decorations were even more elaborate. The rooms would have done credit to a professional

The double arch bridge at Old Falls, a classic of its kind, was demolished in 1952 to make way for a wider, more modern structure.

decorator. In one corner was a sporting scene nicely arranged with fishing rods, tackle and oars.

"Another corner displayed "My Lady's Bower," a hammock laying across the corner and overhung with evergreens; a fan, hat, novel and other articles were scattered about in arrangement that had lately harbored the form of a young lady. In the opposite corner were displayed the colors of the Nautilus Boat Club of Brooklyn. A winter scene displaying snowshoes, sleighbells, muff, etc. was the attraction in the fourth corner of the room. All about were flowers and ferns both pleasing and artistically arranged.

"The supper furnished by the hostess was a feature of the evening and very joyously accepted. After an evening of dancing and merry-making, each person present was presented with a Japanese souvenir."[2]

The nearby Palen Tannery in its own way gave birth to a hotel that has become synonymous with the resort region. During the halcyon years of the tanning industry, Rufus Palen took on a partner, Nicholas Flagler, whose daughter, Carrie Flagler Angel, started a boarding house appropriately named the Flagler House.

In the 1902 "Summer Homes" a squib noted that the house had been in operation for the "past thirty years" as a "first-class boarding house" making it a pioneer resort of 1872. In 1895 it ran this five-line listing in "Summer Homes."

Mrs. C.F. ANGEL – "The FLAGLER HOUSE" *1½ miles from station: accommodates 70; double rooms with board for two persons $16 to $20, single rooms $10 to $14, transient $2; located on a knoll; surrounded by large, well-shaded grounds; lawn tennis, croquet; first-class in every respect. References exchanged. Geo. W. Olcott, 85 William Street, New York; J.S. Coffin, 72 John Street, New York; Edward Kellogg, 243 South Street, New York.*

While Mrs. Angel was peacefully guiding the destiny of the "Flagler" into the first few years of a new century, two Jewish gentlemen, Asias Fleisher and Phillip Morgenstern were just getting their first taste of a small boarding house operation. Finding the activity to their liking, they bought the "Flagler House" about 1908 and by 1909 the resort's "Summer Homes" listing had a different flavor, Kosher.

This general view of the Flagler shows the building, left, built in 1904-1906 and the main building shown here shortly after completion in 1919-20 when the hotel was "kosher" and owned by Fleisher and Morgenstern. The front cover to a very rare promotional piece, left, developed by Mrs. Carrie Flagler Angel, featuring one of the earliest known views of the famous resort. *Courtesy, Steingart Associates; left, Courtesy, Rev. Robert Houghtaling, Historian, Town of Fallsburgh*

THE FLAGLER HOUSE.

FALLSBURGH,

C. F. ANGEL.   SULLIVAN CO., N. Y.

The sign-flanked main entrance to the Flagler during the depression years. Sign at right indicates the adjacent nine-hole golf course, one of the pioneer courses in Sullivan County. *Sullivan County Museum Archives*

The FLAGLER HOUSE — *Fleisher & Morgenstein, (sic), Proprietors. Strictly Kosher; rates $10 to $14. It is a most attractive summer resort; 1½ miles from the station; the buildings are artistically designed, the rooms are fitted with all modern improvements; it has some 30 acres of beautifully cultivated lawn abounding with shade trees; a tennis court and various other facilities for outdoor exercise and amusement; these grounds are beautifully set off by a grove of pine and evergreen trees at the foot of which runs the Neversink River convenient and safe for rowing or bathing; the surrounding scenery is magnificent; the water supply is obtained from a spring on the top of a mountain; first rate table and attendance; special rates for families for the season. Ask for booklet.*

FALLSBURGH   141

The "New Flagler" featured among its many advanced facilities this pleasant sun parlor. *Courtesy, Steingart Associates*

Typical of the semi-abandoned resorts in the Old Falls area is the many-dormered Pollack's Fallsburgh Country Club.

The aggressive team immediately started adding facilities until by 1919, realizing their needs for a larger main house, they started drawing up plans for a large new building estimated to cost $100,000. The new facility was contracted to Tyrrell and Kinnear of Middletown, who began construction November 22, 1919. Thoroughly modern, it boasted hot and cold water and a telephone in every room. On the main floor, a large lobby, a sun parlor, ball room and writing room were "arranged in artistic fashion." The finished structure, with an exterior treatment of stucco, (one of the first in the county to use this material),[3] cost, in typical resort fashion, $75,000 over the original estimate of $100,000. The 80 room, 50 bath resort opened about June 1, 1920. The Flagler House soon became the focal point for banquets and political conclaves in the era before the expanded mass facilities of the Concord, Kutsher's, Grossinger's and others.

The year 1921 got off to a big start with the address of unsuccessful Vice Presidential candidate Franklin D. Roosevelt at the Jeffersonian Dinner before 698 of the faithful but "well sprinkled with Republicans." The local press commented that "the Flagler is the only house probably that could handle such a sized crowd, a testimonial to the enterprise ... of Fleischer and Morgenstern."

The Flagler was also an entertainment pioneer on the borscht belt. In 1928 management built a completely equipped theatre which seated fifteen hundred people and whose electrical switchboard,

The Saxony, formerly the Hotel Glass, captured on film by the author during the High Holy Days of 1969 with some of the season's first guests taking the sun. Built in 1919, it was one of the most modern and elaborately furnished hotels in the resort region. The former Levitt Hotel, below, near the Flagler, sports a capitol-like dome and the crescented dormers, right, identifying it with the prosperity/depression era and its Sullivan County mission motif.

The Hotel Furst, a product of the "Golden Era," was located, before its demise by fire, about midway between Fallsburgh and Woodbourne. *Courtesy, Steingart Associates*

scenery dock and fly loft were comparable with many theatres on the Great White Way. In 1929 the hotel hired the much sought-after "King of the Borscht Circuit," Moss Hart as social director. He had as his chief assistant Dore Schary, who went on to become head of Metro-Goldwyn-Mayer. The once "King Flagler" by 1929 was beginning to feel the competition of "The Grossingers" and their noted social director, Don Hartman, also destined for fame as head of Paramount Pictures. The competition resulted in the elaborate playhouse and the engagement of Hart.

At about this time there was great prosperity in South Fallsburg and along the intervening miles to Old Falls. Small hotels were going for unheard of prices—the Lakeside Inn alone selling for $35,000. The Hotel Glass (today's Saxony) started to add two more stories and it had only opened that July to overflowing crowds. It was to be sold in just two years to Isaac Steingartz for $100,000, one of the largest transactions in Sullivan County up to that time. The Elm Shade put up a $25,000 addition; in fact, the demand for lumber was so great that the Fallsburgh Lumber, Feed and Coal Company could barely fill over half of all the orders. To keep up with the business expansion the firm erected larger sheds and installed another railroad siding. Even chickens were big – Bloom Brothers, chicken dealers, "sold fifty-three carloads of chickens amounting to between $350,000 and $400,000." A new firm of steam fitters, in business only one week, secured over $25,000 in contracts for steam heating.

Things were indeed moving right along in and north of South Fallsburg. In fact, after the turn of the century, the three miles from South Fallsburg to Old Falls blossomed forth with hotels in such close proximity that it became known as Hotel Row. Just north of South Fallsburgh was the Irvington, then the Riverview,[4] the Elm Shade,[4] the Levitt, the Flagler House, Pollacks Fallsburg Country Club, the Hotel Glass (Saxony), the Ambassador,[4] and the Hotel Furst.[4]

The Ambassador was one of those new era hotels that also claimed its share of the banquet circuit, most important during the off-season. Located just down the highway from the Flagler, its Moulin Rouge built in the 1950's was the first real nightclub built at any resort and the beginning of a trend that made the old casino obsolete.

Nothing emphasized the basic ethnic background of the people who built the burgeoning hotel industry as much as the burning of the Blue Mountain House at Old Falls in July, 1931. The fire started when Sabbath candles set on a wooden table and left unattended were believed to have tipped over as they melted and ignited articles on the table.

An aerial view, shot in 1948, showing the density of hotels lining the Neversink River, left, in the Old Falls area. In the foreground is the swimming pool and the pioneer night club of the Ambassador Hotel, shown in center. Today the hotel is gone, marked only by a charred elevator shaft. In the middle distance, the Hotel Glass (Saxony) and in the far distance, the water tank-dominated Flagler Hotel with the very elaborate playhouse facility, left, a near-legendary theatrical center exploited by producer Moss Hart. *Courtesy, Steingart Associates*

The old iron bridge, built in 1903 for the crossing of the Neversink River, is today the intersection of Route's 42 and 52. The J.O. Pierce flour mill later became a popular casino. *Courtesy, Mrs. Bruce Denman, Sr.*

Woodbourne

Woodbourne, like Old Falls, received its initial impetus from the establishment of a tannery complex, one built by Austin Strong in the early years of the hemlock slaughter. It was not until March, 1878, that any reference to summer boarders appeared in the local press — "The Woodbourne Hotel is being fitted up for summer city boarders. We understand that parties from the city have already engaged rooms at this place."

The first three years of the new century brought signs of change to Woodbourne with the new turnpike to the hamlet completed and the toll gates put in full operation with rates of 2¢ to 4¢ for a single rig. In March of 1903 the old covered bridge crossing of the Neversink, built in 1843, was being torn down to make way for a new iron structure. Just a month before the demolition of the covered bridge, a significant release appeared in the Liberty *Register*.

"Hebrews have turned their attention towards Woodbourne and are buying up the purchasable farms in that section. During the past few days they have bought Gus Hasbrouck's farm, one of the best there, for $6200; Wright Holmes' farm for $1700 and the Charles Hommel farm, consideration unknown."

Woodbourne and its tiny sister hamlet of Hasbrouck peaked as "Summer Homes" advertisers in the 1906 edition when 26 resorts were listed. In the 1920 issue, Woodbourne listings dropped to four, indicating not the closing up of resorts, which were still on the upswing, but the lessening of the importance of the railroad promotional publication as a public relations vehicle. More and more of their guests were arriving for their vacation by private car, hack,[1] and bus.

For a number of years after 1878, Sullivan County's businessmen, the resort operators, had depended to a large part on the efforts of the editorial staff of the "Summer Homes" publication and the O. and W. to educate and draw customers; but the rise of the automobile lost for "Summer Homes" much of its impact. Various promotional gimmicks were used to publicize the county's resorts.

In June of 1927 an advertisement appeared in most of the county papers announcing an eight page promotional booklet to be prepared by the

Sullivan County Chamber of Commerce for distribution by New York City papers. Twelve New York City papers carried the booklet containing the names of all the resorts and businesses affiliated with the organization.

The results were felt immediately. The O. and W. claimed they carried nearly 10,000 more passengers than in the previous year and, not so enthusiastically, that automobile traffic increased beyond all expectations. The promotion was repeated in 1928.

The campaign's impressive results spurred the Chamber on to new challenges. A contract was signed in April, 1928, for two huge billboards—one near Hohokus, New Jersey, on Rt. 17 and the other on the Bear Mountain route near New York City. At the end of April arrangements were made with radio station WABC to announce fishing conditions in Sullivan County in a fifteen minute slot from 7:45 to 8:00 p.m. Pressure from the Chamber and the willingness of resort owners to pay for advertising also prompted four of the leading New York papers to run special summer resort numbers in May and June, some of them with vacation guide booklets.

The 1872-73 Sullivan County Business Directory featured the landmark Woodbourne House in a full-page spread.

The old Woodbourne Post Office at the corner of Rt. 42, left, and Rt. 52, foreground. Second building down Rt. 42 is the historic Hotel Fischer, today's Armstrong. Courtesy, Rev. John Carter.

In 1905 the Mountain Top House, near Woodbourne, was prosperous under the proprietorship of Myron D. Depew, manifesting itself into a double-porched addition in 1913. Erected in 1900, the resort burned to the ground on May 2, 1932, while being prepared for the seasonal opening. *Photograph by Howard Wood, courtesy, L. Komitzky*

The Knoll, a Woodbourne showplace in 1900, was managed by Dr. J.A. Munson. Overlooking the prison flats, the handsome structure ultimately changed hands, became the Woodcrest Villa, and finally burned down in December, 1968. *Courtesy, Rev. John Carter*

By 1927, county orientated organizations, such as the Sullivan County Chamber of Commerce, were starting to explore alternate promotional schemes that would divorce the resort region from dependency on the New York, Ontario and Western Railway's "Summer Homes" publication. This is a typical advertisement that appeared in the June 2, 1927, Liberty *Register*.

To the Hotel Proprietors of Sullivan County

The Sullivan County Chamber of Commerce has contracted for an extensive advertising campaign in eight different Greater New York newspapers beginning Sunday, June 5th. An elaborate booklet devoted to Sullivan County as a whole, has been arranged and is now in the hands of the printer for delivery on June 15th. This booklet will be distributed to thousands of people who are prospective Sullivan County guests. If you are a member your name and the name of your hotel will be listed in the booklet. Join now. Send your membership fee, before June 7th, to

F. W. Meusgeier at Roscoe, N. Y.

The Merritt House, operated by Silas Merritt, posed their summer boarders, with the exception of one disinterested guest and a dog, for a rather formal portrait before the lens of Hurleyville photographer Howard Wood, at the turn of the century.

August Guntlow's Mountain Spring House operated a depot wagon for the convenience of its guests, some of whom interrupted their unhurried vacation activities to sit for photographer Howard Wood and his Kodak.

The Hotel Fischer, background, was always a favorite stopping place for the annual summer appearance of performing bears and the arrival of the wheel-operated hurdy-gurdy, here shown below, just around the corner from the Hotel Fischer. The woman went around the neighborhood with a tamborine and picked up tips from boardinghouse guests and inevitably stopped in at Gus Guntlow's "Curio," just down the street. *Both photographs, courtesy, Rev. John Carter*

Local booster groups like the Swan Lake Board of Trade were formed to promote the business and community interests of the village. Four years later, in May of 1932, the Hotelmen's Protective Association of Monticello met at the Feiner House and arranged to have signs promoting Monticello and its hotels placed in 90 New York subway stations. "Spend your vacation at Monticello, Summer and Winter Resort," they read, followed by the names of about 40 hotels (in three-quarter inch type) printed in the center, with art work of sports framing the sides.[2] Announcement was made in May of 1933 for the sustained cooperative attempt to publicize the vacation advantages of Sullivan County by a group of the leading hotels including the Flagler and Grossinger's. Their campaign consisted of a regular half-hour radio show each morning from 10 to 10:30 over station WOR. A nine-piece orchestra, singers and other entertainers appeared plus a brief talk which described some of Sullivan's advantages with 100 words or so directed to each of the hotels supporting the program.

In addition to resorts, Woodbourne had another industry thrust upon it. In May 19, 1932, announcement was made by the State Prison Commission that a multimillion dollar prison would be built on the flats south of the village. A considerable amount of concern was expressed by the resort operators for fear the proximity of the prison would deter summer business. As it turned out, their fears were unwarranted. One realtor commented "the upswing in real estate values was phenomenal." The red brick prison in the "sixties" is the community's major economic mainstay. Enlarged in the 60's and turned into a narcotics treatment center ... many people laughingly call the tall chimneyed building Hotel Woodbourne.

Ho — for the fair!! Anson and Martha Smith about to depart the Mahlon Donovan place on Rocky Hill for the Grahamsville Little World's Fair with "Peck" Smith standing by, buggy whip in hand.

Grahamsville

From the first arrival of the New York & Oswego Midland rails in Sullivan County, people around Grahamsville[1] were always stumping for a branch line to town. In March of 1889 the Neversink Valley Railroad was the big news around the cracker barrel and pot bellied stove. The line was projected to branch off at South Fallsburgh, go through Old Falls, Woodbourne and Hasbrouck to Neversink Flats, with the further possibility of a line over the drainage divide to Grahamsville. The local press noted that "...if made more easy of access by a railroad, it (Grahamsville) would attract thousands instead of hundreds of city people." Most people in Grahamsville, however, realized that the chances that a railroad would go over the saddle between the two communities were painfully remote.

Through the 1880's there was much agitation for a trolley road. Later, in February of 1889, sentiment revealed a new change of direction with publicity and talk pouring forth for the construction of a turnpike from Grahamsville to South Fallsburgh. The thinking here was that a turnpike would undoubtedly give Grahamsville a "commercial imeptus that would eventually lead to the building of a trolley road." Developers reasoned, with the introduction of "fast coaches" together with the "investment of the capital that would result, Grahamsville would turn from its pastoral quietude into a gay and popular summer resort."[2] But in the 1960's Grahamsville is still a little town that basically has resisted change more than seeking it.

It was an isolated community, particularly in its orientation to the O. and W. Railway; but it did list in "Summer Homes" despite its bumpy eleven mile ride from the depot in South Fallsburgh.

That Sunday morning in 1886 when Pete Reilly paused at South Fallsburgh with his papers, a glance at the current issue of "Summer Homes" would have revealed one lonely listing under Grahamsville, that of Mrs. William M. Porter whose Echo Cottage noted accommodations for five and "free transportation" – probably by farm wagon. The only public transportation available from So. Fallsburgh over the rough roads of that day was by a roundabout route by regular stage to Ellenville – an enterprise of Messrs. Wright and Curry which the press of 1886 reported as "doing a good business."

GRAHAMSVILLE STAGE HOUSE ...

T. O. PORTER, Proprietor,
Grahamsville, N. Y.

Bar well Supplied with good Wines, Liquors, and Cigars.

☞ BOARD by day, week, or month.

On day of Fair, a Conveyance will be run every hour to Fair Ground.

ON THE EVENING OF THE FAIR, THERE WILL BE

A SOCIAL DANCE

A GOOD SUPPER WILL BE SERVED AT MIDNIGHT

MUSIC BY FULTON'S ORCHESTRA.

Every body is invited and a good time anticipated.

In the days of the horse and buggy, the historic Grahamsville House was indeed a busy place, particularly at Fair time. According to Town of Neversink Historian Inez Gridley, some of the proprietors who held open house at fair time were Sylvester Porter, Theron Porter, Dan LeFever and a Mr. Henman. At one time it was the Briggs Funeral Home; today it is Finch's Restaurant and boardinghouse.

Just up the road from the Grahamsville House is the Anapel House where Adam Anapel served as proprietor; and further up was the Sycamore House, also known as the Hawthorne House, with a ballroom on the second floor. Both hostelries have faded and are but a shadow of their former opulence. *Courtesy, Michael O'Donnell*

Grahamsville Fair booklet advertisement announced "conveyance" service to the fair from the Grahamsville House. The Little World's Fair was started in 1898 by S.N. Smith, Joseph Hall, Andrew B. Currey and Gabriel F. Currey and has carried on the tradition of the country fair. *Courtesy, Inez Gridley*

A family gathering enjoys lunch at the Little World's Fair in the days of the horse and buggy. Below, the midway in the days of the automobile stresses games of chance in foreground, while buildings in background house various agricultural exhibits.

This Hudson River bracket phase of gothic revival architecture, (characteristic of works of Calvert Vaux and A.J. Downing) is now the home of the author and was listed in "Summer Homes" as far back as 1884. Operated at that time by John Reynolds, it had accommodations for 20 in a "fine house, high and well ventilated; large rooms; water on first floor; fine grove nearby and daily milk."

As late as June of 1922, public hearings were being held on the application of Oscar E. Doughty for a "certificate of public convenience and necessity for the operation of a stage route by auto bus between Grahamsville and Ellenville, passing through Eureka, Montela and Lackawack."[3] The village folk resisted almost to a man. Most preferred that their community retain its rural-agrarian charm that manifests itself once a year at the Grahamsville "Little World's Fair," an event that started about 1879.

Notoriety of sorts came to Grahamsville's small Lefever's Hotel in July, 1901, when Wilfred Blondin was suspected to be hiding there. Blondin, a French Canadian, was accused of decapitating his wife in Boston three months previously. John Galbraith, a farmer, noticed that the picture in a "wanted" circular in the Post Office looked like a stranger he had seen loitering around down at Lefever's Hotel. A few cohorts agreed and "Blondin" was quickly confined to his hotel room until Boston authorities could arrive. At the end of the resultant newspaper story, one additional development was tacked on. "LATER" "Boston detectives have examined the man and say they are confident it is not Blondin, but farmer Galbraith is positive he is right and still has his man confined in a room at the hotel."[4]

This kind of individual determination manifested itself in February of 1880 when iron was reportedly discovered on Burnt Hill on lands belonging to John Reynolds. Parties from New York contracting for the ore agreed to pay Mr. Reynolds fourteen cents for every ton taken. Comment persisted amongst the town folk that the ore was of no value. Digging continued, however, until specimens of the black oxide of manganese were assayed by the Andover Iron Company and found worthless. Only then did the digging cease and Reynolds seek to add to his lumber mill fortune in a less spectacular fashion. His house, located across the small valley from Burnt Hill, was listed in "Summer Homes" for 1890.[5] His son, George Reynolds, was described as proprietor of a private residence that would accommodate 25 at a rate of six dollars. It was operated as a summer boarding house and listed as such in "Summer Homes" until 1910.

On the road from Grahamsville to Napanoch were two small hamlets, Eureka and Montela,

One of Grahamsville's early industries, the knife factory, started operations in May, 1903, with a force of about twenty men. At 12:30 a.m. on July 27, 1907, G.E. Bryers, living next door to the knife factory, was awakened by a crackling noise. Finding the knife works ablaze, he quickly spread the alarm; the Methodist Church bell was rung and soon all of Grahamsville was on hand to witness the demise of the frame structure.

which boasted some of the finest boardinghouse farms in Sullivan County and operated as such considerably longer than in most other sections of the county.

In Eureka, Mrs. Ora H. Cross conducted a farm boardinghouse; and in Montela, the Butternut Grove House was successfully operated by Ward Dierfelter; even Sundown offered accommodations at the farm of B.D. Kortright.

Grahamsville had the Crawford House, operated by Mrs. E.A. Crawford and considered the principal hotel in the village, which like most commercial hotels in the county also catered to summer folk. Daniel C. Wright and Sylvester E. Porter also took guests as well as C.W. Pierce at his Sycamore House.

It was for the boardinghouse keepers down in the idyllic valley at Montela and Eureka that the summer season came to an abrupt and soggy end one unforgettable August Sunday afternoon in 1928.

It had rained hard the day before but on that dark fateful Sunday, August 26, it came down in buckets. The headwater mountains being saturated, the cloudburst of that Sabbath morning was too much for the already swollen streams.

Down at Eureka was located the popular boardinghouse of Bruce W. Fuller, filled to capacity for, what was up to then, a good summer season. "All fourteen of our city guests were having dinner

The Fuller House, where high waters in August, 1928, terrorized a houseful of summer guests as the silt-laden tide rolled onto the porch and threatened to sweep through the front door. *Courtesy, Bruce Fuller*

GRAHAMSVILLE

A 1937-38 aerial view of the construction of the dam and reservoir between Lackawack and Grahamsville looking west-northwest. In the right foreground, the "core wall" marches down the hillside with another small section starting in center.
The valley road has been cut by the beginnings of the massive earthern fill, just beyond the concrete batch plant. The temporary "shoo-fly" and bridge around the construction site have been broken and the new twin valley roads, left and right, are now completed and operational.
Woodsmen have already started clearing the hillside, right, up to the projected maximum waterline. The Lackawack House, referred to in Summitville Chapter, stood approximately where the dam proper is being erected. In the upper center, the still standing houses of Montela may still be seen while the hamlet of Eureka nestles in the distant haze at the far end of the eight mile long 'Peaceful Valley.' *Courtesy, Albro Brown*

On Sunday, August 26, 1928, the rapidly rising waters of the Rondout Creek carried the barn of Grover Hornbeck across the valley highway and deposited seven autos from his garage further down the valley in various stages of disassembly. *Courtesy, Mrs. Madeline (Ralph) Adams*

when we noticed the stream was higher than usual. Before we finished dinner the rain was coming down in torrents." One guest, a jeweler from Tiffany's in New York, insisted on leaving but ended up stalling-out on one of the rapidly flooding bridges. In but a matter of minutes the car and the jeweler and a diamond stick pin or two went swirling out of sight down the muddy current. Unable to swim, he was swept down stream to be later rescued by the wife of Dr. Urban T. Kemble, a local physician. As the water started rising up to the front porch level, Bruce decided to carry each of his guests a quarter mile to another house on higher ground.

"When all fourteen guests were at the other house, a vacationing police captain, who assisted in the evacuation, proceeded to play a piano but succeeded only in bringing on the tears of the upset lady guests, the situation already aggravated by soaked clothing and wet handkerchiefs. As I recall it, it seems he played something like 'Nearer My God To Thee.'"[6]

In any event, the boarding season ended suddenly that afternoon just two months after the hiring of a man whose employment sounded the death knell for what was known as the Peaceful Valley. Mahlon Wright of Lackawack was the first of an army of laborers to receive notice of employment for work on the new 30,000,000 gallon Rondout Reservoir that would convert the eight miles of lush farmlands into a denuded basin of gaunt foundation walls, tree stumps and meaningless stone walls in preparation for permanent inundation.

An unidentified station agent (perhaps George H. Knapp, Luzon's first station agent, 1872-1913,) waits patiently with the U.S. Mail bags and the delayed up train. B.F. Clark's Waldorf House, background. Building, right, housed the post office and Webster Wilkinson's General Store, while the next was the office of Dr. W.H. DeKay, the druggist, and L.W. Lawrence's meat market. Just up the street, to the left of the horse and wagon, was the studio of Howard Wood, who took this picture from the second floor porch of O'Neill's Hotel.

Luzon

Hurleyville

As Train No. 29 leaned into the super elevation through Smith Hill cut and out on the extended high embankment approach to Hurley station, Pete took count of his few papers left and realized that he had just about enough to get him through to Rockland station (Roscoe). He also might have paid more attention as he passed through Hurleyville[1] had he known it was one of the fastest growing communities in Sullivan County, with a rapidly developing concentration of farm boardinghouses with a great potential for newspaper sales.[2]

For the year of Pete's paper run through Hurleyville there were nine farmhouses listed there and one "out near a lake called Lock Shelldrake (sic) Post Office" — destined to become a resort center of considerable stature and notoriety. At this point in time Charles W. Travis was the only one out at the lake to grasp the idea of a summer resort.

Joseph H. Worden's Hurleyville listing in the 1886 "Summer Homes" announced accommodations for 20, (above average—in 1886 accommodations for most farmhouses was 5) a large lawn, plenty of shade, swings, hammocks, large croquet ground and lots of surrounding acreage. It was the bounty of this lush acreage that influenced a feminine reporter who stayed at the Worden farmhouse to note on one special occasion " ... the ladies had fairly pulled the woods out by their roots so they could decorate the parlors. While flowers, ferns, florals and blossoms and sunflowers and every green thing that grows had been made to beautify in the endless variety of arrangement that only the ladies are capable of." The evenings entertainment among all this plant life "consisted of tableaus, charades etc. and concluded with the usual parlor dance."

By 1907 as many as 34 listings in "Summer Homes" were noted under Hurleyville, with one in particular, Mrs. M. Brophy's Mountain View Farm House, regarded as the one with the most colorful reputation. Known as Brophy's Mad House, it was frequented by the firemen and policemen of New York City who, by reputation, "let their hair down" when they went to the mountains. The house burned down in 1910 but the road on which it stood, Brophy's Road, memorializes its former presence.

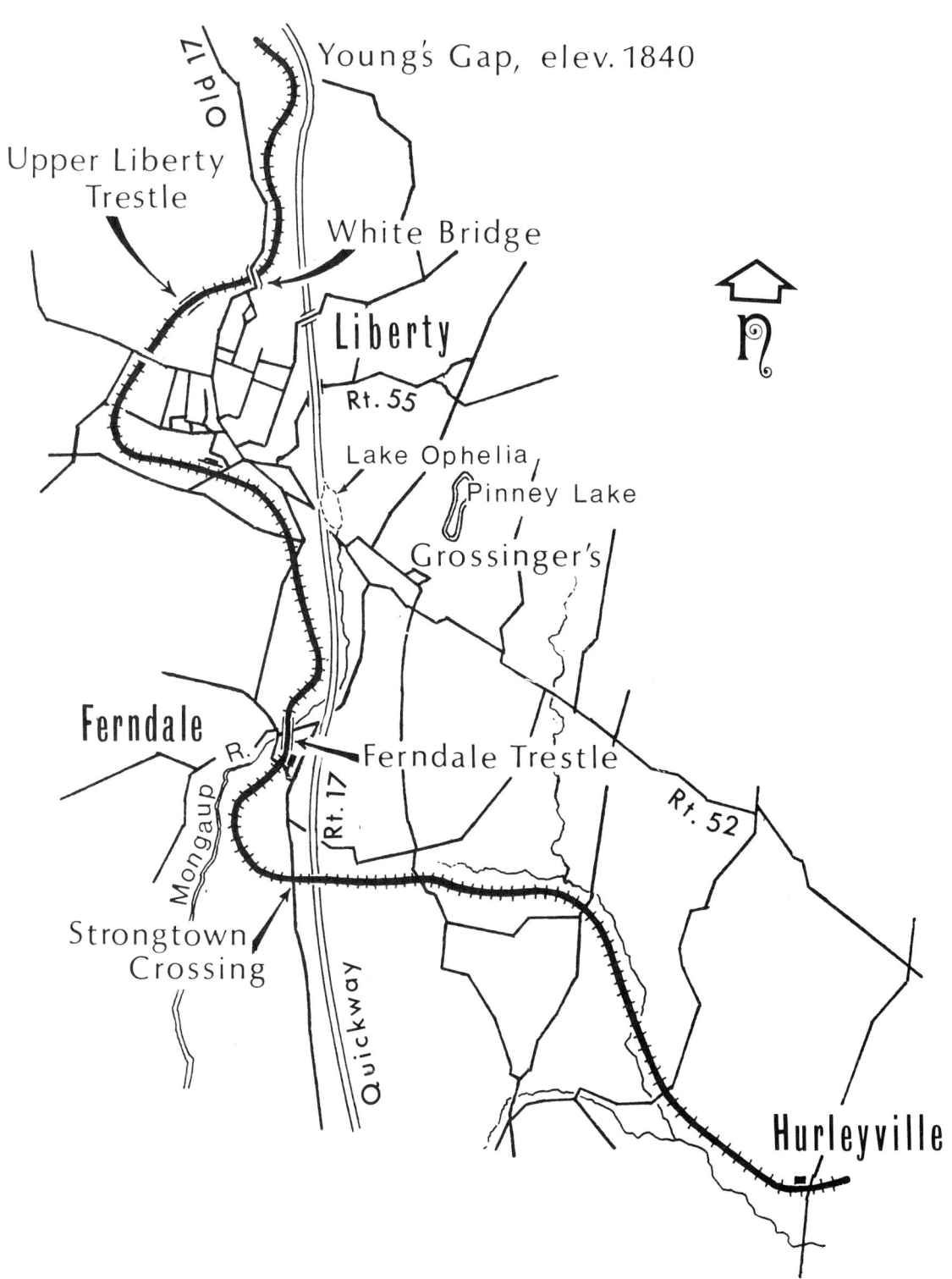

A. Luzon (Hurleyville) depot.   B. Hurleyville creamery.   C. Approximate location of explosion of engine No. 70

The first frame depot and freight house at Luzon, (Hurleyville). The main business area and grade crossing, background. *Photograph by Howard Wood*

A substantial new depot, the dawning years of the auto age and the era of the all-summer vacation. These three facts, confirmed by the steamer trunks on the platform, place this Wood picture in the halcyon years of Ontario and Western passenger service. *Photograph by Howard Wood*

The Christian houses started to pass into the hands of Jewish entrepreneurs about 1910. "The Hotel Waldorf at Hurleyville," read a typical 1912 press notice, "was recently sold to some Hebrews of that village." The trend continued, with a headline of March 7, 1919, noting "HEBREWS BUY SMITH FARM; PAY THIRTY-SIX THOUSAND." The release went on: "It is thought that the new owners, instead of farming it on the scale the farm is capable of (at one time more than eighty cows) they will keep summer boarders."

One hotel that did remain Christian in Hurleyville is Knapp's Columbia Farms Hotel which in 1966 celebrated its Diamond Jubilee.[3] The Elmore House was one farm boardinghouse operation that maintained 48 consecutive listings in "Summer Homes" as a Christian establishment. In its first farmhouse listing in 1895[4] no mention was made of clientele preference since all houses at that time were Christian. After only one year of being a farmhouse it appeared in print with the name it was to carry for many years, the Echo Lake Farm House under the management of Willard Elmore. It was to operate as such until W. Ray Elmore assumed partnership in 1901 (W. Elmore and Son) and jointly to continue their $1.50, three line blurb in "Summer Homes." In 1907 W. Ray Elmore took over and enlarged the house and increased the "Summer Homes" copy to seven lines trumpeting "best beds and elastic felt mattresses" and "illustrated booklet on request."

By 1913 the influx of Jewish operators prompted Elmore to include in the "Summer Homes" copy, "Protestant and Catholic Churches nearby." Progress was also on its way with "hot water heat, acetylene gas light, livery and automobile, running water in all rooms, local and long distance telephones." In 1920 The Elmore House emerged marking the virtual end of the farmhouse as a viable resort-type operation. It continued under "Gentile management" virtually alone in the Kosher South Fallsburgh listings until the early 1940's when its copy disappeared amid a clutter of display ads in the twilight years of the "Vacation Guide" (Summer Homes) publication.[5]

During the halcyon years of its operation, the Elmore House depended on the products of the land as well as paying guests for its economic stability. One of these products, milk, soon became for many farmers a major source of income. Its vital role was emphasized in the opening paragraph for Hurleyville in the 1891 "Summer Homes"—"An important milk station, situated 1,320 feet above the sea." Indeed it was. With completion of the new creamery in December of 1888, it was considered one of the largest and most important

Brophy's Mountain View Farm House became so popular with police and firemen from New York City and their hilarious antics that it became known as "Brophy's Mad House." *Courtesy, Don Battey*

The Columbia House, the oldest continually operating resort hotel in Sullivan County, founded by John Harms Knapp in 1891, was named in honor of the Chicago World's Columbian Exposition held in 1893. This is how it used to be, right, when a summer season at Knapp's Columbia House meant long, lazy August afternoons rocking on the spacious porches overlooking the valley and Hurleyville. *Top photograph by Howard Wood; right, Courtesy, Ben Knapp*

In this period photograph of an unidentified farm-boardinghouse check-in desk, the transition from gas illumination to electricity may be noted in the chandelier and the primitive wiring along the edge of the ceiling, left. Note the makeshift drinking fountain, probably a very up-to-date feature at the time. *Photograph by Howard Wood*

The Elmore House started as a humble farmhouse purchased by the Elmore family in 1833, commencing boardinghouse operations in 1883 and finally closing its doors in 1943. The property was sold to the Town of Fallsburgh for golf course development. *From an early brochure, courtesy, W. Ray Elmore*

milk stations on the line. Its output would be added to the average of 1500 cans per day for 1888 which, for the milk-producing regions of Orange, Sullivan and neighboring counties, aggregated about $9,000,000 for the coffers of the O. and W. At that time milk traffic was increasing at the rate of 20% a year.

This remarkable source of income for the O. and W. began in 1871 when a single car was run on a passenger train from Bloomingburg to Middletown. The first milk train to operate north of Bloomingburg pulled out in April of 1877 with George L. Greer of Walton as conductor.[6] Greer's cooperation with the farmers was such that after his assignment to the new "Night Line" in 1882 he was called back by farmer protest for the milk runs.

Through 1878 milk shipments continued to increase, with over 30 cans from Liberty consigned to Charles R. Gregory of Jersey City, who was one of the first commission dealers in the metropolitan area. Recognizing the importance of the increase over the entire county, the management introduced new cars "set upon improved springs equipped with vacuum air brakes." November and December of 1878 found many of the farmers living along the line busily erecting ice houses to improve and expand the handling of their milk. By April of the following year the regular milk train running from Morsston to Middletown made 27 stops in a distance of 49 miles and carried 250 cans of milk.

By 1900 the movement of milk over the O. and W. had become a prime economic fact of life and was reflected in this milk maid watercolor art on the title page of the 1907 "Summer Homes."

LUZON.   Hurleyville   167

The creamery at Hurleyville was considered one of the most modern on the line of the O. and W. Note wagon just pulling up to the loading dock with three cans of milk. *Photograph by Howard Wood*

Train No. 11 moves north out of Middletown behind class "U-1" No. 256, with a string of eleven empty milk cars in 1937. *Photograph by M.B. Cooke, Courtesy, Gerald M. Best*

DEALERS IN ONTARIO AND WESTERN MILK

NEW YORK

C. Althoff, 419 East 17th St.
Beakes Dairy Co., 206 E. 12th St., 321 Lenox Ave., 109 E. 124th St., 57 6th Ave., 266 W. 53d St. and 98 7th Ave.
J. C. Beckman, 416 W. 46th St.
J. Bellmer, 500 W. 126th St.
Luke Blake, 959 6th Ave.
Borden's Condensed Milk Co., Main Office, 108 Hudson St.; 201-229 E. 34th St., 306-317 E. 117th St.
Paul Boye, 402 2d Ave.
S. S. Brown, 318 Greenwich St.
O. Brooker, 364 W. 52d St.
Burges Bros., 334 E. 9th St.
M. Burgman, 156 W. 31st St.
Busch Bros., 419 W. 54th St.
J. J. Clancy, 1025 6th Ave.

H. Doscher, 332 W. 38th St.
J. Gluck, 511 2d Ave.
G. Guier, 427 W. 48th St.
B. Haase, 432 Pearl St.
L. J. Hall, 1087 Park Ave.
F. F. Hatch, 146 W. 49th St.
F. Honiker, 269 E. 10th St.
S. Horton, 644 6th Ave.
J. C. Hurtzig, 507 E. 76th St.
J. Jones, 357 W. 54th St.
J. P. Just, 162 W. 98th St.
F. Kalb, 517 E. 5th St.
J. E. Keogh, 37½ Carmine St.
A. Koester, 509 W. 55th St.
N. J. Lewis, 303 W. 53d St.
Lieberman Bros., 72 Suffolk St.
J. J. Lydecker, 408 W. 45th St.

Jas. Lyons, 222 E. 47th St.
F. Maulsted, 443 W. 45th St.
McDermott Bunder Dairy Co., 527 W. 38th St., 2214 7th Ave.
H. Meyer, 472 W. 42d St.
T. A. Mills, 350 E. 64th St.
J. H. Muller, 441 W. 53d St.
Mutual Milk & Cream Co., 322-326 E. 103d St.
W. H. Nelson, 210 W. 35th St.
J. Oniel, 454 W. 37th St.
H. Petry, 293 Delancy St.
W. Reese, 118 2d Ave.
J. E. Rosasco, 26 King St.
J. A. Rudolf, 504 W. 43d St.
Sanford Dairy Co., 138 W. 31st St.
H. Schroder, 215 E. 27th St.

H. M. Schwartz, 504 E. 118th St.
N. Smith, 105 Broome St.
Smith Farm Dairy, 464 Columbus Ave.
Standard Dairy Co., 611-613 E. 12th St.
Paul Steffens, 376 W. 126th St.
T. O. Smith's Sons, 672 6th Ave.
Tietjen Bros., 508 E. 118th St.
Tupper Bros., 76 W. 102d St.
Fred. Tutting, 109 King St.
Warwick Valley Milk Ass'n Co., 115 W. 32d St.
A. Westerman, 315 E. 83d St.
H. T. Witt, 418 West 55th St.
F. W. L. Witt, 705 Lexington Ave.

BROOKLYN

Alex. Campbell Co., 802 Fulton St.
Borden's Condensed Milk Co., 98-106 Sterling Place, 942-958 DeKalb Ave.
City Creamery Co., 1201 Atlantic Ave.

Columbia Dairy, 243 South 4th St.
A. Cook, 234 Powers St.
A. L. Day, 339 Sumner Ave.
Empire State Dairy, 502-506 Broadway.

W. M. Evans, 250 Hewes St.
J. H. Holtes, 335 South 1st St.
D. W. Kaatze, 383 South 1st St.
C. Oher, 154 Eagle St.

The R. F. Stevens Co., 338 Adams St.
B. Wecht, 105 DuBois St.
W. S. Weed Ice Cream Co., 1207 Bedford Ave.

UNION HILL, WEEHAWKEN AND JERSEY CITY, N. J.

A. Attig, 404 Jefferson St., Union Hill.
G. Bauneister, East New Durham.
N. Bennevitz, 420 Bloom St., Union Hill.
H. Bonjer, 13 Leonard St., Jersey City Heights.
G. Budde, 306 Kossuth St., Union Hill.
H. Brill, Guttenburg.
J. M. Brill, 71 Bergenline Ave., Union Hill.
J. Draves, 130 Union St., Union Hill.

DuBoise Bros., 685 Ocean Ave., Jersey City.
O. Heuer, 411, Jane St., West Hoboken.
C. H. Helmers, 177 Sherman Ave. Jersey City.
J. Jens, 526 Liberty St., Union Hill.
U. Kaiser, 520 Palisade Ave., West Hoboken.
W. Kroger, 141 Kossouth St., Union Hill.

W. Mahland, 394 Bergenline Ave., Union Hill.
J. Rinhardt, Franklin and New York Aves., Weehawken.
J. Stehler, 728 Spring St., Weehawken.
E. Schmidt, 485 West St., West Hoboken.
F. Schumaker, 70 Seventh St., Union Hill
J. Stiehler, 728 Sipp St., Union Hill.

H. Stockfish, West Hoboken.
F. B. Tietjen, 265 Summit Ave., West Hoboken.
L. B. Upright, 320 Hudson Ave., Weehawken
H. Wolphman, 586 Hudson Boulevard West Hoboken.

The outlets for the O. and W. milk trains in New York and New Jersey were noted in this listing in the back of the 1905 "Summer Homes."

In May the Midland announced a rate charge of 50 cents per 40-quart can, (up 10 cents,) claiming that they could not afford to run the train for less money. A protest meeting of farmers and shippers at the Liberty House resulted in a compromise price of 45 cents.

In January of 1880 a meeting of the milk shippers was called at the Liberty House to form the "Sullivan County Milk Association."[7] It was one year later, about April 1, that the O. and W. commenced running a special refrigerated train from Delhi to connect with the regular milk train at Morsston. The railroad was by this time supplying milk cans for those shippers who needed them, at $4.00 each. By the third week of December, 1891, 17,430 cans of milk were going to the city weekly, 165 cans of condensed milk and 311 cans of cream, with the average price paid for the surplus on the platforms being $1.76 a can of 40 quarts.

Probably one of the most important shipping points on the line was Liberty where on June 13, 1892, 256 cans of milk (10,240 quarts) were shipped, 102 boxes of cheese, 3 barrels of pot cheese and 20 tubs of butter.

The O. and W. was so deeply involved in the transportation of milk by this time that it was offering to "erect and rent, at a nominal figure, creameries at favorable points along its line to responsible parties." The management, to encourage its milk business, pointed out: "When a farmer's wife has once seen the difference in work – between sending milk to New York, and working it up into butter and cheese – she is ever afterwards in favor of the New York business."[8]

The ploy must have struck a responsive cord with the farm-maids because May, 1896, saw an increase of 500 cans a day over the previous year. On July 14, 1898, a record of sorts was made when a train of 24 cars moved 7,200 cans to New York. And so it went year by year, more and more cans and longer and heavier trains: the six year total up to February 1, 1901, a whopping 8,940,971 cans.

Eli Atwell at Mountaindale depot "well remembered three full milk trains down the line a night." The year was about 1913[9] and "the milk trains – the first one that picked up the local milk – went through Mountaindale about 5 o'clock in the afternoon, then there were two later trains that went through here about 6 o'clock at 60 to 70 mph from way up on the northern division. The only stops these northern division hotshots made were Sidney, Walton, Livingston Manor, Summitville, Middletown and Weehawken. They made better time than most of the passenger trains."

LUZON.   Hurleyville   169

The ice houses that farmers built at various points along the line to keep their product fresh needed ice, and many ponds supplied this precious commodity. Brown's pond, about half way between Hurleyville and South Fallsburgh, was the focal point of commercial ice harvesting activity. An almost annual event was the arrival at the pond of the Knickerbocker Ice Company of New York City during the first week of December. The company would erect a housing for an engine to assist in the work alongside of a specially laid half mile of track. Forty carloads of ice would move out daily on the O. and W. to the City where the next summer it would command premium prices over the less pure Hudson River ice. Nearby Echo Lake and Fallsburgh Lake[10] were also harvested and stored to guarantee cold refrigerator cars on the summer milk runs.

Hurleyville (Luzon) has been the scene of some disturbing incidents, particularly for the operating department of the O. and W. One in particular involved the late Will Brock when he substituted for the agent (suddenly taken ill) at Centerville in February of 1901.

"He (the agent) assured me I could handle the work," Brock commented, "but cautioned me to be very careful should it be necessary to deliver a train order."

Since trains were seldom stopped for such purposes, Brock felt secure in taking over for the balance of the day. Brock recalled: "that day was exceptional. As soon as first No. 9 pulled out, the dispatchers started calling for a "31" train order for second No. 9 and I received my first train order for delivery. Second No. 9 proved to be the flanger[11] and needless to say I checked and double checked, even after I had my o.k. complete from the dispatcher. About 20 minutes later I heard the operator at Luzon report that second No. 9 had run into the rear end of first No. 9 near the station, killing two or three people and burning up the coach."

Actually there was one fatality that cold blustery February day. When the flanger, second No. 9, struck the passenger coach it was telescoped and the passengers were thrown to the front end of the car. Almost instantly the passenger coach and a baggage car took fire from the overturned stove, which destroyed both cars. Also lost were 600 pieces of postal matter.

The passengers made their way out of the car by breaking the glass of a window. H.R. Schofield, one of the escapees, later died of severe burns. Train No. 9 in charge of Conductor Oscar Kirby and Engineer Andy O'Neal[12] had orders to pass train No. 32 at Hurleyville and had pulled up to the switch, the contemporary press reporting "...the second section...had no such orders."

Bill Brock recalled: "it proved to be the engineer's fault on second number nine by running through a red block which he claimed he could not see due to snowing and blowing so hard it covered the block signal."

"Perk" Jacobson of Hurleyville recalled a minor accident that occurred during World War 1 when "the unloading chute in the bottom of a coal car broke just after going through Hurleyville southbound and distributed coal liberally along the right-of-way." Perk remembered that a coal famine existed at the time and "the word quickly passed through town and soon wagons closed in on the right-of-way to pick up the wayward coal."

Not all misfortunes at Hurleyville had such beneficial communal results. One of the worst disasters of an operational nature for the railroad occurred to train No. 3 on the long embankment south of town. It was just about 4:15 p.m. on a cold February 13th in 1907 when engine No. 70,[13] upon emerging from Smith Hill Cut at forty miles per hour, was literally torn apart in an explosion that, by word of mouth and photographic coverage, ultimately achieved legendary proportions.

Three trainmen went to glory – fireman Martin Mullen, "... who was hurled into a field one hundred feet away, his head being torn from his body"; engineer J.D. Valquette of Cadosia, who was riding on the engine to 'learn the road' "... was hurled four hundred feet from the track and horribly mangled"; and engineer William Gadwood of Walton, who was hurled into a field later to die of his injuries.

The explosion of the boiler tore the ground beneath the engine as though a heavy charge of explosives had been set off, driving the rails apart for a distance of a hundred feet. The force of the blast also threw the baggage car and smoker down the embankment and the remaining cars from the rails with the parlor car blocking the southbound tracks.[14] Before the tracks were cleared for trains No. 7 and No. 5, the carnage was duly photographed by L. G. Laidlaw of Hurleyville. Laidlaw's pictures became fixtures in almost all 'parlor table' family albums of the area. O. and W. officials approached Laidlaw, while shooting the wreck, and offered him $50.00 for the negatives – an offer which he shrewdly refused. The orders for pictures came in at such a fast rate that the long hours in the darkroom all but ruined the photographer's eyesight.

Hurleyville, fortunately for the present, had several photographers who recorded the great boardinghouse era. In 1886 Graeff and Gardner operated a branch gallery in Hurleyville as an addition to its facilities in Jeffersonville, Grahamsville and Liberty. But perhaps the most compre-

This picture, left, of the blowup of Brook's-built, class "G," No. 70, by photographer L.G. Laidlaw, is perhaps the most famous O. and W. wreck picture of all time. Arrow in distance indicates the location of a section of boiler plate. No. 70 is shown above in better days. *Top photograph, courtesy, Robert F. Harding*

A rare Laidlaw view (Laidlaw and Wood Studios) at the 1907 demise of No. 70, showing the hat-marked site where one of the three badly mutilated trainmen was found.

A slight altercation on March 8, 1920, put snow plow No. 2 at right angles to the main line, threatening Prince's feed store. The plow was back on the tracks in a few hours. *Photograph by Howard Wood*

hensive recorder of Hurleyville and the boardinghouse-spanning region was Howard Wood[15] whose old Hurleyville studio flourished in the early 1900's.

He didn't seem to be ready, however, to record the worst fire in Hurleyville's history on Monday, October 16, 1911. It was discovered about 3:30 A.M. in the Hotel O'Neill by proprietor C.L. Hack, who immediately aroused the guests in the hotel. To control the fire, one of the buildings in town had to be dynamited, but not before O'Neill's Hotel, a meat market, barber shop, two grocery stores, a fruit and tobacco store as well as a barn, shed and ice house were reduced to ashes. No injuries were reported during the conflagration — the only fatalities being nine dogs, trapped in the collapse of various buildings.

Hotels and boardinghouses that burned down during the "Season" were more the exception than the rule. The burning of the Grand View Hotel in Mountaindale, one of the largest in the county, which went up at 3 a.m. on July 11, 1913, was an exception. At the time of the fire there were about 100 guests registered. Luckily they escaped without injury but lost most of their belongings. As a result of the disaster, the local press began calling for tighter fire regulations in hotels and boardinghouses. It put readers in mind of an editorial that appeared in the January 29, 1904 Liberty *Register,* following the Iroquois Theatre holocaust in Chicago,[16] outlining a state law requiring the hotels to be inspected every six months— in January and June. The editorial went on to outline, among other things, the need of escape ropes in every room in non-fireproofed buildings over two stories in height, and proper and timely inspections.

The editorial was quickly forgotten but again brought sharply into focus in May of 1920 when the Max Cohen Boardinghouse near Mountaindale burned, taking two lives.[17] "... the building laths, unplastered because the boardinghouse was still in process of completion, burned like tinder, fanned by a fairly stiff breeze."[18]

It happened again when the Leona House in White Sulphur Springs burned in July, 1922, with 125 guests registered. Then the National Hotel in Bridgeville went up in July, 1924, with no loss of life to its 20 guests.

A thirsty guest going into an unused kitchen at the High Grove House in Woodbourne in July, 1925, saved the lives of many children put to bed early so the parents might "... watch a movie in

Although most farmers elected to take in summer boarders after the New York and Oswego Midland started promoting their facilities in "Summer Homes" in 1878, it seems as though the Hurleyville area had more than their share of agrarian entrepreneurs. This was due in large part to the proximity of ambitious photographer Howard Wood who made sure nobody was left out of his developing trays. The two photographs, above, are examples of his craft, with the Hornbeck farmhouse, right, clearly illustrating how the prospering farmer had to increase his accommodations by constructing a less than aesthetically pleasing addition.

M. Meinhold's Waldorf House commanded a lucrative commercial site opposite O'Neill's Hotel and the nearby depot area. This scene in the 1890's is marked by the pony cart and the nostalgic curved pilsener beer sign.

Facing the Waldorf House across the tracks was O'Neill's Hotel, whose proprietor, "J.D.," made no bones about whose beer and ale he featured. The hostelry was listed in the 1898 Breed's Directory of the New York, Ontario & Western Ry. as the Hotel Brooklyn and noted that the "bar will always be found supplied with Choice Wines, Ales, Beers, Liquors and Cigars." The popular tippling spa was doomed to vanish in smoke along with nine other structures on the night of October 16, 1911.   *Photograph by Howard Wood*

Edward Hope operated not only this well-manicured boardinghouse but also a most lucrative souvenir manufacturing business in an adjacent barn, right rear.   *Photograph by Howard Wood*

An early horse-drawn road scraper of heroic proportions takes its ease, along with the town smithy, in front of his shop, beyond which may be seen the mansard roof of O'Neill's emporium. *Courtesy, Tom Masterson*

peace." Finding the kitchen a mass of flames, he sounded an alarm and the 52-room structure was quickly evacuated of its 60 guests.

Many letters to the editors of the various papers resulted every time a hotel was leveled during the season, commenting that time was running out on fire safety in the resorts. Time was indeed running out and faster than one could imagine.

The fire that changed the fire safety attitudes of resort operators occurred not during the summer season or the High Holy Days but on Washington's Birthday weekend in 1926, when Shindler's Prairie House, located between Hurleyville and Loch Sheldrake, burned to the ground taking 12 lives. The 80-room[19] resort, located on the Hillside Road leading to the Loch Sheldrake-Liberty road, was built in 1912 and remodeled again in 1924 during the "stucco" mania. As too often occurred in early county history, appearance was more important than safety.

The fire is thought to have been started by sparks from a fireplace in which large slabs of wood had been placed by the porter for the night. The fireplace, located in the central lobby on the main floor, stood near the main staircase which wound up three stories, in the center of the building. The flames, starting in the fireplace area, are thought to have swept up this staircase, creating a chimney-like draft. Nearly 50 occupants of the building were trapped by the vortex of flames in the upper hallways or in their rooms by the sudden cutting off of all avenues of escape. The wooden fire escape offering little aid forced many to leap out, sustaining serious injury in the three story drop to the ground.[20]

The porter, Jerry Bastian, perhaps the only man who could give an accurate account of how the fire started, lost his life in warning the guests. Another one of the victims was Julius Jacobson, brother of "Perk" Jacobson of Hurleyville.[21]

"I remember the night of the fire," recalled Perk, "it was bitter cold and windy with the roads badly drifted with new snow. We had just started for the hotel when we learned that some badly burned people had been brought into Goodlemen's Drug Store. One of the burned was my brother Julius. They poured oil on him to help relieve the pain. We got a car and took Julius to Monticello Hospital. I'll never forget that trip. We could not get up the hill past the Columbia Farms Hotel so we had to go by way of South Fallsburgh. As it was, it took us a little over three hours. We had to push the car through so many deep drifts I lost track how many times."

LUZON. Hurleyville

The 400-room Morningside Hotel, between Loch Sheldrake and Hurleyville, was a product of the stucco-era, having opened its doors for the first time in 1920. It burned to the ground in early 1964. *Courtesy, Steingart Associates*

The Liberty *Register* for February 25, 1926, ran this grainy picture of Shindler's Prairie House to illustrate the spectacular Washington's Birthday fire story. Because of the high fire risk in the region and the need to protect the Jewish farmer turned boardinghouse operator, the Associated Co-operative Fire Insurance Companies of Sullivan and Adjoining Counties was formed in Woodridge on April 10, 1913. Samuel Shindler, owner of the Prairie House, was a member of the original Board of Directors.

On the day of the last scheduled passenger run to Sullivan County, the Hurleyville depot was distinctive with its own makeshift Railway Express parcel ramp. *Photograph by Edward H. Weber*

District Attorney Sidney Foster, who had charge of the investigation into the fire protection facilities [or lack of them] of the hotel, immediately set about framing a bill which was to be presented through Assemblyman Maxwell Knapp of Hurleyville to the New York State Legislature. Supporting editorials appeared in all the papers: "No device is too expensive to disregard ... strict regulations of the law should be strictly enforced ... there is no cause to relax in the slightest a perpetual vigilance ... " and so on.

The results of Foster's investigations were presented before a grand jury in order to determine if anyone should be held criminally accountable for the tragedy. On Monday, March 15, witnesses appeared before the panel. After a three-day hearing, the county grand jury chose not to return an indictment against any person in connection with the fire. Five cases for compensation by relatives of deceased victims were started before Referee Burns in Monticello the first week of March. That same week Samuel Shindler, weak and unnerved by the fire, which left him so exhausted that he had to be carried aboard an O. and W. train at South Fallsburgh, left for New York to regain his health.

By April 1 things were moving along in Albany with Assemblyman Knapp preparing to introduce a bill to amend the business law relative to fire escapes on hotels and boardinghouses and to inspections and injunctions. On January 27, 1927, editorials advised the resort industry of the "New Fire Escape Bill" which essentially required boardinghouses and hotels to maintain fire escape appliances in all rooms and more importantly the issuance of a certificate "only after an inspection has revealed that the law has been complied with."

The resorts and fire safety were coming of age.

177

Early risers and a classic Buick touring car patiently await the arrival of the Loch Sheldrake morning mail. *Courtesy, Tom Masterson*

Loch Sheldrake

Hurleyville (Luzon) and Loch Sheldrake are so close together that the boardinghouses and homes strung out along the road between essentially blend them into one.

Hurleyville as the O. and W. detraining point for its sister resort eventually led to the formation in February, 1930, of the "Luzon and Loch Sheldrake Hotelmen's Association" by interested business representatives of the two communities.[1] The railroad and its "Summer Homes" publication did much to bring about this camaraderie.

In the dawning year of 1886 there was but one listing in "Summer Homes" under Loch Sheldrake, but this seeming lack of interest was not to last — the idea of farmers taking guests really caught on because by 1889 Loch Sheldrake boasted ten farmhouse listings, and her tiny neighbor, Divine Corners, had eight; both were sub-headings listed under Hurleyville. Finally in 1893 pressure by the Loch Sheldrake resort operators on the "Summer Homes" people brought about a major resort heading for the listings of Loch Sheldrake as well as Divine Corners. Further, an extensive introductory paragraph of sixteen lines described the Loch (lake) as "... something like a half mile long by a quarter mile in width, and partly surrounded by woods and groves, which, where they border on the lake, present the same natural beauty they did many years ago."

The Loch's promotion in the railroad publication went as high as 28 resort listings by 1907, dropping to 16 in the 1915 issue and five years later to four.

These were the lush years before the competition of the automobile, the bus and the airline. This domination of the transportation field was reflected in the opulently produced "Summer Homes" and accordingly started to subtly reveal itself in the 1898 issue with green-tinted photographs and in 1901 with vignetted[2] photographs and double ruled borders. The 1902 issue sported a full color title page featuring the milkmaid and her pails of milk; a visual theme that was to be featured for many years to come which the railroad believed was promoting one of their chief assets, the fresh milk — healthful environment image.

Loch Sheldrake and Schupp's Loch Sheldrake House, right, in 1890, from the hill that later saw the erection in the early 20's of the Victoria Mansion. *Sullivan County Museum Archives*

They were on the right track, for assets due in large part to milk receipts were such in 1903 that a surplus for the "Summer Homes" budget permitted the commissioning of eight full page 'sepia-tinted' wash drawings of appropriate sporting subjects: golf playing, a horseless carriage,[3] a fisherman on the Beaverkill, a huntsman and hound dog and others, each set off with a four to six line poem.

A feeling of prosperity was invading the editorial rooms of "Summer Homes" which revealed itself in the 1905 issue with nine handsome full color watercolor renderings of scenes along the lines of the O. and W.[4] The 1906 issue was greatly in demand by customers for the purpose of cutting out and framing eight vignette watercolors of general scenes with such titles as "The Old Orchard," "In Parksville" and "Kiamesha Lake." This issue was also unusual in that the page size was enlarged to 7 x 10 from the long standard 6 x 9. This size held through 1909, only to return to the old size in 1910.

By 1915 the publication lapsed into a monochromatic-antiseptic format which clearly stated the great years of the O. and W. were now a thing of the past. If there was more money in 1920, and surely there was, it went for operating overhead and not into the niceties of aesthetically orientated promotional pieces.

The cover art for 1920 was so poorly done that from 1921 on, the photographer's art was depended upon entirely for cover decoration, not without a semblance of monotony. More and more the photos in the book included shots of autos on ever-improving highways with an occasional "... Sullivan County needs more and better highways" finding its way into the accompanying copy. The railroad's euphoria started to crumble when the number of listings decreased consistently through the 20's until by 1930 full-page one-hotel ads started appearing with a large picture of the resort across the top.[5] Boardinghouse and small hotel operators were drifting away from "Summer Homes" listings in such alarming numbers that the format was drastically changed to the one page — one resort with photo format or subdivided display-type ads. By 1933 the depression was making its inroads resulting in a one-page Loch Sheldrake — Hurleyville combined listing of resort facilities.

During its long tenure of publication, "Summer Homes" could indeed be read as a barometer of passenger travel and the economic stability of the railroad company.

In the 1906 issue there were 23 boardinghouses and farmhouses listed at "Sheldrake" including the pioneer resort operator H.M. LeRoy and his Maple Grove House and Maple Grove Casino that boasted the first bowling alley in Sullivan County. An

The earlier issues of "Summer Homes" featured scenes of nature on the covers such as the aquatic hunting scene on the 1881 issue, top, and the dragon fly-frog theme in 1891. The first advertisement announcing the initial issue in 1878, appeared in the April 19, 1878, Liberty *Register*. The June 14 *Register* later reported "the neat and well written little book 'Summer Homes on the Midland,' has made its appearance and is indeed a very handy reference to people in the city who wish to spend the summer months in Sullivan County." *Courtesy, James Garvin*

In 1898 "Summer Homes" appeared in hard cover and was used extensively in the depots at the various resort points as a ready reference book that generally hung on a nail near the ticket window. They were also available for reference in all the leading New York hotels.
Courtesy, Mrs. E.T. Bradford

In 1893, opposite page, the front and back cover featured the dapper summer boarder addressing himself to the ever present milkmaid, while his departing train traces a sooty mark on the distant horizon. *Courtesy, Mrs. E.T. Bradford*

The 1906 issue appeared during the halcyon years when the extensive budget for "Summer Homes" was reflected in the commissioning of this special O. and W. milkmaid watercolor painting for the cover and assorted scenes on the inside. The covers during the 20's, upper right, featured the many scenic faces of the resort region, such as this unidentified waterfall on the 1928 issue. *Both, courtesy, Mrs. E.T. Bradford*

old-time summer visitor writing from Brooklyn recalled: "Free dancing in the casino every afternoon and evening except Sunday, then we went buggie (sic) riding in the suburbs. Wednesday and Saturday evenings, barn dances for the benefits of the haywagon riders who came from the surrounding boardinghouses and farms in Hurleyville and even Ferndale."

Melvin A. Rexford's commanding Overlook, formerly the Hotel Lawrence, which actually did overlook the lake,[6] was a landmark for many years as well as M.G. Roosa's mansarded Roosa Hotel now completely swallowed up by the Evans Hotel.

As far back as August, 1878, the contemporary press recorded the presence of "sixty-three summer boarders in and around Sheldrake"[7] with the July 4th weekend in 1879 "...celebrated to its fullest extent at Sheldrake. The hotel was filled to its utmost capacity and G.P. Wright, the proprietor, had his hands full. At an early hour he refused to take any more numbers for the ball, having then 108 and many from a distance were obliged to go elsewhere for accommodations." It was a weekend of some consequence: "... 500 took supper and 344 horses were fed."

To further promote the region, the O. and W. produced a set of post cards which by August, 1906, were selling well over 100,000 before Labor Day. The cards were available in sets of 10 and were on sale for ten cents apiece at all railroad stations.

East Shore—Loch Sheldrake

LOCH SHELDRAKE
and
HURLEYVILLE HOTELS
LUZON STATION—Sullivan County, N. Y.

Modern Hotels and Camps are situated in this vicinity.
Complete facilities for your diversion; sports of all kinds.
Social entertainments of every character. Nature in all its beauty and grandeur can be fully enjoyed in this section. All Dietary Laws observed.
For information and particulars write to any of the hotels listed below.

Anawana Lodge ....Hurleyville, N. Y.	Loch Sheldrake Rest Loch Sheldrake, N. Y.
Bell House ....Hurleyville, N. Y.	Loch View House ..Loch Sheldrake, N. Y.
Black Apple Inn ..Loch Sheldrake, N. Y.	Lake Shore Hotel .....Hurleyville, N. Y.
Brookside House ...Loch Sheldrake, N. Y.	Midwood Hotel ......Hurleyville, N. Y.
Butler Lodge ....Hurleyville, N. Y.	Miller Gap House ..Loch Sheldrake, N. Y.
Capital Hotel & Camp	Moonglow Inn .....Loch Sheldrake, N. Y.
Loch Sheldrake, N. Y.	Mountain Cliff Hotel
Camp Harmony ....Hurleyville, N. Y.	Loch Sheldrake, N. Y.
Columbia Star House ..Hurleyville, N. Y.	Overlook Hotel ...Loch Sheldrake, N. Y.
Edgewood Hotel ...Loch Sheldrake, N. Y.	Paramount Manor .....Hurleyville, N. Y.
Golden House ....Hurleyville, N. Y.	Pine Grove House ..Loch Sheldrake, N. Y.
Grand View Hotel ....Hurleyville, N. Y.	Pine View Country Club
Hotel Ganz ....Loch Sheldrake, N. Y.	Loch Sheldrake, N. Y.
Hotel Roxy ......Loch Sheldrake, N. Y.	Riverside Palace ...Loch Sheldrake, N. Y.
Hotel Schlesinger ..Loch Sheldrake, N. Y.	Rubel's Mansion .....Hurleyville, N. Y.
Hotel Wellworth .....Hurleyville, N. Y.	Riverview Lodge .....Hurleyville, N. Y.
Hotel Wayside ......Hurleyville, N. Y.	Shady Nook Country Club
Karmel Hotel .....Loch Sheldrake, N. Y.	Loch Sheldrake, N. Y.
Lakeside Hotel .....Hurleyville, N. Y.	Sunset Hotel ....Hurleyville, N. Y.
Lakeview House ...Loch Sheldrake, N. Y.	Victoria Mansion ..Loch Sheldrake, N. Y.
Leroy Hotel ....Loch Sheldrake, N. Y.	West End Hotel ..Loch Sheldrake, N. Y.
Loch Sheldrake Inn..Loch Sheldrake, N. Y.	Wernick House ...Loch Sheldrake, N. Y.

"THE MEETING PLACE OF FRIENDS"

After the Crash in 1929, many resort operators advertised in multi-listings, such as this page in the 1933 "Summer Homes" for the Loch Sheldrake-Hurleyville area.

The pioneer LeRoy House (H.M. LeRoy, prop.), above, which grew into the Maple Grove House and Maple Grove Casino also boasted the first bowling alley in Sullivan County, below. *Photograph left, by Laidlaw and Wood*

This overview of Loch Sheldrake shows the Victoria Mansion commanding the heights at left, with the pioneer Roosa House, (Jim Roosa, proprietor) middle center, and the Hotel Evans, the successor to the Roosa House. *Courtesy, Tom Masterson*

Mel Rexford's Overlook House, the sale of which to Jewish investors in February, 1919, marked the initial penetration of the all-Christian hotel community at Loch Sheldrake. *Photograph by Wood*

In 1919 and 1920 two transactions took place that were most indicative of the transition to a Jewish-orientated resort. February, 1919, saw Mel Rexford's Overlook sold to S. Salrzman for "the consideration of $17,000," and the following year Marvin Leroy[8] sold the "Leroy House" to the Kranuss brothers of New York City for the record price of $50,000. Marvin Leroy had purchased it from his father in 1910 for $15,000, an indication of the increased resort property values and the steady growth of Loch Sheldrake. The Leroy place was one of the oldest resorts in the county, Garrett Leroy being one of the first farmers in the county to turn his attention to the summer boarders in the late 1880's.

Loch Sheldrake never experienced a "village leveling fire" such as many other county resort centers suffered. The area did have an occasional boardinghouse or hotel go up in smoke – with the demise of the Victoria Mansion in July of 1943 one of the more notable. The fire apparently started on the front porch roof of the first floor of the four-story building in the middle of the afternoon. Within 40 minutes the structure, containing 80 guest rooms, large dining rooms, kitchen and other public rooms, was a $75,000 loss. Most of the 100 registered guests were left with "no more than the standard shorts-and-halter attire."

Built and owned by Louis Kelman, it was a shining example of the great hotel expansion "stucco" period of the 1920's; erected about 1923. This remarkable hotel expansion period was also the era of the "rub-out," the slot machine and illegal hooch.

"THEY LOOKED LIKE 'RUBES'; THEY WERE 'DRY' AGENTS."

So read a headline on January 27, 1922. The four actually did look and act like farmers. How was Sullivan County to know their names were Izzy Eisenstein and Moe Smith;[9] "that they wore tiny shields on their suspenders, and that their companions were Agents Fannelli and Stafford?" The agents rode out from Monticello, in a hired wagon, to Bethel, " ... and there, in a barn on the edge of Bethel's burying ground, found one ten and one thirty-gallon still." Thus it was recorded in the press — only one of an endless number of "raids" to enforce the Volstead Act during the hectic days of the Prohibition Era.

This rube guise didn't work most of the time. The agents had to compete with the grapevine and accordingly moved with bewildering rapidity from one place to another.

It all started on January 16, 1920, when prohibition – "a beneficent law of the people, by the people and for the people was written into our

The double-porched Loch Sheldrake House, operated by Albert Schupp, played the field by advertising for summer boarders, salesmen and hunters. The Bullock Diner parking lot now occupies the site of the long-vanished hotel. *Photograph by Wood*

national Constitution."[10] It is not recorded as to how all sections of Sullivan County celebrated the event, but Liberty had a torchlight parade and then a march to the Presbyterian Church for services. The event also heralded the opening of the floodgates of gangsterism to Sullivan County. Immediately, gangsters became the purveyors of illegal "hooch" for the resort crowds.

With their migration to the mountains, intergang "misunderstandings" were inevitably solved by a concrete weighted deposit in Loch Sheldrake, Swan Lake or in some one of the other watering spots. One notorious gangland rub-out came to light on July 31, 1937, when the body of Walter Sage was found floating in Swan Lake albeit tied to a slot machine frame and a thirty-pound stone. Sage was lured to Loch Sheldrake and stabbed to death with an ice pick near a modest resort known as Marion's Cottage. Two years later, on June 1, 1939, it was reported " ... the sash weighted body of a man, who had been shot five times and stabbed seven times, floated to the surface of Loch Sheldrake" during the Decoration Day weekend. The body was identified as Maurice (Frenchy) Carillot, dope peddler and key man in a narcotics ring.

All were victims of Murder Incorporated, a far reaching development of Brooklyn's gangland. Of the total of fifty victims, Sullivan County and its distinguished County Judge, George L. Cooke, were concerned with but five.

Other types of violence shook the good people of Loch Sheldrake. There were, for example, the bandits who in August of 1928 entered the Loch Sheldrake Casino on a quiet Sunday morning "in a fanfare of pistol shots." Their nemesis was Morris "Mike" Steiglitz, the bartender who "acted accord-

Souvenir of Hotel Lawrence

Photo by Laidlaw

HOTEL LAWRENCE was destroyed by fire on the night of October 27, 1904. It had accommodations for 100 guests and was the finest equipped summer hotel at Loch Sheldrake. The proprietor, L. W. Lawrence, has since erected a large amusement hall in Hurleyville, which is now open to the general public.

This sprawling structure was purchased by L.W. Lawrence in 1901 and immediately enlarged and improved into the prosperous Hotel Lawrence. Returning home late on the night of October 27, 1904, the Lawrences built a fire to take off the chill, which led to the hotel's demise. A defective flue was suspected as the cause of the initial attic fire that spread downward devouring all but a few furnishings saved by the Lawrences. *Courtesy, Tom Masterson*

The Capitol Hotel and Camp shown nearing completion in the early 1920's just after its final application of stucco. Like the Hotel LeRoy, it, too, after abandonment was control-burned by the Loch Sheldrake Fire Department. *Courtesy, Steingart Associates*

The Roxy Hotel shortly after completion in 1928 during the ownership of Morris Moskowitz. The hotel, after extensive expansion, became the Green Acres Hotel, formerly of Lake Huntington. *Courtesy, Steingart Associates*

Two brothers by the name of Appel, one with red hair and one with black, decided to go into the resort business. "Red" Appel opened a restaurant (Red Apple Rest) on Route 17 in the Ramapo Valley which has become legendary as a bus and hack stop. "Black" Appel erected an inn near Loch Sheldrake, right, in 1923 in the best tradition of the stucco era. Later the hotel became known as Brown's and expanded beyond the World War II period facility shown below, into a greatly enlarged hotel complex under the deft hand of Charles and Lillian Brown.

Courtesy, Steingart Associates

LOCH SHELDRAKE 189

The abandoned LeRoy Hotel and annex buildings shortly before controlled burning by the Loch Sheldrake Fire Department. The stucco-era hotel property is now the site of the new campus of the Sullivan County Community College.

ing to the traditions of the old school of bartenders of less effete days." Halfway down the room at a mahogany bar stood "Mike" with a handful of money. When he started shooting at the gunman nearest to him, the other bandits turned and peppered the bar and back wall with bullet holes with "Mike" standing tall and straight wreathed in acrid smoke and surrounded by the singing bullets. With one dying on the floor and the other four bandits roaring off in a Packard (probably black) down the road to Woodbourne – "Mike" was clearly the hero.

Occasionally a hold-up would involve an entire hotel. Traveling in a stolen Buick and a Ford roadster, a gang of seven New York gunmen swept down on the Seiken House two miles from Liberty soon after noon on August 16, 1926, and "armed to the teeth with revolvers, held up all of the 186 guests of the house and the proprietors to boot." They posed first as authorities searching for slot machines but, finding none, relieved the guests and climbed back into their cars and tore off " ... firing 15 or 20 shots as they left to keep guests in a quiet mood."[11]

May, 1930, saw five bandits swoop down on the Ambassador Hotel at Old Falls, dash in the lobby and order all in sight to throw up their hands. Eight or ten guests were relieved of their cash and jewelry amounting to over $1700. As quickly as they appeared, the bandits vanished.

And so it went around Sullivan County during the 20's: a 10-gallon copper still, a gallon of alleged whisky, a sample of corn mash and two prisoners near DeBruce in March of 1923. A headline "Troopers seize Huge Still and $800 in Moonshine in Callicoon Center Raid." The front page of the *Register* for February 26, 1925, noted "Chrysler Roadster Loaded with Worse Than Gunpowder (illegal hooch) Seized at Livingston Manor." The purveyor apprehended was claimed to be responsible for "the numerous and rather violent 'celebrations' for which the Manor has been noted of late."

Others read: "Seizure of Gambling Devices at White Lake"

"Racketeer Rivalries End in Duel at Fallsburgh"

"Troopers Find Another Still at Swan Lake"

In the face of mounting criticism of the region's increasing wide open reputation, the dynamic sheriff of Sullivan County, Ben R. Gerow, vigorously proclaimed: "The lid is down on slot machines in Sullivan County and it is going to stay down for the rest of the summer." This was an overly optimistic statement. The previous year (1930) the sheriff had led a considerable number of raids which he claimed had practically eliminated that form of entertainment in the county, but one-armed bandits were common in many resorts into the 1950's. In some circles the 1931 season must have been successful when one considers this headline in the Hurleyville *Sentinel*:

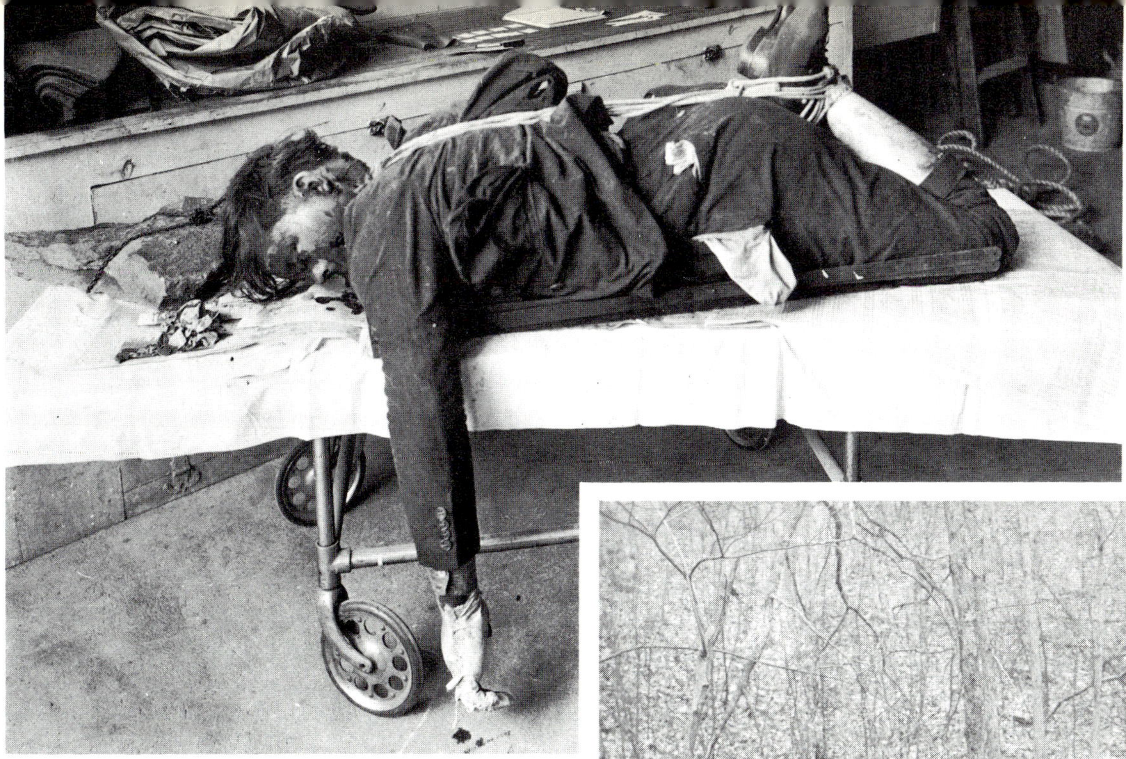

Walter Sage, a Brooklyn gangster, was stabbed thirty-seven times with an ice pick, then tied to a pinball machine rack and deposited in Swan Lake. On July 31, 1937, the body was discovered floating on the lake. In 1940 a grand jury indicted Jack Drucker for the slaying of Sage, but it was not until December, 1943, that Drucker was picked up. On May 11, 1944, County Judge George L. Cooke sentenced the 38 year-old gangster, a native of Sullivan County, to twenty-five years to life in prison.

A stalwart bunch of well-armed 'moonshiners' pose at a still high in the mountains in back of Grahamsville; any two of which might be the well-disguised Izzy Eisenstein and Moe Smith just before executing a well-planned pinch. *Courtesy, Bruce Denman, Sr.*

"Region Still Popular With Gangsters, But Summer Passed Without Fatality."

Editorials were apprehensive when "Waxey" Gordon was apprehended in a cottage behind the "Mansion House" at White Lake. The press screamed about the all-too-true negative image the county was getting. Not too long before, North White Lake had its name changed to Kauneonga Lake in an effort to disassociate itself with the unsavory reputation White Lake had achieved. But finally, before Sullivan County had to change *its* name, (and this was alluded to by many) beer was legalized.

Before it was all over though, the staid New York, Ontario and Western found itself innocently enmeshed with the mobs. It all happened at the sleepy little depot of Winterton, just barely inside the borders of Sullivan County. It seems a consignment of "cereal beverage" to a ficticious William Smith, placed inconspicuously on a siding, was the target for an abnormal number of trucks. Before long their frequent trips along quiet country roads attracted the attention of the authorities. Upon investigation the boxcar was found to contain 78 half barrels of beer. The balance, 150 in number, had already been liberally distributed about the area.

That Sunday it was wet in most of Sullivan County — courtesy of the New York, Ontario and Western.

The first spindly iron trestle at Liberty Falls (Ferndale) and the tannery pond. For the youngsters of Liberty and Ferndale, a dandy exercise in adventure, above, and a popular skating retreat, below.
The engine on the trestle has all the characteristics of No. 4, the first homemade Mother Hubbard to be rolled out of the Norwich Shops in 1898. Its consist — three milk cars and a combine — marks it as a local originating at Liberty.   *Sullivan County Museum Archives*

Ferndale

Liberty Falls

Train 29's run from Hurleyville to Liberty Falls was one thing to Pete Reilly as he contemplated what was left of his pile of Sunday papers, and quite another thing to the Sun's "four cent scribe" who described how the road curved around "... dodging the blackened stumps of clearings and running through swamps whose tall red flowers, cat-o-nine tails stalks and wild roses nod in the breeze that the train stirs up."

Brakeman Edward Firman had an explanation for that when he said "the railroad was built that way to let the passengers see all of a few counties from the car windows at once."

In any event, the train slowed a bit as it neared the Liberty Falls depot and the nearby trestle; in fact, just enough so Pete could glance up the valley road and see an occasional boardinghouse roof piercing the dense groves that gave Liberty Falls its rustic charm.

One page of "Summer Homes" in the year of Pete's run listed three farmhouses with guest accommodations; W.K. Loder, Mrs. W.W. Bartholomew and John Clements, the latter one having been included in the first issue of "Summer Homes on the Midland" in 1878 as J.A. Clements Farmhouse. Listed on the opposite page was the Nichols' Farm which much later was to be purchased by Selig and Malke Grossinger. Ferndale (Liberty Falls) in those bucolic years, was a microcosm of the pioneer farm boardinghouse industry of Sullivan County. By 1910, four "classic" farm boardinghouses were located more or less within walking distance of John T. Clark's famous pavilion on Lake Ophelia – the Clements Lake Farmhouse, Nichols Boardinghouse, The Pinney House and the Ferndale Villa.

The first of these, the Clements Lake Farmhouse, can truly be called one of the very few "pioneer" summer resorts of Sullivan County still extant. Miss Laura Clements and Mrs. David Clements told of the first Clements' arrival in the county about 1811. "They stayed with friends in a log cabin on the hill overlooking the village while their first home was built. It was a two story house built with wide boards. The mantel from the fireplace and the large stones for the horse block and sidewalk were later taken to the new house which was built in 1850. That house was copied from the family home in Fairfield, Connecticut. About a year later the parlor furniture, of black

A. Grossinger's   B. Site of Ferndale trestle   C. Ferndale   D. Ferndale depot

The 1887 "Summer Homes" captured the same restful atmosphere in its illustration of Liberty Falls that Pete Reilly surveyed from his paper-laden coach one year before.

The early Ferndale depot (Liberty Falls nomenclature dropped in 1897), a familiar and welcome sight for those guests bound for the Clements Lake Farmhouse, Nichols, Bunger's Spring Lake Farm House, Mongaup Farm House, the Pinney House, Hill Crest Farm, Ferndale Villa and Grand View Heights. Farm resort operators differed on the one or two-word spelling of farmhouse.

FERNDALE 195

The Clements Lake Farmhouse, above, as it appeared during the heyday of its operation. The low two-story section, left, was the original home built in 1850; the peaked section in the center was added after the Civil War, while the large three-story structure was completed in time for the 1902 season. A rare stereopticon view, left, of an unhurried game of croquet before the resort's two expansion periods. *Courtesy, Mrs. David Clements*

A period picture of a typical Clements Lake Farmhouse bedroom as it appeared at the turn of the century. The furnishings were part of a consignment purchased by Civil War Col. Addison Clements for his new Clements House, a distinguished Liberty hotel built about 1870. *Photograph by L. Jack Agnew*

walnut, arrived from Newburgh after a tedious haul by horses over the Newburgh-Cochecton Turnpike."

The first of three additions was constructed just after the Civil War, making it possible for the energetic J. Newton to undertake the entertaining of summer guests in 1872. As the boardinghouse business prospered, the old farmhouse was expanded by a three story 34' x 60' addition ready for the 1902 season. The main house could now accommodate 50 guests in 25 rooms. Later a guest house was built to help take care of the ever growing number of boarders. Now completely modernized, it is known as the David Clements house.

The guests arrived on one of three trains from the city. There was the 2:40 p.m. on Saturday, and at 7:25 arrived what Laura called the "husbands train," since all the husbands arrived on that one to spend the weekend with their families who were up for the entire season. All of these trains ran in three and four sections. "Some came in on the 'Chicago Express' that arrived at 9:40, a through night train with Pullmans that stopped at Liberty."

The house operated big three-seaters to meet the trains, generally at Liberty. "Later when T.B. and consumptives were scaring some people we would also run a three-seater to Ferndale for those people who were sensitive about Liberty and its association with the disease." Having a limited number of wagons, Mr. Clements frequently hired a Tally-Ho[1] and four white horses from Wickham's Livery Stable in Liberty for taking guests to ball games at Monticello and outings at Kiamesha Lake and Loch Sheldrake.

Everyone had his job to perform at the farmhouse. Miss Laura had the responsibility of growing fresh flowers for placement about the house at all times. Even the lake across the road made a contribution other than floating boats — it floated geese, the feathers of which Grandma Clements stuffed into pillows for the guests.

The original 1850 part of the house still has the parlor furnished just as it was at the turn of the century. It is occupied only occasionally in summers by members of the family, the addition being partitioned off and used for storage. The early furnishings have survived due to a twice-a-year ritual. It seems that there were two sets of furniture — the family furniture and the summer folk furniture. In the late spring the parlor "family" furniture would be moved out to an apartment in the new wing — even to the taking up of the red rose Brussels carpet — and the summer furniture moved in, the ritual of course reversing itself in the fall.

TO PROVIDE A CHEAPER RATE

For business men, having families in the country, and who desire to visit them a certain number of times during their sojourn, the following rates have been made for a ticket, from New York, good for six round trips.

THESE TICKETS WILL BE SOLD ONLY TO HEADS OF FAMILIES

BETWEEN

June 15th and Sept. 1st.

They will be good only for a continuous passage at any time and on any passenger train up to Oct. 31st, 1887. They are not transferable, and good only for party whose name they bear. These tickets will be on sale only at the

Gen'l Pass'r Agent's Office, 18 Exchange Place, New York.

West Cornwall	$9.60	Mountain Dale	$19.85
Orr's Mills	9.60	Centreville	21.00
Meadow Brook	10.10	Fallsburgh	21.85
Denniston's	10.35	Hurley	22.70
Genung's	10.60	Liberty Falls	24.45
Rock Tavern	11.30	Liberty	25.00
Burnside	11.55	Parksville	26.45
Campbell Hall	12.25	Livingston Manor	27.90
Stony Ford	12.75	Rockland	28.00
Crystal Run	13.00	Cook's Falls	29.40
Mechanicstown	13.20	Trout Brook	31.30
Middletown	13.20	East Branch	32.10
Winterton	14.00	Fish's Eddy	32.85
Bloomingburgh	14.40	Hancock	34.50
Wurtsboro	16.65	Cadosia	36.40
Summitville	17.55	Rockrift	36.45
Phillipsport	18.10	Walton	36.70
Homowack	18.67	Hamden	37.15
Ellenville	19.85	Delhi	37.80

J. C. ANDERSON, Gen'l Pass'r Agent.

The 1887 "Summer Homes" noted this special "heads of families" rate card for trains which came to be known as the "husbands trains."

Entire families would come up year after year for the whole season which ran about six weeks. In some respects it was much like a second home to many that came. They would be shown to their old favorite room, even their old "knock-around hat" would still be hanging just where they left it at the end of last year's Labor Day weekend. The Rev. Dr. Hyde summed it up nicely when he recalled to Miss Laura, "I could leave off reading, place a bookmark at the spot, place it on a table and know full well when I came back the next season the book and bookmark would be just where I left them."

One event looked forward to by one and all was the annual Coaching Day Parade held in Liberty toward the end of August. "We generally entered some kind of decorated rig and occasionally won," recalled Laura. "I remember one year we had all the little children placed around a very colorful May Pole on a hay-rigging. I can still hear the

Joshua Gerow's Ferndale Villa as it appeared after the mansard roof was removed to allow for the construction of a fourth floor to accommodate the ever increasing number of summer guests. *Courtesy, Mr. and Mrs. Paul Allen*

As a novel means of promoting his lumber yard business, Joshua Gerow erected a ladies' outhouse comprised of rare and exotic woods from his extensive inventory. It was a small replica of the main house before the mansard roof was removed. Joshua Gerow, Jr., recalled: "Father's friends always contended that the privy was the most elaborate in the entire country — it was paneled inside with black walnut and the seat was made from a two-inch thick mahogany plank." *Line drawing by author, based on sketch supplied by Joshua Gerow, Jr.*

children shouting 'we won, we won, we got the prize' as the hay-rig broke over the top of the hill below the house."[2]

And so it came to pass that the good years of the Clements Lake House were to come to an end with the sending out of notices to all of the old friends that there would be no 1937 season. "Father had been ill for quite some time when we decided to send out the notices. In July of that year he died. I shall always think that closing the house was a contributory cause to his sudden passing away."

So ended 64 years of continuous boardinghouse operation — a near record in the annals of the boardinghouse industry.

One of the boardinghouses that shared in much of the seasonal activities with the Clements Lake House was the landmark Ferndale Villa[3] erected in 1879-80 by the forty-year old Joshua Gerow for his new bride.[4] At the time the Ferndale Villa was built "Josh" was in the lumber business with Uriah S. Messiter, one-time proprietor of the Liberty House and the giant Hotel Wawonda. Naturally the Villa reflected his interest in the lumber business through the use of many different types of fine and exotic woods. Beautiful paneling was used throughout with the front doors of solid black walnut as well as the stairways.

Ferndale Villa, according to family tradition, was named by Mrs. Joshua Gerow for the verdant ground cover of "lady ferns" in the large grove of trees that once stood where Howard Johnsons, Sullivans and the Triangle Diner are now located at the intersection of Routes 52 and old 17.

The historic old Ferndale Villa still stands, right, opposite the Liberty Holiday Inn, still in use as employee quarters for Grossinger's Hotel. The present interior no doubt differs considerably from the nostalgic setting, below, of the back parlor at the "Villa" during the era of the acetylene hanging lamp and the potted fern. *Courtesy, Mr. and Mrs. Paul Allen*

The now vanished Lake Ophelia has been replaced by the Rt. 17 Quickway (white lines) and the lower regions of Grossinger's ski slope. *(See key map below).*

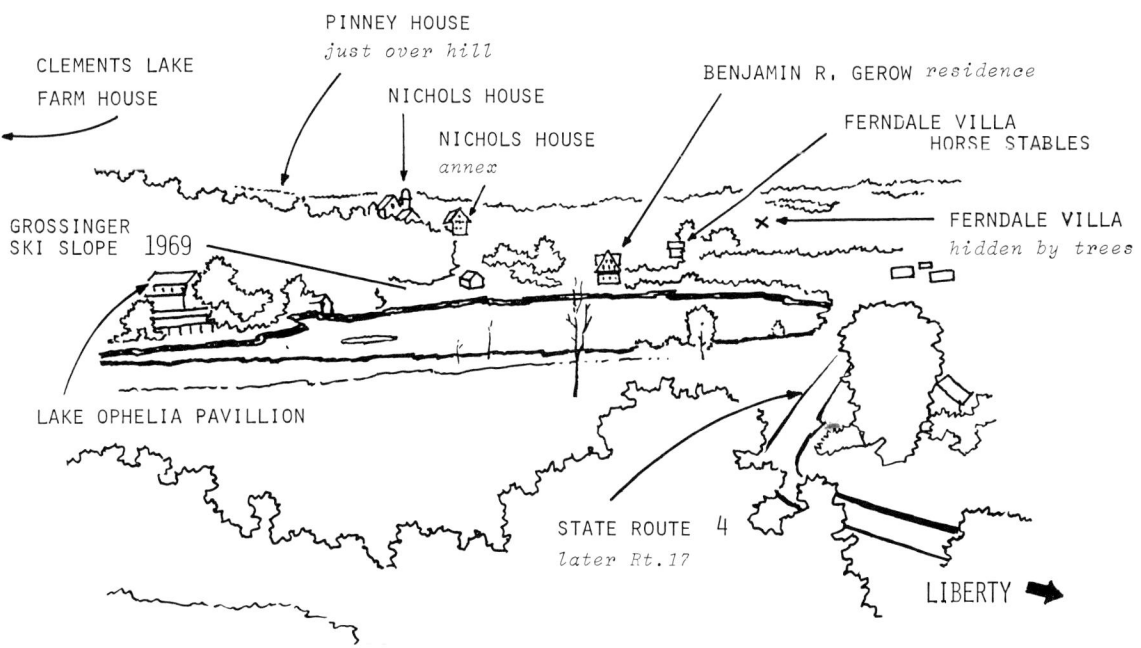

After years of publicity as Ferndale Villa, the O. and W. decided it was such a nice name that they would rename Liberty Falls, "Ferndale." Joshua got so mad that he engaged a lawyer to fight taking his name of Ferndale, but, knowing full well he couldn't win over the powerful O. and W., he dropped the suit.

A part of the lush grove across the road from the main house was cleared in June, 1897, for an 80 x 100 foot lawn tennis court. Earlier, in April of the same year, light lines were extended from Liberty down "to the handsome boardinghouse of Joshua Gerow."[5] However the electric company charged such exorbitant rates that "Josh" refused to electrify the villa — continuing to use acetylene gas and kerosene lamps. Whether the courts were illuminated is not recorded; if not, it is probably just as well since the grove surrounding the courts were liberally festooned with the hammocks that were a tradition with guests at the Villa. They came for a rest and the hammock was a very important partner to that end. The guests who came back year after year purchased their hammocks, one for each member of the family; and, when they arrived, "Josh" would get them out of winter storage and tie them to their favorite trees.

Before the tennis courts and the proliferation of the hammocks, the area across from the Villa was known as "Gerow's Grove." Dances were held there, typified by the extravaganza held on Saturday, July 28, 1883, which commenced at 4:00 p.m. with a concert by the Stevens Concert Co. of Middletown "... featuring their Grand Orchestral Organ, which is said to be one of the most wonderful reed organs in the country." Free stages operated back and forth between the grove and Liberty for every part of the extended program.[6]

A nearby attraction for the boarders at the Ferndale boardinghouses was Lake Ophelia and its famed pavilion.[7] The structure, built during the winter of 1901-02 for John T. Clark, was in its day the largest dancing facility in the county.[8] The sprawling pavilion contained eight bowling alleys, a roller skating rink, pool and billard tables and the dance pavilion was large enough — in the words of Ben Gerow — "to accommodate 36 square sets."

A boardwalk traced along the shoreline making a promenade in fashionable attire an evening's obligation. During the day one could row in any of the more than 75 rowboats, or in season go on a prickly blackberrying expedition to the island in the middle, or one could simply sit on one of the two levels of porches and order sodas and lunch. An early morning porch fire, on October 19, 1911, was discovered by "Red" LaBar who gave the alarm. Of undetermined origin, the fire soon reduced the popular pavilion to ashes.

Those who wished to imbibe didn't miss the passing of the pavilion since it was "dry,"[9] as were most of the Ferndale boardinghouses. On more than a few occasions "Josh" had to take a couple of wagons up to the Liberty House to bring home guests who celebrated Saturday night a bit too much.

The Nichols boardinghouse, operated by J.B. Nichols, and the Pinney House also occasionally had to collect a guest or two at the commercial hotels in town. Both boardinghouses had been built about the same time. The first Nichols House was completed about May, 1890, and the first 'hard luck' Pinney House in 1892, a large wing being added three years later.

E.E. Pinney had hard luck with his house. The 30' x 40', three story structure, perched atop a commanding elevation overlooking the present site

Lake Ophelia was a favorite with ice skaters in the winter as was the nearby pavilion with the summer boarders in the Ferndale area. *Photograph by Otto Hillig*

The first Pinney House, above, erected in 1892 with a large wing added in 1895, burned in October, 1898. Shortly thereafter a new and larger Pinney House was constructed, shown, right, on a brochure cover. The impressive structure measured 64 x 108 feet in area with an extension of 26 x 44 feet, utilizing 150,000 feet of hemlock, with accommodations for 175 guests. Every sleeping room was equipped with electric warning bells and fire escapes, but no sprinkler systems. *Courtesy, Herbert Sprague*

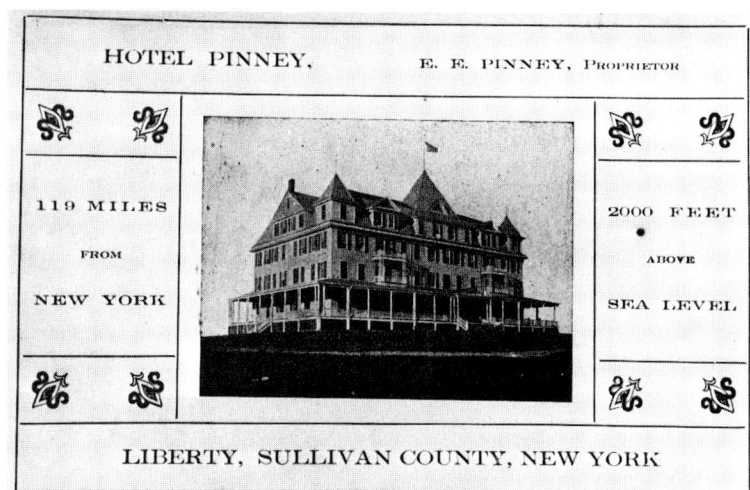

of Grossinger's, had accommodations for 100 to 125 guests, "a costly gas machine ... and hot and cold spring water throughout."[10]

Mr. Pinney was sitting in the house, engaged in reading a paper, when the Rev. Father McKenna informed him that the building was on fire. The October, 1898, fire, originating from a defective kitchen flue, quickly levelled the structure. One month later the press noted that architect Frank Cotter had completed detailed plans for the New Pinney House. Another fire, October 29, 1903, saw the handsome pile with its 264 feet of porches reduced to ashes.

The neighboring Nichols House also had a fire ... on only one occasion, however ... flaring up January 18, 1897, as the result of a defective chimney flue. Immediately plans were made to rebuild and on February 26, 1897, all the details on the New Nichols House – one that was destined to become the core structure of one of the most famous resort hotels in America, The Grossingers – were released to the local press.

The new Nichols was not a rectilinear mass as were most boardinghouses and hotels; but, rather, its architect, Frank Cotter, designed a rambling structure embellished with a porte-cochere, two balconies and a distinctive circular tower.

There was a well-trodden path between the Nichols and the Ferndale Villa worn by the hundreds of guests who over the years walked to the casino at the Villa for Saturday evening home talent shows and up the hill for Sunday evening services at the Nichols. The casino boasted a [square] Steinway piano, a good-sized stage and seating for 150 to 200 people. There was no Saturday night admission charge but a tambourine was passed around to help defray costume or prop expenses.

The Nichols House, below, designed by architect Frank Cotter, departed from the box-like concept to present a multi-peaked and turreted structure with distinctive porte-cochere. Later purchased by Selig and Malka Grossinger in 1919 (their second hotel, having opened their first, Grossinger's Kosher Farm, in 1914) it was soon expanded, right, to include a large annex building, left. The landmark turret may be seen just over ridge of original building. Today's modern complex has completely engulfed the Cotter-designed structure. *Courtesy, Mrs. Bruce Denman, Sr.*

The "famous water hazard" at the Grossinger's golf course. By 1929 the hotel had grown to a number of annex buildings; the dining room was twice its original size; guest capacity exceeded 500 but most importantly, the bank account showed $100,000. This nestegg softened the depression and helped implement Harry Grossinger's plans and ultimate construction of the championship golf course he had so long dreamed of. The course was completed in time for the 1932 season.

The Lakeside Inn, once located on Grossinger property and owned by Max Fish and operated by Charlie Berkowitz, vanished in a blaze about 1955 that, according to longtime Liberty fireman, Dewey Borden, caused the building to suddenly "fold up like an accordion," narrowly missing a number of volunteer firemen. *Courtesy, Steingart Associates*

During the unhurried 1880's and 90's, activities such as this "straw ride at Liberty Falls," pictured in the 1895 "Summer Homes," were a looked for and greatly anticipated vacation event.

Besides the community church services on Sunday evening there was the 'Sunday exchange' the Ferndale houses had with other hotels in the Liberty area, an ancestor of the round robin meal plans of contemporary Miami Beach hotels. "If grandfather had ten guests who wanted to eat on a certain Sunday at the Walnut Mountain House, he would drive them over in the old fringed surrey for the day. Generally the following Sunday a group from the Walnut Mountain House would come to the Villa for dinner and the day. The Sunday dinner groups went as far as the Maple Grove House in Jeffersonville and houses in White Sulphur Springs and Youngsville. All the planning for these exchange events generally took place at the post office, where most of the boardinghouse operators met informally when picking up their mail."[11]

When not loafing in the hammocks, frolicking at the Liberty House or promenading around Lake Ophelia — coaching parties and straw rides were the order of the day. Straw rides to Loch Sheldrake for a good time at LeRoy's Maple Grove Casino were generally attended by thirty or forty guests; and if there weren't enough from the Villa to go, they simply went up the hill to the Nichols to round out the load.

Kiamesha Lake was always a favorite target for a coaching party and picnic. The August 21, 1896, *Register* recorded an excursion of considerable magnitude that hired "Chas. Stanton's large and commodious four-horse stage and two carriages" to carry 27 ladies and 3 gentlemen. "The ladies endeavored to beg, borrow or steal a few more men on the way but either the men were too bashful or they did not like the looks of the crowd, and the effort was unsuccessful."

Katrina Falls and Mongaup Falls were other popular excursion spots. On Friday, July 22, 1887, for example, a trip to Mongaup Falls[12] was run via a charted Liberty and White Lake stage. The round-trip fare of $1.25 included enjoying the benefits of an accompanying refrigerator wagon loaded with provisions.

In early 1901 there was a great deal of talk about establishing a race track and a meeting was held at the Mansion House which established the Liberty Driving Park Association.[13] Josh Gerow lent support to the undertaking. He wanted new activities for his guests and he was intensely interested in horses and racing.[14] In April, 1903, the stables were enlarged from ten to fifty stalls and arrangements were made to erect a grandstand that could accommodate a thousand people. Two thousand five hundred people turned out for the race course's opening on May 30, 1903, to watch two races run on a slow, wet track. This was largely a shortlived amateur event which died out in 1906.

Ground was broken for the Liberty Driving Park Association track on October 10, 1901, with completion ceremoniously taking place in 1902. The track, "laid out by Civil Engineer Mills of Goshen, was 'regulation,' with two stretches, having a minimum width of fifty feet, while the home stretch was sixty feet wide." In August 1904, the management of the track supplemented its income by selling advertising space on the racing card to various Liberty hotels as well as the New York, Ontario and Western Railway. *Photograph by Otto Hillig*

| HOWARD HATS and WALKOVER SHOES DEFY COMPETITION. Young, Massiter and Dodge. | LAKE OPHELIA Liberty, N. Y. Dancing every Tuesday & Friday Eve's Boating, Bowling, Pool & Billiards W. H. Clark, Prop. | New York Ontario & Western R. R. Special Excursion World's Fair LOWEST RATES OF THE YEAR Wednesday Sept. 21st Special Through Train of Reclining Chair Cars. Seats free and Pullman sleeping Cars to St. Louis |

J. C. YOUNG, PRESIDENT. D. S. HILL, VICE-PRESIDENT. G. W. MURPHY, SECRETARY ELMER WINNER, TREASURER

LIBERTY DRIVING PARK ASSOCIATION.
THURSDAY, AUGUST 18, 1904

JOHN O'BRIEN'S OFFICIAL PROGRAM

No and Name of Driver	FIRST RACE FREE-FOR-ALL PURSE $400	1	2	3	4	5	6	No and Name of Driver	SECOND RACE 2:16 Class Pace PURSE $400	1	2	3	4	5	6	No and Name of Driver	THIRD RACE 2:19 Class Trot PURSE $400	1	2	3	4	5	6
1 Doble	GUY GATON, br s Parker C. P. Doble, Syracuse							1 Allen	SIR ARTHUR, blk g Coatman A. S. Case, Three Bridges, N. J							1 Doble	MEDIA, b m Belmont Prince C. P. Doble, Syracuse						
2 Davis	JIM KENNEDY, b s Formerly King Wilkes R. L. Davis, Brooklyn							2 Davis	JUDGE JOSEPH, ch g R. L. Davis, Brooklyn							2 Murphy	FLORENCE LOWE, blk m Cicerone J. W. Murphy, Glen Cove, L. I.						
3 Nichols	LEO S., ch g Colbert D. H. Nichols, Brooklyn							3 Rhodes	CAPT. SAMPSON, g g Reelection W. L. Rhodes, Guttenburg							3 Rhodes	MIDNIGHT HAL, blk g Black Hal W. L. Rhodes, Guttenburgh, N. J						
4 Graham	ONOTO b m Online A. J. McClure, Albany							4 Hamlin	ROY D., b g Walsingham Hudson River Stock Farm							4 Hamlin	ORA JANSEN, ch m Fillmore by Hambrino Hudson River Stock Farm						
5 Kehoe	BROWNIE, b g Baron Boy John McGuire, N. Y. C.							5 Gosnell	NEWSBOY, g g Curt Gosnell, Chester							5 Gosnell	FANNIE RILEY, ch m Curt. Gosnell, Chester, Pa						
6 Chs. Clute	CAPT. MOON, b g Delmar Lynch Bros., Troy							6 Murray	DEAN SWIFT, br g Gold Lumps J. S. Murray, Chester							6 Rathbun	LILLIE SLIGO, ch m West View Farm, Worcester						
								7 Roland	SIRDAR, g g Baron H BARON H. Jr., blk h Baron H. Moynehan & Baxter, Utica							7 Lewis	LUNDA, b m Norris J. H. Lewis, New Milford Conn						

TIME _____ TIME _____ TIME _____

| GOOD FOR 5 Cents S. & B. | THIS CHECK AND FIVE CENTS GOOD FOR ONE "DREAMLAND" STANDARD 10-CENT DRINK. SEARS & BROCHU, PHARMACISTS, Opposite Post Office. | After the Races go to the LIBERTY HOUSE, Cafe embraces only Best Wines, Liquors and Cigars. New features in Billiard, Pool and Klondike Tables and Shuffle Boards. L. H. LOCHMAN, Prop. J. J. GERHARDT, Manager | MANSION HOUSE FOR BLOSSOM CLUB WM. MURPHY, PROP |

Large scale professional horse racing came to the county with the opening of the Monticello Raceway on June 27, 1958. The trotter track was developed by leading members of the county's business community and hotel owners.[15]

The inevitable ethnic change in the Ferndale area came at the Ferndale Villa in 1912 when the Jacob Selig family rented a room. Selig's Christian wife engaged the room at Gerow's where the husband was not welcome. But the area's resorts needed new business and the next year the Frank Eisenberg family took accommodations at the Nichols. "That first year was rather unpleasant," Mrs. Allen recalled, "but the following year Mr. Eisenberg came to Josh and rented a cottage for three months" at a reported $1,000 per month. They took it from Memorial Day till Labor Day and stayed every year for the next five years. This structure is now Grossinger's Honeymoon Cottage.

In these pre and post World War I days most immigrants were still young — most having arrived in the 1890's and 1900's. Many were, however, tied up in the movement to return Jews to the land or a need for a healthier atmosphere which was the motivating factor in the Grossinger settlement. A number of places were sold, including the Ferndale Villa and the Nichols House. Mr. Nichols had died about 1914 and the house was being operated only half-heartedly by Mrs. Nichols when the Grossingers, who were already running a successful roominghouse operation, came along in 1919, bought the house and laid the foundations for a legend.

Kantor's Pharmacy in Ferndale, below, was known far and wide for its "always pure, fresh and cold, Ice Cream Sodas." This warm weather mecca lured youngsters from Liberty on expeditions across the Ferndale trestle, right background. Alas, it all came to an end on June 16, 1913, three days after the big Liberty burn, when the popular soda parlor burned along with Sam Steigert's bottling business, Lewis Hirsh's grocery store, M. Katzmer's candy store, and other community businesses, right. *Courtesy, Mrs. Bruce Denman, Sr.*

Ferndale had its almost required fire on Monday, June 16, 1913, which destroyed most of the town.[16] Although the fire came close enough to scorch the O. and W. depot; service on the line was not interrupted. The Night Line was the only train remotely affected when it " ... halted south of the station and proceeded past the fire with some trepidation."[17] It is well the trestle crossing the Mongaup River and its valley was iron and not wood, as it was when originally built.

Noted Liberty photographer, Otto Hillig, recorded this rare view of the removal of the old Ferndale trestle. The new plate girder trestle, started in 1900 and completed August 1, 1901, was built 19 feet north of the old trestle. Here the old box trusses are being removed with the aid of falsework over the old tannery pond. The Ferndale depot is out of picture, right. *Courtesy, Mrs. Medwin Benton*

The bridge, one of the most impressive on the line, seemed to stay "new and handsome," at least to the writers of "Summer Homes." The 1878 edition noted, "The railroad strikes the valley of the Mongaup at Liberty Falls, crossing it on a trestle 100 feet high and 1,100 feet long, the scene from which is inspiring." It wasn't 'new and handsome' yet, just an old wooden crossing but by October, 1881, increased locomotive weights led to the letting of contracts for a new iron bridge that would cost $45,000.[18] The 105 foot high iron bridge, completed about October, 1882, was immediately opened to traffic. By 1900, heavier locomotives and larger capacity coal cars once again necessitated the rebuilding and strengthening of all the bridges on the coal route, particularly those on the section between Rockland (Roscoe) and Middletown.

The new Mongaup River bridge was built nineteen feet north of the old one on new abutments sunk by the coffer dam technique, the deepest being eighteen feet below the water in the tannery pond below.[19] Construction workers in the pond had to dig through 8 to 10 feet of discarded hemlock logs, stumps and residue from a pioneer tannery once located at Liberty Falls. Burke Brothers of Scranton, Pennsylvania, started the masonry work in November, 1900, and completed it August 1, 1901. The plate girder viaduct of twenty-one spans, supported by ten towers of four legs each (aggregating 1,400,000 pounds) was erected by the Rochester Branch of the American Bridge Company.

"On Sunday September 1, train No. 9, the Long Milk, ran across the new steel viaduct at Liberty Falls."[20] Later, on the same Sunday, engine No.

The Ferndale trestle, above, after double tracking, (note alternate staggered in-and-out support bents) with a consolidation towing a coal drag plus an assortment of high cars.

The Ferndale-Liberty area was also the site of another major trestle—the upper Liberty trestle—which stood for many years as a classic example of wooden bridge engineering. On the distant hill stands the Fern Cliff House while directly below are the beginnings of the Hillside Greenhouses Co.

Jim Shaughnessy, skilled railroad lensman, zeroed in on an F-3 diesel inching across a now badly neglected single track trestle, a year or two before abandonment.

The high-speed lens of noted Sullivan County photographer, Paul Gerry, froze the downward plunge of a span of the Ferndale trestle during scrapping operations. Had W.J. Martin of the O. and W. Passenger Department had his way in 1890, the bridge section would have made quite a splash. At that time a high dam was proposed across the narrowest part of the Mongaup Valley below the trestle, to form a lake (Liberty Lake) which was to be stocked with game fish with special one-day excursion runs planned from the city.

Southbound train No. 12 leaving Ferndale and its towering trestle on May 19, 1940. *D. Diver Collection, Cornell University.*

206, one of the "heavies" out of Mayfield Yard in Carbondale, Pennsylvania, hauling thirty loaded coal cars, passed safely over the new bridge enroute to Middletown. It was the first of the new engines over the line from Cadosia to Summitville.

Through the years the daredevil stunt of the "Huckleberry Finns" of Ferndale and Liberty was to cross the trestle before a train would come along. It was a normal Sunday afternoon event for boys and girls to walk from Liberty to Ferndale across the trestle, have a soda at Kantor's Drug Store and take the train back to Liberty before supper time.

On April 4, 1913, a team of horses tried it. Freightened and running wild on the Monticello road, they cut past the depot and out across the trestle covering about a hundred feet of the crossing before they fell through. One horse had its leg so firmly wedged between the ties it took considerable time to get it loose, delaying the "Night Line" about twenty minutes. The accident happened directly after a southbound freight had passed.

That team was luckier than Charles Rose's horse at Livingston Manor which broke loose from a cutter in January, 1922, dashed successfully across one bridge but fell through the second; the forelegs slipped through just in time to meet the "Scoot" in charge of Engineer A.B. Carruth and Conductor A.E. Jones in a qualified "cornfield meet." The cowcatcher of the engine was so badly broken it had to be replaced by a new one. It took an hour to extricate the dead animal's carcass from the cowcatcher and forward trucks of the locomotive.

The strategic importance of the Ferndale trestle was pointed up in April, 1917, when, following President Wilson's address to the extraordinary session of Congress, sixteen servicemen were assigned to guard it against sabotage. Co. A of the 71st Regiment, consisting of over one hundred men, guarded the O. and W. from Mountaindale to Cooks Falls with eight assigned to the upper Liberty trestle and two to the White Bridge-Route 17 highway crossing at the edge of the village.

Housing for the men was solved with an empty barn or untenanted house and three meals a day sufficing nicely, at the regular army contract price of 75 cents a day. The good boardinghouse keepers of Liberty failed to show the concern for the servicemen that they did for the summer vacationists.

The first Liberty House, built in the early 1860's, became the headquarters for the New York & Oswego Midland Railway surveyors and construction crews. At porch corner, Uriah S. Messiter, proprietor, stands at left, surveying the rutted Main Street and two delivery wagons used to transport Kalamazoo Stoves from the railroad freight house to farmhouse customers. Methodist Church shows, right background. House site is now occupied by the Liberty Professional Building.   *Courtesy, Dewey Borden*

Liberty

The Era of the Great Hotels

At Liberty, Pete Reilly jumped down and threw a bundle of papers to Thomas Head, who sat poised in his wagon ready to take them around to the "chromo-colored boardinghouses" in the neighborhood. Even the genial station agent, Ike Post, took forty extras to sell before church time.

Pete's paper run in 1886 was at the dawn of Liberty's great hotel era. "Summer Homes" that year listed only 30 boarding or farmhouses under Liberty and quite a few of them were in the Ferndale area. During July of 1888 the Saturday Half-Holiday train which generally had on board 50 to 200 husbands — up to spend the weekend with their families in the era of the two-month all-season vacation — was running to Liberty with two locomotives and thirteen crowded cars. Even today many hotels offer a six- or eight-week package deal which includes all week accommodations for Ma and the kids and weekend privileges and a two-week stay for Dad.

On August 3, 1889, the Half-Holiday arrived with 400 aboard, hauled by two locomotives, a sight that was becoming commonplace on weekends. In the first weekend in August, two years later, the number of summer boarders embarking for Sullivan County was 1,502; the heaviest train being the Half-Holiday Mountain Express carrying 600 passengers occupying 16 coaches.[1] By August of 1896 a typical Saturday would see 800 detraining at Liberty with over 400 pieces of baggage to be dumped unceremoniously on the platform. On July 3, 1897, trains 1, 3, 7 and 15 each totaled between 450 to 500 pieces of baggage and 1,000 to 1,500 passengers per train — now running in multiple sections. The trains in early May were also becoming so crowded that they, too, were running double headed and in sections.

As the years of the early 20th century passed, there was no let up in the constantly increasing passenger loads. For example, on July 15, 1904, it was reported in the press that "...thus far this season 3500 more people have been carried out of Weehawken than it had transported up to the corresponding date last year." It was obvious by

213

A. White Bridge Crossing B. Site, upper Liberty trestle C. Liberty depot D. Dashed line — location of former Lake Ophelia at foot of present day Grossinger's ski slope.

On July 22, 1887, the following press release appeared in the Liberty *Register:* "R.B. Whittaker photographed Liberty last Friday morning from two different points. One picture taken from Ernhout's Hill shows the whole village and the other from the cemetery shows the southern portion of the village."

The view from the cemetery, left, shows the Presbyterian Church, center, with the box-like Clements House to the right. In this pre-hotel era panorama, the Clements House dominated the hotel scene. To the left of Lake Street is the large winterized water tank on the O. and W. right-of-way. To the right of the Lake Street crossing is the freight house-like original passenger depot. Walnut Mountain looms in the background.

Whittaker's view from Ernhout's Hill shows a church dominated village; the Presbyterian Church, dead center, then the Baptist Church (burned 1913), the Methodist Church and the Roman Catholic, in that order. Dimly in the upper right corner is the wooden upper Liberty O. and W. trestle. The O. and W. siding in the foreground leads into a structure, left, that also shows in the Hillig overview, (page 217), as the oblong wooden building, left. The Clements House mansard roof shows over the Presbyterian Church roof while the steeple apex cuts through the original Liberty House. Whittaker later contributed many pictures for inclusion in the pages of "Summer Homes." *Left, Sullivan County Museum Archives; right, courtesy, Herbert Sprague.*

the turn of the century that a train of 16 coaches containing 900 passengers on its way to Sullivan County barely raised an eyebrow. Two-thousand people detraining at Liberty on a Saturday afternoon to be picked up in one of the 125 to 175 boardinghouse wagons, surreys and buckboards that crammed the area around the depot and down Clements Street, was commonplace. Actual tabulations for June, July and August of 1901 indicated "over 10,000 tickets were sold in New York offices to persons stopping off at the Liberty station."

The late William "Bill" Brock of Liberty recalled "... one train running in three sections ... and selling $7,520 worth of tickets on one Labor Day at $2.40 per ticket. Our sales at that time averaged about $5,000 per day until the season was over." This was at a time when there were "... eight passenger trains per day in each direction and more on weekends, besides a coal train on an average of one every hour from Mayfield to Middletown and return; also three milk trains daily in each direction, three through freight trains in each direction daily plus a local freight in each direction daily except Sunday."

The local press believed the region to be at the dawn of an era of unbelievable prosperity. The July 26, 1889, *Register* noted: "Many new houses built during the past year were thought to be adequate to accommodate all whom (sic) might come but the actual test of their capacity shows that there is YET ROOM FOR SEVERAL MORE FIRST CLASS BOARDINGHOUSES. What Liberty now wants is two or three houses with a capacity of accommodating 200-300 guests each."

The growth of passenger travel pointed up the need for a new station at Liberty. The O. and W. sent Chief Engineer Lewis D. Fouquet to Liberty in July of 1892 to select the site for the new station which Bradford Lee Gilbert, the noted railroad station architect, was commissioned to design.[2] By October the contractors, Lindsley Brothers of Middletown, had a crew of carpenters enclosing the building in a rush before winter set in, the finishing work completed by A.P. Underwood of Otsego County. In the Spring of 1893 the new depot was opened. Liberty celebrated. As one prominent businessman remarked, "we complained, begged, threatened and finally settled down to patient waiting for years, all of the time being assured by the railroad people that we would get it in time."

The building the community got was a semi-precious architectural gem with eight foot high walls built out of field stone (*a la* the work of Henry Hobson Richardson) on which the moss had been left. A massive fireplace, of the same boulders, dominated the waiting room wall opposite the ticket windows.[3]

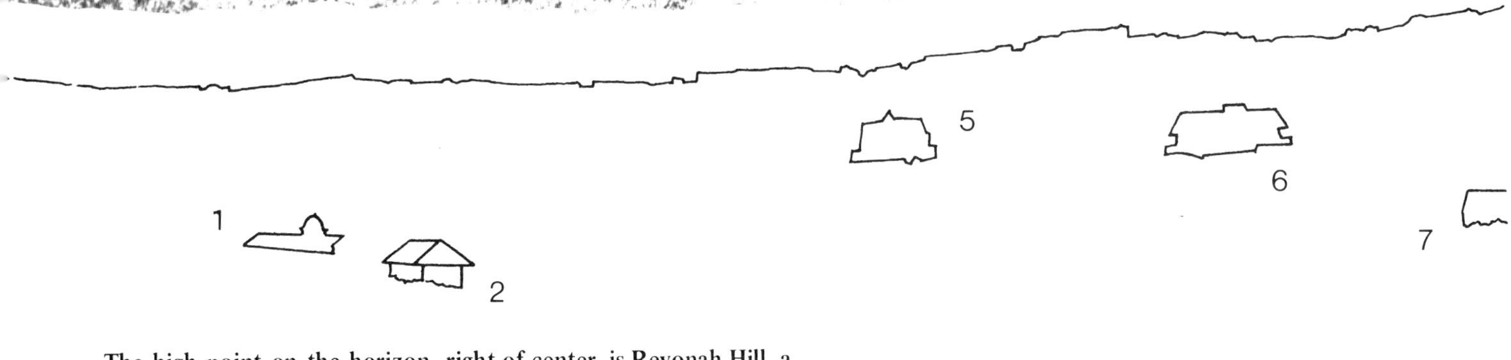

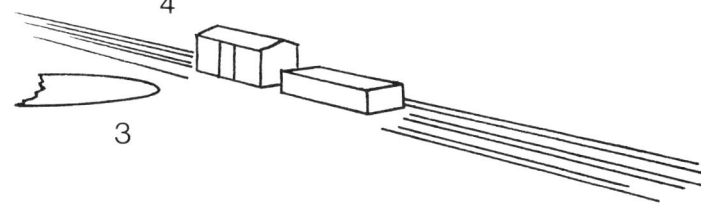

The high point on the horizon, right of center, is Revonah Hill, a commanding elevation that in 1889 was owned by A.J.D. Wedemeyer. Here, on these seven hundred acres, he planned a "high class hotel" and a colony of cottages around a lake upon whose surface was to be placed a "fleet of boats." The O & W was so impressed with A.J.D.'s grandiose plans that they planned a depot just for the resort at the Buckley Street crossing at the base of the hill. [Revonah is a reversal of the letters in Hanover, Mr. Wedemeyer's birthplace in Germany.] *Panorama by Otto Hillig (about 1900)*

1. New York, Ontario & Western Depot
2. Freight House
3. Turntable
4. O. and W. mainline
5. Hotel Monitor
6. Ye Lancashire Inn
7. Hall House (Lenape)

8. Music Hall (burned, 1913)
9. The Swannanoa
10. Fern Cliff Manor
11. Catholic Church
12. Methodist Church
13. Liberty House
14. Presbyterian Church
15. Mansion House
16. Old School (burned, 1913)
17. Upper Liberty trestle
18. Hotel Wawonda

LIBERTY Part 1   217

The inauguration of the new depot, described as most attractive in its graceful outlines, beauty of finish and complete construction, almost coincided with the opening of the hulking Hotel Wawonda which was perched on a hillside across the village of Liberty directly opposite the station's porte cochere.

That same year the new Pinney House was nearing completion, a year later Ye Lancashire Inn opened and the Swannanoa followed over the winter of 1895-96.

Liberty, besides experiencing a construction boom in the 90's ["There has been no time in the history of the place when there has been more building going on than at the present time"][4] was in the midst of a population explosion. It added nearly 1000 new residents between 1896 and 1897 bringing its year-round population up to 3,537.

The gateway to all this hustle and bustle, Gilbert's masterpiece, unfortunately stood only three years before burning to the ground on October 17, 1896. The fire was discovered by night operator Edward Brochu at ten minutes to five, after the fire had already made considerable headway and was out of control. By next March, 1897, an almost exact replica of the burned building was constructed.[5]

During the rebuilding period, the O. and W. proposed to give Liberty an ornamental fountain if the village would furnish the water gratis. Free water, indeed water under any conditions, was not available until 1899 when the Liberty *Register* announced that if "you [the O. and W.] are still addicted to the art habit, we have the permission to say that our village officers are similarly situated with regard to water ... and that we are now ready to meet you for the fountain, with the fountain, and by the fountain."

1891 saw the arrival of the first street sprinkler to wet down the dirt streets in dry weather. The townsfolk commented on the ability to breathe air once more instead of dust. The vehicle's only drawback was that there was no adequate water source for it, but this was soon remedied. In June of 1893 the waterworks were completed at a cost of $20,000 with subscribers on the water main obligated to make a "semi-annual payment in advance, of fully $400." Before snow started there would be 100 taps. Now the press began calling for electric lights and a stone crusher, the crusher to prepare the native stone for distribution on the dusty streets.

In January, 1896, a telephone network connecting, by various routes, Liberty to Mongaup Center,

Photo copy of the original architect's rendering of the Liberty depot by the office of railroad station architect, Bradford Lee Gilbert. The rendering was made in 1892 and the station completed just in time for the Wawonda excursion.

LIBERTY

VIEW OF LIBERTY

In Sullivan County, New York

120 Miles from New York City

FARE $2.40

By New York, Ontario and Western Railroad.

1578 TO 2400 FEET ABOVE TIDE WATER

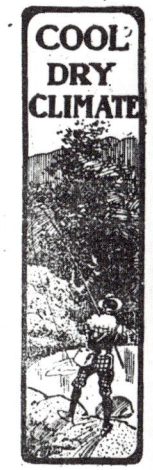

COOL DRY CLIMATE

ONE of the most popular summer resorts in the East. The elevation ranges from 1,578 to 2,400 feet above the sea. From many of the mountain summits that border the village on the north and west, the views are unsurpassed, the eye reaching to the nearest horizon, the Catskills, twenty miles distant to the north and east; to the southward the Shawangunk Mountains, and westward a distance of fifty miles along the Delaware River. From these vantage points may be seen twelve to fifteen beautiful lakes.

The village has a resident population of 1,800, a complete sewer system and water supply, a well organized fire department, a bank, opera house, numerous stores, handsome residences, many of which belong to prominent New Yorkers, six churches—Episcopal, Catholic, German Lutheran, Presbyterian, Baptist, and Methodist.

For those seeking **HEALTH, RECREATION, REST or PLEASURE** Liberty offers every opportunity

Every modern convenience is embodied in the construction and improvements of the leading hotels, and the boarding-houses offer many attractions. There are also many desirable cottages to rent.

FOR TERMS AND BOOKLETS ADDRESS

HOTE

U. R. MESSITER	Hotel Wawonda	ING @ CO	Revonah Mountain House
WM. S. ELEE	New Libe		The Hall House
Dr. A. P. BUCKLEY	The Buckley		Mansi
E. E. PINNEY			Pinney

BOARDING-HOUS

WASHINGTON BROS	Summit House	J. E. C	Grand View Heights
J. O. NEWKIRK	Walnut Mountain Farm House	CHAS. A SYREEN	Syreen House

Real Estate Agent, **THEODORE WINTHROP WESTON**

Liberty advertisement, sponsored by the hotel and boarding house operators, that appeared in the New York *Evening Post*, Saturday, June 1, 1901. For added impetus, the newspaper adopted the overview of Liberty shown on pages 216-217.

Train No. 1, running extra, pausing at Liberty behind Schenectady-built 4-8-2 No. 409. The Livingston Manor Lumber Co., left, is the former Lennon House, see below. *Photograph by M.B. Cooke, Courtesy of Gerald M. Best*

The ornamental fountain erected by the railroad in conjunction with the Liberty Improvement Society. The society, organized on December 6, 1893, undertook many community-wide projects. In the far distance is the Hotel Wawonda and, right, the steeple of the Baptist Church which burned in 1913. To the left of the steeple is the old school, also consumed in 1913 in a separate burning. The Lennon House, below right, was operated by John C. Lennon for many years and acquired a high standing with the traveling fraternity throughout the state. The hotel was built about 1869 by John Schaefer, an immigrant from Germany. The third floor was added by Lennon in 1896. *Photograph left, by R.B. Whittaker; below, Sullivan County Museum Archives*

This Hillig original, copied from a lantern slide, shows the Liberty depot in all its pristine newness. The freight house, background, was built in October 1899 to accommodate the ever increasing amount of railroad-generated business. *Photograph by Otto Hillig*

Monticello, South Fallsburgh, Woodbourne, Jeffersonville and Grahamsville was inaugurated. The press urged the boardinghouses and hotels: "It's a good thing. Push it along."

But the electric lights created the biggest stir. At dusk on Wednesday, June 9, 1897, Anna Sharpe, the five year old daughter of J.H. Sharpe, head of Sharpe Electric Equipment Company, flipped the switch that turned on about 100 lamps in the business places along Main Street. A few weeks later the village's 70 new electric street lamps (20 were privately owned) were lighted. The Liberty Methodist Church was illuminated with 50 bulbs. In those uncertain days its chandeliers were equipped to be both electroliers and oil lamps. The Hotel Wawonda had 10 bulbs and the Mansion House and the Register offices also had their own lights. A. McPhillamy's Ice Cream Parlor, the gastronomic craze, also had a light.

In October of 1889 work was begun on a sewer system but the *piece de resistance* of civic improvement was provided by the O. and W. in mid-summer of 1904 when its men stationed at the depot crossing were given uniforms, blue blouses and caps — the caps bearing the inscription 'CROSSING WATCHMAN' and the blouses sporting brass buttons. This touch of opulence took note of a managerial sensitivity to "image" as well as reflecting the financial stability of the New York, Ontario and Western in the dawning years of the Twentieth Century.

The road realized that its future growth would be based on increased population in the area it served and to help its long range goals it sought to stimulate a building boom in the 90's by offering to "carry materials and persons employed on building construction for that purpose free of charge."

One group taking advantage of the railroad's generosity was the partnership of George Young, J.C. Young, U.S. Messiter and Warren L. Scott, who in September of 1891 began the construction of what would become the largest hostelry in Sullivan County, the Hotel Wawonda. The foundation of the main block of the hotel was completed

The Syreen House (Pleasant Valley Farm), like so many turn-of-the-century resorts, evolved from simple farmhouses as discernible by the barnlike addition, right.

The above resort was noted in the 1896 "Summer Homes" as the Mecca; in Fred Sprague's small picture book of "Indelible Photographs," published in 1893, it was listed as the Guildersleeve House, (purchased in 1894 by Charles O. Hayden, renamed "Mecca," 1894 Summer Homes) while photographer R.B. Whittaker, on a grouping of resort photographs, identified it as the Messiter House. The 1890's saw a number of picturebooks issued, one of the handsomer ones being distributed by photographer M. Aldrich in 1899. *Courtesy, John Joyner*

The Hall House as it originally appeared before the addition of a brick extension and name change. The modernized hostelry of Modified Georgian style was named the Hotel Lenape (after the Lenni Lenape Indians), the plans for which were first revealed to the public in July, 1927. The Liberty landmark closed its doors as a hotel, Saturday, January 24, 1970.

The Buckley, an early resort hotel that in 1899 boasted accommodations for 75 guests, still stands today at the corner of North Main and Buckley St.

by November 1. A large force of carpenters was soon busy building the first story framework of what would be a four story 42' x 180' structure with a 40' x 135' wing. Once the building was enclosed, construction moved rapidly. By May the New York Electrical Engineering Co. was installing an electric call bell network and the latest patent improved fire alarm system. There was also to be a system of pneumatic speaking tubes connecting each sleeping room in the house with the office. On June 3, 1892, the press reported "the rooms are filled with furniture and carpets and today the work laying the latter was commenced." The 139 cars of material used in the construction were moved onto the site over a specially built O. and W. siding – the white pine, originating in Georgia, arriving free of charge.

The structure was impressive, girdled with 650 feet of broad verandas, its eight large public room fire places "to take off the chill and give cheerfulness on cold days," with a billiard room, bowling alley and telegraph office to round out the appointments.

By June 17 what were described as French cooks and bakers were arriving from New York on the Sullivan County Express and within one month they would be serving over 200 diners on an average Sunday.

A fine 12-page promotional brochure was produced (eight photogravure pictures and four pages of descriptive matter), but it was outclassed as a promotional device by the excursion Uriah S. Messiter, the genial manager, had arranged for June 12, 1893, with the O. and W. management.

"We are on the broad and breezy verandas of the Hotel Wawonda, four hours and 118 miles, as the track winds, from our Brooklyn homes, and two thousand feet above them," wrote a special Brooklyn *Standard-Union* correspondent on June 12, 1893.

The reporter was only one of more than 26 newsmen representing papers and trade journals who had accompanied the first O. and W. All-Vestibule Limited daily express to Liberty.

As a publicity stunt to play up the healthful, bracing Catskill Mountain ozone (as some of the writers preferred to call the air), the special also carried 24 prominent doctors from the New York – New Jersey metropolitan area.

The special actually was the maiden run of a new O. and W. name train, the "Sullivan County Limited," planned to run daily, leaving Weehawken at 3 p.m., and returning the next morning with a 9:55 arrival designation. This time card would afford executive husbands a rare overnight mid-week visit to their families who were spending the summer in the mountains.

The special consisted of six cars: a baggage car, three "perfectly appointed" vestibule coaches (which under a special order had been outshopped by the Ohio Falls Manufacturing Company), the

The Liberty Brass Coronet Band that met the Wawonda special at the depot received generally favorable reviews with the exception of that by the New York *Morning Journal* newsman who reported "the guests were met by a lot of carriages and the Liberty Brass Band which mutilated the fresh mountain air until dust from the numerous vehicles got down in their horns and choked them off." It was an era when virtually every community of any consequence had its coronet band.

Wawonda

The impressive Hotel Wawonda, erected by a combine consisting of George Young, J.C. Young, U.S. Messiter and Warren L. Scott in 1891-92. The largest structure in Sullivan County fell on hard times, due to the influx of T.B. patients to the area.

The spanking new Mother Hubbard-type locomotive, No. 140, built by Dickson Locomotive Works in April 1893, hauled the special to Liberty and the Wawonda for a gala celebration. The event exploited not only the Wawonda but also heralded the inauguration of the first O. and W. All-Vestibule Limited daily express to Liberty.

The arrival of the press excursion in 1893 found the Wawonda parlors decorated with a typical over-abundance of American flags. The opulently furnished hotel came to a fiery end, right, in June, 1914, in one of the largest single structure fires in Sullivan County history.

Pullman "Parthenia," and President Fowler's private car. Although a last minute development kept Fowler from making the trip, he made sure liquid refreshment was available at the Hotel Wawonda.

In Liberty, the first sounds of the "140's" whistle was the signal for the brilliantly-attired Liberty Coronet Band to strike up. The depot was crowded with local celebrities and the carriages provided for the trip to the Hotel Wawonda.

Exact time of arrival of the special is subject to conjecture. The time card stated 12:45 which the Brooklyn *Eagle* scribe, evidently by luck, subscribed to. The New York *Morning Journal* reporter read 12:30 while the scribe from the *Sun* was running a bit late with a 1:05 p.m. Perhaps the liquid refreshment dispensed on the way up fuzzed the numbers on the dial of the official clock to the extent that the *Daily Railway Times* took the only safe way out by recording simply that Liberty was "reached in time for dinner." The dinner was superb as was the entire program with U.S. Messiter being named 'prince of hosts' by the reporters.

The house developed an enviable reputation through the years. Many weekends saw all 300 rooms occupied; the mile long twenty foot wide bicycle path around the hotel congested by tandems and the precarious high-wheeled "ordinary." In 1898 the bowling alley was partitioned into rooms to help meet an increasing demand for accommodations.[6]

In April, 1903, D.W. Dieter of Brooklyn leased the hotel and promptly engaged Clarence Masten to paint the largest building in Sullivan County for $600. To spark up a fading image its transportation equipage was updated with the purchase of an

Swannanoa

The Swannanoa, built in 1895 by Fred Schrader, was the setting for the many spectacular masquerades and receptions. The hotel, 40 x 36 feet, is said to have cost $27,000. It could accommodate between 100 and 140 when it burned, below. At the time of the fire, it was in the process of redecoration. The entire roof was ablaze when the fire company arrived, the fire spreading downward leaving part of the first and second floors intact. *Courtesy, Ontario Hose Co. No. 3*

automobile, an "up-to-date tally-ho coach and several pretty pony turnouts."

The considerable investment made by the builders in fire equipment paid off in September of 1907 when a fire in the reception hall fireplace ignited the roof. A house hose rushed to the spot on the roof – a fire ax – a hole – and the fire was dispatched. Well that it was, since the fire alarm in Liberty, the Baptist Church bell, as well as other village church bells were already ringing for the Sunday morning services.

On June 4, 1910, the Wawonda was sold at public auction. The Liberty *Register* of the time reported that originally " ... it was patronized by a very wealthy class of people coming mostly from New York City, Philadelphia and Washington. Frequently the guests brought their entire families, carriages and stewards, staying for the whole season. A year or two after the Loomis Sanatorium was established, the number of wealthy people who had before visited the hotel began to stop coming."

In 1911 the management was taken over by J.F. Warner at a time when patronage had dipped to a new low. On Tuesday, June 9, 1914, between 1 and 3 o'clock a.m. a fire of unknown origin leveled the sprawling hotel sending flames 300 feet into the night sky, lighting up the surrounding hills with an eerie glow that revealed hundreds of huddled spectators.[7]

There were no guests in the house at the time, only J.F. Warner and Charles Flood, employees who made their escape through the windows. Flood, on the second floor, "scaled down the side of the hotel via window blinds." The fire had started mysteriously in the rear near the kitchen when there were no controlled fires in the building and with the electric current still turned off.

The handwriting was on the wall – Two years before in April, 1912, the popular Swannanoa burned and September, 1920, saw the demise of Ye Lancashire Inn. The disappearance of the grand hotels from the Liberty scene was a distinct loss to the commercial and social life of the community.

In November, 1893, during the halcyon years, Ye Lancashire Inn, the Mansion House, Buckley, Ferncliff, Mecca, DuNord, Monitor and other resort hotels joined with other interested parties to form the Sullivan County Coaching Day Association.

During the summer a coaching day had been held under the auspices of the officers of the civically orientated Liberty Reading Room organization. It had created considerable local interest, although many felt that it should be sponsored by those more closely connected with the boarding-house keepers' interests and the pleasure of the summer boarders.

The association's first meeting was held at the Liberty House on November 25, 1893, and a formal organization was created.[8] August 23, 1894, was set aside as the first official Coaching Day. Within two years Coaching Day parades became *the* event of the summer season with a reported 10,000 people witnessing a mile-long procession of seventy-five or more beautifully decorated wagons in Liberty as well as outstanding parades being held in Hurleyville, Monticello (10,000 were supposed to have witnessed the parade there also) and one planned for White Lake. Bloomingburg came through in later years with parades of thirty rigs.

Bands, decorated bicycles, and saddle horses competed along with carriages in various categories: Most Handsome, Most Grotesque, Boarding

THE OFFICE OF "YE LANCASHIRE INN."

"Ye Lancashire Inn."
Liberty, Sullivan County, N. Y.

F. W. Lancashire & Co., Proprietors.

●

OPEN ENTIRE YEAR

●

Steam and Hot Water Heat.
Electric Light.
Modern Improvements.

F. H. SCOFIELD, New York Representative,
1 Madison Avenue.

NO CONSUMPTIVES TAKEN.

This advertisement which notes 'no consumptives taken,' ironically appeared in the special "Winter Homes" publication for the winter 1899-1900, promoting the area for the afflicted. The nearby presence of other T.B. facilities discouraged old customers, resulting in the hotel's ultimate conversion to a consumptive war veterans rest hospital.

Ye Lancashire Inn

Ye Lancashire Inn earned a reputation as a Cuban retreat due in part to the sojourning of Rosita Sardinia, daughter of a wealthy Cuban, who was later to marry into the family of the King of Spain. Pierre Lorillard of tobacco fame was a regular guest as were Mrs. Augustus P. Gardner, daughter of U.S. Senator Henry Cabot Lodge of Massachusetts and, as a child guest, Cesaer Romero. The Inn was built in 1893-94 by Jacob Matzinger for Frederick William Lancashire, who operated it until 1908. On August 27, 1920, fire was discovered, right, issuing from the roof and top floor of the structure by Fred Mauer while passing by in his delivery wagon. The 75 to 80 war veteran patients were safely evacuated along with some furnishings while the building burned from the top down.

The house rig, below, was used to meet trains at the depot. In 1896 the management catered experimentally to the winter trade outside the village, but it proved unsatisfactory. *Courtesy, Ontario Hose Co. No. 3*

Mansion House

The Mansion House, above, was built about 1870 as the Clements House, original structure, right, by Civil War Col. Addison Clements. By 1892, under the proprietorship of Charles Morton, the house was fast becoming a popular retreat with Brooklynites. In 1896 a four-lane bowling alley and dance hall were added. The landmark house on South Main Street (just west of Presbyterian Church) ended its days as the Yendes Inn — at the time, Liberty's oldest hostelry. *Courtesy, Mrs. David Clements, right, Dewey Borden, above.*

House with largest number of turn-outs and so on. But if 1896 was big, 1897 was an event that locals felt left even the *blase* New Yorkers gasping for adjectives. Considered one of the biggest Coaching Day Parades on record with an estimated 15,000 to 18,000 people lining Main Street to witness "one hundred and fifty decorated wagons and quite as many decorated buildings."

"From Lake to Buckley Street on Main Street, a distance of three-fourths of a mile, not only were the people standing five to twenty deep, but every window, porch, or other accessible elevation along that part of Main Street were doing their utmost as grand stands; even the proprietors of the Music Hall sold all the 'head room' at the windows in the hall at 50 cents per head, and many other people along the street with a pecuniary turn of mind were wishing for once they were living in glass houses."[9]

Nearly every house and business place along the line of the parade was decorated as well as many others about town lending a most festive atmosphere. A parade it was and that day, appropriately enough, the 'grand old lady of Liberty,' the New Liberty House, came home with the first prize for 'Prettiest Float".[10]

The New Liberty House was indeed the Grand Dame of Liberty and far outlived the other giants of her time. She was, when originally built across the street, one of the few drummers' hotels which had the class and service to attract the resort orientated traveler. An example of her quest after

230

Hotel Du Nord

It was a fine day in August 1898 when John and Katie Dohrmann herded their Hotel DuNord guests out front for a group portrait just before departure for the Coaching Day Parade. The imposing hotel, typical of the hotels of Liberty, showing little disposition toward the crescented falsefronts that later decorated the 'mission era' hotels of the county.

The first meeting of the Sullivan County Coaching Day Association was held in November, 1893, to initiate planning for the first Coaching Day Parade the following summer season. The event in 1894 was duly photographed, right, on upper Main Street and subsequently appeared in the 1895 "Summer Homes" publication.

Fern Cliff House

The Fern Cliff House had its grand opening on Monday evening, July 6, 1896, with special stages carrying guests from the Post Office in town. Under the proprietorship of Mrs. D. Wihltman, the name of the house was later changed, about 1900, to the Revonah Mountain House.

This formal portrait of elegantly attired ladies and mature, hirsute gentlemen, represents the official guiding force behind the 1907 Liberty Centennial celebration. Among the community leaders shown are white-mustachioed Joshua Gerow and wife (first row, second and third from left), and derby-topped Arnold J.D. Wedemeyer (front row, seventh from left).

The Centennial Arch, below, erected in front of the Baptist Church, right, out of picture, as part of the Liberty Centennial Days celebration, June 11 and 12, 1907. James Goodsir's drygoods store is shown just above the arch and above that, with arched windows, the Young, Messiter and Dodge department store, today's Sullivan County National Bank building. All the buildings on the left side of the street were wiped out in the great June 1913 blaze including the Music Hall building, extreme edge, and the white Hasbrouck block, over the American flag. Surrounding communities also participated in the Centennial Days by sending decorated floats (wagons) as witness this presentation from White Sulphur Springs, above. *Photograph by W.H. Beebe, Monticello, courtesy, John Joyner; top, courtesy, John Joyner.*

style were her typical Saturday evening 'Hops.' One of which, held July 27, 1888, was described by S.O. Journer, Society editor for the Liberty *Register:*

"Early in the week a limited number of invitations were sent to guests of the various houses in town and on the appointed evening about one hundred people assembled in the ball room and parlors where they were warmly greeted by the Liberty House host and hostess pro tem. A moment later the famous Nutting Orchestra of Middletown filled the house with "Rock-a-by Baby" and everybody glided lightly away to the swells of that very electrifying waltz. At 10:30 o'clock groans were heard issuing from the dining room, where everybody rushed to ascertain the cause, not a little apprehensive that medical aid would be required, but the alacrity with which the large tables were relieved of their heavy burden of daintily prepared refreshments soon dispelled all agony and smiling with refreshed vigor all again repaired to the ball room, where the glowing faces, graceful, prettily attired figures and buoyant spirits conveyed even more eloquently the pleasure of all present than did the warm expressions spoken as the guests reluctantly departed while the shades of Saturday were falling fast."

The Liberty House's saga begins in the 1860's when it was operated by Sheriff Melvin Wells. He was followed by George R. Brown who later sold the house to Alfred Messiter, the proprietor when the New York and Oswego Midland Railway was built through Liberty.

The namesake hotel soon became railroad headquarters for the contractors and their clerks. The first train arrived in Liberty Falls in January, 1872, an occasion celebrated by the railroad's provision of a free dinner and an excursion to Ellenville. The inevitable speeches were made by Henry R. Low, Dewitt C. Littlejohn[11] and others who "tried to lift the veil of the future and show the flowery land, which they claimed laid beyond." In July of the next year, 1873, rail service to Liberty was initiated.

Apparently the "flowery land" was already a reality. Flora Parsons Clements[12] reminisced: "when the first train pulled into Liberty proper, the trainmen were throwing bouquets of flowers from the platforms at the ends of the cars to the crowds lining the tracks." A few months later, in October, 1873, only the memory of wilted flowers remained as the inadequately financed line went into receivership. In 1880 the road was sold to Conrad N. Jordan and reorganized as the New York, Lake Ontario and Western.[13]

The road had failed because it was caught up in the Panic of 1873, a severe national depression triggered by the failure of J. Cooke and Company, but in fact the result of an orgy of post-Civil War expansion especially of railroads.

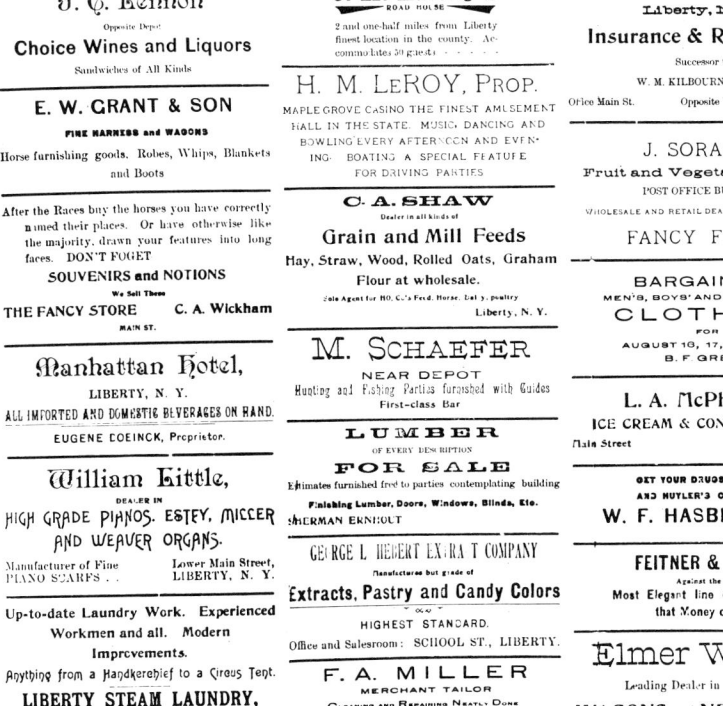

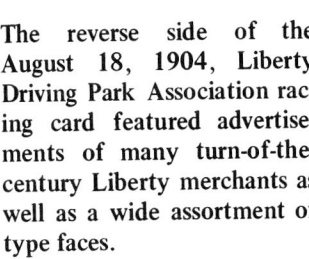

The reverse side of the August 18, 1904, Liberty Driving Park Association racing card featured advertisements of many turn-of-the-century Liberty merchants as well as a wide assortment of type faces.

Liberty House

Probably one of the most famous of Sullivan County's hotels was the bandstand-Porges block-flanked *New* Liberty House, which opened to the public on January 20, 1896. With the development of State Route 4 between New York and Binghamton, it became the popular half-way overnight stopping point for early-day automobilists.

It was from these humble beginnings that the legend of the Liberty House started in the 1860's. Here the venerable old hostelry seems about to be inundated by the snows of the Blizzard of 1888 or the big storm of February, 1893. *Courtesy, Del VanEtten*

The fine appointments of the New Liberty House were known and appreciated far and wide as note the home-like parlor, left, and its fireplace and piano. The check-in desk, above, and its glass-covered cigar case, which was a might too handy for cigar smoking fireladdies as they dashed up the stairs, right rear, with their hoses to battle the downward burning flames. *Both photographs, courtesy, Herbert Sprague*

The barroom of the Liberty House played a distressing role to the management when in August 1925 the United States Marshall padlocked the doors for violating the Federal Prohibition Act, (Volstead Act). The action was rather useless since, according to the press, the barroom was used "largely for storage." *Courtesy, Herbert Sprague*

On April 3, 1926, the quiet of a Sunday afternoon in Liberty was shattered when the cry of 'fire' was heard in the J.C. Young Hose Company house. Before night fell, the Grand Dame of Liberty was a shambles, marking finis to a colorful chapter in the annals of Sullivan County hotelkeeping. At the height of the blaze, fire fighting forces heroically kept the Porges building, right, in photograph below from igniting, even though it was reported someone was opening windows in an effort to initiate combustion of the vulnerable structure. *Courtesy, Ontario Hose Company No. 3*

Prospects were dismal for other local businesses as well. Failures were alarmingly frequent. Contractor Delos E. Culver who had built the road didn't pay sub-contractors, sub-contractors didn't pay laborers, laborers didn't pay boardinghouse keepers and the latter didn't pay merchants. It would be almost ten years before Liberty would completely recover from the depression. A harbinger of better days was noted in the local press in August, 1879, which recorded that " ... hundreds of Summer boarders are located in and around the Village of Liberty. Nearly all the summer boardinghouses are full while others are crowded."

Then there was the tax problem.

In 1874 the financially hard-pressed towns, which had floated bonds for the construction of the railway, were authorized to tax the road. The original act under which the railway was constructed exempted it from taxation for ten years after completion, but George M. Beebe, who was a Member of Assembly in 1874, had the law, an apparently unconstitutional device, amended. The receivers resisted aand finally one day in March, 1875 " ... all the rolling stock was run out of the state", and not a wheel turned on the road for over sixty days. The tax problem was finally settled and about the first of May, 1875, trains began to roll again.[14]

Through all of the railroad 'labor pains' the Liberty House provided a base of operations for the aborning railroad. The railway office was located in the basement, conveniently nestled between the barroom and the billiard parlor-beer saloon. The bar was a payday favorite of the railroaders.

Elections, town meetings and mass meetings were held at the Liberty House. During railroad times railroad laborers, with no right to vote, were run through the railway office, posted on answers to questions and sent to the polls where they were challenged and generally driven off without voting.

In April of 1878 Uriah S. Messiter acquired the Liberty House from his father and immediately enlarged and improved it. Then in 1885 he sold it to Thomas H. Houlihan who built the larger structure across the street whose grand opening took place on January 20, 1896. A full page in the 1896 "Summer Homes" was devoted to the new building. "It contains 78 large, airy, light sleeping rooms, without an objectionable room in the house ... it was built after the plans of a noted New York architect (Frank Cotter) and has all modern improvements, including open fire-places, steam heat, gas, electric bells, speaking tubes, fire alarms in every hall, baths, the best sanitary plumbing, pure spring water, cellar under the whole house, fire escapes, etc." As the years passed and the house increasingly became the civic and cultural center of Liberty life, additions including a casino and bowling lanes were built on the rear.

In 1901 the hostelry was sold to William S. Parmelee, only to be re-acquired the next year by Uriah S. Messiter who managed it for two years selling it to G.W. Murphy in time for the 1904 season. Murphy lasted but a short while, selling the sprawling hotel to Herman C. Lohman who made a considerable quantity of money from the business. After Lohman's tragic death,[15] his brother John sold out to George W. Rockwell, former operator of the Rockwell House in Monticello.[16]

Rockwell was not a new broom that swept clean, and few changes were made during his tenure. Tom McCormick remained as chief clerk of whom the *Register* wrote: "the house could hardly be without the services of 'Tom.' " The amiable Grover C. Bonnell was in charge of the livery and barns and John Manion saw to it that guests were transported from the O. and W. depot: carriage in summer, sleigh in winter. The sleigh was drawn by a big black horse that had a propensity for going to sleep and falling in his tracks. Special props were ordered for use when the 'big black' tired of waiting for a "delayed" O. and W. train.

Perhaps the most poignant of all annual events held at the house were the October meetings of the GAR veterans of the 143rd New York Volunteer Infantry Regiment. In 1909, 34 veterans slapped backs, shook hands and relived the Battle of Peachtree Creek and Sherman's 'March to the Sea'. By October, 1923, the ranks had thinned to 18 and by October 13, 1925, the roll listed only eight in attendance. It was their last reunion at the old spot.

The Liberty House burned down on Sunday, April 3, 1926. A little before five o'clock that Sunday afternoon all was quiet at the J.C. Young Hose Company house. Dewey Borden was taking his ease with some of the boys, when a very excited citizen dashed in to report that the top of the Liberty House was in flames.[17]

The chemical hose truck, driven by Dewey, pulled up to the building a moment before the actual fire whistle was sounded, "yet even as early as this, the whole top of the hotel was in flames."[18]

Paul Allen of Kenoza Lake observed that it "just seemed to burst out all over." This phenomenon, also noted by fire officials, led to speculations of arson. Rumors spread rapidly that black powder or some other flammable material had been distributed liberally about the attic.

Rumor or not, the fire had gained fantastic headway by the time fire lines could be established. The fact that the hotel was the only building to burn was due to calm weather and the excellent work of the firemen under the direction of Chief Norman Rampe.

"When we ran in the front door of the house," recalls Borden, "there sat 'Willie' Greenspan and a bunch of his cronies in the card room playing pinochle, completely unaware of the fire in the attic." Meanwhile, hose after hose was carried through the lobby and up the stairs in back of the check-in counter with its squared-glass cigar display case. As virtually every fireman passed the counter on his way up to the fire lines, he would reach around and grab a handful of the Havana filler's — that is until Chief Rampe happened to witness one of the hosemen make a fast withdrawal.

"It was an enraged chief," Borden recalled, "that stormed up the stairs and one by one demanded of the men that the cigars be returned to the display case." All of the stogies were returned only to go up in smoke within the hour — to the enjoyment of no one.

By the time darkness fell an estimated 500 people were crowded along Main Street to witness the end of a landmark, the site of many Lincoln Day dinners and the building from whose balcony President Theodore Roosevelt once addressed a cheering throng.

The one village structure that seemed eternal was the old depot up the hill just off Lake Street. It seemed to be in constant motion, particularly in the summer months with the crowded trains disgorging their humanity into the jammed-up wagons and three-seaters that virtually immobilized Lake Street in both directions.

It was the scene of hackmen arrested by O. and W. police for violations of trespass regulations, and even the setting for a suicide in 1910 when Joseph Ostrich shot himself with an old-fashioned 44-calibre colt revolver near the Express Office.

There were the times that crowds jammed the area in front of the station to welcome politicians during campaigns. In October, 1924, Theodore Roosevelt, Jr., the Republican candidate for Governor of New York, came to town. On a balcony of the Lennon House, before a crowd of 1500 persons, he projected the question, "Are we going to permit Tammany to build up a great machine in this state and to dominate our lives?" That November, Democrat Alfred E. Smith was elected governor.

There were fatal accidents at the crossing by the depot but there were also incidents which were beyond belief such as the experience of "Gid" and "Dutch," two noted characters who attempted to cross the tracks while drunk. Their brush with death in front of southbound No. 2 caused their auto, a Star runabout, to be ground to pieces and lodged under engine No. 3, which was standing on a parallel track. Station Agent Bill Brock recalled "as soon as 'Gid' was extracted he was pronounced dead and laid on the ground to be turned over to the undertaker and while 'Dutch' was being pulled out [from] between the driving wheels, the undertaker arrived but found 'Gid' had got up and walked away unbeknown to anybody around. 'Dutch' was finally extracted and after gaining consciousness allowed 'The damn Star is good no more' and walked away without visible injury."

It was an era when virtually every "Summer Homes" listing boasted of its location on a "rise of ground," an important factor when malaria was

New Features
At the
LIBERTY .. HOUSE

Just completed and now open, the new

CASINO

Daily Concerts
Morning   Afternoon   Evening

BOWLING   ALLEYS
Billiards   Pool

Refreshments Served a la Carte from 8 to 11 P. M.

DANCING
Tuesday and Saturday Evenings.

Herman C. Lohman,   Prop

The Liberty House management, constantly striving to improve their facilities, trumpeted the latest improvements in this August 26, 1906, Liberty *Herald* advertisement.

A 1900 issue of Ainslee's Magazine thumped the healthful elevation of the Liberty area with distinguished physician recommendations. Even with the agrarian charm of the milkmaid illustration, this advertising theme led eventually to the inclusion of advertisements from many private citizens who converted their large homes into rest centers. Typical was "The Liberty Home" on Champlin Ave., a street which quickly became lined with such facilities.

still prevalent. A wag writing in the Brooklyn *Standard Union* of June, 1893, commented: "some way they have all got a rise of ground — they are built that way."

It was a time when a veteran of the Civil War could buy a piece of land and "one year later sell it to a Vassar College professor and get a 100% advance over his price the previous year."

They were simply heady years for the mountain resorts.

But they would soon peak out and to some degree the Ontario and Western would be to blame.

In the 1890's copy appeared, at first subtly and then in raucus tones, in "Summer Homes" trumpeting information on the treatment and cure of lung diseases. Although the healthful air and remarkable elevation of Liberty was emphasized virtually from the beginning as one of the primary reasons for going to the mountains on the O. and W., it wasn't until 1889 and 1890 that a feature, "What Medical Experts Say," appeared recommending the "immediate neighborhood of Liberty, N.Y., as one of the best regions for consumptives" backing up their assertion with a thick sheaf of endorsements from medical experts in the New York area.[19]

The treatment of pulmonary diseases received its first impetus in the Liberty area when Dr. Alfred L. Loomis in 1895 bought land on a high elevation a few miles out of town on the road to White Sulphur Springs as the site for a medical institution. During the early part of 1896 construction went apace, an electric light plant was installed and 125 men and many teams were involved in grading

A NEW BOARDING HOUSE
"THE LIBERTY HOME"
44 CHAMPLIN AVE. (Burns' Residence)

The whole building has been thoroughly renewed and very specially equipped for a limited number of select guests. The treatment is to be that of a real home plus the skill of a trained personelle. Now open for enlistment or inspection by the general public.

J. L. BRUCE, Proprietor.

The Loomis Sanitarium's Administration Building was built by J. Pierpont Morgan in 1896 and stood but three years — a victim of fire on October 14, 1899. The Casino, background, among other things, housed recreational facilities. In June, 1901, Ontario and Western train No. 1 carried 175 physicians from the New York Post-Graduate School to the Loomis Sanitarium, below, for a study of the renowned facility. *Photograph, top, by Whittaker and Aldrich*

the grounds. On June 1 the Loomis Sanitarium for consumptives opened under the auspices of the Episcopal Church with "a housekeeper, two servant girls on hand and Dr. Davis of New York, the physician in charge." The rate expense to each patient was $5 per week for board and any medicines at wholesale rates. The O. and W. cooperated in the enterprise by charging patients going to the sanitarium a special $2.25 rate, the regular fare being $3.09.

One month before the official dedication the O. and W. brought out a special pamphlet titled "Winter Homes" (4" x 8") whose object was to "direct the attention of physicians and those of their patients afflicted with lung and throat troubles to a region within 3 3/4 hours' ride of New York." The publication, averaging about 42 pages, continued to appear annually in the late fall until the winter of 1905-06 when consumptive backlash in Sullivan County reached crisis proportions.

By 1901 Liberty boardinghouse keepers and citizens petitioned the O. and W. to "eliminate all sanitarium and hospital advertisements from the 1902 issue of the 'Summer Homes' book." The management readily agreed. The local press, when reporting this, added appropriately: "Now let the advertisers leave out of their advertisements all references to consumption and religion and it will be better all around."

Fresh air, being an important factor in the treatment of tuberculosis, many of the small cabins were designed for cross ventilation in virtually all directions for all seasons of the year. These winter and summer views appeared in the 1904-05 issue of "Winter Homes."

Are your Lungs or Throat affected?

If so, go to Sullivan County, New York; you can get there in a ride of three hours from West Englewood, on the

NEW YORK, ONTARIO & WESTERN RAILWAY.

Don't go to Colorado or North Carolina at a large expense. The world-famed lung specialist, Dr. A. L. Loomis, through a long series of experiments, demonstrated that the climatological conditions of this section, in winter or summer, were far better for the cure and prevention of phthisis than any point in the west or south. He located, near Liberty, N. Y., the Loomis Sanitarium, and the great number of cures effected bear out his judgment.

The most prominent throat and lung specialists in New York and Brooklyn send their patients there.

The region is 2,000 feet above the sea; there are no fogs, no stagnant waters, no poisonous vapors, and malaria is unknown.

Send a two-cent stamp for a copy of "Winter Homes," giving a list of the sanitariums in and about Liberty, or six cents in stamps for a "Summer Homes," giving list of the farm and boarding houses for the summer months, to

J. C. ANDERSON, Gen'l Passenger Agent,
56 BEAVER ST., NEW YORK CITY.

The cover of "Winter Homes," for the season of 1898-99, featured an 'Ozone carrying' doctor. The first press release promoting the initial issue of ten thousand copies of "Winter Homes" appeared in the January 15, 1897, Liberty *Register*. Both "Summer" and "Winter Homes" were advertised in local publications such as the advertisement, left, slanted for West Englewood, New Jersey residents.

Opposition to consumptives was virtually non-existent when "Winter Homes" first appeared, with the possible exception of a release appearing in August of 1896 replying to negative comment "that there is no cause for anxiety upon the health of the community ... the fact is that this sanitarium is located at Liberty is the best guarantee possible that Liberty is the healthiest place to be found in the East."

On November 20, 1896, about one hundred and fifty invited guests were present at the dedication of the Loomis Sanitarium including J. Pierpont Morgan, an avid Episcopalian and the friend of many bishops, who had arrived aboard a special train that left New York at 10 o'clock over the Erie road. The train consisted of two Pullman cars and the president's car and was switched onto the O. and W. tracks at Middletown at which time conductor George Close took charge of the train for the run to Liberty. The special, pulled by engine No. 139 with engineer John W. Harvey on the right side, made the run from Middletown to Liberty, a distance of 41 miles, in 54 minutes.

The dedication services were conducted by Bishop Potter of the Protestant Episcopal Church who extended recognition to Mr. Morgan for his gift of the administration building (cost $75,000). Constructed of stone, 276 feet in length and three stories high, the building contained offices, pharmacy, laboratory, reception room, library, solarium, dining room, kitchen, laundry and living rooms for the house physician, matron, nurses and staff of helpers. Other institutional buildings included the Casino, a two story building for amusement and five cottages: The Sloane, Watson, Walker, Martha Lester and Irvin.

A few years later tragedy struck. On October 14, 1899, a fire was discovered in an upper room on the west end of the administration building and within three hours nothing but stone walls and chimneys were left. Firemen at Liberty's Hallock Hose Company, knowing of no place to attach

their hose at Loomis, bundled several hundred feet of lawn hose, a score of fire buckets and other fire fighting paraphernalia in a large wagon furnished by Postmaster Winner and headed for the scene of the fire.

Practically all the loose furniture on the ground floor and some in the upper floors was saved, but the vital boiler, engine dynamo and electric lighting plant were ruined. Alfred L. Sweeney, Manager of the Liberty Light and Power Co., immediately set up emergency lighting for the cottages and construction crews started erecting temporary buildings. In April, 1901, Morgan came through again when he purchased the entire plant of the Liberty Electric Light and Power Company and presented it to the Loomis Sanitarium. Under the new arrangement the sanitarium would receive free the current for its six hundred lights and by furnishing lights to the village would derive a steady income.[20]

In 1902 and 1903, letters occasionally appeared in the papers as distinguished doctors and boardinghouse operators threw brick-bats back and forth over the subject of consumptive treatment in the village of Liberty.

Resistance was, however, steadily mounting. By December of 1904 a request for permission to establish another sanitarium was denied with Judge George H. Smith commenting that "greater precautions should be taken to prevent the indiscriminate entertainment of persons afflicted with the disease in private families." Further, "that its (Sullivan County) summer business had already been injured by the reputation it had as a resort for invalids and that our people must now choose whether they want a health resort or a pleasure resort."

An editorial asked "why must the village suffer to be given a 'black eye' because certain boardinghouses with all the outward appearances of sanitariums exist in the very heart of the village?"[21]

Resolutions were passed requesting action be taken to remedy the conditions.[22]

Probably the whole problem was best summed up in the Von Unruh Sanatoria Inc. proposal for a sanitarium on Walnut Mountain. The Town Board of Liberty met and was of the opinion that the application should be granted. Town merchants such as James Goodsir, obejcted: "To support the proposed sanitorium was the beginning of the end of the summer business in Liberty."

At a hearing in November, specialists from Saranac Lake and New York testified against the alleged Von Unruh "cure."[23] Even the operators of the small boarding farmhouses made their objections heard loud and clear. C.P. Gregory, J. Newton Clements of Ferndale and D.H. Clements spoke for the Grange.

In January, 1917, the headline: Dr. Von Unruh and his Cure Head Elsewhere," wrote finis to the controversy.

In July, 1918, the Liberty Village Board posted notices calling attention to the spitting ordinance. Police were instructed to arrest offenders but

Typical of the "health" advertisements run by the Ontario and Western — this one appearing in the New York *Evening Post* for June 1, 1901

uniformed police were sometimes at a disadvantage, "the board has now put on a plain clothes officer with instructions to give special attention to spitters."

As Dewey Borden recalled the big years of the sanitariums, "there were two things that seemed to upset the folks in town the most, not to mention the skittish visitors — the sight of patients walking the streets expectorating in little boxes called 'sputum cups' and the other was the practice of the cheaper sanitariums to hang their bedding out the windows on every sunny day much to the distress of the neighbors."

This concern over the spreading of germs resulted in a "Swat The Fly" contest in July, 1912, sponsored by the *Register*. The winner was Dewey Borden reporting a 'kill' of 67,000 with a grand

"Winter Homes", 1901-02

Liberty photographer, R.B. Whittaker, recorded John Dwyer's new house for the special Mid-Summer Souvenir Edition of the Liberty *Register* in August, 1899. Originally known as the Woodland Manor, it later became the Linden Manor and subsequently catered to T.B. patients. *Courtesy, Herbert Sprague.*

total of 114,481 by all the contestants (runners up, Charlie Hoos, 34,451; Willie Hegemann, 9,630; Walter Lancashire, 2,700; Maxie Cink, 400; L. Armand, 200).

But for all the concern over the spread of disease and the growing number of private homes being converted into sanitariums in the village, the Loomis Sanitarium continued to grow, experiencing both good times and bad. In 1926 they were the feature of the entire issue of the magazine "Outdoor Life," which gave the history and operation of the institution in most glowing terms.

Disaster struck a second time in August, 1922, when an upset can of grease ignited and gutted the eastern end of the main building. Within thirty minutes of the arrival of the Liberty fire forces under Chief Rampe, the blaze was declared under control, saving much of the building and keeping the loss to $30,000.

This burning of the administration building was not marked by an historic rescue as was the first burning in 1899. At the height of that blaze two trolley engineers working nearby on the new right-of-way of the Liberty and Jeffersonville trolley line raced into the inferno and rescued the wall-mounted memorial slab. Unfortunately, the success of the Liberty and Jeffersonville Trolley line did not match the success of the rescue of the memorial slab.

The "on again-off again-Finnegan" story of that trolley line started in 1896 when the Jeffersonville *Record* reported there were "capitalists in the field

LIBERTY   Part 1   245

Little is discernible today of the graded right-of-way of the Liberty-Jeffersonville trolley line. This rather obscure section behind the structure is located on the sag just before the grade swung behind the Loomis Sanitarium.

who are willing to build the road if the people will subscribe the right-of-way and about $25,000 in cash."

By the first of the year (1897) Jeffersonville, Youngsville and White Sulphur Springs had agreed to donate $10,000 of the amount, with Liberty the remaining — and therein was the rub. As the Liberty *Register* for January 22, 1897, noted, "Liberty, for once is delinquent in matters pertaining to home welfare, and is behind in donating the remaining $10,000 necessary." By the middle of February only $3,775 of the $10,000 had been raised by Liberty.

Despite the delinquency of the Liberty fathers, April 19, 1897, saw the Liberty and Jeffersonville Electric Railroad Company incorporated in Albany.[24] The survey had been completed the same week and several hundred poles and 2,500 ties had been distributed along the right-of-way from Jeffersonville to a point east of Youngsville. A year later, in January, 1898, it was reported that additional poles " ... will be delivered along the line of the road on sleighs and will be put in position this spring," also noting 3/4 of the grade as being completed.

It seems that much of what the press reported as accomplishment just wasn't fact. For example, on October 27, 1899, the Register noted "we are assured that the construction work on the road bed will positively be commenced within a few weeks and vigorously pushed during the entire winter." A year and a half before, three fourths of the grade had been reported as completed.

The few bridges to be built were to be constructed strong enough to carry the weight of the heaviest cars and engines on the O. and W. line. This would enable the electric company to carry not only coal, milk and miscellaneous freight through in O. and W. cars, but would also permit the running of passenger cars through from New York to Jeffersonville. It would also render feasible the use of O. and W. snow plows and engines in case of snow blockade.

In March of 1900 control of the road fell into the hands of Sheffer, Rannie and Co. of New York and two months later work was commenced on the Liberty and Jeffersonville "trolley railroad" by contractor W.P. Craig — an old refrain to the ears of the people of Liberty.

The O. and W. also had its engineers in town to give the trolley company a grade and right-of-way to the Liberty depot — even a contract for the erection of a 25 x 100 foot car house was let to Frank Cotter.

A discouraging portent was noted as late as July, however, as it was reported that a flat car used for hauling dirt and gravel was being pulled by a *horse*.

A year later a contract was signed with the Honk Falls Power Co. After May 10, 1901, not much was heard from the trolley line until June 2, 1911, when the optimistic "Trolley Prospects Bright" was bannered on the front page. Key people, including R.B. Mingle, were in town to determine the advisability of its completion.

The Liberty Business Men's Association held meetings when Mr. Mingle announced "The old trolley proposition is dead ... and that the old company will not be reorganized with the intentions that an entirely new company be formed."

At a meeting in March, 1912, the Liberty Business Men's Association was asked to raise an additional $1900, just one month before the Certificate of Incorporation of the Sullivan County Railroad Company was filed in Albany.[25] Once

Station rigs lined up, horses' blinders to tail gate, through the station plaza and down Lake Street — a crowded platform made even more cluttered with the 'all-summer' steamer trunks — indeed the great days of the Ontario and Western when its classic depot was the epicenter of Liberty and a resort region.

again, on April 5, 1912, a published story reached an unbelieving public announcing that work would be commenced on the construction of the road by the 15th of May.

In August there was another road block—the Public Service Commission refused the application for an electric road claiming there were too many grade crossings and the curves and grades did not meet the requirements of the Commission. By October a new certificate of incorporation along with a new name — the Liberty and Callicoon Railroad Corporation—was announced, with its official approval by the Public Service Commission forthcoming in January, 1913.

In February the old 'chestnut' was back in Liberty's lap with this ultimatum: "If Liberty co-operates, Road Will Be Built ... either the necessary amount of stock must be subscribed now or the project will be abandoned."[26]

Mr. Valentine Scheidell of Jeffersonville commented at a Liberty Business Men's Association meeting that there was no trouble raising the amount necessary in Youngsville and Jeffersonville. It was essentially the $2,000 still outstanding on the $10,000 from Liberty. The money never did materialize.

In June, 1913, contractor William P. Craig deferred any further effort on the project due to illness in the family, summing up "it will keep until we are ready."

It kept until June, 1917, when Craig arrived in town to tear up the two and one half miles of steel rail between Liberty and Loomis. This was all that had been completed since 1896. Before he left Liberty he announced with bravado his plans for a new charter from the Public Service Commission for a line from Liberty to Kenoza Lake. As far as is known this was the last Liberty ever heard from contractor Craig and the trolley line project.

LIBERTY OPERA HOUSE
ONE NIGHT, TUESDAY AUG. 20
THE NEW
Black Patti
TROUBADOURS

Headed By the
ORIGINAL

BLACK PATTI
(Sissieretta Jones)
Greatest Singer of Her Race

EVERYTHING NEW
INCLUDING
"TUTT" WHITNEY

— AND —

40 OTHERS 40
IN REFINED
COMEDY, VAUDEVILLE, OPERA
SINGERS, DANCERS UNSURPASSED

Prices .25 .50 .75 $1.00

Seats on sale at Opera House Box Office Sat. Aug. 17

The New Black Patti Troubadours were featured at the Liberty Opera House (Music Hall) in this August 16, 1907, Liberty *Register* advertisement. The large frame structure at the corner of Chestnut and Main Streets was the cultural and social center of Liberty in the dawning years of the twentieth century.

Liberty

The Great 1913 Fire and After

Liberty and its Ontario and Western depot was much like the hub of a three spoked wheel: one hub, Jeffersonville; another, White Lake; and the third, Neversink.

Neversink, as one of the three dependent spokes radiating out from the "hub" of Liberty, keenly felt the economic loss of Friday, June 13, 1913, when the business heart of the resort center was reduced to ashes.

The Liberty fire, which ultimately involved eight mercantile establishments, started in the rear of the Music Hall in the center of town at the corner of Main and Chestnut Streets. The Music Hall, built by A.J.D. Wedemeyer, was the cultural center of the community and bore witness to the local birth of the entertainment phenomena of an era — the motion picture.

"Those who attended the [grand] opening of the Music Hall Monday evening, aver that the Hall is not only music to the ears but music to the eyes and a place altogether lovely."[1] Quite naturally the Liberty Coronet Band was on hand for the festivities and appropriately an address of welcome by A.J.D. Wedemeyer and a major address by George H. Carpenter — considered "one of the ablest speeches that has ever been given in Liberty."

In 1897 the "Projectoscope," an early motion picture device, was featured, prophetically showing "burning stables with smoke issuing from the burning interior and horses coming out of the door, one after another in a perfect semblence of reality." Also in the same program appeared, "the Irwin-Rice kissing scene representing a man and woman going through every variety of the osculatory process, struck a responsive chord with the majority of the audience and its repetition was demanded with emphasis."

The programs on the stage of the Music Hall ran the gamut from the Park Sisters "and their skill in executing the coronet and quartet," to "A Knapsack Tour of the World" — a graphic lecture. In March, 1901, it was "The Illustrated Lecture on Paris and the Exposition of 1900." In June, 1898, the Alonzo Hatch electro-photo musical or "moving picture", was the big event along with occasional receptions and hops.

Main Street in 1900, showing the flagpole-peaked Music Hall, and in the far distance, the protruding Hasbrouck block. The horse and carriage, left, is parked in front of A. McPhillamy's popular ice cream parlor. *Courtesy, Mrs. Fanny Edwards*

The Music Hall and block of buildings wiped out in the June 13, 1913, conflagration. On the horizon are two of the Liberty resort hotels; Monitor, left, and Ye Lancashire Inn. The small peaked extension on building, right, hangs out over the entrance to B.E. Misner's store, closeup, opposite page. In 1904, the Music Hall's builder, A.J.D. Wedemeyer, sold the structure to department store operator B.F. Green, who after the 1913 blaze erected the present Green Building. B.F. Green was brought to America from Russia as an illiterate boy by Charlie Green. Charlie, a Jewish peddler who, by hard work and abandonment of his given name (Nathan Federgreen) struck it rich in Sullivan County.

B. E. Misner's confectionery store, doomed by the 1913 burn, faced the Baptist Church, whose reflection shows in the plate glass window. *Courtesy, Mrs. David Clements*

At the height of the blaze, the steeple of the Baptist Church across Main Street caught a spark. The low water pressure, putting the initial fire beyond the range of the hose lines, necessitated a bucket brigade. Under the command of Rev. Ralph Thorne, the brigade nearly succeeded but soon the roof was ablaze, then the main sanctuary.

Once in awhile an engagement was a flop – "the Garrick Theatre Co. closed an unsuccessful three nights' engagement ... business being exceedingly poor."[2] Then there was the time Field's and Hanson's minstrels had to cancel their date at the Hall because of the high prices asked by the Ontario and Western for switching their cars.

On Monday, June, 13, 1904, Keough and Snyder's Twentieth Century Moving Picture and Vaudeville Company's presentation "The Great Train Robbery," was presented, a 12-minute epic considered to be the first American-made feature film. It also brought to Liberty for the first time, Edison's "Marvelous Kinetoscope Machine." Nine years later, on June 13, 1913, the final curtain came down.

Eight mercantile establishments burned out with a loss of $200,000. One area resident reckoned June 11 to be his lucky day. On that Wednesday "Pim" Morgan moved out of his third-story flat in the doomed Hasbrouck Block. For the rest of the tenants and businessmen it was indeed a bad-luck Friday the 13th.

"The fire whistle was just starting to blow," recalls Dewey Borden, "when I looked up the narrow alley between the Roosa Building and the Hasbrouck Building to see flames roaring out of the Sherwood Stables at the far end. Seems it was about 4:45 in the afternoon." The alarm was reportedly turned in, however delayed, by Bill Weber, a resident in a tenement adjacent to the stables.

LIBERTY Part 2 251

EXTRA The Liberty Register EXTRA
THE LEADING NEWSPAPER OF SULLIVAN COUNTY

Vol. XLIII. No. 39 — Liberty, New York, Saturday, June 14, 1913 — Price Five Cents

HALF OF LIBERTY'S BUSINESS SECTION WIPED OUT BY FIRE!

Most Destructive Conflagration Ever Known in History of Town. Opera House, Baptist Church, B. F. Green's, Jafnel's Pharmacy, Kniffin's Stationery Store, B. E. Misner's Grocery Store, Roosa & Lancashire's, James Mance's Pharmacy, Wm. Fahrenholz's Stationery Store, Roosa & Lancashire's Barn, Hasbrouck's Apartment House, Sherwood's Barn and other smaller buildings burned to ground; Very Little of Contents of buildings Saved. Other buildings greatly damaged.

Total Loss Will Reach From Three to Five Hundred Thousand Dollars. All Will Rebuild at Once.

Many Merchants are Utterly Ruined; Fire Started in Roosa & Lancashire's Barn About 4:30 O'clock; Flames Spread with Incredible Speed; Firemen from Nearby Towns Heroically Respond to Call. Total Insurance Will Not Reach over $75,000. Entire Business Section Was in Grave Danger; Great Many Houses Were on Fire; Rumor of Death Is Untrue; Firemen Often Risking Their Lives Fought Valiantly; Some People Injured. Wild Excitement as Whole Village Is Threatened.

Fighting with the courage and bravery of Spartan heroes, in the heat of Hell, the Liberty firemen and firefighters from nearby towns, who heroically responded to the call for help, yesterday afternoon between the hours of 4:30 o'clock and 7, combatted the most terrific and most destructive conflagration known in the history of the town of Liberty.

Only one other fire in the history of Sullivan County that could possibly equal it was the great fire at Monticello a few summers ago. Nearly an entire half of the business section of Liberty was wiped out. For some time the entire business section of the village was in grave danger of destruction. Within less than half an hour after the fire had started the whole business block extending from the corner of Main and Chestnut Street north to W. F. Hasbrouck's dwelling was a raging furnace of flames.

The origin of the fire is unknown. It started in the barn and storehouse of Rosa and Lancashire, which is situated in the rear of their large grocery store. Thomas Washington had only a short time before unloaded a load of hay in the barn. With such incredible speed did the flames race that they had gained uncontrolable headway before the firemen had hooked their hose to the hydrants. The place in which the fire started was thickly surrounded by frame buildings that were easy prey to the flames. The firemen were hardly aware that the fire had started before the flames had raced over the entire block.

Burning fragments of wood were blown in all directions. Some of these were blown across the street, landed on the tower of the Baptist Church, Goodsir's store, which is owned by Isham Young, the Lyric Theatre, owned by John Durbee, and these buildings broke out in flames. With no less than twelve large buildings in flames it was a mighty proposition that the firemen had to cope with.

The buildings that were entirely destroyed were as follows: The big corner building owned by B.F. Green, in which were located, the Opera House, Jafnel's Pharmacy and Mr. Green's clothing size, C. A. Sprague's two large buildings, occupied by stationer Kniffin, grocer B. E. Misner, and on the second and third stories where dwelt George Huber, Elmer Kniffin and other families; Wilbur Roosa's building, occupied by Roosa & Lancashire's, the leading grocers, and on the second and third stories of this building different families lived and their entire belongings were destroyed; the barns of Roosa & Lancashire and W. F. Sherwood and the Baptist Church. Practically all the contents of the above buildings were entirely burned.

Considerable goods were taken from B. F. Green's store but it was badly damaged and this morning may be seen littered along the streets. All along the line on Main Street and at many nearby dwellings the contents of the houses were packed up and placed in the streets. Special police were on guard last night. Four horses were saved from Sherwood's barn by Henry Kost and Ed. Davis.

Estimates from men well qualified to judge place the entire loss at from $250,000 to $500,000.

Such estimates are from such men as Wm. H. Hand, Isaac Fox, David B. Hill, H. D. McLaughlin, Charles Crawford, etc.

Total insurance (average estimate of insurance dealers) is placed at not exceeding $75,000.

Mr. Green is the heaviest loser. To a Register reporter he stated that his loss will reach $60,000.

Insurance was carried as follows: Green, $8000 with Beck, $2000 with McLaughlin and $7,000 with Wm. D. Hand. Only last January Mr. Green cancelled a further policy of $6000. Jafnel carried $3000 with Beck (to fair), Kniffin carried a total of $1000 with Beck on his stock in store and household goods; B. E. Misner carried no insurance; C. A. Sprague carried only $1500, Wilbur Roosa, who estimates his stock loss at $6000 and store loss at $10,000 carried $3,000 insurance on stock and $4000 on building; James D. Mance carried $1000 with Hand (will not cover loss); Wm. Fahrenholz carried $1500 with Wm. H. Hand; Hasbrouck carried $2400 with McLaughlin and $1600 with Hand, Goodsir had stock insured for $1000 with McLaughlin and $2000 with Hand, Baptist Church, small insurance with Church Association, Mr. Durbee, owner of Lyric Theatre carried $1,600 with Hand. There was also insurance on Isham Young's building and Sherwood's barn.

H. J. Sarles, whose store windows were broken, carried $500 plate glass insurance with McLaughlin. Mr. Jafnel says that he had just put in $6000 in fixtures, etc., in his corner drug store recently purchased.

Green and Roosa stated last night that they will rebuild immediately. It is very probable that the entire block wiped out will be rebuilt with in the summer.

The alarm at the power house was not sounded until the fire companies were at the fire. Company No. 1 was the first on the scene and hooked on the corner hydrant, the other companies soon followed. The prevailing need for more hose for the present companies was demonstrated. As the great blaze raged fiercely and the efforts of the village companies seemed but of little avail, a cry for help was sent to neighboring places. Too much praise can not be given for the quick response to that cry. The following fire companies of different towns rushed into Liberty in the order named; Hurleyville, Livingston Manor, Monticello, Jeffersonville, Callicoon, Lake Huntington, and Roscoe. All of the above companies came with fire fighting appliances. Youngsville and Ellenville sent men. Within twenty minutes from the time the call reached Middletown, 250 firemen were at the station. They came in a special train as far as Summitville; where they were notified that the fire was under control and they returned. Livingston Manor firemen, under the leadership of Chief Robinson, came in James Stevens automobile and in special train (50 men). Monticello firemen, under their leader, Chief August Hotens, came in a number of automobiles (50 men). The quick response of brother firemen and their hard and able work was most heroic they have the heart-felt gratitude of Liberty's people.

Many a brave deed was done by the fire-fighters. The heat was unbearable. Many of the firemen are burned so that their flesh is raw. So hot was it where men stood holding the nozzle of the hose that water had to be frequently poured on them to keep their clothes from burning. We cannot give special praise to anyone, every fireman was a hero. When the cry was raised that lives of people were endangered on the upper floors of the Hasbrouck building, there were a score of men ready to risk their lives in going through the building.

There was a persistent rumor shortly after the fire that a woman who lived near Roosa & Lancashire's was burned to death. This is untrue. The woman referred to probably was an elderly woman, the mother of Mrs. Pierpont, who was seen at the window. She was an invalid and was carried to safety. Fred Schoemaker, who was at work on the Baptist Church belfry, was overcome, but his condition is not serious. Rev. Ribaca had his leg badly strained. There were several overcome by the extreme heat; some received minor injuries but no one was seriously injured.

The aid of the out-of-town firemen came in the nick of time. The Liberty men after having stood the heat of the roaring furnace for nearly an hour were weakening one by one as the help arrived. Without giving quarter for crashing walls nor flying gines the firemen fought nobly. Several streams were on the blaze, which accounted for the lack of the usual high pressure. Water had to be continuously poured on the home lying on the ground to keep it from burning.

When the fire first started it was thought of but little consequence but within ten minutes its treachery was fully realized. As the awful blaze rushed on and on, continually breaking out in new places and as Goodsir's store and the Baptist Church burst out in flames, the people were nearly panic-stricken. Mattresses, bedding and all kinds of household furniture were thrown from the second story of more than a score of houses. For a time it seemed that Davis Brothers' meat market in the rear of the Sarles store must go, but by hard work it was saved, although on fire several times. If fire had gotten headway in this building the entire block of frame houses down to the Poollman House and possibly further, would have probably burned. To the north the brick meat market of Frank Mauer was a barrier and had it not been for this brick building the residences of W. F. Hasbrouck, Dr. C. S. Payne, and the business block still further to the north would also have been licked up by the flames. Davis market was damaged to the extent of about $300. Dr. Payne had his valuables moved, expecting that his home would go. On the other side of the street matters were serious. With the Baptist Church entirely enveloped in flames and the fire eating its way into Goodsir's store, hopes were almost abandoned for the saving of buildings on adjoining property. To the north Schraders restaurant and the Register office were in great danger, as they caught fire at different times. Employees of the Register standing on the roof with a garden hose probably saved the buildings to the north of Goodsir's. It was with great

(Continued on Page 2.)

EXTRA! EXTRA!
BERL BROWN, EMPLOYED IN COON BROS. SAW MILL AT GROOVILLE MEETS HORRIBLE DEATH

Bert Brown, 22, met a horrible death at the saw mill of Coon Bros. at Grooville, formerly Emmansville, above Livingston Manor, yesterday, (Friday) morning when he accidentally fell on a large circular saw and was cut completely in two. Mr. Brown's work was to guide the boards from the rack after they had been cut. While handling one of the boards he was suddenly drawn to the saw which entered his left thigh near the hip and going upward cut its way through the young man's body through to the skull.

Opposite, one of the few times in history when the Liberty *Register* devoted the entire front page to a local story. *Courtesy, the Liberty Register*

The 1913 blaze at its height, showing the lawn in front of the Baptist Church littered with display cases and merchandise moved out of the B.F. Green department store, left background. The B.E. Misner store remains may be seen just to the left of the hanging electric wire, right. The last remaining wall of the Hasbrouck block, captured on film shortly before its collapse, left. The spread of the fire was stopped by the cement block liquor store, right.

Liberty's first fire truck was this homemade converted Stoddard Dayton auto developed in the winter of 1913. On board, (L to R), are Ben Gerow, Walter J. Randall (driver and chief), Norman H. Rampe, Joseph Rinaldo, Gurnsey Rampe and Byron Grant. The development of the truck by the Liberty Hose and Truck Co. was done in secret. Planning a coup, they set fire to a pile of rubbish at Clem Smiths on No. Main Street and had an alarm sent in for which they were all set. The secret was well kept and they had their laugh on the other two companies when they arrived dragging their carts to find that the Number 2's had the fire out. *Courtesy, Ontario Hose Company No. 3*

As flames tore through the 112 foot long Roosa & Lancashire grocery and fruit store, emergency calls went out to surrounding communities; and soon Livingston Manor Hose Co., arriving on a special O. and W. train, was on the scene, quickly followed by Mountain Hose Co. of Monticello, Jeffersonville Hose Co. and the Lake Huntington Hose Co.[3]

When it was apparent that things were out of control, willing hands set to moving merchandise out of Green's Clothing Store, located in the Music Hall building. "You never saw a bunch of guys move so fast," recalls Borden, "as they carried out showcases, racks of clothes and assorted merchandise and piled it up on the lawn across the street in front of the Baptist Church."

After sweeping the Hasbrouck Block housing the James B. Mance Pharmacy and the William Fahrenholz stationery and news store, the advance of the flames up Main Street was finally halted by the concrete-block Hasbrouck's Liquor Store.

The great holocaust of 1913 occurred in the dawning years of the age of the automobile. Just two years previously the sale of an automobile in town was actually a news item: "Ben Gerow has sold a Cadillac touring car and a Ford 'runabout' to Wm. S. Merwin of Hazel. This will make four Cadillacs and five Ford automobiles this spring."

By 1919 reckless driving in town and particularly on the road to Youngsville provoked an editorial in the Register aimed at the high speed cutting-out and cutting-in passing of its citizens on Main Street by the summer visitors. "Some night, unless cut-outs are closed, a peeved citizen is going to arise in his wrath and hurl a brick at a thoughtless, selfish driver."

High speed driving on the road to Youngsville was so bad that "many persons will not venture out along the state road Saturday nights ... fenders [guard rails] along the state road between Youngsville and Liberty, broken in more than twenty places, show either that cars are excessively subject to accidents or else that drivers who have been to Youngsville are." The traffic count continued to increase in Liberty through the 20's until by 1932 on a given Saturday in August over a 12 hour period (7 a.m. to 7 p.m.), 7,525[4] vehicles passed a given point on Main Street.

One means of conveyence that was rendered obsolete by the increase of motor vehicles was the farmer and his sleigh. Traditionally, in winter, roads had been packed down with snow rollers, but automobiles had different demands. By 1929 Ralph Lindsley[5] threw up his hands after a year of plowing roads and leaving several inches of snow on the road with the hope that this would make

Liberty's famous citizen, Otto Hillig, photographer and trans-Atlantic aeronaut shown here on road just outside White Sulphur Springs, whose landmark White Sulphur Springs House shows, right. Doubtlessly he was returning to his Liberty darkroom to develop pictures shot in the tiny resort community. He was recognized as one of the resort's leading photographers and did considerable illustration work for the "Summer Homes" publication. The unidentified photographer at the unidentified crossing, below, might be Liberty photographer R.B. Whittaker who also did considerable work along the line of the O. and W. between 1888 and 1896. *Courtesy, John Joyner; below, D. Diver Collection, Cornell University*

Locally, Otto Hillig was known by his conspicuous hilltop 'castle' which stands today (1970), gaunt and vandalized, a far cry from this personalized Christmas card view, left. Hillig achieved international fame and put Liberty and Sullivan County on the map when on Friday, June 19, 1931, he flew the Atlantic in the "Liberty," (piloted by Holger Hoiriis, left), with Copenhagen, Denmark their goal, but landed instead at Krefeld, a small town near Dusseldorf, Germany.

A turn-of-the-century Fourth-of-July Automobile Parade featured the venerable old Champlin Avenue Hose Company No. 23's hose cart. Otto was a great champion of such automobile activity, being devoted to the horseless carriage and its inherent "speed." In August, 1907, Otto unintentionally made the social notes of the Liberty *Register* when the paper announced the sale of his automobile: "This will be gratifying news to owners of shade trees, live dogs and shining marks of all kinds. Congratulations will be hardly in order, however, until Otto deposes and says he intends to remain carless." A month later Otto relented and the September 13, 1907, *Register* revealed in a front page story the delivery to 'fearless Otto' of a seven passenger 1907 Haynes.
Courtesy, Ontario Hose Company No. 3

Northbound passenger train, above, crossing the upper Liberty trestle on the approach to the site of the White Bridge Crossing, shown below (abutments, left and right) with a heavy freight drag about to pass under the new bridge. The train, headed by engine 407, was running late due to engine trouble on a cold February 11, 1940. The stiff grade leading to Young's Gap necessitated the inclusion of an in-train pusher, right of distant upper Liberty trestle and a tailend pusher, out of sight in hillside cut. *Both photographs, D. Diver Collection, Cornell University*

The 'Crawford,' engine No. 38, a 4-4-0 built in December, 1871, by the Baldwin Locomotive Works, was the first inspection engine on the O. and W. In this rare photograph, engineer Henry McEway is shown in the cab and George French, brakeman, in the gangway. *D. Diver Collection, Cornell University*

Official inspection engine No. 26 with Bill Leddy, fireman, left, and engineer Jack Harvey, at Middletown in 1893. Known as the "Glass House," it was destroyed by fire on Wednesday, February 9, 1921, when it rounded a curve in a cut at Champlin's switch (near Liberty's upper Buckley Street crossing) and collided with a "pick-up" freight comprised of a locomotive tender and caboose, on the southbound track. Contemporary reports claim the fire started from a stove in the overturned caboose which engineer LeVan and conductor Rockwell had spotted ahead in time to slacken their speed before the impact. Also aboard were three officials; Wells D. McQueen, Supt. of Southern Division, roadmaster Talmadge and maintainence-of-way engineer Heiderthal. All the woodwork was ablaze by the time the fire engines arrived.

the roads passable for sleighs and for trucks and cars as well. Ruts developed to bare asphalt, the remaining ridges of snow froze so hard that the plows could not bridge them, thereby leaving the roads in a condition beneficial to neither sleigh nor car. Superintendent Lindsley summed up "the day of the horse and sleigh during the winter has passed, apparently, and nothing but trouble awaits them today on our modern highways."

This era of "modern highways" was also giving the O. and W. much to think about — particularly one antiquated bridge at the north end of town built in 1901 at a cost of $2,000. Known as the "White Bridge" — a dangerous crossing of the O. and W. approachable by a zig-zag right-angle configuration — it had passed through a less than adequate alignment modification in 1925.[6]

Its inadequacy was dramatized by the death of Mr. and Mrs. Josiah King on September 2, 1931, when their automobile could not negotiate the left angle turn and "the wheel scraped the baseboard [curbing] and the car lurched through the flimsy and rust-eaten pipe railing" to crash top down on the railroad tracks below. A flurry of editorials and public outcry for elimination of the 'death bridge' resulted in some vocal activity by the Public Service Commission in April, 1932, but no corrective measures were taken.

One editorial opined, "Hard times — not only for the railroad, but for the state as well — is probably the chief reason for reluctance in taking this deadly condition out of Route 17."

It remained for Morris Moskoff's failure in August, 1932, to negotiate the curve — removing 20 feet of railing and dropping to the tracks below — to bring the deadly condition sharply into focus. Public opinion demanded action. Through the various resultant hearings, the O. and W. objected to being even partially assessed for a new bridge, pointing out that since the passing of the Grade Crossing Act in 1926 they had eliminated 28 grade crossings at a total estimated cost of $775,514, 50 percent of which had been borne by the railroad. With the White Bridge costs, the line would be forced to go into the red.

In March of 1933 the people of Liberty circulated a petition expressing "friendship of the village for the railroad and a general local feeling that the users of the bridge and not the railroad should pay the cost of reconstructing this death trap." Upstate automobile clubs were also circulating petitions urging the Public Service Commission to act.

A collision between two trucks on the bridge's curved approach in June, 1933, put three in the hospital and an editorial in the paper taking its title

The deserted and infamous O. and W. White Bridge Crossing, west of Liberty, is today marked by rusting pipe railing and meaningless concrete abutments. The newer old Rt. 17 bridge shows in the distance.

from Shaw's *Saint Joan,* "How Long, O Lord, How Long?" Finally, the July 27, 1933, *Register* trumpeted success: "Relocation and reconstruction of the White Bridge ... will be made entirely at the expense of the State Highway Department."

While the O. and W. management was seeking to get the State of New York to pull its chestnuts out of the fire it was also plunging ahead with a new freight handling system in Liberty for the entire territory between Mountaindale and Hancock. The plan called for the shipping to Liberty of all freight in less than carload lots (LCL) directed to stations between Mountaindale and Hancock. From Liberty, the freight was to be trucked to its destination by Killian's Transfer.

The arrangement,[7] which became effective May 3, 1932, proved to be a most successful venture under the direction of Ralph E. Wright. By the morning of May 5 there were 14 carloads of freight disgorging about 70 tons of L.C.L. into the 10 trucks of the Killian Agency. The only resistance to the service came from Monticello merchants who first were inclined to oppose the operation but soon decided to give it a fair trial. Its success in Monticello, as elsewhere along the line, brought about its expansion in January, 1933, to include freight destined for Kingston, Middletown and Port Jervis.

The mighty O. and W. was paying homage to the economical efficiencies of trucks as a media of transportation and no doubt many in the managerial heirarchy saw only too well the handwriting on the wall.

This R.B. Whittaker classic from the John Joyner collection shows springs-owner Benjamin Willey, in the top hat, tippling, no doubt, a glass of the mineral water, while surrounded by guests from one of the many nearby farm-boardinghouses.

White Sulphur Springs

Robertsonville

Had the Liberty-Jeffersonville Trolley line been built, White Sulphur Springs would surely have been an important stop on the line.

It was originally known as Robertsonville,[1] until the craze for new names came along as a lure to summer boarders. In 1870 the place boasted a store, hotel and post office and was the center of a thrifty farming community. George W. Robertson operated the hotel which was the center of community life.

In December, 1891, the Rev. Jesse Schafer of Newburgh chanced to visit White Sulphur Springs and left a few random notes. "A wagon ride of five miles to the west in mud and mire through a most romantic country, and over hill and dale, on Friday morning, brought me to Robertsonville — now named White Sulphur Springs.

"This is a little hamlet, situated in a lovely valley and consisting of a Post Office, two stores, a Methodist Church, several farm houses (which entertain summer-boarders) and a new and capacious boardinghouse, owned by a Mr. Ernhout of Liberty (White Sulphur Springs House), which will suitably accommodate 150 guests. Nearby is a sulphur spring of wonderful medicinal and remedial properties, which is becoming renowned."

"Summer Homes" proclaimed that the odorous water "is used with the most gratifying results for all kidney diseases, dyspepsia and impure blood, and will cure all skin diseases and nervous debility, loss of appetite and torpid liver. Also will give great relief in all cases of rheumatism, dropsy, scrofula and chronic diseases."[2]

In the 1885 "Summer Homes"[3] the mineral springs were noted as the property of Mr. Benjamin Willey and it wasn't until 1889 that the White Sulphur Springs House was erected with 244 feet of wide verandas to fully exploit the springs.

The hotel immediately became one of the most popular resorts in Sullivan County. 1900 publicity described the grounds — "A boardwalk has been laid from the house to the springs, along which may be found many a cozy nook, rustic benches, etc. Within a few feet from the spring is a beautiful fall of water, a small trout lake, summer houses, rustic bridges, maple grove, apple orchard, bowling alley, lawn tennis and croquet grounds."

In 1914 White Sulphur Springs was struggling to

The main street in White Sulphur Springs showing Hanofee's Garage, left, and the Lawrence House in distance. Looking toward Liberty, right, showing the White Sulphur Springs House in distance and the Methodist Church, left. *Top, courtesy, John Joyner; right, photograph by Otto Hillig*

The Leona Hotel (Fischer), was demolished in 1964, virtually the last of a list of resorts that included the Lesser Lodge, Eagle's Nest, Victoria and others. *Courtesy, Steingart Associates*

The original Lawrence House, above, owned by Brunso Robertson, burned and was replaced by the four-story structure, below. The landmark hotel subsequently was abandoned with the wrecker's bar performing the *coup de grace* in 1964. *Both photographs, courtesy, John Joyner*

WHITE SULPHUR SPRINGS 263

Henry Ernhout's famed White Sulphur Springs House was the pride of the community. Much of its popularity hinged on its proximity to the equally famous "springs." It has since fallen on hard times, right, and stands as a haunting reminder of the golden years when the springs was a mecca for health seekers. *Top, courtesy, John Joyner*

John Joyner, Postmaster at White Sulphur Springs, prizes this hand-written menu, in use when the 'house' was under the proprietorship of Ada Maffett. The main reception hall, below, as photographed by Otto Hillig. *Lower, courtesy, John Joyner*

WHITE SULPHUR SPRINGS HOUSE
MRS. ADA MAFFETT, Proprietor

...Menu...

Thursday August 26-1909
Breakfast
Bananas   Fruit   Stewed Prunes
Cereal
Cream of Wheat   Egg O'See
Broiled
Sirloin and Tenderloin Steak
Fried
Ham and Eggs
Potatoes
Hashed Brown
Ribbed   Ham and   Fried
Poached on Toast
Omelette plain or with onion
Bread
Hot Rolls
Dry & Buttered Toast
Coffee   Tea   Cocoa   Milk

The boardwalk constructed through the woods connecting the White Sulphur Springs House to the springs. The springs glen, left, above the original bath house (later burned), was crisscrossed by rustic bridges. The two-story section laundry was used for drying towels. *Left, photograph by Otto Hillig, courtesy, John Joyner; above, courtesy, John Joyner*

The 1900 issue of "Summer Homes" featured this nostalgic view of summer visitors "taking the waters." A feature story in the September 4, 1914, Liberty *Register* headlined "2016 DIPPED IN THE SULPHUR WATERS." It went on to note "...this is the largest number thus far in the season of any previous year in the history of the springs."

The shady and cool glen just below the springs proper in 1876, below. Today the same location is violated by piles of lumber and junk. By close comparison the same rock configurations may be noted. Impedimenta in the stream below has considerably raised the stream level today, lessening the drop of the falls as shown in the above view.

have electricity run into its resort houses and community — summer boarders had been complaining for quite some time.

It was reported that "bolder boarders who feared not the darkness and nightly traveled the walk to the springs, they too have suffered from the lack of light. White Sulphur is the home of mischievous youth, who, glowing with the expectation of hearing a heavy body hit hard earth, frequently stretched wires and ropes across the forest-boarded path just high enough to trip the victims feet."

In 1906 there were just five other resorts besides the White Sulphur Springs House listed in "Summer Homes," with 1915 recording a near record of nine establishments. By 1930 only three saw fit to advertise. One of the three was the Hotel Leona, a hotel of considerable stature at the "Springs."

Disaster struck the "Springs" in May, 1921, when during the early morning hours flames consumed the large garage of Martin Hanofee and eleven automobiles. Before the J.C. Young volunteers from Liberty could get there, the fire had spread to the J. Heifech Hardware store (just opened) and a large dance hall. The garage and dance hall, nearing completion for the summer season, were badly needed in the village for the convenience and amusement of summer guests.

The Jeffersonville House, under the proprietorship of Augustus Grouten, boasted the usual barroom and dance hall. Grouten also built the first hotel at nearby Kenoza Lake (Pike Pond). *Sullivan County Museum Archives*

Jeffersonville

Jeffersonville took a giant step forward in the first week of August, 1887, when it was linked to Liberty by telegraph. "The line is not only a great benefit to the O. and W. and the people along the new telegraph line, but it is a necessity as well." On September 7 the Walnut Mountain House tied into this line. The 'drummers' hotels in Jeffersonville were no doubt among the principal business places to benefit from the line.

The first commercial hotel in "Jeff" to open its doors to the summer city guest was the Beck in 1882. The house "contained 45 well-lighted, airy sleeping rooms, with high ceilings and large, well-ventilated halls."[1] The Beck's stage met trains daily (except Sunday) at the O. and W. Liberty depot from 12:00 to 2:00 p.m.

Unfortunately, John Beck had only five years more to operate his hotel. By December 21, 1912, the Beck had accommodations for between 150 to 200 guests, but fortunately was empty that cold night when Mr. Beck placed an oil lamp in the bathroom on the second floor to keep the water from freezing in the pipes. It is believed the oil lamp exploded; but, in any event, Mr. Beck had just enough time to arouse his sister-in-law, Miss Christine Ruppert, and make an escape from the second floor. Two hose carts were brought to bear, but it wasn't until the water pumps in Bollenbachs' grist mill were set in motion that the pressure increased enough to save adjoining buildings.

The old Jeffersonville House had many colorful proprietors, including Charles Stanton, whom the late Historian, Charles S. Hick, recalled as being a horse lover, and in those days that always meant race horses. "He kept some in his stable and to them he devoted all the care and attention he was able. He took one of his favorites into the barroom to clip the hair from it. A drummer came to the hotel to get a room, opened the barroom door to face a horse and walked back out believing he had made a mistake and gone into the stable."

Barrooms must have done quite well, particularly in 1897 and '98 when a spot check of bills as furnished by the hotels and saloons in town revealed that in a village of five hundred souls, 3,000 kegs of beer a year were consumed.

A fire in the Eagle Hotel was the reason for the demise of a large portion of the business community in the early morning hours of May 10, 1918. It started around the pantry or kitchen of

The spectacularly situated Walnut Mountain House, located just outside Liberty on the road to Jeffersonville, could boast one of the first hotel telegraphic connections to the outside world. W.B. Holmes of Ellenville purchased the mountain (elev. 2100') in 1886 and commenced construction in September of that year. The Holmes family moved in in May, 1887, and commenced taking summer guests. Within a week over 40 guests, mostly from New York and Brooklyn, had engaged rooms for the summer.

The Eagle Hotel on a gala day long gone, when it promoted its interest in hosting automobile parties, note banner, to a disinterested crowd of coaching day parade fans doubtlessly wondering when the parade will start.

The main street in Jeffersonville showing the Eagle Hotel, left in photo above and below. It was the first structure to disappear in the 1918 fire; its owner, Thomas J. Conlin, later went on to the Jeffersonville House as cafe operator. Many of the buildings on the left side of the street, above, vanished during that wild night. *Top, courtesy, John Joyner*

Nearby Youngsville and its meat market apparently provisioned the Jeffersonville House as revealed in this rare photograph from the collection of the late Nellie White.

Jeffersonville had its own brewery in 1873 which reflected the concentration of early settlers of German extraction in and around the community.

the hotel and spread so rapidly that it was only "through the dexterity of the local firemen in running a ladder up to a window" that the hotel bar tender, George Metzger, was rescued from his third floor window. In quick succession the fire spread to the Goubelman Building on the south and then to the Lichtig Building. On the north, Eddie Homer's cafe and residence went up along with Beck's Department Store. Becker's large drug store, with an immense stock of goods, and its steel sheeted walls stopped the flames but not before the store was gutted. To the rear of the hotel the fire spread to the garage and machine shop of Holmes and Martin, destroying six automobiles.

Sam Shapiro, operator of the New York Store was so convinced his place would go that he pressed a couple of trucks into service and began moving his clothing, shoes, etc. up the street and dumped it off at Mrs. Brand's barn. Alas, his store did not burn but when he moved his goods back he found he was shy fourteen or fifteen suits of clothing, a bundle of women's dresses and a lot of shoes and other articles.

Historian Hick recalled George Beiling's quest for a name for his boardinghouse near Youngsville.

The Jeffersonville Coronet Band arrayed in front of the Mansion House, a Jeffersonville landmark, under the proprietorship of J.D. Sherwood when it advertised in the 1873 Sullivan County Gazetteer and Business Directory, below. *Courtesy, Nellie White*

The hamlet of Kenoza Lake (3½ miles from Jeffersonville) showing the Kenoza Lake Hotel, right, and the historic, cupola-topped Fern Hotel, center. On February 19, 1890, the United States Post Office Department notified Pike Pond Postmaster Blake G. Wales of approval of the name change to Kenoza Lake. It became official on April 29, 1890. The name change came about when one of the first summer boarders at Pike Pond came to Postmaster Wales (Wales being a fan of the poet Whittier) and suggested a change in name. Wales already having a fancy for Kenoza from Whittier's poem, "Kenoza Lake," set the bureaucratic wheels in motion. The area to the left later became the location of Feinberg's Edgemere Casino and boardinghouse. *Courtesy, John Joyner*

The Montana Cottage was typical of the summer accommodations around Kenoza Lake during the era of the Ontario and Western. *Courtesy, Kenoza Lake Store*

The Kenoza Lake Hotel gaily decorated for festivities that suggest a wedding party, replete with an abbreviated brass band. The first hotel at the lake (Pike Pond Hotel) was built before 1872 by Augustus Grouten and when the above photo was taken it was under the brief joint proprietorship of Philip Behrman and George DeLap in 1906. In November 1923, a fire leveled the structure in about an hour, consuming everything except a cigar case and cash register, saved from the barroom. The nearby Jeffersonville Fire Department is credited with saving the little village from possible extinction.

"Since he had three apple orchards on his farm, someone suggested Orchard Grove House." Mr. Hick remembered they often had "eighty to a hundred boarders, and where so many could be accommodated seemed a mystery. The orchard was filled with hammocks. There was no such thing like a power washing machine — wash tubs and wash boards were in abundance. Many of the families did their own washing in a building back of the boardinghouse or under the shade of the orchard tree."

In June, 1910, William J. Harding, when writing a letter, noted the activity of preparation and anticipation of the summer boarding season.

"The vanguard of our summer visitants has begun to put in an appearance. The housewife washes her windows, airs her rooms, cleans her cellar and scrapes the rubbish from the corners. Pater familias rakes the front yard, carries the settee to the porch, puts a screen before the closet and surveys the improvement with a smirk of satisfaction. The man who looks to making money by 'riding the boarders' washes his wagons, greases his harness and carefully scans his last summer suit to see if it will do another season."[2]

Numberless seasons passed for the oldest and seemingly the most durable hotel in Jeffersonville, the Mansion House, which started out in the early 1840's as the private residence of Sidney Tuttle. Later, Granville Porter added to it and gave it its familiar name. Through its many proprietorships, one of the longest and most respected was that of Mr. and Mrs. William Knell, who maintained the venerable old structure for over forty years. Mrs. Knell died in 1943 and the hotel closed, to be purchased by the Karadontes family of Jeffersonville the following year.

The front desk was finally closed by the wrecker's bar in 1966.

Regatta Day at White Lake, on August 5, 1898, found the "sheet of water" alive with craft of all kinds and the double-porched lakefront facade of Grey's Casino swarming with a crowd that seemingly threatens the imminent collapse of the structure.

White Lake

Hotel Arlington burned to the ground, August 19, 1905 at 2:30 a.m., 150 guests, no injuries.

As an increasing number of resorts opened at White Lake, the need for a new road to the lake, preferably from Liberty, was all the more pressing. Heretofore, the only way to reach White Lake had been by way of Port Jervis, and a stage ride of eight miles from Monticello, necessitating a change of cars at the first stop and a tedious and less than smooth ride from the latter place.

On June 9, 1882, it was announced in the local press that a new road between Stevensville and White Lake will be commenced "as soon as planting is out of the way." Barely a year later, handbills were distributed, asking: "What has become of that favorable public improvement — a new road between Liberty and White Lake?"

Construction was started and in March, 1886, at a meeting of the Liberty and White Lake Turnpike Road Company[1] held at Stevensville (Swan Lake), announcement was made that the Turnpike Company headquarters would henceforth be the office of George H. Carpenter in Liberty.

Construction on the 'pike' proceeded satisfactorily with June 1, 1886, set as the target date for completion. Finally, on Friday, June 25, a special excursion of park drags, three and four seaters and just plain wagons made the official formal opening tour from Liberty to the Prospect House at White Lake for a sumptious banquet of green turtle soup, turkey, sirloin of beef and lamb.

By July, accounts of rides over the turnpike were appearing in all of the area papers. One reported the erroneously named Tally-Ho as presenting a "very lively appearance. On each of the four fine horses before the coach is attached a string of bells, a pair of boots and 'tassels on their boots.' This together with the coaches buggler (sic) and the crack of Gus' marvelous whip makes harmony not altogether displeasing to the ear."

Bethel was soon clamoring for a mail route over the line of the stage — a copy of the *Register,* for example, took three days to reach the community. Whether or not papers and express were expedited,

WHITE LAKE TALLY-HO.

The White Lake Tally-Ho as illustrated in the 1887 "Summer Homes." Some readers commented on the circuitous route followed which took it past the Hudson Highlands and Hudson River sidewheelers, background. The following year the steamboat was deleted from the art; the river and mountains remained. Still finding it hard to justify the mountain and a river of such proportions on the way to White Lake, the management eventually deleted the controversial details in later issues.

the route did become a popular byway for 'straw rides.'

"The carry-everybody wagon, liberally upholstered with straw, with a be-belled four-in-hand, started from the residence of Mrs. E. Carpenter as the mellow gloaming waned into foolish moonlight. How eighteen persons could manipulate the space of a No. 12 wagon so that the occupants were only one deep was a serious mystery until one of the ladies discovered that Mr. Conklin was suffering his feet to 'hang off.' "[2]

Up until 1889 most of the houses at White Lake maintained their own stages to pick up guests at the Liberty depot. In March, '89, an agreement was signed by nearly all those engaged in White Lake enterprise giving the stage proprietor, Charles Stanton, exclusive control of all passenger traffic between the two points; the one exception being unless specifically requested by a guest.

By 1892, however, the Van Wert brothers[3] had put in a daily line of stages between the two points. In the fall of 1893, word was around that the O. and W. was thinking about building an electric road from Liberty to White Lake. "Positive word" came from White Lake a bit later that "surveyors will in a few days commence locating the route."

'White Lakers' had had a taste of 'rail fever' on October 24, 1892, when a number of gentlemen from White Lake and Mongaup Valley met at the Lakeside House to perfect the organization of committees in the interest of the White Lake Railway Co.[4]

The company was to extend from Monticello to White Lake and eventually Jeffersonville. The bonds were to be guaranteed by the Philadelphia and New England R.R. Co. which would operate the line as an extension of the Monticello branch.

As with most Sullivan County trolley projects with endless gaps in their progress reports, so too was the case with the Liberty-White Lake line. It wasn't until March, 1896, that the trolley line was again in the news, this time with a line from Liberty to Stevensville being proposed. The power of Stevensville Lake with another power house on line would energize the overhead trolley wire system.

The attitude of the people at White Lake was spelled out in a letter-to-the-editor in April, 1897, when a 'White Laker' fumed "that the people in this neighborhood will not put up one cent for railroads. The people have been fooled so much that in the building of railroads they won't have anything to do with anything pertaining to railroads."

And that was that until February 18, 1898, when the following squib appeared in the papers, "now that the trolley line from Liberty to Jeffersonville is well along – why not have one to White Lake?"

Hope bloomed eternal in Sullivan County – particularly when it came to trolley lines.

When the New York and Oswego Midland brought out its first issue of "Summer Homes on the Midland" (1878) it made no reference whatsoever to White Lake. By 1881, the lake was adequately listed: twelve resorts were noted for an area that "for half a century has been a favorite resort for sportsmen, invalids, pleasure-seekers and clergymen."5

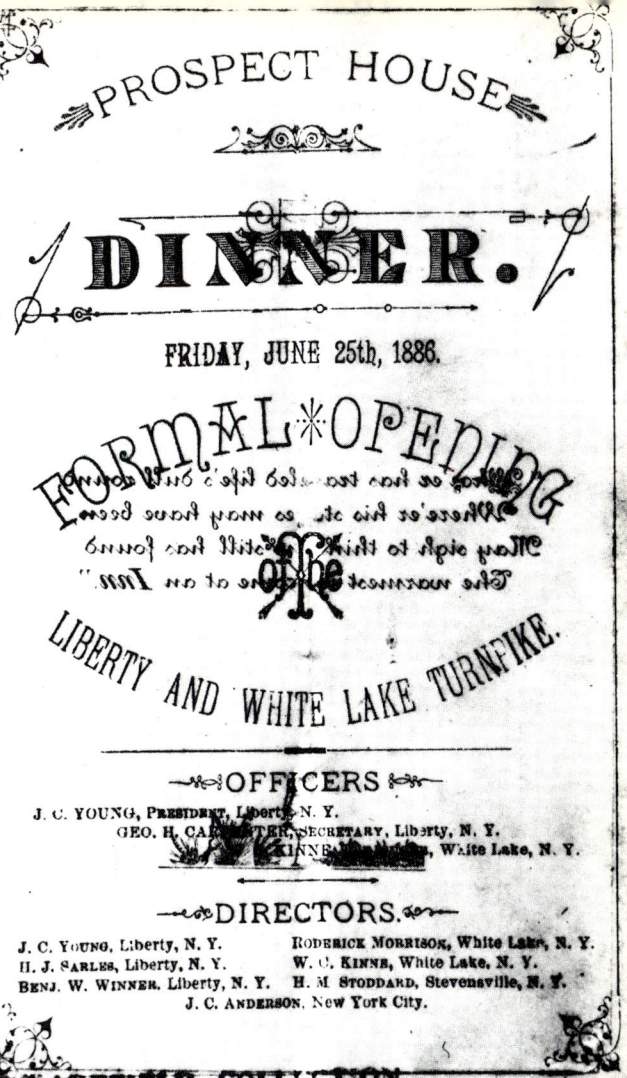

The special program and menu printed to celebrate the formal opening of the Liberty and White Lake Turnpike. The sumptuous repast was served at W. Chester Kinne's Prospect House, below.

WHITE LAKE 279

1899

PROPOSED SCHEDULE OF

SUMMER STAGE LINES

BETWEEN

New York, Lake Kiamesha,

White Lake and Stevensville

CONNECTING WITH

New York, Ontario & Western R'y.

W. M. TIEL,
Traveling Agent,
Middletown N. Y.

J. R. DUNBAR,
Gen'l East. Agent,
371 Broadway, New York.

J. C. ANDERSON, Gen'l Pass. Agent.

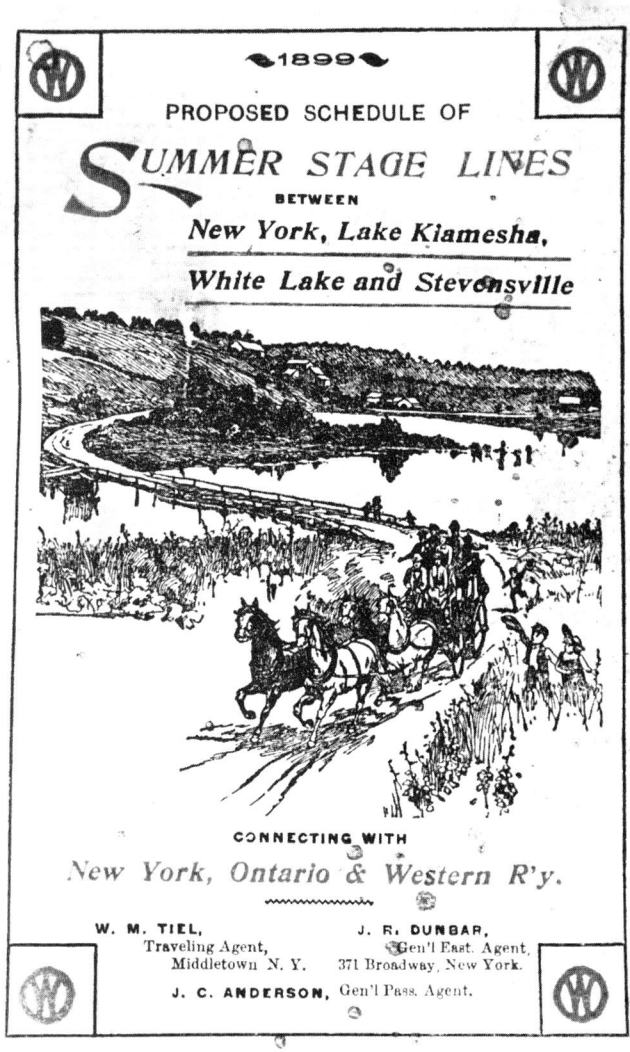

The importance of the stage line to Stevensville and White Lake was pointed up by this specially issued timetable in 1899. *Courtesy, Robert Rosch*

A classic view of the White Lake stage just before departure for Liberty. Trunks were carried on the bracket at the rear of the rig, left.

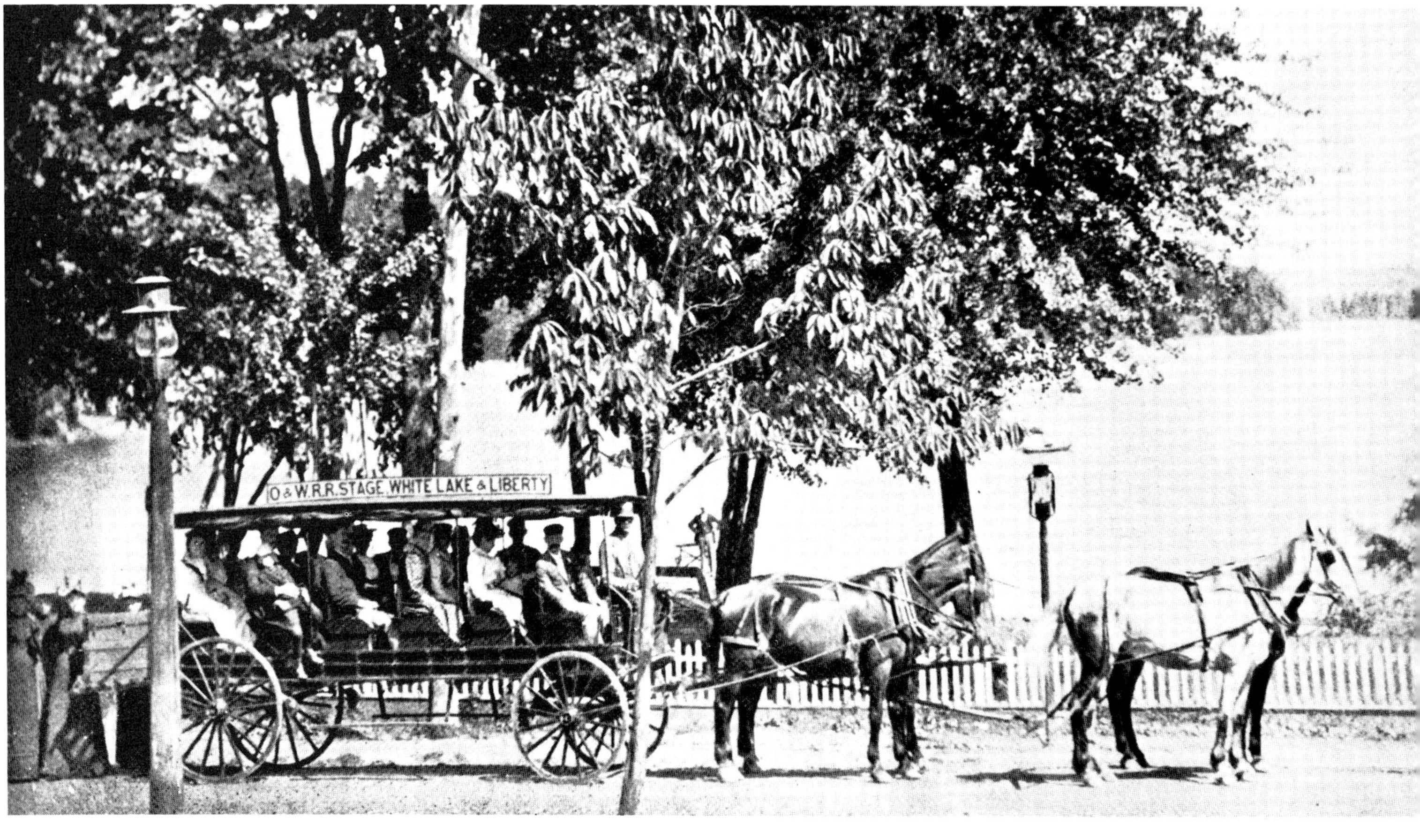

White Lake derived its name because of the clarity of its water and the many areas of white sand which are clearly visible in this aerial view of the lake. Always an enjoyable part of a visit to the lake was a ride on the "Queen" shown, right, at Lewis' Grove landing. The launch commenced its run at Grey's Casino and would pick up vacationers at the various docks, which on the west shore were exceedingly long due to the shallow water. Rt. 17-B stretches across the bottom third of the picture. The former Liberty and White Lake Turnpike terminates at Rt. 17-B, right side, and runs in a diagonal jog out of the picture, top center. The housing development, upper left corner, just above Amber Lake, was the location of the West Shore House. *Courtesy, Sullivan County Tax Map Department*

One of White Lake's recreational qualities was dramatized by an event in 1843 when Lewis Piatt caught a trout that weighed eight pounds and fourteen ounces. A sketch of the fish was drawn on a board at the old Lake House and ceremoniously hung over the door. In the same year, James B. Finlay employed an Indian to take black bass from Lake George and introduce them to the crystal clear waters of White Lake.

In 1845 Finlay built the first hotel for summer boarders.[6] The business did not pay until the 'grande dame' of White Lake, the Mansion House was built by D.B. Kinne. Grove Hotel was erected in 1866 and two years later the Sunny Glade Boarding House was constructed by Capt. William Waddell.

In 1885 the Prospect House was opened by W.C. Kinne. One of its first official functions was the banquet marking the opening of the Liberty and White Lake Turnpike. The broad verandas, the large parlors, the ample halls and the large and well-lighted dining room all contributed to the daily pleasure of guests.

The beautiful scenery was keenly appreciated by the noted artist A.F. Bunner, a member of the American Academy of Art, for whom Kinne built a large studio on the grounds for the artist's summer use.

It was a time when special writers from New York dailies, like the Brooklyn *Standard Union* in 1892, descended on the region to describe the scenery: "sloping farms, framed in groves of natural beauty, up to the very summit of Mount Sherwood, as it looms up into the serene heavens" or the "smoky range of the Shawangunks is lost in the glades and forests of the mysterious Neversink." One wonders if the good people of Liberty appreciated the literary flavor of "to the northward, Walnut Mountain stands out like a wart on the face of nature."

But for all the romanticism, (if warts can be called romantic), hotels blossomed around the lake in great profusion almost overnight. Facing the lake from a high rise of ground was the Laurel House. The Van Wert House kept by F.B. Van Wert "is so situated that a clear view is obtained of the country for miles in any direction." At the intersection of the turnpikes from Liberty and Monticello is W. Van Wert's Willard House from which "a clear, cross-cut view of the lake at the south end is obtained." The Hoffman House was located on the north shore "in such a position as to afford clear and attractive views of the lake to its most southerly point." Sherman Ramsay's Ramsay House was located at the north end of the lake where "the breezes are strong and pure and never unpleasant." J.E. Gray's White Lake Spring House — "scenery is picturesque and has afforded many subjects for the canvas of artists." "On a rise of ground" was located the Lake View Cottage (one of a thousand resorts so geographically located and identified), operated by William Sturgis.

And so the feature story in the Brooklyn *Standard Union* went on, summing up the full page story with the highly successful operation of John J. Van Orden and his West Shore House.

John J. Van Orden and his wife (Ida Van Vactor), met at the Mansion House where they were employed. In 1882 they purchased the 40-acre tract where the West Shore House was located (now the site of the White Lake Homes) from John's older brother, Charles, who had purchased the property in 1867 from Roderick and Sara Morrison.

During their tenure, Ida Van Orden did all the business and correspondence, and daughter Lila rode bareback down to the Post Office with the mail each night. They were alert to taking advantage of advertising their accommodations for 40 guests in the "Summer Homes" publication. In

The Mansion House, one of the pioneer hotels at White Lake, still stands (1970) (however virtually unnoticed, due to an obscuring stand of evergreens.)

The West Shore House shown in its second stage of development. The original farmhouse, to the left of the above structure, virtually lost its identity when the third expansion took place between 1905 and 1907. During the horse and buggy era, the house had its own hand-lettered depot rig, below, right.   *Courtesy, Muriel VanOrden*

Shakespearean actor Frederick Warde was furnished with a log cabin retreat, "Wardesden," by the management of the West Shore House.

WHITE LAKE   283

The Kensington, of plain frame exterior treatment, never made the transition into the stucco era as did the Fulton Hotel, insert below. In the 1920's the Fulton emerged with a new stucco exterior, interior renovations and a new name – The New Empire Hotel. *Lower photograph, courtesy, Steingart Associates*

The Kenmore, replete with seemingly endless porches, balconies and a commanding tower, unhappily burned to the ground in 1947.

Typical of a decorated craft at White Lake during Regatta Days is this Lake Huntington extravaganza, festooned with Japanese lanterns for afterdark "strutting."

The Sylvan Grove House at North White Lake, hard by the Liberty-White Lake Turnpike, below, has changed but little since the turn-of-the-century photo, above. *Photograph, below, L. Jack Agnew*

The usual summer vacation group portrait — a looked-forward-to souvenir for the long winter months. This 1890 posing at the West Shore House is typical. *Courtesy, Muriel VanOrden*

1889 guests seemed to have ambition, their copy noting "charming walks and drives." By 1891 things were slowing down a bit with "abundance of shade in adjoining grove, provided with seats, swings and hammocks; piazza around the house." The "activities" must have been agreeable since accommodations rose to 75 by 1896 and to 90 in 1910.

One of the first guests at their original West Shore House was Frederick Warde, famous Shakespearean actor who made his debut in England in 1867. When carriages met O. and W. trains at Liberty, one wagon went along just for Warde's baggage — the thespian generally arriving with 10 to 15 pieces of luggage. Warde had an old log cabin (called "Wardesden") he used as a study near a lily pond on the shore of the lake.[7]

In 1919 the Van Ordens sold the West Shore House to Swartz and White, during whose management the house became a favorite of vaudeville stars Paul Whitman, Russ Columbo and Joe E. Brown.

The operation went through two other ownerships before the fateful February morning in 1957 when a passerby noticed the windows lit up by flames. A quick alarm brought out the Kauneonga Lake, Mongaup Valley and Smallwood forces, but not before the fire had ruined the entire top floor of the two and one half story building. The ruins were eventually torn down to make way for a housing development.

Somehow or other things had been different at White Lake for quite some time before Joe E. Brown showed up for a stay. It wasn't like it was at the turn of the century. By 1887 there were so many people and resorts that a magazine — the White Lake *Season,* edited and published by W.S. Barstow and printed at the Liberty *Register* office, found a ready market.[8]

Nearly every day during those busy days there were ball games, foot races, tub races, and sack races; but perhaps the events that were looked forward to with the most anticipation and brought "the lake" the greatest amount of publicity were the boat parades and regattas.

The season was running long when in October, 1886, the annual illuminated boat parade was observed and regarded as "superior to all of the praise given heretofore."

Optimism ran high in the early 1880's. "White Lake, with a little more enterprise capital, would soon be the leading summer resort of the state." By October, 1886, "White Lakers" were sounding a bit like Liberty boosters a few years hence, when the lament was heard "...if parties could erect a house that would accommodate 500 guests, we feel confident in saying that it would easily be filled."[9]

Alas, White Lake was destined to remain a resort of small hotels, and boarding houses.

The big one was never built.

In 1896 the management of the New York, Ontario and Western featured the above photograph in that year's issue of "Summer Homes" under the caption, "Going to the Post Office." The event proved of such consequence that the Liberty *Register* on April 24, 1896, noted in a front page release that "our old friend William DuBois and party of Stevensville," were currently appearing in "Summer Homes."

Swan Lake

Stevensville

In 1886 there were six resorts listed in "Summer Homes" for Stevensville (detrain at Liberty Falls). In 1890 pressure from Charles Stanton, the stage operator on the Liberty and White Lake Turnpike, caused Stevensville to be dual listed under Liberty as well. There were 13 establishments listed for that year, six accessible from Liberty Falls and seven from Liberty.

In 1907 Stevensville was a well established and bustling summer spa with resorts like the Crystal Spring House, Halcyon House, Alpine House, Goff's Mountain View House, The Criterion, and the Kilcoin Hotel all clamoring for the summer vacationer.[1]

Stevensville received its name from the Stevens brothers who operated a sole leather tannery at the lake until it burned in 1856. One of the brothers, Daniel T., rebuilt it and continued operations until around 1873. About 1895, Alden S. Swan arrived at the lake and immediately started acquiring reality holdings.[2] By the time of his death (1917) he owned the Swan Lake Mills, Rock Spring Lodge, Horseshoe Lake Farm, Swan's Casino and of course the lake.[3]

One of the big seasonal events of the county occurred at Swan Lake's Norton's Casino when Joe Dealy's vaudeville presentation took to the boards. The annual event started about 1910 and included top-notch bands for dancing as well as exceptional vaudeville. By the 30's Norton's was putting on the Monster Mardi Gras for the guests staying at the now large 'Sullivan County-mission' hotels. On commanding heights overlooking the lake were the Commodore, the Stevensville Lake Hotel and the Swan Lake Hotel.

In June, 1932, the Commodore Hotel caught fire from a short circuit in a porch ceiling. Early discovery of the fire and prompt and effective

An early artist's impression of the Liberty, Stevensville, White Lake stage that appeared in the 1891 and subsequent issues of "Summer Homes." The stage is shown here leaving Stevensville for Liberty, having just passed over the primitive causeway. The hill, left background, later became the location of the President Hotel, with further hotel development taking place on the hill, background and right, out of picture.

The Swan Lake boat livery, left, was the early morning target of fishermen bent on a day's pickerel fishing. Considered in 1907 as one of the best pickerel lakes in New York State, it was "...estimated that from 500 to 1000 pounds of pickerel were taken daily from its waters." A fleet of 100 St. Lawrence skiffs stood ready for those interested in just boating. *Photograph by Otto Hillig*

Gazetteer and Business Directory of Sullivan County, 1872-3

Hunting and fishing proved to be a great attraction to the Stevensville area. Here man and beast and trophies posed for posterity and a "Summer Homes" (1896) photo caption, dubbed, "A Day's Hunt in Sullivan County, 162 Rabbits and 57 Partridges." It would seem after a few seasons of this magnitude the hunter and his dog would soon be looking elsewhere.

The Halcyon — one of the first hotels of consequence at Stevensville. Under the proprietorship of M.F. Keogh in 1907, the hotel advertised in "Summer Homes" that it "commands a magnificent view of the surrounding country in every direction of from twenty to thirty miles."

Two landmark hotels at Swan Lake – the Stevensville Lake Hotel and the Swan Lake Hotel. Progress was the downfall of the Swan Lake Hotel, below, when it caught fire during the installation of an elevator. *Both photographs, courtesy, Steingart Associates*

The President Hotel — on the heights overlooking the dam and nearby boat livery. Part of the community of Swan Lake shows in the background. *Courtesy, Steingart Associates*

NORTON'S CASINO
SWAN LAKE, N.Y.

2 BIG NIGHTS

| Sat. Eve. | Sun. Eve. |
| September 5th | September 6th |

JOE DEALY'S MONSTER
MARDI GRAS

Sensational Attractions
Expensive Prizes

DANCING WITH
Ticker Freeman's Californians

No money will be spared on these two nights to hold the best dances I have ever given in this County.—JOE DEALY.

SOMETHING DOING EVERY MINUTE

Norton's Casino, Swan Lake, September 5th and 6th

Watch for Opening Date of
JOE DEALY'S VAUDEVILLE
At Liberty Theatre, Liberty, N. Y.
It will be a Knockout Show
Opening Date to be Announced very Soon

A typical Norton's Casino advertisement that appeared in the July 3, 1931, Liberty *Register*.

work by the Swan Lake and Liberty firemen saved the hotel from destruction as 125 guests stood around with their personal baggage piled about them.

The Swan Lake Hotel was not so lucky. This hotel, built by Henry W. Siegel, was in the process of having an elevator installed in 1954 when a fire broke out on the first floor and quickly roared up the open elevator shaft. Because of the enormous draft created by the unenclosed shaft, the hotel was soon a smouldering ruin.

The builder, Henry W. Siegel of Ferndale, along with Jacob Kretchmer of Woodridge had purchased the holdings of the Swan estate in 1921 for about $85,000. The press at the time commented that "Siegel and Kretchmer have purchased a property with great possibilities for development, having a large number of ideal sites for hotels and bungalows..."

Great possibilities the property did indeed have. Siegel went on to build the famed Commodore and Stevensville, thereby leading Swan Lake from the time of the farm-boardinghouse into the era of the big hotel operation.

If one were to try to find one photograph that would best illustrate the leisure and unhurried atmosphere of the Sullivan County resort region during the era of the Ontario and Western, this picture of the W.H.H. Williams (Maple Grove) House near the old covered bridge above Neversink would surely be one of the front runners. This was one of the pioneer boardinghouses in the county, along with the Flagler, having been purchased by Mr. Williams in May, 1881, from a Mr. Herron, who later operated the Herron Cottage.

Neversink

"As one approaches the village from Liberty, he passes along a deep ravine many hundreds of feet, at the bottom of which flows this river, [the Neversink] famed as one of the finest trout streams in the state, with water clear as crystal, stones and even pebbles visible a long distance from the banks."[1]

New York, Ontario and Western passengers bound for this resort sometimes got off at Fallsburgh and took a stage up the Neversink River from Woodbourne or the alternate route over the turnpike from Liberty.

The first resort on the upper Neversink River was the Maple Grove House owned by a Mr. Herron until May, 1881, when W.H.H. Williams bought it and "thoroughly outfitted it for the accommodation of about 100 boarders." In his first full year he had between 40 and 50 summer boarders; by July of '86 he was catering to 100 guests. In the winter, when not "practicing dentistry in his leisure time," Williams was busy talking up a new turnpike to Liberty.

The turnpike talk was temporarily sidetracked by a railroad proposition in 1889 when the Neversink Valley Railroad proposition rose in meteoric optimism only to drop out of sight by the end of the year. The survey was run connecting with the O. and W. at the Centerville bridge (Neversink River trestle) instead of at Fallsburgh because of the improved grade and a free right-of-way.

It was planned that the Neversink depot would be located on the lower end of Johnson's flats where the Riverside House is located. The Liberty *Register* for July 5, 1889, suggested that "there is every indication that the Neversink Valley Railroad will be built."

By December, 1889, the project had run its course. "Since there is little or no prospect of a railroad to Neversink ... it seems to us [that] the Neversink people should shorten the route to the O. and W. by building a good turnpike to Liberty."[2] On April 24, 1890, at an informal meeting of the stock subscribers, the enterprise was officially named the "Neversink and Liberty Turnpike Company"[3] and by August, 1891, the work, under the charge of C.M. Bonnell, was at work in Grant's woods between George Crary's hill and the road running by the John A. Clement's farm.

The little hamlet of Neversink boasted the Neversink Hotel and above, the Edgemere House. The Edgemere, under the proprietorship of Charles E. Freer, was a practitioner of the summer boarder mass-portrait souvenier photograph. Also in the heart of town, the Riverside House, left and below left, (behind the horse and buggy). The main street was dominated by the Milton VanKeuren store, right, later to burn to the ground on May 13, 1904 taking with it the adjacent Cross Brothers store. The intense heat cracked the plate glass windows of Denman's Store, extreme left, as well as the windows of the Riverside House. *Middle photograph, courtesy, Mrs. Benjamin Bertholf; lower photograph, courtesy, Mrs. Bruce Denman, Sr.*

Sky Farm, built and operated by H.J. Spargur, went through a number of expansion periods and survived good times and bad to emerge into the decade of the 70's, right, a ghost of its former elegance. *Photograph, top, by Albert E. Cawood; courtesy, Don Battey*

The progressive little hamlet even had its own brass band, posed here in front of the Methodist Church. *Courtesy, Mrs. Bruce Denman, Sr.*

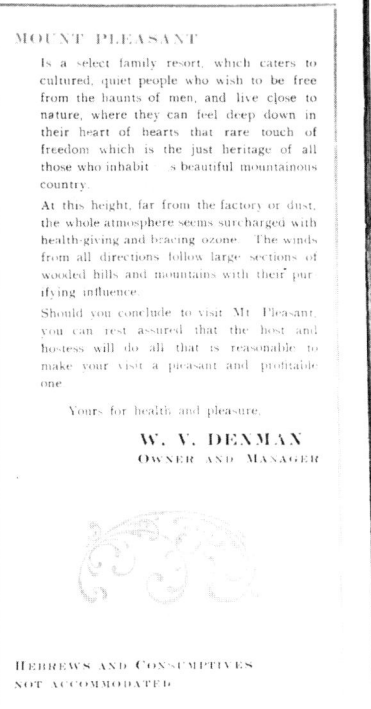

The Mount Pleasant House, operated by W.V. Denman, issued a small descriptive brochure of the resort's facilities, typical of many such pocket-sized promotional pieces issued by the small Sullivan County boardinghouse operators. *Courtesy, Mrs. Bruce Denman, Sr.*

The Herron Cottage at Neversink is a typical example of the out-of-scale size the so-called "cottages" were wont to grow.

At the time the turnpike construction was moving ahead, the Neversink Driving Park at Dan Pierce's track announced a series of horse races for August 18, 1891.[4] The meet, attracting between eight hundred and a thousand race fans, began at 1:00 p.m. A great many of the bettors at the track were Brooklynites and many of these were staying at the Spring Brook House. The resort was famed for its progressive euchre parties which were long remembered by its guests. "The parlor and dining room showed the careful attention of the ladies in the profuse decorations of foliage and wild flowers, while the grounds were brilliantly illuminated with many colored Japanese lanterns. The music for the occasion was furnished by Freer's Neversink Orchestra and during the evening the Scribner brothers furnished an elaborate collation, which was enjoyed by all."[5]

Probably one of the most spectacularly situated houses was that operated by W.V. Denman. The Mount Pleasant House stood on the brow of a hill overlooking the village of Neversink, "fully five hundred feet above the valley."

The view was so awesome it prompted a guest, William J. Hampton, to write a piece for the local papers in which he told of a landscape painter who stood near the broad veranda. Saying nothing, the artist suddenly but reverently removed his hat. Those who saw him asked why he did it. He replied, ' because of the majestic panorama, nature's handiwork spread out before me.''

The scene of Neversink, as viewed from the Mount Pleasant House, above, is now inundated by the impounded waters of the Neversink Reservoir of the New York City Board of Water Supply. The white line on the hill indicates the approximate high water mark of today's reservoir. The steepled Methodist Church may be seen in the center. *Courtesy, Paul Denman*

The Neversink covered bridge, which was once blown down and replaced, eventually burned down in May, 1923, of suspected incendiary origin. *Courtesy, Mrs. Benjamin Bertholf*

It was indeed a time of reverence for the great out-of-doors; even the brochure advertising Mr. Denman's boardinghouse reflected this — "the whole atmosphere seems surcharged with breath-giving and bracing ozone. The winds from all directions follow large sections of wooded hills and mountains with their purifying influences."

In November, 1896, while taking the "ozone," vacationers also had the added attraction of a flood which swept away the large iron bridge spanning the Neversink River directly below the Denman piazza, a number of people having left the bridge barely a moment before it went down.[6] The village in 1903 depended on lumbering in the wintertime for its livelihood. The mill had a shingle factory annex, where large quantities of shingles were turned out for a village consisting of a grist mill, five stores, two blacksmith shops, one church and two or three "temperance hotels."[7]

For all its pious qualities, however, it was a doomed village. Today its abandoned foundations lie hidden under the impounded waters of the Neversink Reservoir of the New York City Board of Water Supply.

Parksville, at the juncture of the Little Beaver Kill; flowing out of the hills, left, combined with the primary drainage stream, right, emanating from Young's Gap, have always been a critical problem for the little community in times of sudden cloudburst and unusually heavy spring thaws. Also under constant threat were the tracks and right-of-way of the Ontario and Western. *Courtesy, John Joyner*

Parksville

When Pete Reilly's paper train slowed going through Young's Gap, a "thoroughbred native" standing at the trackside was handed a paper. He looked at the date, saw it was Sunday and said: "You're the stuff, begosh!" At Parksville the brakeman became so enthusiastic about seeing a Sunday paper he jumped out into the rain and sold twice as many papers as Pete. "He came back to the caboose, wet and proud, with a handful of nickels."

The little resort village where this business transaction took place was one with a varied background.

In 1886 "Summer Homes" listed five resorts[1] – four farmhouses and one village residence for Parksville. It described the community as a "small, pretty village in the heart of the trout country" where guides could "be found near the station, who will, for a small consideration, accompany anglers to the best fishing grounds." This same copy was used through each succeeding issue until 1929 when angling was played down. Parksville was now being hawked as a "delightful region in which one can rest, swim, hike and sleep in peace."

The prettiness and peaceful qualities came under fire in a 1932 editorial that noted "for a car to get through (Parksville) on Route 17 in the summer without hitting half a dozen objects on the road is a miracle," and at a later date, in a press interview with the postmaster, the auto junkyards, deserted stores and buildings came under fire, pointing up the dramatic contrast to the original image sketched by the "Summer Homes" copy. The depression was on.

For all the changes that time and Route 17 made, it remained the center for a number of resort hotels – Grand Hotel, Klein's Hillside, New Brighton, Paramount, Transville, Prospect Inn and the Breezy Hill Hotel.

The crown jewel of the Parksville area is a resort that was first listed in "Summer Homes" in 1923 – the Young's Gap Hotel. The resort story began in

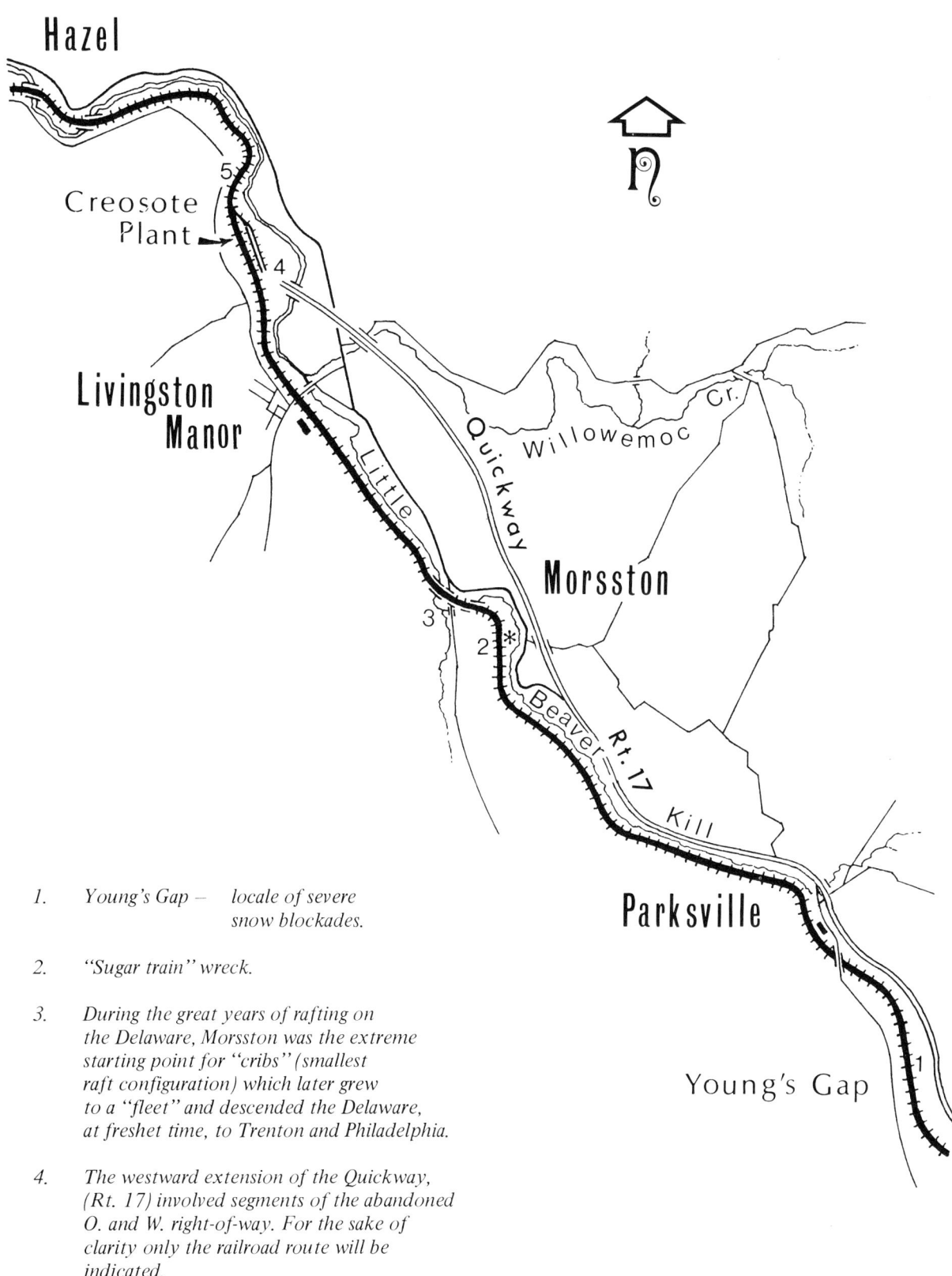

1. Young's Gap — locale of severe snow blockades.

2. "Sugar train" wreck.

3. During the great years of rafting on the Delaware, Morsston was the extreme starting point for "cribs" (smallest raft configuration) which later grew to a "fleet" and descended the Delaware, at freshet time, to Trenton and Philadelphia.

4. The westward extension of the Quickway, (Rt. 17) involved segments of the abandoned O. and W. right-of-way. For the sake of clarity only the railroad route will be indicated.

5. May 29, 1929 Mud slide wreck at Mott's Flats.

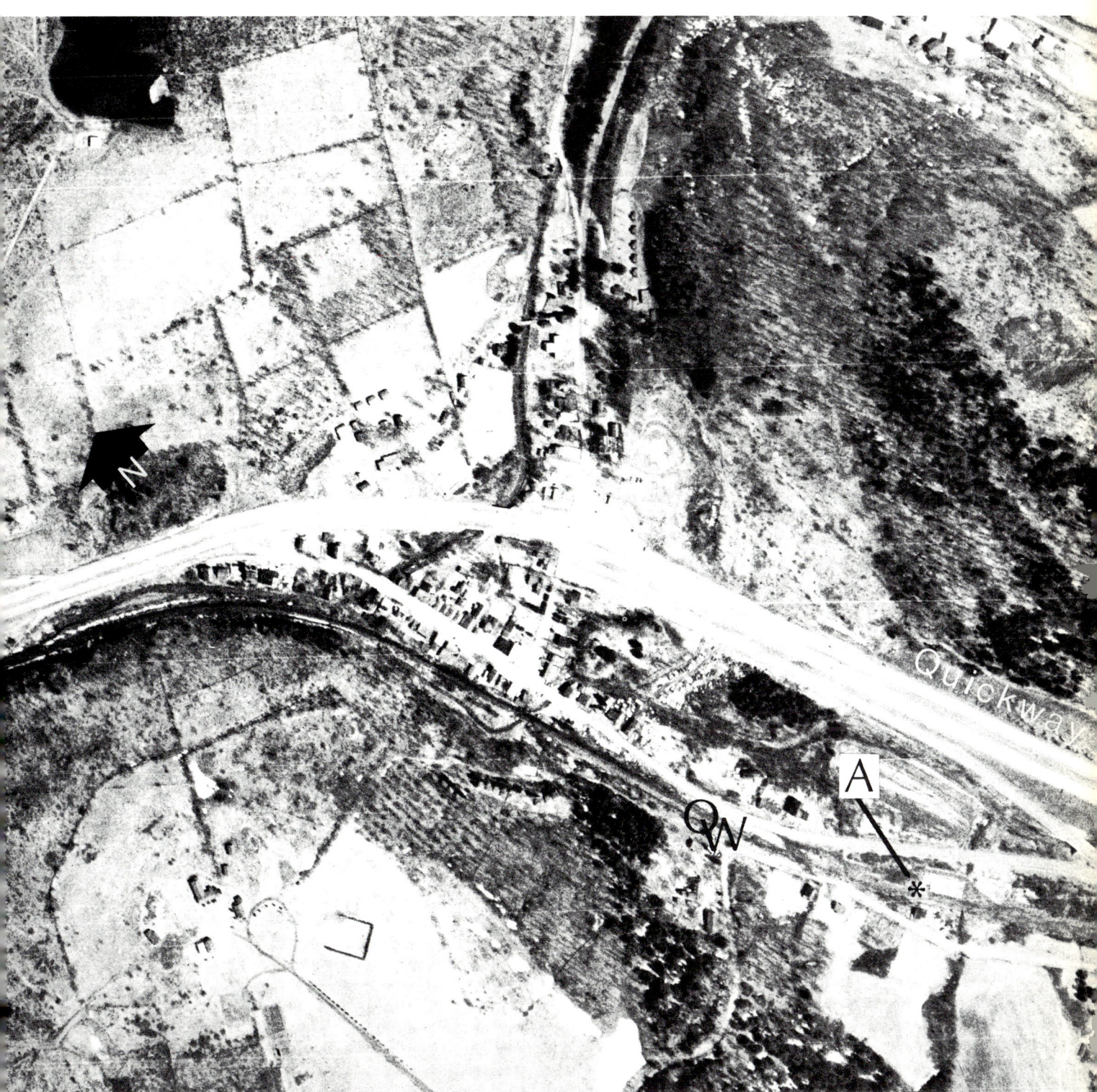

A. *Site of Parksville Depot*

April, 1915, when dynamic partners, Louis Gelberg and Joseph Holder, first came to Liberty and bought a nineteen room home. They found the boardinghouse industry in town restricted and in 1922 moved to Parksville, purchased the property of Mrs. Josephine Armstrong and proved themselves leaders in the industry by being the first in the area to secure electricity from the village of Liberty when other hotels were content with kerosene and candles. They first saw the value of large rolling lawns, of concrete swimming pools, and they were among the first to consider building up a winter business.

By 1928 their new four story main building of light-faced brick featuring a swimming pool, gym, sun parlor, ballroom, tailor shop, barber shop and accommodations for 400 guests was opened – a reaffirmation of the prosperity of the Twenties.

The resort, first in the county to use steel and brick construction as well as first with an elevator, closed its doors during the 1967 summer season.

The "Roaring Twenties" opened with a near record, if not a record, for the O. and W., when in October of 1920 the management reported that a record 297,000 tickets were sold to points in Sullivan County – 25,000 more than in any previous year.[2]

In the early part of the decade (1922-23) business warranted the purchase of ten Mountain type locomotives constructed by the American Locomotive Company which were the line's backbone up until the end. At the same time the O. and W. also ordered 20 new passenger coaches, four combination passenger and baggage cars, three baggage and mail cars and three all steel baggage cars.

On the 4th of July weekend in 1925 many of these new cars were pressed into service to bring in the more than 12,000 vacationers on Friday and used again in the 18 special trains needed to return them to the city.

One alarming note in the local press, insofar as the O. and W. was concerned, was the capacity business done by the bus lines which was twenty percent more than the previous year.[3] The O. and W. was starting to show the erosion of the competition when in February, 1928, the famed "Night Line" of 25 years duration was taken off because of operating losses.

A few months before the debacle in 1929, the local press was trumpeting the installation of swimming pools at many of the hotels and the practice of engaging orchestras and social and athletic directors to make the hours more attractive to the guests. Tennis courts were also the rage with hotels installing them in the front lawn so all could see the added athletic facility.

This mania for over-expansion of the physical plant contributed to the financial difficulties of the early thirties which were characterized by a 600 signature petition presented to Governor Lehman in February, 1933, which sought to "remove penalties for non-payment of taxes and provide for tax payments in installments." Assemblyman Benjamin Gerow accompanied a committee to Albany, selected at a mass meeting at the Flagler Hotel in Fallsburgh attended by more than 1,000 resort operators.[4] Spokesmen at the meeting claimed "ninety percent of the hotels in Sullivan and Ulster were in straits." Much of the financial bind was created by the seasons developing into what the operators termed a "week-end season." They also complained of the high cost of foodstuffs in Sullivan as compared to neighboring counties.

The depression caused resort prices to drop, but, in 1932, even with reduced rates, the industry reported business roughly 33 percent lower than 1931, a summer when a polio epidemic in New York City sent people running to the mountains, if at all able, or at least sending their children to camps.[5] Those who did come were not as carefree and free spending as in earlier years. Hotel keepers reported that in many cases guests haggled over rates. The pinch of the depression also limited the casual spending money. This kept most of the guests at the hotel resulting in a hue and cry from the local merchants.

The business card of a 1920-era boardinghouse operator; this one located in Cooley, a vacation area near Parksville, *Courtesy, Herb Mussman*

The original William Young farm homestead on the site of today's abandoned brick and steel Young's Gap Hotel, right. Mrs. William Young is shown at the left. Later, in 1922 during the ownership of Josephine Armstrong, the property was purchased by Louis Gelberg and Joseph Holder. *Courtesy, William R. Baldwin*

Frank Lindhardt's Hotel Earlington, aside from featuring Ballantine's Export and Lager Beer, listed in the 1907 "Summer Homes," "fine parlor, hot and cold water, baths, pool room, cafe, gas in each room and barber shop." *Photograph by Howard Wood*

The stock market crash in 1929 and its economic implications, plus increasing doubt in the effectiveness of individual advertising in "Summer Homes," resulted in this single-page group Parksville listing, right, in the 1930 issue — sponsored by the Parksville Hotel Men's and Boarding House Association.

HOTELS OF PARKSVILLE

Issued by the Parksville Hotel Men's & Boarding House Assn., Parksville, N. Y.

Name of House	Proprietor	Accommodate	Phone-LIBERTY
"Avigail"	J. Budow	75	662-J
Ambassador Hotel	Levitts Bros.	150	728-R
Breezy Hill House *	L. Pachaneck	200	725-W
Belmont House	I. Finger	180	57
Conklin Hill House	Ph. Tarr	80	Tel. Conn.
Charam Hill House *	M. Charam	100	727-R
Edgewood House	Henry S. Fidell	80	727-J
Fiddle House *	Harry Fiddle	125	726-W
Flamenbaum House	N. Flamenbaum	60	726-M
Fleisher House *	M. Fleisher	125	1093-F-13
The Glory	M. Eisenberg	175	1076
The Grand Hotel *	J. Schmidt	150	262
Highland View House	B. Schwartzman	150	940
Highland House	D. Smith	125	731-R
Hillcrest View House	Fleisher & Schwammer	150	726-R
High View Mountain Hotel *	O. Tanzman & Son	125	Tel. Conn.
High View Hotel *	H. Holdstein	125	727-M
Ideal Summer Resort	B. Tanzman	80	681-W
Klein's Hillside Inn *	L. Klein	225	1185
Lincoln Hotel *	Peltz Bros	150	951-J
Maple View House *	Max Siegel	120	724-W
New Brighton Hotel *	Ben Cohen	100	951-R
New Mountain House *	Guttman & Weiss	150	723
Parksville Mansion *	S. Siegel	60	728-M
Prospect Inn	L. Orseck	125	724-M
The Park Inn	Goldfarb	100	727-W
Perl House			1180-81
Paramount House	Gasthalter Bros.	175	726-J
Overlook Hotel	I. Resnitzky & Sons	120	718-J
Ridge Mountain House	M. Welkowitz	150	696-W
Sunny Brook House	L. Nasofer	100	724-J
Spring Lake Hotel	K. Hurwitz	120	Tel. Conn.
Sunrise Hotel	Friedman & Weinstein	175	111-J
Shady Grove House	A. Novick	75	1061-M
Wallach Farm House *	Max Wallach	175	725-M
White Star House *	Max Budoff	150	1079-M-21
Young's Gap Hotel *	Gelberg & Holder	600	700
Kaufman House	J. Kaufman		
Westin House			

The Jewish Dietary Laws are observed by all on the above list.

* Star next to name denotes open all year.

Operationally speaking, many of the hotelmen were able to force their employees into agreements whereby the latter received compensation in proportion to the amount of business transacted. In some cases employees agreed to work for their maintenance alone.

As a paradox, there were a few rare prosperous operators like Jack Weiss of Perlwyn Lodge who in 1932 reported the best summer business in six years. He credited it to a more extensive advertising campaign, which was exactly what the editorialists had been thumping for for a number of years. "It must be remembered that the business which is now done comes without any extensive or planned sales effort. What tremendous improvements would not an intelligent and sustained advertising campaign produce!"[6]

The O. and W. had been doing this kind of thing through their "Summer Homes" almost from the beginning but summer patronage in August, 1931, was none too good. President Joseph H. Nuelle reported "Busses and private automobiles have made inroads in our passenger traffic, but we have effected economies by operating fewer passenger trains and increasing loading." One month before this utterance the bus companies reported 320 bus loads of passengers with one bus company reporting that it transported 1900 passengers on one given Friday.

In 1932 the road did increase net earnings 64 percent[7] which was due entirely to the increase in the anthracite coal haulage which made up 70.62 percent of total tonnage. But for all the loss in passenger revenue the road did not seek aid in 1932 from the Reconstruction Finance Corporation, but in fact contributed to the local economy by employing 98 men in the raising of track between Parksville and Livingston Manor.[8]

Twenty-one years before, in June, 1911, the project had been initiated at Young's Gap when the railroad eliminated an exceptionally dangerous grade crossing. During construction a guy rope had suddenly snapped about 7:30 p.m. dropping a 90 foot span weighing 10 tons from the forty foot high embankments into the cut. The span settled on the northbound track tying up traffic in both

Y-2 locomotive No. 457 working upgrade from Parksville through a wintery landscape to the Young's Gap drainage divide. *From original oil painting by Manville B. Wakefield*

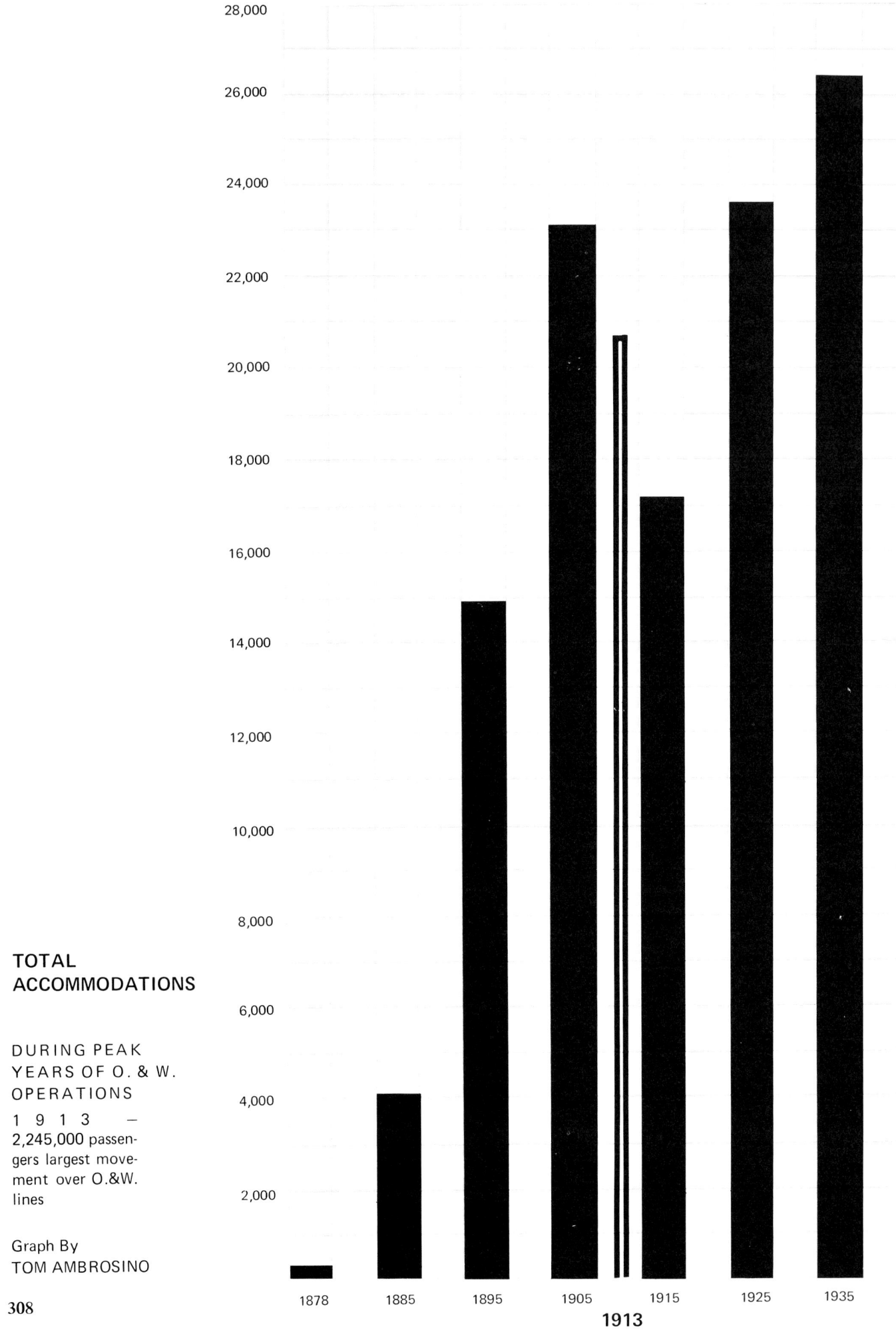

TOTAL ACCOMMODATIONS

DURING PEAK YEARS OF O. & W. OPERATIONS

1 9 1 3 — 2,245,000 passengers largest movement over O.&W. lines

Graph By
TOM AMBROSINO

308

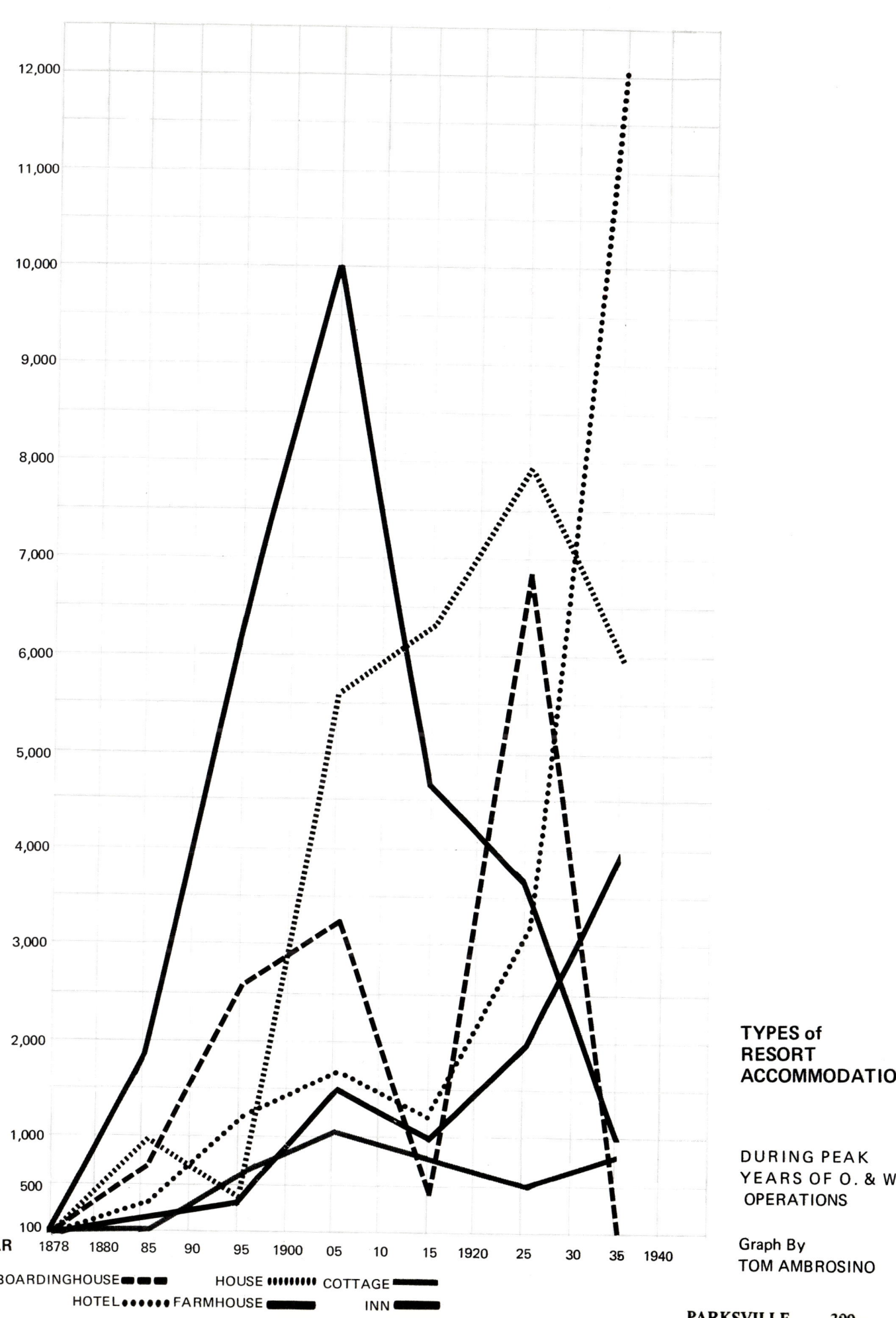

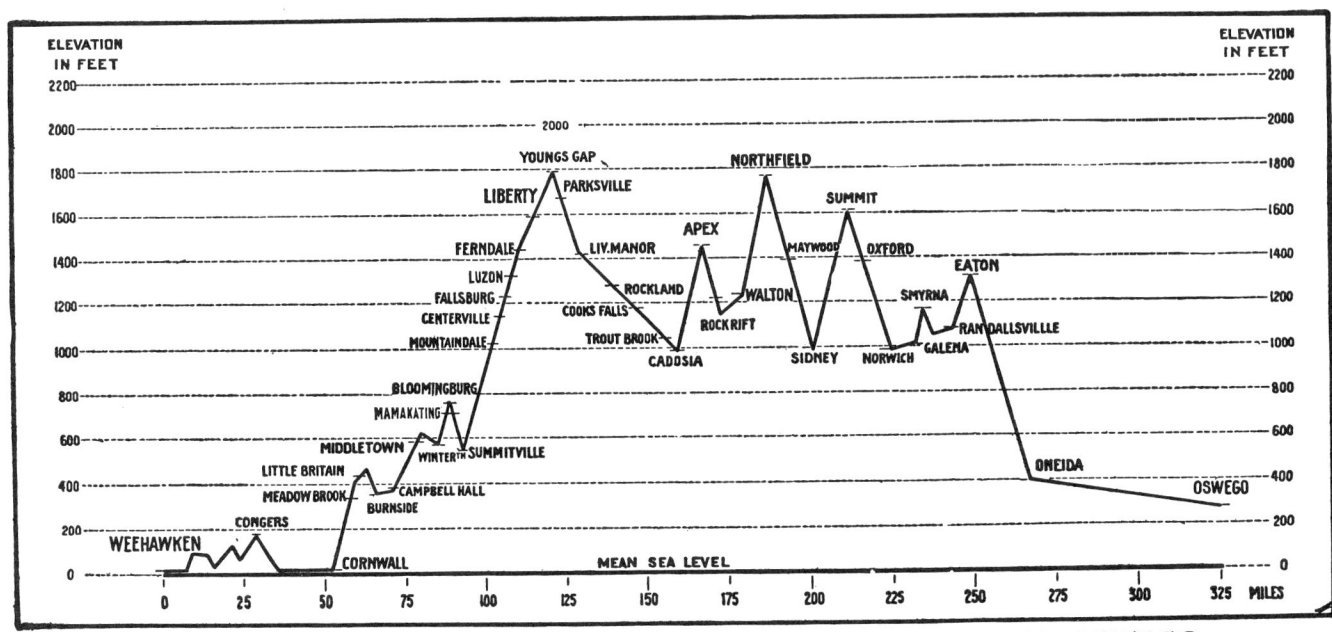

PROFILE SHOWING ELEVATION OF TRACKS WEEHAWKEN TO OSWEGO.

A quick glance at the above profile will indicate the maximum elevation at Young's Gap on the O. and W. as slightly less than 1800 feet. Actually the United States Department of the Interior, Geological Survey (Livingston Manor Quadrangle), records the 'Gap' as 1840 feet above sea level. *From "Winter Homes."*

directions until midnight when the six delayed trains, including the "Scoot" and the "Night Line," were permitted to proceed.

Parksville and Young's Gap (they were sometimes thought of as one because of their proximity) were the scenes of activities other than those generated by boardinghouse operators. In January, 1880, Edward Washington guaranteed the railroad that he would ship such large quantities of wood over their line that the O. and W. put in a special switch and siding at the "Gap." In the 1880's and 90's Parksville was a center for quantity shipping of small spruce trees that were sold in New York City as Christmas trees. The trees were gathered wild and when the stock was depleted the industry died.

About 1883 Messrs. Lawrence and Durland of Orange County opened a creamery at Parksville that became a model operation on the line of the O. and W. By 1891, the creamery, then under the superintendency of Mr. and Mrs. Charles Early, was receiving 210 cans of milk daily and shipping 175 cans a day out over the lines of the O. and W., the surplus being processed into butter and cheese.

Parksville had its share of fires. The blaze in May, 1882, wiped out the drug store of George S. Lord, five buildings all owned by the firm of Thomas Crary and company and the well filled O. and W. ice house. At the height of the summer season in August, 1925, a fire started in a barn to the rear of the Farmer's Cooperative Store in the center of the principal business block and proceeded to burn down seven buildings, all more or less dilapidated.

The geographical entity Young's Gap is notorious in Sullivan County for its weather. In February of 1893 a blizzard struck that was the equal of the "Blizzard of 1888." Snow commenced falling Tuesday evening at six o'clock and by Wednesday morning the "Night Line" was able to get through the gap only with the aid of a snow plow. An hour later the "Scoot" attempted to come through the gap but it was now again drifted full and consequently lifted one of the rear passenger cars from the rails. "Shorty" Vaughan, the good-natured, good looking, 300-pound conductor on the "Scoot," attributes their failure to the fact that he was on the forward end of the train, leaving it insufficiently ballasted in the rear. The engine uncoupled and ran to Liberty to pick up 150 shovellers who worked all day throwing it out as fast as it drifted in. By nightfall no headway had been made and the passengers were unloaded and put up at village hotels. With these additional overnight guests many of the hotels in town were unexpectedly filled to capacity.

Working in the "Gap" with the shoveling crews could be a serious proposition as section boss Flynn found out when the edge of a twenty foot high snow pile suddenly gave way, precipitating the

Young's Gap, showing the Rt. 17 Quickway and a short section of the abandoned O. and W. right-of-way, left edge, just before it enters one of the numerous rock cuts. It was the frequent rock cuts and winters' drifting snow that created difficulty in maintaining train schedules.

Bucking through a side-hill cut in Young's Gap, following the great 1914 blizzard. Progress was impeded by a stalled train, below, being cleared of snow by a crew of O. and W. shovellers. *Both photographs by Otto Hillig*

No. 185, a Dickson locomotive built in 1893, slowly comes to light, above, while in another part of the 'Gap', left, a brace of cabooses stand locked in monumental drifts. *Both photographs by Otto Hillig*

The 1914 blizzard paralyzed other parts of the county and complicated other forms of transportation, as witness the oxen struggling down an otherwise deserted Broadway in Monticello at the height of the storm. *Courtesy, John McKenna*

helpless snow fighter down the bank and wedging him between the driving wheels of a stalled locomotive. The snow covered him to a depth of about four feet; and, although it was some time before he could be shoveled out, he did manage to survive, although considerably bruised.

The *Register* in floridly describing the blizzard of February, 1899, remarked that "this patch of moss-covered rock and velvet sod, known as Sullivan County, evidently has been the door mat for every storm entering the county during the past century." And no doubt the O. and W. management was thoroughly convinced that each one started and ended at Young's Gap, filling the deep cuts with hard-packed drifting snow. In December of the same year that Pete made his paper run, a blizzard struck that not only tied up the line at the 1,840 foot high pass, but also at Champlin's Cut on the approaches in back of Liberty. The "Night Line" stalled out in the cut as did a snow plow dispatched to its rescue. Middletown sent another plow and work train which released the almost completely submerged train at 10:00 the following morning.

At one particular cut in the 1899 "howler," the snow, from ten to twenty feet deep, forced the rotary plow to tunnel a short distance, back out, and then after "caving in" the tunnel thus made, commence again.

In 1914 Sullivan County was hit with a one-two punch blizzard, tying up Young's Gap tight with drifted snow and stalled trains. Train No. 3, northbound, due at 4:45 p.m., arrived several hours late Saturday afternoon and advanced as far as Young's Gap, where it finally gave up the fight, and was stalled. The passengers were transferred to another train about 10 o'clock. The stalled train was unable to get out until 3:30 Sunday morning.

Even with the extra width of the double track cuts in 1914 it was exceedingly difficult to maintain wintertime operations through the "Gap." Before double tracking it was virtually impossible. The problem was so acute that when the project of double tracking was actually undertaken by the management, the section from the "Gap" to Parksville was given first priority.[9]

The urgency for double tracking on the southern division was brought about by the increased coal

The Young's Gap-Parksville area was subject to other types of interruption to rail service, such as this rail-bender between the depot and the old Rt. 17 overpass, background. The B. and O. boxcar reportedly contained a load of dynamite. *Photograph by Otto Hillig*

Double tracking employed the use of this venerable Bucyrus steam shovel, above, and a stationary steam engine-operated hoist somewhere in the valley of the Beaver Kill.

Double tracking achieved major proportions when the many bridges and trestles underwent widening operations. The substantial trestle at Cadosia, above, nears completion (Cadosia depot in the background) while below, the newly poured concrete abutments and piers of the Delaware River crossing await the steel erectors. The Erie mainline tracks cut under the single track bridge on the opposite bank. *Both photographs, Sullivan County Museum Archives*

Locomotive No. 227, the Roscoe afternoon train on the western flanks of the Young's Gap divide — the date, July 15, 1939.   *Photograph by John P. Ahrens*

traffic generated by the Scranton Division, which was officially opened on Monday, June 30, 1890.[10] South of Cadosia the congestion was compounded by the necessity of running some trains in six sections. Extra pushers with night and day crews were placed at Livingston Manor to assist the heavy drags up to the "Gap." The increased business was such that schedules were virtually impossible to maintain.

The first manifestation of things to come was the new Liberty Falls trestle built in 1901 to heavier tonnage ratings. In 1902 President Fowler announced "recommendations to the Board of Directors that 107 miles of the main line between Cadosia and Cornwall be double tracked."[11] The work was to be done gradually, "covering a period of three or four years ... to be paid for from net earnings."

In November, 1902, work was commenced on the double tracking of the upper Liberty trestle.[12] Other bridges were being given attention in this regard — the crossing at Fish's Eddy being completed in January, 1903. At this time, O. and W. civil engineer H. G. White and his assistants were establishing three-year headquarters on the second floor of the Livingston Manor station for the purpose of establishing grade on the line from Fallsburgh to Cadosia.

In March, 1903, the contract for the section from Parksville to Livingston Manor was awarded to the Crary Construction Co. of Binghamton.[13] A factor which lent impetus to the project was the talk in May, 1903, of the O. and W's becoming the New York connection for the Canadian Pacific Railroad. The O. and W. managers noted the double tracking as a vital factor in the plan, as well as the building of a line from Port Jervis to New York City so as to be independent of the West Shore.

With or without the Canadian Pacific stimuli, the coal tonnage did continue to increase, making the dirt fly on more and more sections of the line during 1903. Double tracking gangs were working the section between Bloomingburg and Summit-

The now vanished Parksville depot as captured by lensman Edward H. Weber. The original configuration of the depot (built in 1892), illustrated on the chapter heading page, can still be detected.

ville in February, as well as between Fallsburgh and Liberty and the section from East Branch to Cadosia. In May the double tracking between Middletown and Winterton was opened and by September, 1903, the three miles between Luzon and Strongtown was operational.

The year 1904 saw the many pieces falling rapidly into place — the sixteen mile segment from Summitville to Middletown was opened for service in February, Fish's Eddy in June and Livingston Manor to Roscoe in December. One of the last contracts to be let was from a point just below Young's Gap through Liberty to Strongtown crossing.

It is well that double tracking was completed in the dawning years of the 20th century. With the flood tide of anthracite just over the horizon — the O. and W. was ready.

Locomotive No. 3, the "Chenango," built by the Rhode Island Locomotive Works in 1869, is shown in this rare photograph at Livingston Manor preparatory to taking on water. Engineer Edward Clark stands near the gangway. Also shown are conductor Edward James, trainman George Close, and Art Conkling by pilot, left. *Courtesy, William Capach*

Livingston Manor

As Pete rolled into Livingston Manor on No. 29 all he could remember was the man in Weehawken who told the newspaper scribe on the same train that this is the place where 1,250,000 baseball bats are made each year.

Maybe it was this unique product of the local industry that had something to do with the village inhabitants' voracious appetite for the Sun and its sporting section.

A village of sportsmen it indeed was — from the time when the entire valley belonged to Dr. Edward Livingston.[1] As the first "Summer Homes on the Midland" explained it — "here was his residence with conservatory attached, and a little way off, approached by a double row of maples, his hot house and bowling alley. In front of the house was a fountain, and on the other side a library building, where the Doctor used to read and paint."

In that 1878 issue the place was listed as Morsston.[2] Extraordinary trout fishing on the Beaverkill and Willowemoc was noted as being a prime attraction of the area. Locals including Emmet Sturdevant, Matt Decleer, the Jones Brothers and Murdochs opened boardinghouses to accommodate fishermen out after the elusive "brookies." As the '78 "Summer Homes" asked "Who has not heard of Murdoch's on the Beaverkill?"[3]

Many had, including clergymen, lawyers and businessmen from New York City. They had all "eaten motherly Mrs. Murdoch's cakes and maple syrup during the last twenty-five years, and had gathered new strength and health from absorbing the perfect air as one struggled along the stream, and then come home, with a full basket, wet and hungry, to absorb his own trout as they came crisp and hot from her skillful hand."

One could also go to Mead's, Merwin's or Weaver's or Tripp's and also Flint's — all of them catering to the "artist of the dry fly" or wet if you dared. By the year of Pete's Sunday visit, there were six resorts listed — each one stressing the "excellent trout fishing." It certainly should have been "excellent" since the N.Y. & O.M. management in 1878 saw fit to have over 1,500,000 brook trout and a large number of lake and California trout distributed throughout the region. Again in 1884 more than 300,000 O. and W. sponsored brook trout were put in the streams of the county as well as 900,000 more the year of Pete's arrival at the "Manor."[4]

In 1890 J.C. Anderson, passenger agent, made application to the State Fish Commission for 346,600 trout fry and again the following year for 600,000 more trout fry. That same year a bill introduced by George M. Beakes to establish a fish hatchery in Sullivan County passed the Assembly and the following February, U.S. Messiter introduced the bill in the State Legislature. Out of this legislative effort emerged the DeBruce hatchery at the headwaters of the Willowemoc.

The fame of these waters spread far and wide; and, with the ready availability of the automobile, the sparkling water courses were soon overpopulated, posing a threat to many land owners whose holdings framed tempting fishing pools — not the least of which was the articulate Edward R. Hewitt of the upper Neversink River near Halls Mills.

Hewitt, through the pages of the local press in May, 1920, informed the citizenry that his waters would be open to the local Sullivan County residents but closed to hotel visitors and summer boarders — and those fishermen so qualified "are requested to use the fly and not bait."

The courtesy did not work. In an April, 1923, *Register* he pointed out that "during the season of 1921 the stream was poisoned several times" and in 1922 "the stream was again poisoned and dynamite was used in all the large pools several times." He added that permits would be issued "only to those persons whom I know to be good sportsmen" and those who can be "identified and vouched for by some other citizen."

This naturally stirred up a hornet's nest of controversy through editorials and letters-to-the-editor particularly focusing on the stated point of the opening of a stream that "has been open from time immemorial," and whether "large local trout streams can be legally posted."

This furor was all but eclipsed when on August 9, 1923, a young Boy Scout from Liberty (Albert Hadden), bound for a vacation day's enjoyment, was dismayed to see the lower Willowemoc's surface dotted with innumerable dead fish floating downstream.

The special fish car, 'Adirondack,' shown here on the builder's (Gilbert Car Company, Troy, N.Y.) transfer table. Built at a cost of $4,213.60 in 1891, it was finally taken out of service in 1927. One of the largest consignments of fingerling trout to Sullivan County arrived at Monticello aboard the 'Adirondack' in September, 1919. Aboard were 182 cans of large native fingerling trout from the State Fish Hatchery at Bath, consigned to John J. Burns, President of the Monticello Rod and Gun Club. Insert shows the can-filled interior of the unique railway car. *From a cut in the Fish Commissioner's Annual Report for 1902.*

A. Site of Sherwood Island Park   B. O. & W. Depot   C. Locomotive Turn-around "Y"

The Livingston Manor depot erected to replace the two-story frame structure built in June, 1882, as illustrated in the chapter heading. The second floor of the original structure was the three-year headquarters of the engineering corps in charge of the double tracking project. Below, No. 404 loads Weehawken-bound passengers on a warm August day in 1932. *Top photograph by Howard Wood, Sullivan County Museum Archives; lower photograph by John P. Ahrens*

After due investigation and an accusing feature story in the February, 1924, *Field and Stream,* it was theorized that some sort of poison had been released from the acid factory at Willowemoc. Whether by accident or design, the evidence did not constitute legal grounds of sufficient value to prove the guilt of the acid plant.[5]

Whether or not the negative publicity for the county was a factor is not known, but a positive follow-up was the approval of the purchase of the locally known Beaverkill tannery farm in October, 1926, to be preserved as a state park and campsite area. Known today as the Beaverkill State Campsite, it is one of the finest fishing grounds in the county.

Much credit must be given to the O. and W. management for their foresight in laying the groundwork in Sullivan County for what became one of the classic trout fishing regions in the world.

The Ontario and Western may have set the stage for a fisherman's paradise but the founding Edward Livingston gave little thought to the railroad's progressive role when in the peculiar wording of his will he provided an annoying thorn in the side of the railroad management which finally suppurated in 1923.

The lands on which the railroad bed, station house and freight house stood were originally a farm left to nephew Charles Octavius Livingston, who executed a warranty deed of the property to Medad T. Morss, who in turn conveyed it to the New York and Oswego Midland. Three years after the death of Charles Octavius, his son, Victor Livingston, began an action of ejection against the railroad company because of a clause in the original will of Edward enjoining his nephew (Charles Octavius) from selling the farm or parting with it, stating that it was his desire that it should remain in the possession of his family.

The decision was determined in favor of Victor with action immediately instituted to condemn the lands for railroad use. An appointed commission determined the value of the property upwards of $150,000, with the O. and W. claiming the only amount that could be awarded was the value of the land for farming purposes. After a long, drawn out trial the commissioners awarded $15,000 for the land and $49,000 for the structures upon it, to Livingston.[6]

In November, 1923, the decision of the Appellate Division closed the case. Had it been decided differently it could have made half of the landowners of Livingston Manor homeless.

Generally speaking though, relations were good between the railroad and the community — one notable exception occurred in September, 1914.

For some time the soft coal nuisance and the "holdup" at the Main Street crossing had been creating ill will between community and railroad but it remained for the indiscriminate blowing of locomotive whistles to really set things off. A movement was initiated by citizens to bring the matter before the Public Service Commission.

Admittedly, the "Manor" was a busy rail point — it being known as a "register station," where all trains must stop for orders, from the "Chicago Express," down to the slowest coal drag. As the local press noted, "some of the more capricious men-at-throttle seem to find much pleasure in tooting the time of day to a brother engineer while passing and others apparently take great enjoyment about 3 a.m. by adding a nightmare to the natives' peaceful slumbers with a "go-ahead" lullaby that is long and loud enough to wake the dead ... they all seem to come into and go out of the village with a vengeance, if the hullabaloo of their siren may be taken as an indication of the engineer's feeling."

There were numerous crossings that did necessitate frequent soundings of the whistle; one of which — a thousand feet north of the station — was the scene in 1897 of a tragic, but typical accident for the times: a collision between a train and a horse and wagon.

Engineer Harvey Moore on the southbound mail train No. 2 first saw George Fries and his 'valuable team,' when his horses were jumping frantically

Railroad lensman John P. Ahrens recorded Mother Hubbard No. 251 in August, 1932, while taking on water before departure for Weehawken.

Making the customary stop at Livingston Manor, Class Y-2, No. 456, of 4-8-2 wheel arrangement, performs the necessary ritual at the water plug. The 'Manor' was a vital point on the O. and W. — pusher crews were maintained 24 hours, the Cornwall way freight started there, the Cadosia "pick-up" terminated there — all this necessitating a turn-around wye, fire cleaners, three water plugs, operators 24-hours a day, coaling station, freight house and a restaurant in the depot. *Courtesy, Ellenville Public Library and Museum*

with Fries endeavoring to guide them into the fence at roadside. When the engine, running about twenty miles an hour, had approached within twenty-five feet of the crossing, the horses again jumped frantically onto the track and turned directly toward the engine as it struck them. Fries was found more than a dozen feet from the track and about one hundred feet from the crossing. He lived about twenty minutes after the accident. His horses were carried one hundred feet from the crossing and about a dozen feet from the track, one on either side — a grisly confirmation of a "cornfield meet" between a team of horses and an iron horse.

Tragedy occasionally interrupted the normal activities of the railroad employees and their families. Probably no other O. and W. orientated family suffered the loss that the "Manor"-based Dutcher family experienced.

In 1916 Robert Dutcher, a trackwalker, was killed by a passing train. Ten years later and three miles south of the spot where he died, brother Rufus, also a trackwalker, was struck and killed by a northbound extra. A southbound extra was passing at the same time and it is thought that Dutcher's attention was so fastened on the freight approaching from the front that he did not hear the warning sound behind him.

The final blow came at the end of August in 1931, when another brother, John Dutcher, riding a "speeder"[7] to work with five other men, crashed into the rear of the Cadosia pusher engine at Hazel and was killed.[8]

The right-of-way through the valley of the Willowemoc, with its endless bridges and exposure to high water and ice, was always a challenge to the maintenance-of-way crews.

In October, 1881, near Westfield Flats, carpenters had just about completed repairs on a damaged bridge when they prematurely permitted a train to cross. The bridge collapsed, taking an engine with four men on board followed by seven freight cars down fifteen feet into the stream.

Cloudbursts were another problem. In July, 1902, two severe thunder storms met over Parksville and proceeded to raise the Willowemoc River fifteen feet in five minutes. Three bridges between Parksville and Livingston Manor gave way, holding up the Chicago Express, and No. 10, the long milk. South of the blockade, Express No. 5 and the Mountain Express No. 7 were also held up. Before arriving at the washout, train No. 10 ran into a mud slide causing little or no damage, a dramatic contrast to the tragic results of a cloudburst in the Shandelee section above Livingston Manor in the latter part of May, 1929.

The wagon-rutted main street at the 'Manor,' showing the former Treyz Company Store, left, and down the street, the Manor House. The opposite side of the street, below, was dominated by the Hotel Sherwood. Ice jamming near the junction of the Willowemoc and Little Beaver Kill on March 22, 1912, right, caused the rain-swollen stream to flow down village streets, liberally distributing ice floes as it went. *Top and lower photograph by Howard Wood, photograph, right by Otto Hillig*

The day before Memorial Day in 1929, train No. 10 struck a rock and mud slide and derailed. Before the train could be slowed sufficiently, it struck the crossover switch for the Federal Creosoting Company plant on Mott's Flat and plunged down the embankment. Fireman George S. Freer was killed instantly. Note specially hooped gondola cars, background, for carrying railroad ties. *Courtesy, Mrs. Leonard Sherwood and Wilfred F. Smith*

The dismembered remains of No. 44 (train No. 3) after its derailment at White House Curve, two miles north of Livingston Manor on June 26, 1909. The spectacular wreck claimed the lives of Chester "Rube" Vandermark, engineer, and Les Dougherty, fireman. *Courtesy, Gerald M. Best*

The "Sugar Wreck," about 1906, at a point 2½ miles east of Livingston Manor showing the Morsston House in the background. The jumble of cars included seven carloads of sugar, and as Town of Rockland Historian, Herb Mussman, recalled, "...I don't believe a bag of sugar was sold locally in the stores for over two years." The overalled man in the center is Melvin Blade, section foreman.   *Photograph by Otto Hillig*

The derailment of train WA-1 on March 28, 1939, also demolished this recently completed overpass on the outskirts of Livingston Manor.   *Courtesy, Oscar O. Bennett*

Feeder streams poured torrents into the Willowemoc, and in some places just north of the Manor the high waters deposited a substantial amount of mud and rocks on the right-of-way. At about 6 p.m. on May 29th the Long Milk struck some of this mud, the locomotive riding through it unnoticed by the crew until the wheels of the wooden freight car behind the tender rode up on the mud and struck a large rock dislodging the front trucks, all of which carried 200 feet to a switch; its mechanism throwing the car and the locomotive from the tracks. Riding the locomotive down a 20-foot bank into a muddy swamp was the fireman, George S. Freer, who died instantly from a crushed skull. Frantz B. Romer, engineer, and Datus C. Francisco, head brakeman, both of Middletown, were found dazed in a state of shock and rushed to the Liberty Hospital by the first rescuers from the Manor.

Times were not always tragic in Livingston Manor – its famed Sherwood's Grove was often the target for many joyous clambakes and reunions. On September 8, 1887, 10,000 people attended the 5th Annual Reunion of the Veterans of Sullivan County. "The excursion trains were crowded to the uttermost. The one from the north brought about 700 people, while the one from the south with two engines and nine passenger cars carried 1,010 people, of whom 170 came from Ellenville, 150 from Fallsburgh and 200 from Liberty."[9] At 10:30, jovial John H. Divine took the speaker's stand and warmed the boys up. Thus opened a day of reminiscence, partaking of the "abundance of good things prepared for them by Purvis Post," dancing, merry-go-round riding and, of course, peeking at the "risque" dime museum.

SHERWOOD'S ISLAND PARK,

THE BEAUTIFUL

Clam Bake and Picnic Grounds,

SITUATED AT

LIVINGSTON MANOR, N.Y.

MERRY-GO-ROUND, REVOLVING SWING, TOWER SLIDE, DANCING PAVILION, OPERA HOUSE, RACE TRACK
DANCING EVERY SATURDAY EVENING.

J. F. SHERWOOD, PROPRIETOR.

Publicity card issued by John Fanton Sherwood for his popular recreation center. *Courtesy, Mrs. Leonard Sherwood*

"At the junction of the Little Beaverkill and Willowemoc and entirely surrounded by water, is an island of some forty acres, known as Sherwood's Grove, a favorite and popular resort." The resort, thus described in the 1893 "Summer Homes," hosted the Millard Division #104, Order of Railroad Conductors giant clambake two years before in August, 1891. Every train arriving at the Manor was packed to capacity with the Middletown delegation arriving—260 by excursion train and 240 by regular train. Three hundred people arrived from Liberty with representatives from every village for a distance of 50 to 75 miles packing the grounds to a record attendance of from 5,000 to 6,000 O. and W. railroad employees and their families. Special excursion trains were operated from Delhi, Scranton, Carbondale and Middletown—each train stopping at all way stations.

A typical Bill of Fare for one O. and W. Conductors Clambake held in 1904 included 68,000 clams, 1600 pounds of spring chicken, 1000 pounds of blue fish, 500 watermelons, 14 barrels of sweet potatoes, 35,000 ears of corn, 560 quarts of milk, 100 pounds of coffee, 180 pounds of butter and 400 loaves of bread (plus 75 cases of ptomaine poisoning and 96,000 doses of Epsom salts.)

An early summer church outing at Sherwood's Island Park with the Ladies Aid waiting patiently to serve what would appear to be an anticipated capacity crowd. *Courtesy, Mrs. Leonard Sherwood*

Special excursion trains were a popular railroad feature in the 1880's and 90's. The early "Summer Homes" had listings in the back noting all regularly scheduled excursions. The 1886 issue noted twenty-six such trips to places as diversified as the Thousand Islands, Asbury Park and Lake Minnewaska.

In 1903 a special excursion was run to Washington, D.C. as well as one on July 12 of the same year to Coney Island, where during the preceding winter $1,500,000 had been expended in creating a world's wonderland by the sea called 'Luna Park,' which was considered the largest and most magnificent amusement resort on earth.

Even the spectacular $3,000,000 Poughkeepsie Railroad Bridge of the Central New England and Western was excuse for a rail-boat excursion in October, 1900. The grand and palatial steamer, the "Mary Powell," was boarded at Cornwall for the run north past Newburgh to the bridge at Poughkeepsie. The excursionists then rode over the bridge on a special train. In addition to all this, the boat then continued north to Kingston Point, touted as "the most beautiful park in central New York State" — the round trip fare: a modest $1.50.

In 1933 the rail-boat excursion was revived in a September trip via the Hudson River Steamboat Company's "Benjamin B. Odell" for a run down the Hudson and a sightseeing tour around New York harbor.

Probably one of the biggest excursions ever run was also one of the biggest disappointments. The May, 1903, trip was by rail up the Kingston branch to the awaiting "Mary Powell" and a fast ride to Albany for the purpose of a lengthy inspection of the $20,000,000 Capitol building.

The popularity of the excursion was so far beyond the expectations of the company that it

Uncovering the bake pit; the big moment at a typical clambake at Sherwood's Island Park. *Courtesy, Mrs. Leonard Sherwood*

was completely swamped. Liberty, for example, was apportioned one hundred tickets which were sold out a half hour before the train arrived. People from White Lake and Jeffersonville never had a chance. There were twenty-six carloads landed at Kingston Point one and a half hours after the scheduled departure time for the "Mary Powell;" and, on account of low tide, the trip up the river was unusually slow, cutting the three hours promised in Albany down to about twenty minutes. The O. and W. carried nearly 2000 people along with two or three hundred from Kingston made it possibly the largest party the "Mary Powell" had ever carried.

O. and W. excursions were popular with members of the Masonic Order who traveled to visit the Masonic Home in Utica or to New York City to attend Grand Lodge.

The one excursion conducted by the O. and W. in early June was deliberately tailored to the Sullivan County resort season by affording city dwellers an opportunity to go to the mountains early and 'size up' the accommodations and make reservations. One run in June, 1892, carried 700 ticket holders for the trip to Sullivan County resort points and, hopefully, early reservations. This promotion must have been a forgotten one-shot event. On June 2, 1932, the *Register* announced the O. and W.'s "new plan of special one-day excursions designed to give New York City people an opportunity to come to Sullivan County and select their boarding place for the summer."[10]

In 1893 there were listed in the Livingston Manor area 20 summer resorts and by 1910 an all-time high of 62 places were noted in "Summer Homes." The Manor was the key detraining point

The Trojan Lake Lodge, located atop a mountain, would accommodate 200 and was one of the pioneer resorts in the area. Michael Steinman and his brother-in-law, Simon Goodman, bought 171 acres from Albert and Mable Townsend on February 8, 1912. They later acquired more property and eventually a lake was built on the property. Few of the 25 or so resorts about the 'Manor' during the time of the O. and W. remain — exceptions being the Waldemere and Edgewood. *Courtesy, Steingart Associates*

for boardinghouses in Beaverkill, DeBruce, Lew Beach, Parkston, Shandelee, Craig-e-Clare and Grooville.

The year 1908 saw the establishment of the first Jewish boardinghouse in the Manor — a five-room house full of holes that was later to become the Beaver Lake Lodge. Fannie and Julius Lichtman built Beaver Lake from a small boardinghouse to a large (for the 1920's) resort, mostly by their own labors.[11] "When we first came to the Beaver Lake property," said Mrs. Ida (Lichtman) Gluck, "there was a five-room house full of holes and a barn. My father and Harry Wood (of old Morsston) built all of the buildings in the resort."[12] Beaver Lake Lodge, like so many of the other family resorts, became a victim of the big resorts in the 1930's and 40's; its various buildings being torn down in the 1960's.

By 1920 listings for the region dropped to 20 and in 1923 hotel keepers and proprietors of boardinghouses in and around Livingston Manor, sensing a need for regional improvement, organized an association for promoting their business. "The first problems to be tackled are better electric light service, better telephone service and better railroad service."[13]

The year 1923 was a far cry from the halcyon year of 1888 when the Clay Hotel, part of which contained the old Manor House of Dr. Edward Livingston, underwent redecorating and ornamentation by James A. Kay, "the well-known decorator of Livingston Manor, who is doing it in first-class metropolitan style."[14] It was a classic of that now vanished breed of depot-hotel with its sample room for the commercial travelers to set up their displays of wares. The hotel had all the amenities with four sitting rooms, a large dining room and "all of it heated by steam." Managerial pride manifested itself in that prime necessity, the bar, which in the publicity accounts of the period was noted: "in point of beauty will surpass any in the county."[15] The old hotel, later known as the "Baldwin House," was demolished (about 1952) by John Roseo, who built a house from the salvaged wood.

THE P. H. WOOLSEY HOUSE,

JOSHUA TERWILLIGER, Proprietor.

LIVINGSTON MANOR, SULLIVAN CO., N. Y.

The P. H. Woolsey House was expressly for the Summer Trade--it is not a hotel.

1,600 Feet Above the Sea.   129 Miles From New York.

The P. H. Woolsey House is situated in the beautiful little village of Livingston Manor, on the line of the Ontario & Western Railroad, one of the most pleasant spots among the hills and mountains of Sullivan County. Being located at the forks of the Willowemoc, Beaverkill and Cat Brook, it is a most desirable place for lovers of trout fishing; while these streams with their deep pools, rocky cascades and pretty waterfalls, together with Mount High Point, towering several hundred feet directly in the rear of the house, and Elk Mountain, also within easy access, affords endless opportunity for pleasant rambles amid wild and romantic scenery. Shaded walks and strolls; convenient to churches; only five minutes' walk from depot and post-office; no malaria and no mosquitoes. Situation healthy, being at an altitude of 1,600 feet above the sea. House new and elegantly furnished, rooms large and cool, large double parlors, shaded verandas, etc. Will accommodate 75 guests. Table first-class in every respect. Plenty of fresh milk, and vegetables of all kinds in their season. Good livery accommodations connected with the house. The house is supplied throughout with pure spring water.

There are two morning trains leaving daily for New York at 5 and 6.30 o'clock; and two evening trains from New York arriving at 7.30 and 10.45 p. m. Also an afternoon mail train each way daily.

Take New York, Ontario & Western Railway from foot of Jay or West 42d St.

For further particulars of this summer resort, refer to J. C. Anderson, Gen. Passenger Agt. O. & W. R. R., 18 Exchange Place, New York, or address the proprietor,

JOSHUA TERWILLIGER,
Livingston Manor, N. Y.

The P.H. Woolsey House "at the forks of the Willowemoc, Beaverkill and Cat Brook," as it was advertised in the 1890 Thompson and Breed's Directory of the New York, Ontario and Western Railway.

The White Roe Lodge gave Danny Kaye his first break and set him on his way to the title, "King of the Catskills." His first job was as part of the entertainment staff in 1933 at the age of twenty. He appeared in one play a week and a different variety show every evening. Entertaining commitments at breakfast, lunch and dinner necessitated all-night rehearsals.

Cooke-built locomotive No. 302 is featured in this oil painting by artist-historian, Manville B. Wakefield. Pushers No. 324 and 403 urge a July, 1939, symbol manifest freight across the Little Beaver Kill trestle east of the Manor, left, on the heavy grade to Young's Gap. *Original oil painting, collection of Michael Koch; photograph, left, by John P. Ahrens*

A nostalgic look back at the grade crossing in Livingston Manor on a pleasant spring afternoon. A crossing, duly watched by an ever alert crossing guard, while the ornate observation platform of a crack O. and W. limited moves out of the frame, left. The A.P. DuBois general store, right, a business landmark for years, commenced operations when the railroad came through in 1873. The store discontinued business in the mid-1920's. Louis DuBois, son of the founder, lived across the street from the store in the "showplace of town." *Photograph by Otto Hillig, courtesy, John Joyner*

A ghost still lingers at the 'Manor' — waiting patiently for oblivion.

The native woods of the surrounding countryside stimulated much of the enterprise of Livingston Manor. John Fanton Sherwood began his mill on the raceway in back of the island in 1868. With a secondhand hand turner from Big Indian, he started making table legs out of maple. From this start he progressed to twenty-two hand turners and made other articles such as Indian clubs, dumbbells and baseball bats. Until 1900 all Spaulding baseball bats were made at Sherwood's plant. In 1916 the considerably enlarged enterprise was completely wiped out by fire but later rebuilt to turn out first grade ten-pins of rock maple with a capacity of over five thousand per day.

Hand-made wooden scoops were carved from cherry and maple for use in handling grain and later became the safest type of shovel for use in powder mills. "Scoopers," as the hand-carvers were originally referred to, became a derogatory term in later years when Jewish summer boarders started moving into the resort region. When the locals would refer to the boarders as "kikes," the Jews would in turn refer to the locals as "scoopers."

Up-train No. 6 pauses at Roscoe, hauled by Dickson locomotive No. 132, a Mother Hubbard-type hog, scrapped in 1929. There can be little doubt that there are a number of creel-carrying passengers on the platform with their sights set on the upper reaches of the Beaver Kill and the elusive brown trout.   *D. Diver Collection, Cornell University*

Roscoe

Rockland

It was a weary Pete Reilly who cracked an eyelid when No. 29 came to a halt at Rockland about 9:00 a.m.[1] He swung off the cars at the station with the few papers he had left and proceeded to inquire about the best fishing spots while dispensing papers.

Like her sister community of Livingston Manor, Roscoe was also highly regarded by sportsmen; but in 1886 the "Summer Homes" listed only one resort, the 25-room W.B. Cochran Boarding House as operating in the town. By 1909, however, there were 36 summer resorts listed; the grandest being "Lake Wood Farm." The resort was opened in 1887. It burned in 1897 and was immediately rebuilt on a grander scale by J.F. Wood and later expanded (1912) by Henry W. Bassett. Its many noted guests included John D. Rockefeller, Sr., who visited it each season for many years.

Lake Wood Farm's history ended with a fire in May, 1932, which was very similar to the one which destroyed the original hotel in 1897. When the resort was being redecorated, a fire started on a top floor. Crackling flames were the first intimation workmen and painters, who were eating their lunch, had of the fire. The upper floors of the building were ablaze. The mammoth L-shaped, 115 room structure with a frontage of 200 feet overlooking Lake Florence was a smouldering mass of ruins by nightfall — the loss was estimated at $100,000.[2] The depression precluded its being rebuilt.

The community of Roscoe itself was catastrophically disrupted by a fire on November 19, 1916, when an overheated stove set fire to Balsey Fuhrer's bowling alley at about two o'clock in the morning. An alarm was quickly sounded but a gasoline stove in the bowling alley exploded making it impossible to extinguish the fire, which spread rapidly to the adjoining buildings.

Half an hour later the fire fighters believed they had the blaze well under control when the water pressure suddenly dropped. While help was being sought in Livingston Manor and Liberty, the flames raced through the Voorhee's Dry Goods and

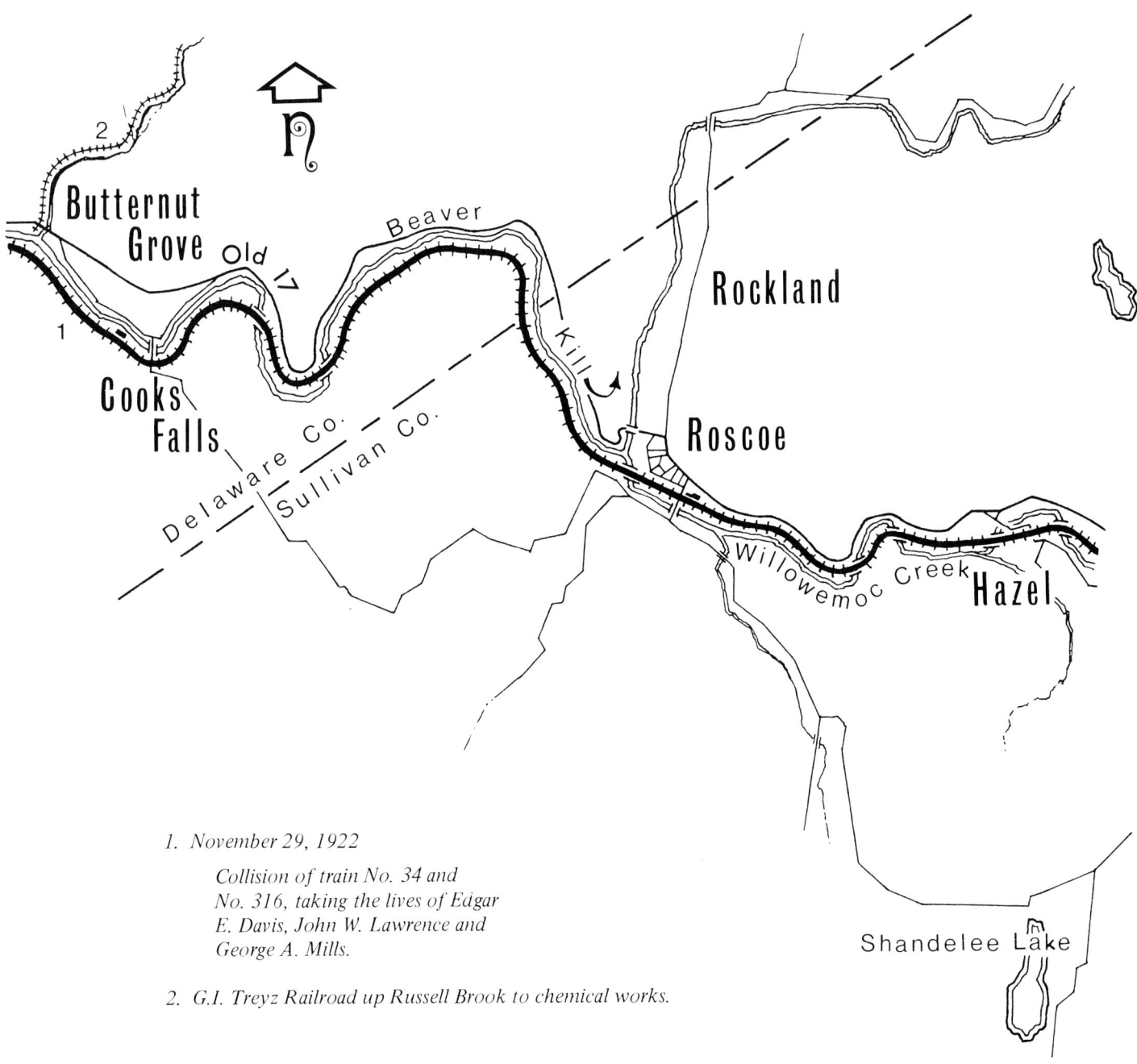

1. November 29, 1922

    Collision of train No. 34 and No. 316, taking the lives of Edgar E. Davis, John W. Lawrence and George A. Mills.

2. G.I. Treyz Railroad up Russell Brook to chemical works.

A. Roscoe depot, since demolished to make way for the Rt. 17, Quickway

B. Turn around "Y".

The substantially built Roscoe depot which featured a unique trout weather vane, top left. The finney ornament was presented to the railroad by J.S. Underhill in April, 1896. After abandonment of the railroad, the weather vane mysteriously dissappeared. A corner of the Beaverkill House shows at left. *Photograph by Howard Wood, Sullivan County Museum Archives*

Ontario and Western No. 249 leaves Roscoe on a warm August afternoon in 1932 headed for the 'Manor,' where coaches and a parlor car will be put on for the run to Weehawken. *Photograph by John P. Ahrens*

Brooks-built locomotive No. 76, posing for a formal portrait with crew at Roscoe. This shiney high-stepper is of the same type as No. 70 that blew up at Hurleyville in 1907. *Courtesy, Gerald M. Best*

A post card scene in Roscoe entitled "A Street Scene (1840-1909), Roscoe, N.Y." which featured a dramatic contrast in modes of transportation. At the extreme left edge, a small portion of the stone Roscoe Bank may be seen. It was this structure that halted the spread of the 1916 flames down the street after the nearby Faubel House was reduced to ashes.

The landmark Beaverkill House, across the street from the depot (corner of roof, right), was a victim of the November, 1916, conflagration. *Photograph by Howard Wood, Sullivan County Museum Archives*

The Campbell Inn, built in 1898 and operated by Jefferson Campbell at the time Howard Wood snapped this picture, boasted a 184 foot long, twelve foot wide veranda that overlooked the "valleys of the famous Beaverkill and Willowemoc trout streams and the villages of Roscoe-Rockland lying at the confluence." In April, 1932, Harry Campbell (son of founder, Jefferson) sold the inn to James F. Wood.

The original Lake Wood Farm, above, which burned in 1897, was replaced by the imposing structure, right, which was reduced to charred ruins in May, 1932.

The Tennanah Lake House operated by A. "Pete" Wolff advertised in the 1907 "Summer Homes" and boasted accommodations for 80. The above photograph was taken at a much later date after considerable enlargement. *Courtesy, Steingart Associates*

The Rockland House was supplied with all its milk, eggs and vegetables from its own 100-acre farm. Not one to quibble over rates, its advertisement in the 1907 "Summer Homes" noted in the last line of copy, "...do not answer this advertisement unless willing to pay the price named."

Railroad station architect Bradford Lee Gilbert's precariously perched summer cabin in the upper Beaver Kill, where he frequently secluded himself when thinking through one of his lucrative design commissions.

The date, September 10, 1953, and Edward H. Weber was there. It is well indeed that he was; for today all is gone, replaced by an interchange on the Rt. 17 Quickway in the heart of Roscoe. It almost became a library—but to no avail.

Millinery store on the north, and the Shaw and Dreher hardware store on the south, thence to the Faubel House. The stone Roscoe Bank checked the flames at that point, but meanwhile the blaze swept across Stewart Ave. gutting the "Beaverkill House" located opposite the O. and W. depot, whose windows were smashed by the intense heat.

Still no water. It was then that firemen decided to use dynamite and they blew up a part of the James Fitzgerald house and built a pile of debris to halt the spreading flames. Meanwhile, a fracas was developing at the depot in Livingston Manor where 50 firemen had assembled to ride a special train to Roscoe, but the O. and W. dispatcher in Middletown refused to order said train. After 20 minutes of delay, the men went in their own cars with several lengths of hose in tow.

The settlement of the loss, placed in excess of $175,000, was complicated by vandals who stole most of the goods moved beyond the reach of the flames.

On the upper reaches of the Beaverkill was Banks' Hotel, which boasted the first nine-hole golf course in Sullivan County.[3] The appropriately named resort was by coincidence popular with bankers from the investment houses in New York City who came up to play tournaments and fish. Built about 1913, the hotel's grounds rambled along the Beaverkill and encompassed some tempting pools which also made the resort popular with fly-casters. Mrs. Paul Allen of Kenoza Lake, once a secretary in a bank in New York City, recalled many of the bank officials "rushing on Friday afternoon for the ferry to Weehawken and the O. and W. for a weekend on the Beaverkill at 'Banks'."

Cadosia depot, where the Scranton Division left the main line for the lucrative coal fields of northeast Pennsylvania. The nearness of the O. and W. to the Erie mainline at Hancock warranted the services of a transfer bus, shown here waiting for passengers at the 28 X 90 foot structure erected in 1901. One day the chain drive snapped as the bus neared the summit of the rather steep hill leading to the Cadosia depot. With 52 passengers on board plus luggage, the driver, Clem Myers, had the presence of mind to turn the steering wheel hard right and swing into the drive to the Mountain House with no damage done. *Courtesy, Oscar O. Bennett*

Roscoe West

Fish's Eddy Depot

The line west from Roscoe into Delaware County followed the tortuous convolutions of the Beaverkill, a region of scenic grandeur, but one that railroaders dreaded because it was fraught with appalling maintenance problems.

At Cooks Falls the Beaverkill drops over a series of cascades. Nearby stands the imposing Mountain Lake Hotel owned in 1910 by V.A. Francisco, a member of the family that dominated the resort region of Cooks Falls. They also operated the Sherman House (Sherman A. Francisco), Sylvan View House (M.J. Francisco) and Butternut Grove House (James O. Francisco).

The configuration of the stream near Cooks Falls was conducive to the formation of ice jams during spring thaws. One such jam which occurred in March, 1888, one mile north of the falls was of such scale that the oldest raftmen on the east branch of the Delaware could not recall one to surpass it. Nor could the railroad recall worse conditions. The backed up water overflowed the right-of-way and washed out the embankment, piling the ice ten to twelve feet thick for a considerable distance along the O. and W. right-of-way.

A dynamite crew was brought in to break up the ice but with tragic results. Several blasting holes were prepared while four men tended a fire nearby thawing out dynamite cartridges placed in a large heavy zinc pail. As the contemporary press reported " ... the four men had gathered as closely as convenient around the fire watching their foreman, who was bending over to check a fuse, when the four cartridges over the fire exploded with terrific force and a report that was heard several miles distant." The pail was pulverized in a thousand pieces leaving the "right knee joint" of Irving Stewart "entirely open and disconnected, while the knee pan was broken in a hundred pieces."

Shortly after the explosion, a special train was dispatched to Liberty for Dr. W.S. Webster, an O. and W. physician, who, along with Doctors J.A. Miller, R.C. Tuthill and F.T. Wheeler of Roscoe, found it necessary to amputate Stewart's leg[1] as

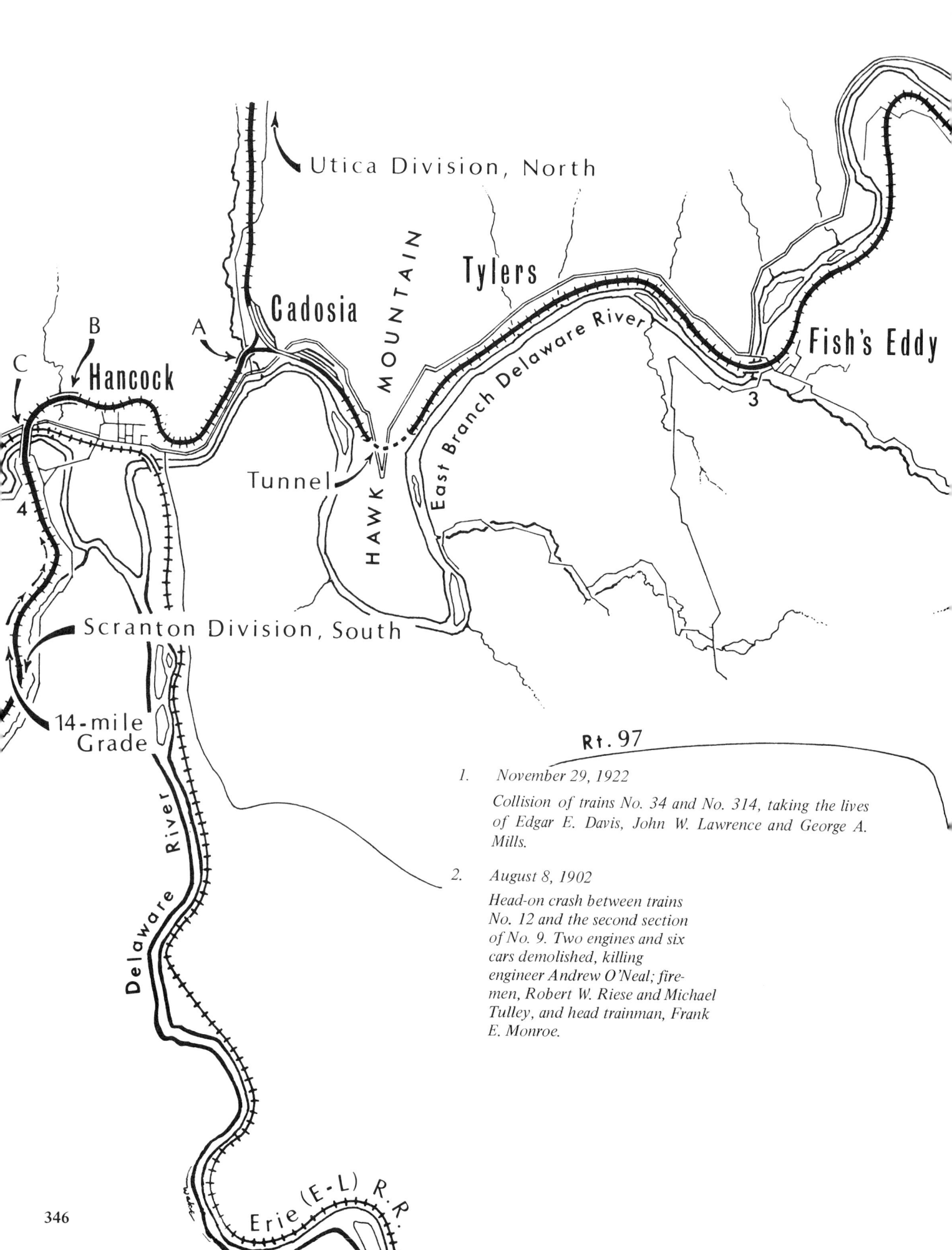

Rt. 97

1. *November 29, 1922*

   Collision of trains No. 34 and No. 314, taking the lives of Edgar E. Davis, John W. Lawrence and George A. Mills.

2. *August 8, 1902*

   Head-on crash between trains No. 12 and the second section of No. 9. Two engines and six cars demolished, killing engineer Andrew O'Neal; firemen, Robert W. Riese and Michael Tulley, and head trainman, Frank E. Monroe.

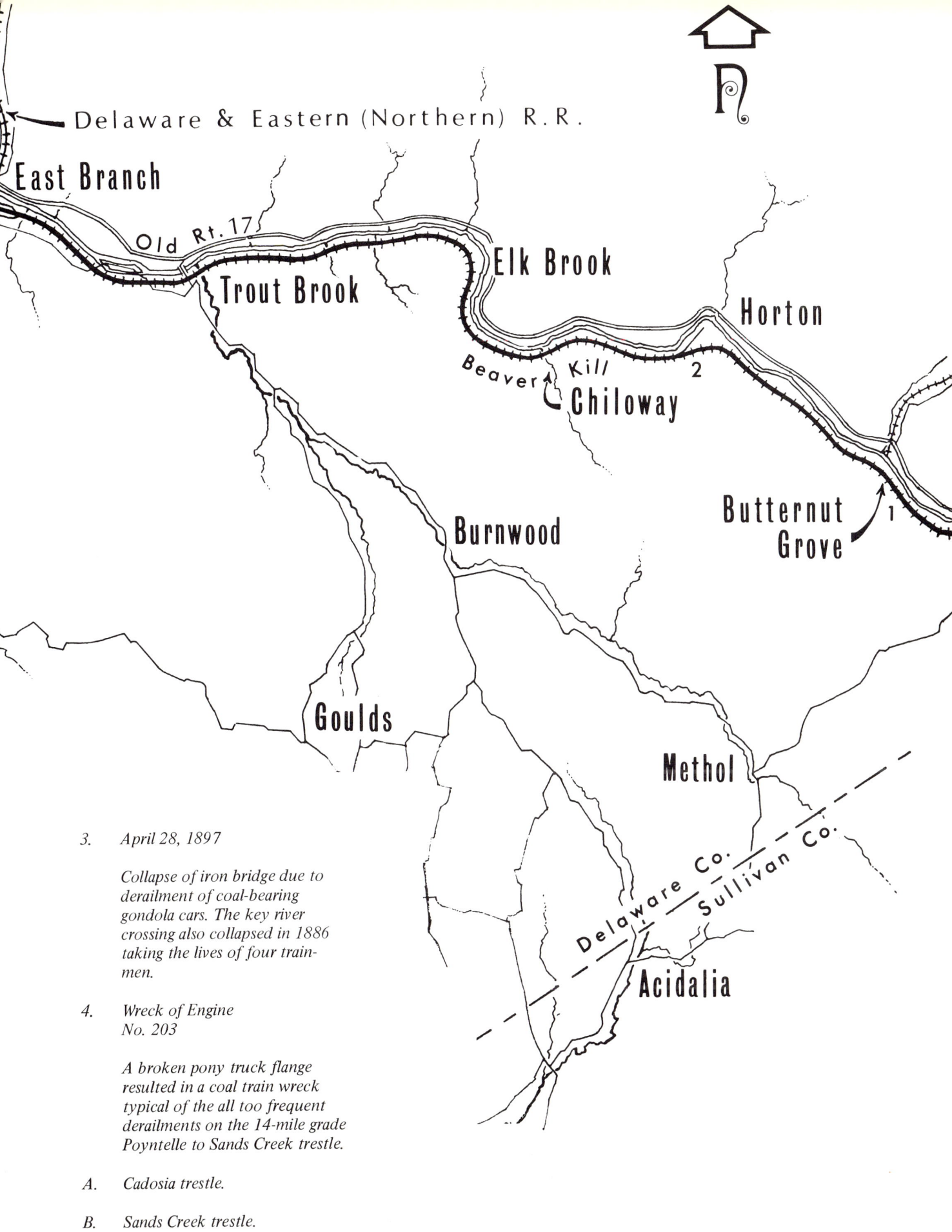

3. April 28, 1897

   Collapse of iron bridge due to derailment of coal-bearing gondola cars. The key river crossing also collapsed in 1886 taking the lives of four trainmen.

4. Wreck of Engine No. 203

   A broken pony truck flange resulted in a coal train wreck typical of the all too frequent derailments on the 14-mile grade Poyntelle to Sands Creek trestle.

A. Cadosia trestle.

B. Sands Creek trestle.

C. Delaware River trestle (standing, 1970).

Opposite, a westbound diesel freight banks on the superelevated curve approaching Cooks Falls in the twilight summer of 1956. *Photograph by Jim Shaughnessy*

A rare view of the Cooks Falls covered bridge, top, and a classic study of the later-built suspension bridge. The bridges connected the major portion of the community with the O. and W. depot facilities, opposite bank in lower photograph. *Lower photograph, courtesy, Gerald M. Best*

The west bound lanes of today's Rt. 17 Quickway along the Beaver Kill are built on the former right-of-way of the O. and W. This spectacular scene, just west of Roscoe, shows Delaware County in the distance; the actual county line denoted by a marker — black spot along right shoulder of road.

well as the right leg of Thomas Brehony, the workman who was preparing to dynamite.

The washout adjacent to the ice jam was filled in and a temporary trestlework constructed so that trains might pass safely. It took a week before the channel was finally opened, due in great measure to the reluctance of potential workmen to labor in and around the blood covered ice.

At Horton's Switch, two and one-half miles north of Cooks Falls, there was a head-on collision on August 8, 1902, so disastrous as to be rated one of the worst in the history of the line. Engineer Andrew M. O'Neal of train No. 12, the southbound milk,[2] had orders to meet the second section of train No. 9, which was running as train No. 11, at Chiloway, two miles north of the scene of the accident.[3] O'Neal ran by the switch at that point, the presumption among railroad men being that Engineer O'Neal, normally on trains No. 9 and No. 10 which were usually given the right-of-way, forgot that he was on another train and assumed he had a clear track ahead.

Train No. 11, the northbound milk, was in charge of conductor Starr Church, with engineer Benjamin St. John at the throttle. The consist of seventeen cars, loaded with empty milk cans and bottles, had just passed Horton's Station, running at slow speed through the curve at Treyz's Switch.

Approaching it, running at full throttle was train No. 12. The noise of the terrific impact carried up and down the valley like a clap of thunder.[4]

Upon investigation it was learned that train No. 12 was operating without air brakes or an attached air whistle. When the train ran by its passing siding at Chiloway, conductor Duclon, having no air whistle and no means of signalling Engineer O'Neal of the error, dispatched one of the brakemen out over the train to the engine. He was about halfway when the crash came.

The incredible boiler telescoping of engines No. 143 and 144 (trains No. 11 & 12) near Horton on August 8, 1902. Lafayette Bennett, father of Oscar O. Bennett, was 'deadheading' (riding as extra cab passenger) in engine, left, but jumped just before impact. *Courtesy, Ethel Schafer*

Workmen dig into spilled coal in effort to extricate the crushed body of engineer Edgar E. Davis. By turning the picture sideways, the vague shape of the shattered caboose of train No. 316 may be discerned. *Photograph by Otto Hillig*

Disaster struck again in November, 1922, when freight train No. 34 southbound from Oswego collided with extra coal No. 316 from Mayfield Yard (Pennsylvania) which had stopped to cool a hotbox [5] at Cooks Falls. According to reports, No. 34 had been flagged about 1200 feet from the rear of the standing freight but nevertheless continued at full speed into the caboose of No. 316, reducing it to splinters. The camelback type locomotive was hurled to the right, striking the 40-foot wall of solid rock, dragging with it the coal tender and two freight cars, crushing Engineer Edgar E. Davis of Middletown in his cab.[6]

At the I.C.C. investigation Cecil Davis, son of engineer Davis of No. 34, testified for his father. He claimed his father died "at his post of duty like a man. The position of his arms," according to the testimony, "showed he was doing his duty as they were toward the boiler. I looked the engine over before they raised it — it was in reverse." [7]

Two surviving landmarks at Cooks Falls are V.A. Francisco's monumental Mountain Lake Hotel, overlooking the Beaver Kill, and the abandoned company store of wood acid manufacturer George I. Treyz.

This wreck, about 1945, a half mile south of Cooks Falls was considered to be the costliest in the railroad's history. Wreckmaster McCormack stands in center, hands on hips, with the "where do we start" expression on his face. It was at the height of the summer season as evidenced by the scantily attired sight-seer and scattering of kids. *Courtesy, Oscar O. Bennett*

On April 15, 1948, NE-6, powered by newly delivered diesel engine 822 under the command of engineer Ray Finch and conductor George Bullis of Middletown, came to grief 1½ miles north of Cooks Falls near milepost 142. Occurring between 4:30 and 5:00 on a dark morning, the lead diesel had passed over a large rock which started to grind at the vital running gear of each unit in succession cutting and dragging as it went. Propelled by the momentum of the heavily loaded freight, the switch point at the Cooks Falls siding jammed the rock, throwing the locomotive and about 17 cars into a jumbled mass. Wreckers were brought in from the Delaware, Lackawanna and Western Railroad and the New Haven to clear up the mess. *Courtesy, Oscar O. Bennett and Alice C. Muller*

The little railroad constructed up Russell Brook by G.I. Treyz to connect his chemical plant with Butternut Grove across the Beaver Kill from the O. and W. (See map, page 336). *Courtesy, Oscar O. Bennett*

Horton : Chiloway

Horton and Chiloway were points on the O. and W. that were virtually devoid of any association with the resort industry. The communities existed because of the acid industry which developed after the Civil War while the tanning activities peaked out. The industry's raw material was hard wood: beech, birch and maple. The three main products of the distillation process were wood alcohol (methanol), acetate of lime and charcoal.[8]

"The first plant," according to Harry Treyz of Livingston Manor, a member of a family who played an important role in the industry, "was built in 1849 near Binghamton at Milburn — now known as Conklin — and owned by the Brookdale Chemical Company."

In 1878 the Acidalia plant was built by the King Brothers at a time when there were but seven known factories in the United States.[9] Later, in 1881, the Kings started a second plant at Fernwood. Essentially a small-time operation, its seven pairs of retorts used 10½ cords of wood a day.

In the spring of 1883 a general, but brief, recession occurred in the industry. Charles Armstrong of Long Eddy announced he would close his acid factory "as soon as the wood he has on hand is used up." Many of the other factories followed suit because the prices for wood acid had fallen so low that it was no longer profitable to manufacture. A few years later conditions changed.

By 1887 new factories were springing up all over the hills of western Sullivan and eastern Delaware Counties. In November and December, Stoddard Hammond was pushing hard to get his plant at DeBruce finished so that he could begin production in the spring. In December, Augustus Dodge of Rockland, the owner of 800 acres of Woodland, announced his plans to start immediate construction of an acid factory on Spring Brook. (Ownership of large tracts of land, of course, was a vital factor in the wood chemical industry.)

In September, 1896, (a year when nine-tenths of all the wood acid manufactured in the United

Remains of the charcoal acetate-carrying tramway-suspension bridge, left, erected by G.I. Treyz to connect the railhead to the Butternut Grove O. and W. sidings across the Beaver Kill. Shown inspecting the stark cable and piers is retired O. and W. engineer Oscar O. Bennett of Hancock. The Luzerne Chemical Company factory at Horton, above, showing the piles of wood used in the distilling process.

Some idea of the enormous quantities of hard woods needed may be gleaned from this faded picture of G.I. Treyz's woodyard near Cooks Falls.

The now vanished chemical factory at Acidalia. Mr. Eugene F. King erected the first factory in 1879, the second in 1881, and, according to Town of Delaware Historian Valleau C. Curtis, "the two factories used five thousand cords of beech, birch, maple and hard woods a year and from them derived the products of acetate of lime, wood alcohol and charcoal." In 1882 the post office was installed and Acidalia received its official name meaning the "City of Acids." *Courtesy, Mrs. Fanny Edwards*

States was made in Sullivan and Delaware Counties, N.Y. and Wayne County, Pennsylvania), the local press reported the purchase by Arthur Leighton of "all the available lands between Trout Brook (Peakville) and Cooks Falls" and the imminent "erection of a large acid factory near Chiloway." In December of 1896 Mr. Leighton, then known up and down the line of the O. and W. as the "acid king," had purchased the Holcomb factory at Cooks Falls and proceeded to install steam to cheapen the cost of manufacture. In the early 1900's many big plants sprang up, making it increasingly difficult for the smaller plants to do business.

During World War I the business got a much needed shot-in-the-arm with the increased demand for its products, particularly in the manufacture of explosives and embalming fluid. A rapid expansion period followed with the enlargement of plants and the opening of closed plants.

Encouraged by the demand, research chemists came up with synthetics equally as good and much cheaper, resulting in a sharp decline in natural production at the close of the First World War. For many years thereafter the old acid factories became marginal operations at best until their equipment finally wore out and was sold for junk.

There were spurts of optimism, such as the reopening of the Cadosia Acid Factory in 1932 by the Keery Chemical Company. This plant, directly or indirectly, employed 100 men from chemical technicians to woodchoppers, teamsters to road builders. Then there were the few who held on well into the 20th century, such as the Treyz Brothers at Horton whose operation finally closed in 1948. The site of the Treyz plant at the big bend in the river is now sliced through by the four-laned Rt. 17 expressway.

Loading bluestone at Elk Brook, showing George Baxter in center, Harry Kane on right and William Reynolds, operator of the stone dock, on the tracks. The acid plant and O. and W. station are discernible in the distance by the three smokestacks. The factory was established by Arthur Leighton who also operated plants in Methol, Horton and Cooks Falls. At the time of his death in 1900 there were about forty houses as well as warehouses and the factory at Elk Brook. *Courtesy, Ethel Schafer*

The H.M. George, opposite, of the newly form[ed] Delaware and Eastern on what would appear to be h[er] maiden voyage into East Branch. The Delaware Hou[se] was later built on the site of the house, bac[k]ground. *Courtesy, William Capach*

Trout Brook, (Peakville Post Office), was once a prime shipping point for princess pine and maiden hair fern to the metropolitan area. The Buckley acid factory at Trout Brook used the progressive steam method for condensing the acid in 1883 when other chemical plants were loath to invest in the new process because of a depressed market. The bustling little community also consigned large quantities of bluestone and lumber, top photograph, to the O. and W. freight agents. Note Huyler's chocolates sign over Peakville Post Office doors, lower photograph. *Both photographs, Sullivan County Museum Archives*

East Branch

As William C. Harris, editor of the *American Angler,* wrote in the early 1890's, "For the delight of black bass anglers, using either artificial flies or natural bait, there is no water surpassing the east branch of the Delaware at its junction with the Beaverkill."

In 1893 East Branch, located at the junction of these two famous anglers streams, could by no means be classified a summer resort center. The village had a drummers' hotel, the Hotel Jones; J.H. Bull's "pleasant country home;" The Maples, managed by A.J. Francisco; and Col. W. Martin's palatial Pines built in 1888 on a promentory fifty feet above the confluence of the two rivers.

The area's economic ease was considerably altered with the coming of the Delaware and Eastern Railroad which went into operation on October 23, 1906. The line constructed to Margaretville with 17 stations on its main,[10] and three on its Andes branch, crossed the Beaverkill near where the stream joined the Delaware and then connected with the O. and W. at East Branch.

After about two years of operation as the D. and E., the line went into bankruptcy and was reorganized as the Delaware and Northern.

The right-of-way through East Branch was straight track — an unusual occurrence in the curving valleys of the Beaverkill and Delaware's East Branch. Fast freights, especially bridge traffic,[11] moved through at remarkable speeds, on one occasion, at least, with tragic results, as recalled by former Delaware and Northern employee Joseph Rider.

"I had just finished lunch and was passing the time of day on the freight house steps when a northbound string of coal empties came rumbling by pulled by one of the big 450 Class engines and at a fast clip, the noise from the empties drowning out all conversation. O. and W. station agent Arthur Gordon had spotted a flaming hotbox in the string of empties, not too far ahead of the caboose. As per a recent directive of the O. and W. ordering all station employees to catch the eye of someone of the crew and notify them if a hot-box

ROSCOE WEST 357

Number 3, the A.C. Fairchild of the original Delaware and Eastern Railroad, undergoes the indignity, at Andes, of having her tender re-railed. Also at Andes, lower, D. and E. engine No. 1, the F.F. Searing, poses in 1905 with Les Avery, second from left, Louis Sanford, conductor, fourth from left and Roma Fitch, at right with shovel. *Both photographs, courtesy William Capach*

The Hotel Delaware saw the golden years when East Branch was the transfer point between the O. and W. and the D. and N.

Cooke-built locomotive No. 409 pauses with train No. 9, at East Branch sometime in the final years of steam. *Courtesy, Gerald M. Best*

exists or if something else should be dragging, Gordon was dutifully running down the southbound track trying to catch the eye of someone in the caboose.

"No one had noticed the oncoming southbound fast freight, the rumble of the northbound empties drowning out all sounds of the "hotshot." Mr. Gordon was struck and killed by the southbound freight right before our eyes not more than three or four steps away. It was a fifty-car train and before a full stop could be made, they had gone the length of the train plus eight hundred feet."

The strange thing is that it was the only time Mr. Rider had ever seen two fast feights going in opposite directions at the same time on the East Branch straightaway.

The last timetable issued by the D. and N., No. 121, was effective September 28, 1941, with the last passenger train, a gasoline-driven car, running from East Branch to Arkville in mid-October.[12] Twenty years before the end came, the little line had been immortalized on celluloid by the Vitagraph Company of America in a five-reel "epic" made in July, 1921, called "Single Track," which starred Corrine Griffith. All the exterior scenes were shot along the right-of-way with one of the trestles, for one reason or another, completely repainted. This was one time when the maintenance-of-way sheets for the D. and N. reflected a repair with the tab picked up by a motion picture company.

The grade crossing of the D. and N. with Rt. 17 (State Rt 4) was the scene of frequent altercations between locomotives and autos. This badly dented roadster rests in the shadow of Col. Martin's palatial mansion, The Pines, once the showplace of East Branch. Today the area shown is part of the Rt 17 Quickway, East Branch interchange. *Courtesy, Joe Rider*

ROSCOE WEST 359

This is how it used to be as passengers and express between the O. and W. and the D. and N. met at East Branch. Delaware and Northern No. 5 and its consist, right, waits patiently for the arriving southbound O. and W. passenger train. Today the same setting reveals the old depot standing guard over the macadamized main street of town.

Fish's Eddy

A derailed coal gondola car in April, 1897, resulted in this jumble of steel trusses and smashed coal cars. A temporary wooden trestle system was erected, below, while a new bridge was being fabricated. The locomotive shown is the ill-fated No. 70, later to blow up at Luzon (Hurleyville). *Courtesy, Gerald M. Best*

Fish's Eddy, a one-time heavy shipper on the O. and W., received short shrift from the railroad. A case in point was the inadequate depot facilities and the controversy it stirred up in 1878 — particularly in light of the $15,069 worth of paid freight local business shipped out over the Midland lines.

The town and the area it served produced railroad ties, lumber, bluestone, and during the great era of the tanning industry, tan bark. The largest tan bark producer, U. S. Tyler, alone shipped three hundred and forty-nine carloads over a three-year period.

But for all this economic support to the railroad, "the waiting-room, baggage-room, ticket office and freight room are all in one." The correspondent for the *Register* from Fish's Eddy recorded, "but one short bench is all the convenience in the passenger

Some idea of the one-time prosperity of Fish's Eddy is realized by the presence of two hotels; the Fish's Eddy House, left, and the George Harrison-operated Central House. The big fire of 1929 wiped out the Fish's Eddy Hotel as well as Finnigan's General Store, the Maccabee Hall, the post office, the Winter residence and the Platt garage and dwelling. It was reported that, just before help arrived from Hancock, East Branch and Roscoe, 18 buildings were in flames at once.

An overview of Fish's Eddy long before the burn of May 10, 1929, when lumber mills lined the stream, when its two hotels at left, above, catered to a substantial O. and W. passenger trade and the upper part of town was a vast wood storage yard for the booming acid-chemical factory, right.

High waters plagued the O. and W. maintenance-of-way crews such as this flood in 1901 or 1902. The photograph, taken by an O. and W. telegrapher, shows the approaches to the highway bridge, inundated, right. The object in the water between the bridges is the newly built foundation for a new jail. The village fathers, impressed with the precarious location in times of flood, immediately abandoned the project. *Courtesy, William Capach*

shed, and if that is occupied, you are left to take your choice between a bag of feed and a buzz saw."

The railroad's crossing of the East Branch of the Delaware at Fish's Eddy was poorly built, and in 1886 the northerly end span dropped into the river taking the lives of four trainmen. One O. and W. veteran recalled the bridge collapse story he heard as a fledgling trainman. "It was a heavily laden coal train that came uncoupled. The engineer, being aware of the situation, slowed down slightly to permit the loose cars to catch up. They did, right on the first of the three spans, the impact derailing the cars and demolishing the span."

In 1897 the same bridge, apparently shoddily rebuilt, again collapsed — however, with no fatalities. The train of empty gondolas left Middletown at 11:00 p.m. in charge of Conductor F.A. Day and Engineer John Henry Warner and at 3:20 on the morning of April 28, while running slowly over the bridge (with the intention of entering Lewis' switch), a car derailed, knocking out an end post of the 140 foot long middle truss span causing it to drop into the river taking along eleven cars.

The transfer of passengers around the wrecked bridge brought a great flurry of activity to the little community, but nothing in comparison to the commotion on Saturday May 10, 1929, when nine buildings went up in a $75,000 conflagration.

Fish's Eddy never really came back — the lumbering operations were gone as was the tan bark business and it would be only twenty-eight years before the flanged wheel and iron rail would vanish from their front door.

Today one of the last remaining vestiges of the railroad still serves — the old railroad trestle is a one-way bridge connecting the sleepy little village to the Route 17 expressway across the river.

Two views of the now vanished north portal of the Hawk Mountain tunnel. Top photograph shows a one-man scooter and when compared with the photograph, opposite page, it would appear Hawk Mountain and its control tower were a favorite congregating point for the three-wheeler set. Just above the keystone of the arch, visible, lower photograph, the railroad placed a plaque commemorating the contractors and officials of the railroad company. *Courtesy, Oscar O. Bennett*

Hawk Mountain control tower, a vital railroad facility for the safe operation of trains through the short single-track bore.

Hawk Mountain

Hawk Mountain, about a mile from Cadosia, has witnessed engineering marvels from the 1870's to 1968. The high rattlesnake-infested mountain spur has through the years been a challenge to civil engineers. Even after the Oswego Midland crews blasted a tunnel through the barrier, the railroad was barred by frequent rock falls within and slides without.

A near miss occurred in November, 1878, when a multi-ton rock fell from the roof of the tunnel just missing the mail train by a few seconds. The rock entirely blocked the entrance to the tunnel necessitating the transfer of passengers by stage over the ridge. Less than a month later, while masons were building an arch at the point of the rock fall, another rock dropped killing laborer Walter Allen instantly and seriously injuring Smith Denman of Summitville and William Potts of Hancock.

Despite the installation of tunnel lining, rock falls were a common occurrence, but generally damage was modest. For example, on Saturday, April 10, 1903, Engineer Patrick Larkin on train No. 6 spotted a rock and had time enough to slow up and gently push it along until the train finally stopped. The only damage was a badly dented pilot.

The old stage route over the mountain ridge, dangerous enough with the horse and buggy, became, with the coming of the horseless carriage, one of the most dangerous sections of highway to drive in New York State. The deadliest point was the 100-foot hairpin curve at the ridge of the rocky outcropping and its hazardous approaches.

To remedy the situation, the State Department of Public Works announced on November 10, 1932, that it planned to replace the sharp curve on the top of Hawk Mountain with a separated lane on

ROSCOE WEST 365

Looking out the east portal of the Hawk Mountain tunnel from the rear of "speeding" westbound train No. 37, on February 4, 1940.

two levels — a unique solution in its day for the elimination of the dangerous curve. The curve had been constructed as part of the original New York State Route 4 in 1911.

In 1966-67 the Route 17 expressway was sliced through the ridge of the mountain with the aid of hard rock drillers from the Rockies, carving a new chapter in engineering achievement at Hawk Mountain. The 6.4 mile cutting, blasting and filling job cost 12.5 million dollars, a remarakble price when compared to the 1.2 million construction costs of the entire 1911 State Route 4 from Middletown to Binghamton.

The great engineering marvel of the 1870's was buried by the massive approach fills of the 1966 highway cut. First the south portal and then the north portal of the O. and W. tunnel vanished. The disappearance of the north portal took with it the keystone and the engraved dates, and the names of engineers and officials of the road in that bygone era of railroad expansion.

The Route 17 Hawk Mountain cut, a triumph of highway engineering that obliterated the west tunnel portal — to left of and below curve, left. Cadosia yards and its mountainous coal piles were once the landmark features of the distant valley. *Courtesy, Bob Wyer, Bob Wyer Photo Cards*

The busy and vital Cadosia depot, nestled in the "V" formed by the Scranton Division track, left, and the mainline track to Oswego, right. The train shown is backing up the mainline with empties to pass over the "Y" track, background, for movement down the Scranton Division. *D. Diver Collection, Cornell University*

Cadosia : Hancock

Cadosia was the most vital junction point on the New York, Ontario and Western; here the coal line to Scranton branched off from the main line to Oswego and crossed a gracefully curved trestle to nearby Hancock and the Delaware River crossing.

Hancock and Cadosia, twin communities, were linked together, first by horse-drawn stages and then by auto busses. By 1888 transfer traffic from the main line of the Erie to the main line of the O. and W. at Cadosia had increased to the point where a special O. and W. ticket office was established in the community's leading hostelry, the Hancock House.

When the first auto busses arrived to replace the stages, they were chain driven, a feature which resulted in frequent upsets when a chain link snapped. But it was not the transfer of passengers to Cadosia that focused attention on that sleepy little hamlet but the tempting lure of 'black gold' to the south of the Delaware valley.

As far back as 1881, the O. and W. management began eyeing the coal beds of northeast Pennsylvania when they contemplated a route down the Bashas Kill to the lower Neversink valley to cross the Delaware River at or near Port Jervis. The plan was to have the route surveyed and partially graded for the Lehigh and Eastern road, following it down the Delaware valley past Milford and thence to the coal regions.

In 1889 three short lines in northeastern Pennsylvania, the Forest City and State Line, the Hancock and Pennsylvania, and the Scranton and Forest City railroads ran their last as independent entities. By June, 1890, they were merged with the aid of British and Dutch investors into the Ontario, Carbondale and Scranton, a wholly owned subsidiary of the O. and W. running from Cadosia to Scranton.

The road was formally opened to freight traffic on Monday, June 30, 1890, with the run of an

Birdseye view of Cadosia showing the depot, right foreground, the "Y" and trestle, just above and the water tank, center foreground. The Junction House, P.E. O'Rourke, prop., left of depot, was popular with the trainmen, while the mansard roofed Mountain House and cupola-topped icehouse, immediate left, offered a bit of resort atmosphere to the sooty rail center. The two houses over the Mountain House still stand — all the rest are gone, replaced by the Cadosia-Hancock Rt. 17 Quickway interchange. The depot still survives, below (1970), visited now and then by retired (and nostalgic) O. and W. crews and an occasional O. and W. buff.   *Courtesy, Oscar O. Bennett*

official inspection train headed by President Thomas P. Fowler in his private car, the "Warwick." The fifteen member party riding in the Pullman "Albemarle" left Hancock Junction at 8:00 a.m. that Monday morning with "breakfast and subsequent meals being served in the president's coach."[13]

A guest on board who was a member of the editorial staff of *The Coal Trade Journal* wrote that the road "is already in excellent shape for so new a line, having no sharp curves, tunnels nor deep cuts ..."[14] Dinner was served on the return trip from Scranton and "evidence was afforded of the smoothness of the newly built road, the crockery and glassware resting as quietly in their places as could be desired." This account was written of course, before the pounding of Moguls and Consols with their 65 and 70 loads of coal in tow. The Ontario breaker at Peckville produced the first car of coal for the new line the day of the formal opening.

By March, 1893, coal was moving out over not only the routes to Oswego, Middletown and New York City, but also to New England from the docks at Cornwall via the transfer boat "Hart"[15] to the New York and New England docks at Fishkill (Beacon). The arrangement to New England did not last too long due to the difficulty of navigating the Hudson in winter.

On November 14, 1893, announcement was made of a new traffic arrangement whereby O. and W. coal would move to Campbell Hall for its junction with the Poughkeepsie Bridge system and continue over that line to the main line of the New York and New England.

Portion of the Cadosia coal storage yards showing the steam plant and loading and unloading equipment. Today, the route 17 Quickway covers the entire storage area. *Courtesy, Oscar O. Bennett*

The Cadosia-Hancock area was indeed a region of trestles. Left, is the curving single-tracked Cadosia trestle, with a string of 'high cars' southbound on the Scranton Division. Cadosia depot and yards in background at base of the hill. The panorama at right, shows the Delaware River bridge, left, just after double-tracking, and in the distance the curving Sands Creek trestle with a steam-spouting freight approaching from right. The Hancock depot is just out of picture, right. The tops of the skeletal bents of the original (and longer) single-track Delaware River bridge stick out of the new fill for the double-tracked approach. (The start of this filling operation is shown on the following page.) The old single-track bridge abutment is visible just to right of the new concrete underpass. The years 1910-1912 saw the entire Scranton Division double-tracked. *Photograph right, collection of Robert F. Harding; courtesy Oscar O. Bennett*

The almost abandoned Hancock depot, above, six years before abandonment. In January, 1911, business was so good that the entire Scranton Division was undergoing doubletracking. Widening the cut at the Hancock depot, right, was typical of the handwork involved. *Top photograph by Edward H. Weber; right, Sullivan County Museum Archives*

Mother Hubbard-powered work train backs slowly out on single tracked Delaware River bridge from Pennsylvania side. Shovelers, right, move fill off flat cars for development of second track approach embankment. *Sullivan County Museum Archives*

The July 2, 1890 issue of the *Coal Trade Journal* announced that the new firm of Dickson and Eddy would be the sales agents for the O. and W. Mr. Dickson was a son of the late Thomas Dickson, who was for many years with the Delaware and Hudson Canal Company and its president at the time of his death.

The *Coal Trade Journal* noted with the opening of the Scranton Division that approaches to the Delaware River valley constitute a "grade of 14 miles, 84 feet to the mile, which will facilitate the movement of coal laden trains." Indeed it did, but perhaps not always to good advantage. This derailment of all-wooden coal cars at Starlight, about 1925, required the services of a big hook and an "Orry" class "P" locomotive, out of Mayfield Yard. *Courtesy, Oscar O. Bennett*

Locomotive No. 203, with Merton Lupton at the throttle, suffered a broken pony truck flange resulting in this twisted pile of smashed coal cars which required the services of two "big hooks" and three days of feverish activity. *Courtesy, Guy P. Twaddell*

The trestles on the 14-mile grade (Poyntelle to Sands Creek) were frequently responsible for spectacular pileups such as this derailed runaway of locomotive No. 201 at Starlight which claimed the life of Mel Whiting about 1903. The Delaware and Hudson Railroad, below, was often called upon to supply power for nudging the ponderous Mayfield-based "big hook" around. This costly altercation near Lakewood involved engineer August "Gus" Ihlefeldt, and fireman Merle Jacobs. *Courtesy, Oscar O. Bennett*

As the coal tonnage grew, the need for more powerful locomotives became increasingly apparent. George W. West, Superintendent of Motive Power of the O. and W. set to work on a project which culminated in the production of the Consolidations (Consol), two of which emerged from the Cooke Locomotive and Machine Company shops about September 1, 1900. The 100-ton locomotives were immediately put to work hauling coal on the Scranton – Hancock run. The mammoth machines were not allowed past Cadosia until two old bridges on the main line were replaced. The standard engines on the O. and W. before the Consols weighed 66-tons and, on a grade of seventy feet to the mile, were capable of drawing only 530 tons. The new Consols could draw 900 tons on the same grade. The success of the new engines and burgeoning business prompted the O. and W. management to order six more in March of 1901, plus 575 coal cars.

For all the improvement in motive power ratios, the grade (85 feet to the mile) down to the Delaware was a factor that continually took its runaway toll. An uncharacteristic, non-fatal and innocuous incident occurred in July, 1901, when train No. 229 stopped at Starlight and lost air pressure because of a leaking air hose. Engineer Mell Whiting noticed the condition and started walking to the rear to tell the trainmen, when the tonnage started to roll. Swinging to the top of a gondola and frantically dashing over endless piles of coal to the engine cab, he found the train completely out of control. Engineer Whiting "opened the whistle wide, thinking to warn trackmen and others of his coming. He then waited for the crash but it did not come. The men on the work train at the Delaware River trestle ... heard the whistle and roar of the runaway train and hurriedly started for Hancock to get out of the way. At Sand's Creek trestle above Hancock the runaway was only a car's length from the work train. Whiting finally brought it to a stop near Leonard's crossing. The distance from Starlight to Hancock is six miles and the run had been made in less than five minutes."[16]

Taking charge of a full tonnage train of coal from Mayfield Yard to Middletown in the days of steam was an experience an "old hogger" was not soon to forget. Oscar O. Bennett of Hancock, a retired engineer, who worked on the O. and W. from 1920 to 1957, recalled the procedure involved to move a consist to the storage piles at Middletown.

"We would start out with a Y-2 (451-460) on the lead equipped with two 8½ x 4 inch cross compound pumps, two Class X pushers (351-362) and a Class P kicker (pusher) (201-220). Leaving Mayfield Yard we moved out to Forest City, a distance of 10 miles, at which point all the locomotives took on water. At Stillwater, the kicker cut off on the fly and returned to Mayfield Yard.

"At Poyntelle (the summit) the train was stopped to disengage the pushers and set up as many retainers as the engineer requested, generally twenty or more. Leaving Poyntelle we began the the longest, steepest grade east of the Rockies, down to the Delaware River. At Jones' Fill[17] we stopped to let down the retainers so as to make the run over Hancock sag[18] between the Delaware River bridge and Cadosia, a distance of three miles.

Oscar O. Bennett points toward the rock cut where a head-on collision on September 10, 1902, resulted in the death of the fireman. No. 217 allegedly pulled out of Preston Park siding against orders. Eluding the attention of the station operator, the train crossed the Preston Park trestle (pier remains in valley) and collided with No. 203.

The Alpha and the Omega — Mayfield Yard, above, starting point of endless coal drags bound for the extensive storage tracks at Middletown, right. *Top photograph, courtesy Jim Shaughnessy*

"At Cadosia a thorough inspection of the train took place—coal, water, sand and a clean fire in the locomotive. After servicing we began the thirty-one miles up the river to Livingston Manor. If, in the engineer's judgment, he could not make the Manor in one hour and five minutes, it was imperative he get water at Cooks Falls. If he did stop at Cooks Falls, another hour was lost. Arriving at Livingston Manor the lead engine took on water and another pusher. There was 24-hour pusher service at Livingston Manor in three 8-hour shifts.

"Cutting the pusher at Young's Gap we began the descent of the 29-mile hill to Summitville. It was a heavy downgrade to Ferndale trestle with good running ground to Mountaindale and heavy downgrade on Red Hill to Summitville.

"We took on water at Summitville and picked up a pusher to Bloomingburg Tunnel. Cutting the pusher on the fly at the entrance to the tunnel we passed through the mountain to High View then down the hill to Winterton, across the trestle and upgrade to Fair Oaks and on to Middletown and a cup of well-earned coffee at Seeholtzer's Restaurant."

On September 10, 1953, Edward H. Weber of Virginia elected to take train No. 1 on the O. and W. to Roscoe. Camera in hand, Ed duly recorded the trip, particularly the turn-around at Roscoe, and returned with pictures of the train and crew. It was the last regularly scheduled passenger train out of Sullivan County. The train was made up of one baggage car and two open-end observation cars. Shown above on the observation deck of car No. 82 are trainman "J.J." Moroney, left, and conductor "Charlie" Robinson.

Epilogue

Abandoned Lake Wood Depot, originally Winwood. Before railroad, known as Como

When Frederic E. Lyford, newly-appointed trustee for the New York, Ontario and Western in 1937, walked into the offices of Otto Kuhler, well-known industrial designer, he got a pleasant surprise. There, spread out on the design tables, was a comprehensive presentation for a "streamlined train" for the ailing O. and W. passenger service.

Kuhler, anticipating a need, set about designing the train along very tight budgetary lines. The passenger equipment used during the early depression years had not been upgraded and was now becoming shopworn and even less attractive to the traveling public. Automobile and bus service was cutting into the once lucrative business of moving passengers to Sullivan and Ulster resorts.

Knowing the austere budget that the O. and W. would have to adhere to, costs were budgeted at a modest $8,500 for the upgrading and modernization. In April of 1938 the local papers reported, "the train under construction[1] in the Middletown shops will consist of four or five coaches, painted an attractive color, hauled by a powerful locomotive distinctly decorated."

Railway Age for June 4, 1938, commented, "an experiment in merchandising relatively short haul passenger service will be inaugurated by the New York, Ontario and Western on June 24 when it installs its new summer train, "The Mountaineer," between New York City and Roscoe, N.Y., a distance of 135 miles."

Just before Memorial Day in 1938 the "Mountaineer" whistled off and highballed out of the Middletown yards with Bob Hirst at the throttle and Walt Davis holding down the left side. Bob Sherwood, now living in Liberty, who was at that time station agent at Ferndale, recalled that "the Ferndale school was closed for the day so the kids could see Number 1 (the Mountaineer) go through. The platform was pretty crowded with kids and adults when she whistled through."

Response by the public was encouraging but managerial optimism was soon shattered with the advent of World War II. The specially refurbished

New York, Ontario and Western Railway
FREDERIC E. LYFORD, Trustee

ANNOUNCES

"THE MOUNTAINEER"
A NEWLY RECONDITIONED TRAIN

Providing greater comfort and convenience in traveling between

NEW YORK CITY

and the

MOUNTAIN RESORTS

of

Sullivan and Ulster Counties

"THE PLAY GROUND OF THE EMPIRE STATE"

Northbound	SCHEDULES		Southbound	
(Read down)	EASTERN STANDARD TIME		(Read up)	
No. 3 Daily			No. 4	No. 96
A M			P M	P M
	Lv. Cortl'ndt St. N.Y.(ferry) Ar.		.....	.....
11 35	Lv. W. 42nd St. N.Y.(ferry) Ar.		10 15	10 50
11 47	Lv. Weehawken Ar.		10 01	10 38
1 07	Lv. Cornwall Lv.		8 41	9 13
1 57	Lv. Middletown Lv.		7 58	8 35
2 14	Lv. High View Lv.		.....	▲
2 19	Lv. Mamakating Lv.		.....	▲
2 28	Lv. Summitville Lv.		.....	▲
2 47	Lv. Mountaindale Lv.		.....	7 48
2 53	Lv. Woodridge Lv.		.....	7 42
3 01	Lv. Fallsburgh (Monticello) Lv.		6 58	7 34
3 09	Lv. Luzon (Loch Sheldrake) Lv.		6 50	7 25
3 19	Lv. Ferndale (Swan Lake) Lv.		6 40	7 14
3 26	Lv. Liberty Lv.		6 35	7 08
3 38	Lv. Parksville Lv.		6 24	6 56
3 50	Lv. Livingston Manor Lv.		6 13	6 45
4 01	Ar. Roscoe Lv.		6 00	6 30
P M			P M	P M

In May, 1938, this special brochure was issued by the O. and W. management to promote the "newly reconditioned train," Mountaineer. *Courtesy, William Capach*

"The Mountaineer" Parlor Cars

Attractive, roomy chairs in the Early American style make the newly furnished "Mountaineer" parlor cars the last word in comfort and convenience. When you travel with friends, the chairs may be arranged in a congenial group; if you prefer, your chair may be turned to face the window.

No Increase in Fares

You can ride in these luxurious parlor cars for the regular coach fare. The only extra cost is the standard parlor car seat charge. Comfort, convenience, safety and the regularity of railway travel are all yours at a new "low" in cost.

Traveling on "THE MOUNTAINEER" PROVIDES

More Comfort	Less Delay
More Safety	Less Danger
More Relaxation	Less Fatigue
More Room	Less Worry
More Enjoyment	Less Cost

Color Scheme Identifies "The Mountaineer"

You can't miss "The Mountaineer". Its bright orange and Ontario maroon exterior is fast becoming a symbol throughout the territory it serves. Use this new train to travel to and from the mountains.

"The Mountaineer" Coaches

Doesn't the interior, as pictured below, look inviting? The color scheme is the new Ontario maroon on the floor with cream ceiling as a cool contrast. Monogrammed linen seat covers give a fresh, comfortable appearance to these roomy cars.

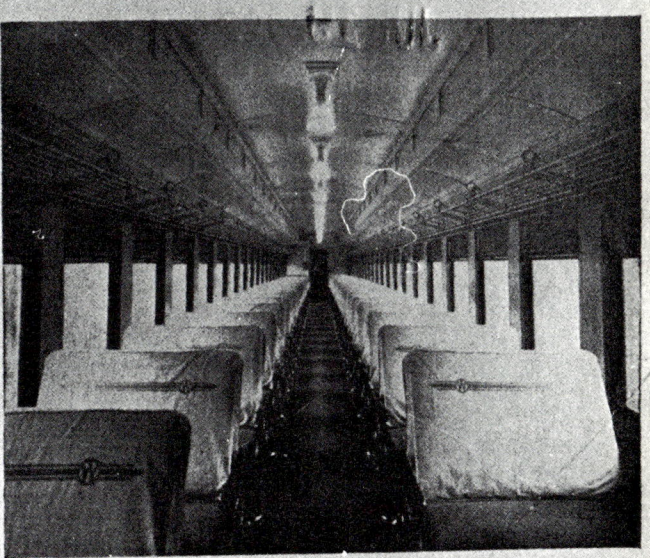

For your convenience the Southbound schedule has been arranged so that you may enjoy the entire last day of your vacation or visit, leave after dinner and still arrive in New York that same evening. Or, for a short shopping or business trip to New York, take "The Mountaineer", spend the night in New York, shop or transact business the next morning, and return on "The Mountaineer".

For further information, consult Ticket Agents or address General Passenger Agent, 370 Lexington Ave., New York City.

The resplendent Mountaineer locomotive, No. 405, pauses with its bright new consist at Livingston Manor, about 4:00 on a warm August afternoon in 1938 — the dawning year of a career that was to be terminated by the Second World War.

equipment was broken up and used in a melange of passenger train operations and troop train service while number 405, the head end power, was pressed into the vastly expanded freight service to end her operating days in that capacity.[2]

The resort region of Sullivan County had its problems during the Second World War, primarily with the ban on pleasure driving that went into effect at noon on January 7, 1943.

Things would get worse. In May, 1943, guests and employees of hotels and large boardinghouses were obliged to turn over their War Ration Books 1 and 2 to hotel proprietors if they stayed in the establishment for seven or more consecutive days.

But it was the transport scene that was the darkest. In May the O. and W. agreed to run two more trains, while the Mountain Transit Company ran only 17 busses as compared with the normal 100 in order to comply with a sudden order by the Office of Defense Transportation to cut schedules drastically.

Taxicabs (or as they are locally known, 'hackers') to and from the city did a flourishing business. Seats in southbound cabs were auctioned at $6.00 and $7.00 each and in Monticello, one of the chief intake and outgo points of the county, fares of $10.00 were reported in contrast to the usual $4.00 rate. From Kiamesha came a report of one operator whose cab was full being halted by a vacationist, who said that he knew where there were possible passengers who would pay double what the hacker was charging the fares he already had. Pretending his cab was disabled, the driver dumped his passengers at a corner, and went back to pick up the other, more affluent, group.

Thousands came by Erie to both Middletown and Port Jervis, rushing for the Sullivan County busses as soon as the trains stopped, many standing in the aisles all the way from the city.

One positive aspect of the transport dilemma was that resorts easily accessible by rail and bus did more business than under normal conditions be-

The handsome 405, (a class Y-1 type, 4-8-2 wheel arrangement) built by the American Locomotive Works in 1923, was the show-off piece of rolling stock of the management. Above, it is shown proudly hauling a railfan special across the upper Liberty trestle on September 24, 1939. Complete dieselization, below, was just over the horizon. The first press release appeared in the Liberty *Gazette* for September 14, 1944, which revealed "plans call for delivery of the first Diesel-electric engine next year. All steam locomotives will be discarded by the end of 1945." The order for 37 diesels, costing approximately $6,700,000, went to the Electro-Motive division of General Motors. *Top photograph, D. Diver collection, Cornell University; below, photograph by Jim Shaughnessy*

The crew of train No. 2, just before the last departure from Roscoe on September 10, 1953. Left to right, engineer Charles Fish; trainman J.J. Moroney; conductor Charles Robinson and fireman "Gus" Ahrenholz. *Photograph by Edward H. Weber*

cause a large percentage of their guests stayed in one spot longer than they would have if automobile travel had been unrestricted.

Freight business was also improved during the war. For the two years, 1942 and 1943, the defense traffic produced a small net railway operating income[3] of $200,000 for the two year period with 1944 the peak year, operating revenues (sales income) up 28 percent over pre-war years.[4] But the boost was not enough to save the ailing line. The railroad company, then in the process of financial reorganization, received an unfortunate blow when a 13-car derailment occurred just south of the Ferndale depot in March, 1943. Much of the consist was war material and, fortunately for the financially strapped line, salvageable.[5]

By 1950 things were indeed bleak with the ton-miles down to 773,105 for 1949 as compared with 1,518,148 during the war-time year of 1943. The share of coal in the operating revenues in 1949 was 17 percent as compared to 51 percent in 1939.

Passenger revenues were suffering too, with a modest $24,917 in the first six months of 1949. At the time of the "Mountaineer" in 1939 revenues were $331,246, a shadow of the whopping $788,000 in 1900. To state it in a more dismal way — in 1949 total operating expenses of passenger service was $388,030 as compared with revenues of $199,304.

In a report prepared for *The Eleven-County Consolidated Committee* by W.C. Kessler of Colgate University in 1950, other facets of the inevitable demise of the "old lady" were brought into focus. One criticism concerned the LCL freight service in the vicinity of Liberty which was characterized as "slow, damages resulting (and) employees sometimes giving poor service in unloading." Although noted as a common complaint against most U.S. railroads, one additional factor that was hurting the O. and W. was the ongoing belief that the line would be abandoned. "All persons dealing with traffic and traffic problems

The Last Years...
a portfolio by JIM SHAUGHNESSY

Fair Oaks

EPILOGUE 383

Campbell Hall

Middletown

One of the last freight train pile-ups occurred at the Fallsburgh depot, left background, on December 23, 1956. A broken rail sent 20 northbound empty cars out of an 89-car train off the track or into an adjacent swamp. After the 1957 closing, the Liberty depot stood silently, above, awaiting the arrival of the scrappers train, shown below at Buckley Street overpass in back of Liberty in June 1958, removing the skeletal remains of the once proud road. *Top and lower photographs by Paul Gerry*

Noted Sullivan County photographer—O. and W. buff Paul Gerry captured the Ferndale trestle under a patina of snow — spring would see the towering 'bents' crashing to the valley floor. By mid-summer the upper Liberty trestle, right, would be half gone. Part of the Hillside Greenhouse complex shows at left edge. *Photograph, right, by Paul Gerry*

One bridge has eluded scrapping, shown here (1970) at a point about mid-way between Roscoe and Cooks Falls known by old railroaders as "Hairpull." The curious name came about as a result of a nearby resident who sheltered two women who were in constant conflict — pulling each other's hair.

EPILOGUE 387

The old order changeth. The above view shows a steam powered 'varnish' and a portion of the old Liberty Highway (State Rt. 4 — Rt. 17), just east of Roscoe. Today it is indeed difficult to imagine the setting as one wisks along on ribbons of concrete around the same bend in the changeless Willowemoc.

The doorway to Sullivan County is still open, however gaunt and inhospitable, as nature gradually returns to claim her own. It will soon be a century since the High View tunnel was opened to become the gateway to an era of bucholic charm and hospitality.

concur in opinion that constant talk of possible or probable abandonment of all or portions of N.Y.O. and W. has had an unfavorable effect upon the desire of present patrons to continue to use the railroad to the present or greater extent." The report added that the negative attitude was discouraging new industry from settling on the line. The report was really a portent of the future. On September 10, 1953, the last scheduled passenger train out of Sullivan County left Roscoe behind diesel engine No. 502.

As circumstances went from bad to worse, attempts were made to form a corporation to operate the O. and W. as a shortline railroad from Middletown to Roscoe or East Branch in Delaware County. Woodridge Attorney Henry Temes was chairman of a Sullivan committee of receivers. A study indicated that it would take $100,000 to begin operations as a shortline railroad.

All to no avail.

The death throes were nearly over when the Sullivan County *Press* for March 21, 1957, headlined: "Receives Order Closing of O. and W."

The last train arrived in Middletown from Norwich at 3:15 a.m. on March 30, 1957, bringing to a close a dynamic chapter in the annals of railroading.

More importantly for Sullivan County, it was a dramatic demonstration of the way in which a railroad could help to transform a region.

From a tannery-dominated wilderness to a leader in the hotel industry — this is the legacy of the coming and going of the New York, Ontario and Western Railway.

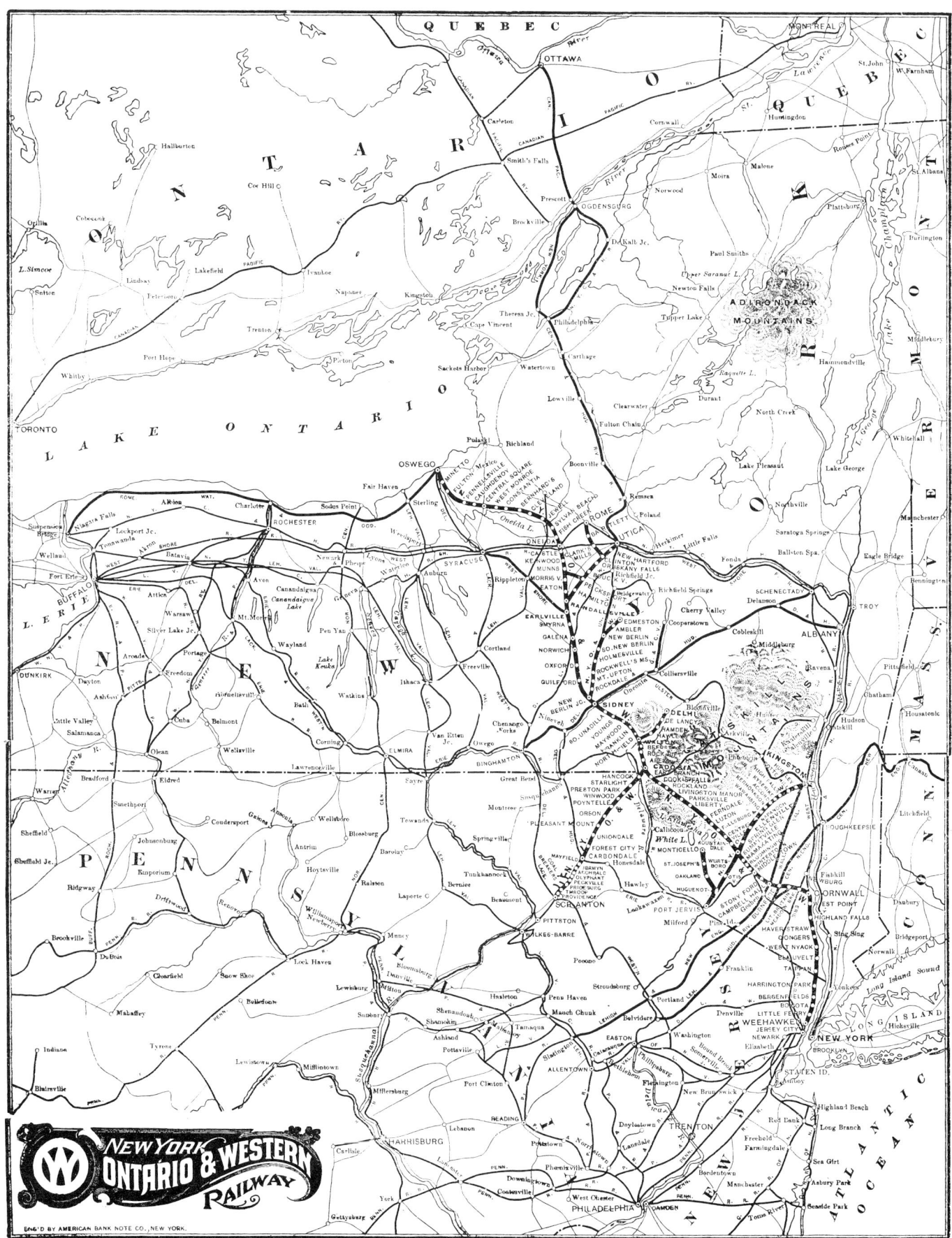

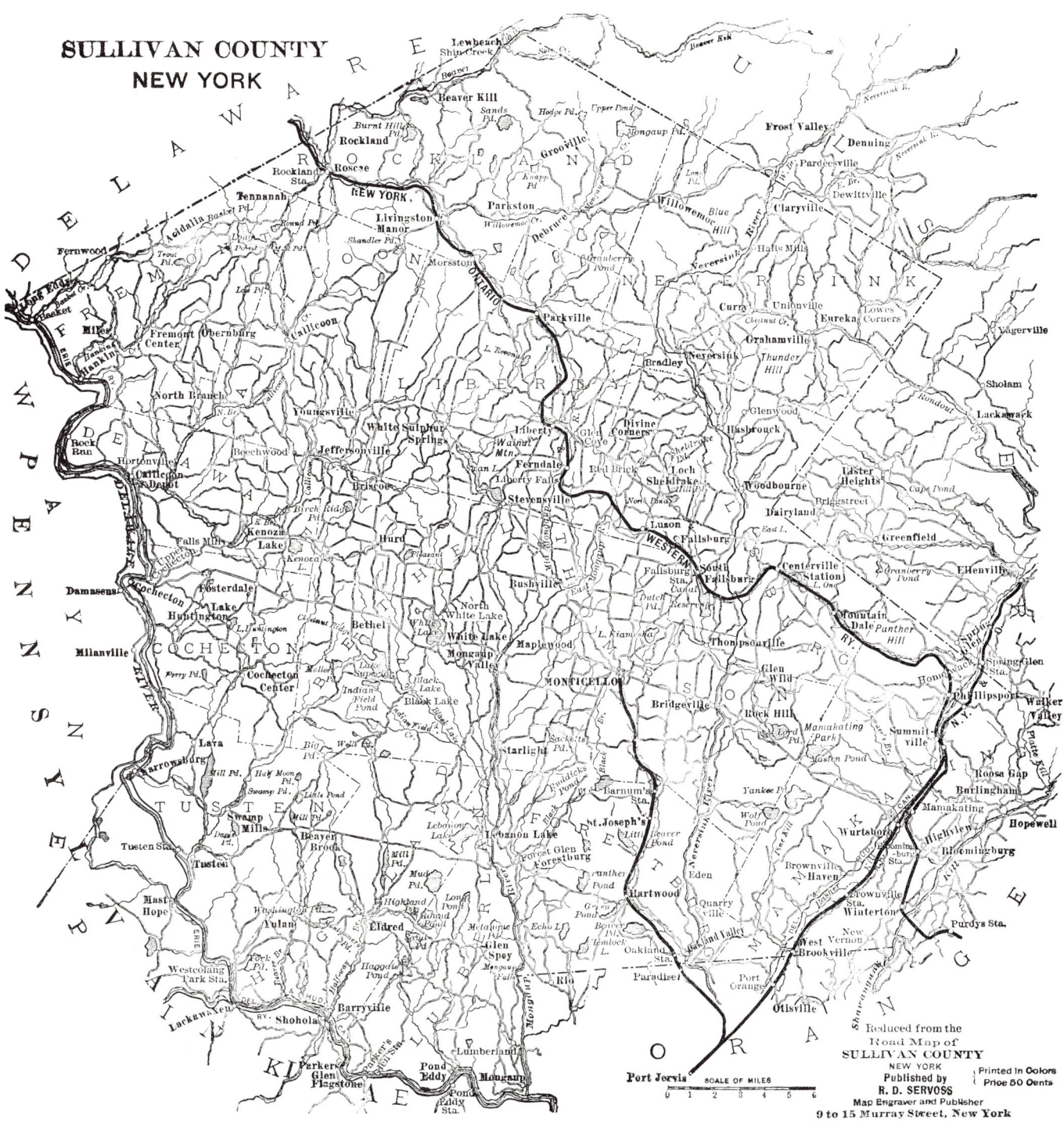

Sullivan County

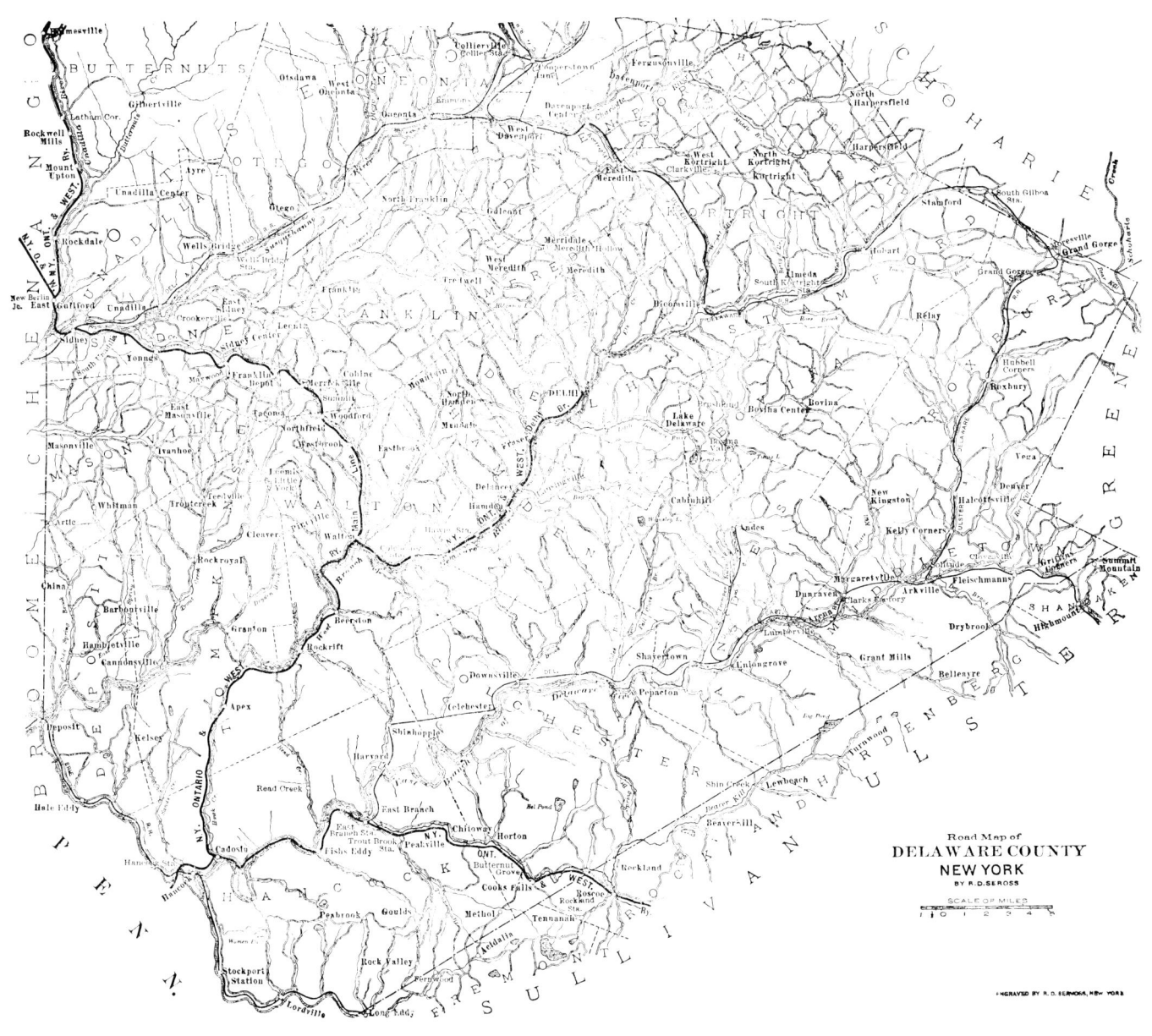

Delaware County

Notes

INTRODUCTION

[1] Translated from the Lenni Lenape indian tribe language meaning a place of red stone hills.

[2] Tusten Depot, Narrowsburg, Callicoon, Hankins, Long Eddy, and Cochecton (Lake Huntington).

TO THE MOUNTAINS BY RAIL
Weehawken to Bloomingburg

[1] First published in the Spring of 1878 as "Summer Homes on the Midland" by the New York and Oswego Midland. In 1880 its cover title was simplified to "Summer Homes" while its title page continued to carry "Summer Homes among the Mountains". By the turn of the century this publication became the most important railroad resort promotional piece in America.

[2] The West Shore and O. and W. officially began joint operations down the Hudson River's West shore when the 1883 timetables treated both companies as one.

[3] Through cars were run over the Wallkill Valley Railroad thence to New York avoiding the annoyance of transfer for Lake Mohonk and Lake Minnewaska travelers. Later, with the completion of the Ellenville & Kingston line, the O. and W. carried patrons to these two points on its own rails.

HIGH VIEW
Bloomingburg

[1] Noted banker and financier who at the time of his death was known as "America's leading Jew" due in great part to the publicity surrounding the Seligman-Hilton affair.

[2] Liberty establishments also stated their preferences with the Hall House, D.R. Bonnell farmhouse, J.B. Nichols & Sons Maple View House (now Grossingers), the J.M. Hill private cottage noting 'Jews need not apply,' etc.

[3] High View Post Office was established for the area around the depot thus taking it away from the Bloomingburg jurisdiction. In July, 1925, the name Bloomingburg was eliminated entirely from the timetables. Up until that time it was listed as Bloomingburg with High View following in brackets. The double listings caused confusion to railroad patrons.

[4] The size of the piazza or porch was a most important architectural dimension of the resort hotel.

[5] Town of Mamakating Highway Superintendent, 1968.

[6] Sullivan County *Whig*, later moved to Monticello to become the *Republican-Watchman*.

[7] Liberty *Register*, January 20, 1927

[8] Liberty *Register* July 7, 1932

[9] Delhi was eager for a bus line to Walton and finally succeeded in having one established. The railroad, losing much of its business, applied for and received from the Public Service Commission, permission to discontinue its branch to Delhi. During the winter it was claimed the bus lines failed to operate on schedule and to give such service as Delhi depended upon. The town appealed for restoration of train service but to no avail.

HIGH VIEW TUNNEL
Bloomingburg Tunnel

[1] Cheaply Built

[2] Class X, single cab locomotives built in 1915 with a 2-10-2 wheel arrangement.
Class Y-2, single cab locomotives built in 1929 with a 4-8-2 wheel arrangement.

[3] Liberty *Register,* October 14, 1904

MAMAKATING
Wurtsboro

[1] The Wurtsboro station referred to here was actually the Mamakating depot on the main line. Henceforth, the Wurtsboro depot will refer to that servicing the village of Wurtsboro in the valley and Mamakating as the station facility on the mountain.

[2] Exclusive summer colony in Orange County, N.Y., founded by Pierre Lorrillard in the 1880's.

[3] The first trail to be so designated a ROAD in the then emerging America.

[4] In 1800 known as Rome.

[5] 1910 "Summer Homes"

[6] Wurtsboro total listings of boardinghouses, farmhouses and hotels: 1886-9, 1898-34, 1910-18, 1920-2 and 1930-5.

[7] Old-time boatmen's spelling.

[8] The local press in the many villages along the line vigorously promoted in January and February the request for advertising copy for the forthcoming "Summer Homes" — February 15th or March 1st generally the deadline. In the 1880's the railroad had a representative [a Mr. Walker] who went up the line to receive advertisements — the press announcing "Go to your nearest station agent or the traveling representative, give him $10 or $20 and a well and truthfully written

393

description of your place...". In 1896 "...not more than 25 words, costs $1.00; not more than 60 words, $2.00; not more than 100 words, $3.00." By 1905 two lines of copy cost $1.50; five lines, $3.00; ten lines, $6.00 and twenty-five lines (Liberty House & Mansion House of Liberty), $15.00. The frequent distortions in descriptive copy would indicate lack of scrutiny or criteria by the agents — particularly in the first two or three decades of publication.

All station agents had application blanks on hand for new advertisers as well as the responsibility [by the 1920's] of securing those ads that were delinquent from the previous year's issue. A typical letter from the Traffic Dept. [Sent to the Ticket Agent at High View.] dated February 26, 1926. "Enclosed please find a copy of last year's "Summer Homes." We have crossed out with red pencil the ads that have been received at this office for our 1926 book. Will you please see what you can do to secure the ads which have not been received, and any other new ones possible? You may accept ads up to and including March 15th."

[9] "On the fly" or "fly switching" is a standard railroad switching procedure when convenient. A train moving at a modest rate of speed uncouples and the powered end pulls ahead past the switch, then the switch points are thrown for the siding and the cars, under their own momentum, move into the siding. Also operable in reverse.

[10] The delegates from Monticello were State Committeeman A.M. Scriber, Chairman; Chairman of County Committee D.S. Avery, Supervisor H.B. Stratton and Village President J.J. Burns.

[11] Henry McNamee, original contractor for the deep uphill cut and extensive downhill fill went bankrupt before completion of the costly project.

[12] Among the Board of Directors of the association were Peter H. Mitchell (Proprietor of Mitchell Inn) of Middletown and H.S. Campbell (proprietor of Campbell Inn) of Roscoe.

SUMMITVILLE

[1] The rolling stock, exclusive of the locomotive, making up a train.

[2] Liberty *Register,* January 27, 1922

[3] S.D. Coykendall, President of the Cornell Steamboat Company, purchased the D. and H. Canal in June, 1899, with all its franchises, rights and privileges for $10,000.

[4] Liberty *Register,* March 23, 1900.

[5] Reference to the Italian construction crews.

[6] Liberty *Register,* October 31, 1902.

[7] Wakefield, Manville B., "Lackawack House: Spa for Tammany Hall." Middletown *Times Herald RECORD,* April 24, 1968.

[8] A long-time resident of the valley and later of Sundown and Wallkill.

[9] Railroaders slang for a headon collision.

[10] Leaping from the cab just before impact.

MOUNTAINDALE

[1] O'Neill was later to expire in the near-legendary Cooks Falls head-on collision.

[2] Liberty *Register,* July 1, 1892.

[3] Liberty *Register,* November 29, 1901.

[4] Hamilton Child's *Gazetteer and Business Directory of Sullivan County"* spelling "Sandburgh."

[5] Its earliest spelling consisted of two words.

[6] An added feature in 1898 was an "Illustrated Summer Homes" with 338, 2" x 3 3/4" pictures of the listed summer resorts and sold for $.25, (the regular Summer Homes was gratis). An additional touch — each picture was numbered and that number was included within parentheses at the end of the copy for that particular resort in the "Summer Homes" book.

[7] In the 1898 "Summer Homes" Paul P. VanBarriger listed his resort as "Idlewile" and as a Christian resort noted "1½ miles to church" plus other data in eight lines of copy as contrasted with the one line in 1899. VanBarriger may have been offered better rates by the Jews or he may have been having a 'tiff' with some of the other farmhouse operators and have done it for spite.

[8] By March of 1903 sufficient numbers of Jewish folk had settled in and around Mountaindale to warrant the banding together for the purchase of a lot with the intent of erecting a synagogue.

[9] Anti-Semitism cropped up in one unusual form as noted in a release in the Liberty *Register* for June 21, 1905. Under a heading, "That Hebrew Sign," the story of the frustration of Abraham Glassman and his boarding house sign was spelled out. One of the first Jewish boarding house keepers in Hurleyville, Glassman erected an advertising sign in front of the Post Office only to find it painted out the next day. Having it repainted, it was again painted out. Again relettered it was erected on a second story porch with an announcement of a $100 reward for the jokester. Next day the sign had vanished entirely. The release closed with "it is probable that one of Pinkerton's best detectives will be put on the case."

[10] Liberty *Register,* February 13, 1903

[11] *Notes and Comment,* Dr. Irwin Richman.

[12] Liberty *Register*, March 7, 1919.

[13] The amendment provides that full and equal accommodations, advantages and privileges shall be enjoyed by all persons within the jurisdiction of the state at all resorts, places of amusement, or of public accommodation.

[14] Yiddish for 'cook alone' or 'cook yourself.'

[15] Last agent at Fallsburgh, March, 1957

[16] Eli Atwell recalls when the Sandburg station burned. "The operator at the station was Ernest Miller, and there was quite a lot of talk they were trying to get the station changed up to Mountaindale but they didn't want it changed as long as they had the station down there. The Sandburg station very opportunely burned and I remember afterwards there was quite a lot of talk that the Sandburg station had had some help to be eliminated."

[17] O. and W. slang for a company investigator.

[18] A vital component in the operation of a turn-out or switch.

[19] Railroad slang for a train on a siding or passing track.

[20] Founder of the Pullman Palace Car Company.

[21] President Ulysses S. Grant was best man at the marriage of Dr. Flurer to Emma. The Flurers came to Mountaindale about 1880.

[22] Dr. Flurer is credited with having performed the first successful head operation concerned with the removal of a bullet from the brain. He was also rushed by special train to the deathbed of President William McKinley in Buffalo for consultation.

[23] Supervisor, Town of Fallsburg, 1970, first elected in 1939.

CENTERVILLE
Woodridge

[1] The abbreviated 1918 "Summer Homes" listed Centerville as Woodridge for the first time.

[2] Brock's experiences along the O. and W. are henceforth chronicled at various points on the line. He was the last station agent at Liberty and died on May 14, 1964, at the age of 81.
Other station agents at the time the line closed down: Summitville, Clyde Budd with Walter LeVan, second trick operator; Mountaindale, Charles Riseley; Woodridge, Chester Phillips; South Fallsburg, John T. Allen, with Emory Patmore second trick operator; Hurleyville, Wesley Hutchins; Ferndale, Robert Sherwood; Livingston Manor, Leonard T. Quinn; Roscoe, Daniel Teller; and East Branch, Fred McMorris.

[3] The practice of turning over cash receipts to a railroad agent on a designated southbound train.

[4] This is pressure created by the slow escape of smoke from the stack of the engine.

FALLSBURGH
South Fallsburgh

[1] The depot was known as Fallsburgh, the post office as South Fallsburgh. In June, 1968, the (h) was officially eliminated by the New York State Assembly. The pre-1968 spelling will henceforth be used.

[2] Reality and image did not quite coincide. South Fallsburgh was not the Switzerland of Sullivan County. People were bitten by numerous mosquitoes and buzzed by innumerable flies. They sneezed, in season, because of the pollen of millions of ragweed plants.

[3] Later Liberty became the prime detraining point for the hamlet of Neversink.

[4] This format was used throughout the book for each major station and the surrounding resort communities that it served.

[5] The original farmhouse operation made the "publicity change" to boarding house status generally upon completion of a new wing to the farmhouse, development of outdoor recreational facilities or the addition of a hand-lettered three-seater for meeting the trains.

[6] The conservative estimate of 80 mph was made by the station agent and people of Luzon (Hurleyville) who lined the tracks and cheered the passing coal car.

[7] Crack all-milk express train originating on the northern division.

[8] The state would pay 49%, the railroad 50% and the county 1%.

[9] Nelson John Chaffee, Donald R. Summerson and Thomas Crispell.

[10] Both were caretakers at the Moneka Lodge — now Pines Hotel.

[11] Postmaster Charles S. Corwin was at the post office after eleven o'clock sorting mail that had arrived on the night train. He left the doomed structure a little before the alarm was given near midnight. The post office was reopened Monday morning at its former quarters on the other side of the O. and W. tracks in the Flynn garage building with a few postage stamps and a money order book Postmaster Corwin had taken home overnight.

[12] Liberty *Register*, April 12, 1912

[13] Identified by weather experts as a tornado.

[14] The Monticello *Republican* for September 17, 1886, reported a proposal by Senator H.R. Low to a group of community leaders "...that if the people would give the right-of-way, furnish the ties, fence the road, and make the preliminary survey, that he [Low] would ensure the immediate building and operation of the road." Although a committee was appointed to raise the $250 needed for the survey, little more was ever heard of this early proposal to connect the two villages by rail.

[15] Hill "16" is high terrain between Kiamesha Lake and the Thompsonville Road which tops out at an elevation of 1600 feet above sea level.

[16] Just two years before [Sept. 1900] a projected trolley line from White Lake to Shohola was very much alive with rights-of-way over two routes secured and contractors making inspections along the route.

[17] Monticello *Watchman*, January, 1903

[18] Traces of the approach fill and some pilings are still discernable on the north side of the creek 1970.

[19] Liberty *Register*, December 9, 1904

KIAMESHA LAKE

[1] Virtually every lake in Sullivan County has been described in "Summer Homes" at one time or another as a "beautiful sheet."

[2] 'Kiamesha' is Indian for 'clearwater' — a quality for which the lake was known far and wide.

[3] Liberty *Register*, August 8, 1913.

[4] Kiamesha Lake has also been a traditional dumping ground for gangland killings and hotel employee murders, and scarcely a year goes by without a quiet little incident on the shores of "the beautiful sheet of water."

[5] In 1895 the first Board of Water Commissioners, [David S. Avery, pres.; Robert McNickle, vice pres.; Jos. L. Reynolds, treas.; M. LaTourette, sec.] appointed about March 26, 1895, entered into a contract with Theodore D. Mead for the purchase of necessary land at Pleasant Lake for a pump house to pump water to Monticello. They purchased a lot 50 foot square with a right-of-way to the turnpike of 30' from a Mrs. Blackwood and a 99-year lease from Mr. Mead over all his property from Pleasant Lake to Monticello for $450.00. Mr. Mead was to have free water in all the buildings which he owned at Pleasant Lake and in Monticello as long as they were in the Mead family.

MONTICELLO

[1] The 1910 Monticello listings noted 67 resorts of which 4 featured Kosher cooking.

[2] One-time gathering place of all fraternal and social events in the Monticello area.

[3] Republican *Watchman*, August 13, 1909.

[4] Republican *Watchman*, August 13, 1909.

[5] The Republican Watchman also burned out on the night of April 26, 1874, Edward F. Curley in his *Old Monticello* recalled "hearing the heavy printing presses and the contents of that office crashing to the ground floor as the supports beneath them gave way."

[6] One of 15 townships in the County of Sullivan and named in honor of William A. Thompson, [March 19, 1803] first judge of the county.

[7] Closed at the time it burned in the 1919 conflagration.

[8] Other turn of the century hotels in Monticello: The Osborn House, the Latourette Hotel, Carlton Hotel, Park View, Fulton House and the Erie Hotel on St. John Street.

[9] The property was purchased at mortgage foreclosure by Adolph Feucht, representing the Argentor Holding Co. of New York for $36,000 in January, 1927.

[10] Located at the northwest end of Wheeler Street (then Maiden Lane) and represented a quarter of a million dollar investment.

OLD FALLS
Fallsburgh

[1] Although officially recognized by the State of Oregon as a holiday in 1887, it wasn't until 1894 that Congress officially declared the first Monday in September a legal holiday.

[2] Liberty *Register*, September 6, 1889

[3] Stucco soon became an architectural craze and along with the false front "crescent" easily marked these hotels as having been built after 1920. This combination of architectural details is sometimes referred to as "Sullivan County Mission."

[4] Hotels destroyed by fire before 1969.

WOODBOURNE

[1] "Hack" is the slang term given to jitney-type rental cars. They can be hired in toto or on an individual seat basis for trips to and from the mountains. There is a whole folklore that has grown up around them. The arguments were sometimes violent over how many suitcases and cardboard cartons travelers were entitled to carry. There were also tales of being driven all over the mountains for two or three hours until a full carload of passengers was acquired.

[2] Emphasis on outdoor sport activity was growing — "Summer Homes" started using full page scenes of outdoor group sport activities in their 1929 issue as contrasted to their heretofore pure scenic photo compositions. In 1932 the cover design featured a collage of athletic activities.

GRAHAMSVILLE

[1] Named for Lt. John Graham, leader of a 1778 expedition that resulted in the Massacre of Chestnut Woods. E.R. Dusinbery introduced a bill in the Assembly in February, 1901, providing for the erection of a monument at the massacre site. A commission consisting of Samuel N. Smith, Reuben D. Carney, James C. Young, G.F. Currey, Gordon C. Grant and Edwin R. Dusinbery of Sullivan County and James G. Graham of Orange County and S.P. Thorn of Ulster County was named to carry out the provisions of the act.

[2] Liberty *Register,* February 17, 1899.

[3] Liberty *Register,* June 2, 1922.

[4] Liberty *Register,* July 12, 1901.

[5] The 1890 "Summer Homes" listed 9 boarding houses, the largest "Summer Homes" listings for one issue.

[6] Interview: Bruce W. Fuller

LUZON
Hurleyville

[1] In the 1886 Summer Homes" it was listed HURLEYVILLE POST OFFICE – *Hurley Station.* Later with Hurley on the Kingston Branch, the confusion between Hurleyville and Hurley manifested itself by summer visitors arriving at Hurleyville and their trunks ending up at Hurley. In Nov., 1902, the railroad asked for suggestions for a new name from the townsfolk. By Jan. 1, 1903, the name Luzon was chosen. The Dr. DeKay family persuaded the railroad to name it Luzon as they had a son in Luzon in the Philippine Islands during the Spanish-American War.
Through the years frequent overtures were made to get rid of the name Luzon, but Luzon Station (Hurleyville Post Office) it stayed.

[2] In the nine years between 1873 and 1882 it grew from a scattering of six souls to a population of 143.

[3] The Hurleyville landmark commenced operations in 1891 under John Harms Knapp. The Liberty *Register* of June 2, 1893, announced "J.H. Knapp of Hurleyville will erect this summer a large boardinghouse to accommodate 150 guests on the hill southwest of that place."

[4] WILLARD ELMORE – Farm House 1½ miles; accommodate 20; adults $5 to $7, children under 10 years $4, transient $1.25; free transportation; high, dry and healthful airy rooms; comfortable beds; views extensive and very fine; plenty of shade; pure air; excellent water; pleasant walks and drives; beautiful lake of nearly 100 acres; fine boating, fishing and bathing; raise own vegetables.

[5] The 1930 issue was the last so titled "Summer Homes." Its new masthead "Vacation Guide," commenced in 1931 and lasted until 1949 – however, in 1948 and 1949, it suffered the humility of a companion piece, same size and format – "the Shortline Guide to Vacationing" released by the Hudson Transit Lines (Bus) (Short Line System).

[6] It took about 6 years before farmers were producing enough milk "up line" to generate a marketable transportation commodity.

[7] This group represented a producing cow population on the N.Y. & O.M.: Winterton–400, Bloomingburg–300, Summitville–60, Centerville & Fallsburg–237, Liberty –450, Parksville–436, Morsston–180 and Livingston Manor–339.

[8] Liberty *Register,* January 15, 1892.

[9] The demand by August of 1913 exhausted the supply of milk cars with many box cars being pressed into service.

[10] In 1919 the Fallsburgh Lake harvest totaled 64 carloads and was stored at Delhi for the northern division milk trains.

[11] A unit mounted at the front end of an engine to force the snow back and off the railroad right-of-way.

[12] O'Neal died in a head-on collision the following year (August 1902) near Cooks Falls.

[13] Press sources erroneously record it as engine No. 72.

[14] The reason for the explosion was never really determined but conjecture suggests an attempt to get back on schedule – linked with low water in the boiler – brought about the demise of No. 70.

[15] At one time Laidlaw and Wood were associated in photographic post card production.

[16] December 30, 1903 – 602 killed.

[17] Tragically, the woman who led all but one of the 30 guests to safety (Mrs. Augustus Emberlin) was a victim when she fell back from a second story window into the flames.

[18] Liberty *Register,* May 28, 1920.

[19] At the time of the fire 46 were occupied.

[20] Prairie House fatalities were: Jerry Bastian, porter,

Hurleyville; Louis Cohen, Bronx; Morris Schorr, Bronx; Julius Hochstein, N.Y.; Abraham Molloch, N.Y.; Max Yankowitz, N.Y.; Harry Miller, N.Y.; Mrs. May Friedman, Brooklyn; Benny Band, waiter, Passaic; Julius Jacobson, Hurleyville; Charles Garfinkle, waiter, Passaic; Mary Dimmeller, chamber maid.

[21] It was by sheer coincidence that Julius was working at the Prairie House that night. He had consented to work for his future brother-in-law, Abe Cohen, who was enjoying a short holiday in New York.

LOCH SHELDRAKE

[1] In March, 1898, a stock company was reportedly formed at Hurleyville with Michael Smith named as president, with the intention of building a trolley line to Loch Sheldrake to be in operation in June of that year.

[2] An irregularly shaped edge to the photograph as contrasted to a squared-off edge.

[3] The first manifestation of this new mode of transportation to appear in the pages of "Summer Homes."

[4] Titles of the paintings were: "Highlands of the Hudson from West Point," "In the Rondout Valley," "Lake Minnewaska," "In Monticello's Shaded Streets," "Neversink River, Woodbourne," "The Old Homestead near Liberty," "White Lake," "Sunset on the Willowemoc" and "Valley of the East Branch."

[5] The first Sullivan County resorts to use this type of display advertising were: White Roe Lake, Kenmore Lake House, Parkston House, Edgewood Inn, the Shelburne and the Elmshade.

[6] The names of many resorts had no relevancy to their location, terrain, or geographical configuration — the 'Overlook' was an exception.

[7] It seems the more glamorous "Loch" came a bit later, appearing in the 1886 "Summer Homes" as "Loch Shelldrake" (sic) with the Chas. W. Travis Farmhouse its only listing.

[8] As spelled in the 1906 "Summer Homes" — contemporary press, LeRoy.

[9] Eisenstein and Smith were prohibition agents noted for their comic-opera disguises used in miraculous apprehension of bootleggers.

[10] Liberty *Register,* January 9, 1920.

[11] Liberty *Register,* August 19, 1926.

FERNDALE

[1] Generally a three-seater, [also known as a park drag], with a fringed top similar to those operated on the Liberty and White Lake stage route which went by the more glamorous calling.

[2] The prize was a set of six pewter cups, once proudly displayed in a china closet in the dining room of the Clements Lake House.

[3] Still standing (1969) on the grounds at "Grossingers," facing Howard Johnson's, and used as quarters for the help.

[4] Prior to 1879 "Josh" was too busy driving cattle back to Liberty from Chicago and Canada, racing and breaking horses. He also held the distinction of being the first man to ship a can of milk over the O. and W. from Liberty to New York City.

[5] This was in May, 1897, when electric lights first came to Liberty. This involved the use of about 200 poles for the service within the village limits.

[6] The grove was rented to organizations for annual outings, picnics and clambakes. The great problem of disposing of the litter necessitated the hitching up of teams of horses to lumber wagons for carting to hidden dumps in the woods.

[7] Lake Ophelia was located on the flats between lower Liberty and Ferndale and has long been filled in — part of it now occupied by the lower portions of Grossinger's ski area and the Route 17 expressway.

[8] First floor 50 x 130 feet, second floor 50 x 100 feet with the south end raised one story above the dancing floor and occupied by Mr. William Clark as living apartments.

[9] The three Gerow boys (Ben, Ralph & Josh, Jr.) moonlighted as soda jerks at the Ophelia Pavilion and for a "little extra" smuggled in jugs of hard cider and sold it for 5¢ a glass. The proprietor, Mr. Clark, was not aware of this but the bribing of the boys by the city boarders was done primarily to "liven up the bowling teams."

[10] Liberty *Register,* October 28, 1898.

[11] Interview – Mrs. Paul Allen

[12] "Once the third highest waterfall in New York State. Above the falls the water had worn a channel about 20 feet wide and 16 feet deep through the solid rock — the waters rushed through these narrow confines and plunged about 20 feet when they met with a temporary obstruction then bounded for three successive leaps into a deep basin at the bottom of the chasm. Total fall being from 80 to 90 feet." (Liberty Register, July 15, 1887) The falls were blasted away and a power dam erected — first power generated on July 2, 1923.

[13] Officers: J. Chandler Young, President; D.S. Hill, Vice President; George W. Murphy, Secretary; Frank Barber,

Treasurer; D.B. Wickham, Dr. H.P. Deady, W.F. Hasbrouck, Elmer Winner, W.H. Murphy – Trustees.

[14] His dedication to horses was epitomized when his son Benjamin brought home from New York the first horseless carriage seen in Liberty and was refused a parking space in the barns or stables for fear the contraption would infect the horses. Ben's mother made a large blanket which was draped over it for protection. This was the start of Ben's abiding interest in the auto and gas station business. Today's Gerow Ford Agency is an important county dealership.

[15] The 1958 Board of Directors: Sidney Sussman, Chairman; Frank E. Devlin, President and General Manager; Morris Abraham, Exec. Vice President, Joseph Fersch, Treasurer; Benjamin Slutsky, Secretary; Milton Kutsher, Donald Hammond, Harold Reynolds, Herbert Sakofsky, Paul Grossinger, David Levinson, and Paul Killian.

[16] Originating in butcher Morris Wolff's living room from an oil stove, it quickly engulfed nine business and residential buildings, several barns and smaller buildings, sweeping both sides of the street clean for nearly the entire distance between the O. and W. station and the foot of the hill. The fire was considerably overshadowed by the June 13, 1913, holocaust in nearby Liberty.

[17] Liberty *Gazette,* June 19, 1913.

[18] In June, 1882, one of the few fatalities occurred during the construction when Liflet Stratton, a carpenter employed by the Passaic Rolling Mill Co., the iron work contractors, was instantly killed when a brace fell and broke his neck.

[19] The bridge design was planned by General Superintendent Edward Canfield on surveys run by Louis Douglas Fouquet of Middletown.

[20] Liberty *Register,* September 13, 1901.

LIBERTY
The Era Of The Great Hotels
PART 1

[1] Whether or not the "Summer Homes" for that year had anything to do with the increased business, the issue did represent an investment of $6,000 by the O. and W. management, a marked increase over previous years.

[2] Bradford Lee Gilbert was considered one of the country's leading railroad station architects when in 1892 he designed his masterpiece – the Illinois Central Station in Chicago. Later, about 1899, he was in charge of the modernization of Commodore Vanderbuilt's Louvre-inspired second Grand Central Station.

[3] The completed 29 x 60 foot structure had cost the O. and W. management $12,000.

[4] Liberty *Register,* March 13, 1891.

[5] Within two years (Oct., 1899) a new freight house (24 x 100) would be erected and in April of the same year a new water tank opposite the station would be built.

[6] Two years before, the Mecca, also a Liberty hotel of considerable note, converted its lanes into a playroom. It appears that bowling alleys fade quickly by the mid -1890's in the larger hotels.

[7] "Officer Colwell turned in the alarm from the Liberty House, Liberty Hose and Truck Company No. 2 was first on the scene followed soon after by Company No. 1 and Company No. 3."

[8] President, A.J.D. Wedemeyer, Vice Presidents: J.C. Anderson, Gen. Passenger Agent, N.Y.O.&W.; W.H.H. Williams, Neversink; George Rockwell, Monticello etc. with all corners of the resort region represented through the naming of sixteen more 'vice presidents.'

[9] Liberty *Register,* August 27, 1897

[10] The press recorded "..it consisted of a sailboat with sails spread to the breeze and occupied by the captain and crew. The yellow and white float was drawn by six white horses, richly comparisoned, with yellow and white harness and blankets, the latter each bearing in gold the inscription, "New Liberty House" ...the boat trimmed in yellow and white cloth and more than 159 chrysanthemums."

[11] Low and Littlejohn were prime movers in the early years of the N.Y.&O.M. Low, an able attorney, member of the State Senate and a persuasive debater; Littlejohn, a dynamic platform speaker, was also Speaker of the Assembly as well as Chairman of the influential Committee on Commerce and Navigation.

[12] Mother of Miss Laura Clements and the hostess of the Clements Lake House.

[13] Under local notes in the February 6, 1880, Register appeared the memo "Remember 'tis the New York, Lake Ontario and Western Railroad now." It wasn't too long before the 'Lake' was dropped.

[14] It was with the resumption of service that one train in particular started its run from Summitville to Liberty and back, made up of a combination passenger-baggage car and an engine which was described as "scooting along over the rails like a shooting star." Some fellow, with a flair for naming things, dubbed it "the Scoot" and Scoot it remained down through the years, a piece of Sullivan County vernacular for "generally" dependable service and sentimental association.

[15] Herman C. Lohman was instantly killed on Sunday, August 24, 1913, by an Erie express train while crossing the tracks in Callicoon.

[16] George Rockwell conducted the county seat landmark for eighteen years until it burned in the 1909 fire.

[17] In response to a call for a meeting at the Register offices in March, 1886, the first fire company in Liberty became a reality. It was started with a membership of 28 and was known as "Watkins Engine No. 1."
On January 15, 1901, the Ontario Hose Company was organized, with Walter J. Randall its first president.

[18] Liberty *Register*, April 15, 1926.

[19] Seven years later many of these same letters were still being published with few, if any, changes in the copy.

[20] Mr. Morgan gave James Chandler Young, a leading townsman, one share of stock and Mr. Young attended meetings of the light and power company in Mr. Morgan's office as a representative of the citizens of Liberty.

[21] Liberty *Register*, April 25, 1913.

[22] The problem eventually reached other parts of the county. In April, 1913, the Callicoon Town Board of Health adopted an amendment to the sanitary regulations relating to tuberculosis and the barring of same from Jeffersonville before these cases "in the long run doom summer visitors to Jeffersonville, much as it did to the great resort hotels of Liberty."

[23] Von Unruh's discovery allegedly would cure incipient cases of tuberculosis to the extent of 100% and 80% of more advance cases. Dr. Herbert M. King, chief physician at the Loomis Sanatorium when called as a witness for the town board, told of writing to competent specialists at Saranac Lake and New York City, none of which passed favorably on the alleged Von Unruh "cure." The Von Unruh Sanitoria Inc. was composed principally of New York Rosslyn M. Cox, former Mayor of Middletown, and Mr. Dennison, of the firm of Dennison and Sons, paper manufacturers of New York as Treasurer. The company was incorporated October 1, 1916, at a capital of $500,000.

[24] Directors: Frank Lober, Wilhelmena Lober, Minnie Lober, Louise Lober, Kate Lober and Thomas Loomis of New York; Charles W. Wilfert, Conrad Metzger and Charles Homer of Jeffersonville.

[25] Local directors: Wm. Kohler, Jeffersonville; J.C. Young, H.J. Sarles, Charles B. Ward, Isaac Post, Isham Young and Frank Bridges of Liberty.

[26] Liberty *Register*, February 14, 1913.

LIBERTY
The Great 1913 Fire And After
PART 2

[1] Monday, October 23, 1893.

[2] Liberty *Register*, October 3, 1902

[3] A quick call went out to the Summitville O. and W. depot where a stop signal prevented 200 Middletown firemen from completing their role as participants in an early example of mutual aid on a large and long distance scale.

[4] This was an increase of 2,066 over the same period one year before.

[5] Supt. of Highways, Town of Liberty.

[6] The White Bridge crossing was at the beginning of the steep grade leading down into the heart of Liberty. This grade was the scene of a runaway milk tanker on Saturday, July 24, 1954, which came to rest in front of the J.C. Young residence after taking three lives, injuring fifteen people and wrecking fourteen vehicles.

[7] As an illustration — freight loaded in New York City at 4:00 on an afternoon is delivered to the merchant before 10:00 the next morning.

WHITE SULPHUR SPRINGS

[1] In 1885 and for sometime thereafter the "Summer Homes" publication incorrectly spelled it ROBINSONVILLE. It was first listed as White Sulphur Springs in the 1891 "Summer Homes" — Post Office changed to White Sulphur Springs on December 23, 1890.

[2] *Analysis of Springs:*

Chloride of Sodium	Nitrate of Potassa
Chloride of Potassium	Alumina
Bicarbonate of Soda	Sulphate of Soda
Bicarbonate of Ammonia	Sulphate of Magnesia
Bicarbonate of Magnesia	Sulphate of Potassa
Bicarbonate of Iron	Carbonate of Lithia
	Organic Matters
	Carbonate of Acid Gas

[3] Although the presence of the springs was noted, there were no resorts listed in the 1885 "Summer Homes."

JEFFERSONVILLE

[1] "Summer Homes," 1907.

[2] "Early Summer Boarding in the Town of Callicoon" by Charles S. Hick, Sullivan County *Record*, July 13, 1944.

WHITE LAKE

[1] Officers: J.C. Young, Pres.; George H. Carpenter, Sec, Liberty; W.C. Kinne, Treas., White Lake; Directors: J.C. Young, Liberty; Roderick Morrison, White Lake; H.J.

Sarles, Liberty; W.C. Kinne, White Lake; Benjamin W. Winner, Liberty; M.H. Stoddard, Stevensville; J.C. Anderson, N.Y.O. & W. Ry., New York City.

[2] So wrote S.O. Journer, a "tongue-in-cheek" feature writer of the resort area in the late 1880's.

[3] Operated the Van Wert House (F.B. Van Wert) and the Willard House (W. Van Wert).

[4] Officers named at Port Jervis on August 11, 1892: Roderick Morrison, Pres.; J.F. Callbreath, Jr., Monticello; Secretary; B. Ryall, Port Jervis, Treas.; R. Morrison, White Lake, Treas. for survey expenses.

[5] By the 1884 issue, "clergymen" was dropped from the copy. From a very early date no intoxicating liquors were served at the resorts surrounding the lake making it popular with the clergy but unpopular with some others.

[6] Operated by Simeon M. Jordan, George B. Wooldridge and Stephen Sweet.

[7] In November, 1876, while playing Marc Antony in the Brooklyn Theatre, Warde noticed that a bit of scenery in the "gridiron" was aflame from a gas jet. Cutting several lines from his speech he had the curtain lowered and quietly gave the alarm. The fire was extinguished. The following week during the engagement of Kate Claxton in "The Two Orphans," scenery in the gridiron again caught fire — this time gutting the theatre with a death toll in the hundreds.

[8] The first issue: June 29, 1887 — $2.00 for summer edition of 12 numbers sent by mail — 20¢ per copy. Each issue contained a photograph of some choice bit of Sullivan County scenery, a page editorial, article on photography, local items, extras, "White Lake maxims" and most importantly of all, lists of guests stopping at hotels in Liberty and White Lake. These were picked up by other papers under such headings as "Summer Arrivals" and "Our Guests." *"Season"* also recorded the crowded conditions at the lake. "The boarding houses here are all filled and applicants are turned away in large numbers."

[9] Liberty *Register,* October 20, 1886.

STEVENSVILLE
Swan Lake

[1] Fishing tackle was provided season guests without charge as a lure for the summer vacationer and to also help promote the excellent pickerel fishing at the lake. The author recalls as a boy journeying to Swan Lake with his father, Manville J. Wakefield, to enjoy the pickerel fishing.

[2] In 1861 Mr. Swan had invested in the oil business and by 1904, as president of the Rubber Goods Manufacturing Company, purchased the oil and grease business of Cooke Brothers and three years later incorporated the business under the name of Alden S. Swan & Co. in New York City.

[3] Mr. Swan's memory was perpetuated on January 15, 1927, when the Post Office was officially changed from Stevensville to Swan Lake.

NEVERSINK

[1] Random notes by an enthusiastic visitor to the village of Neversink in 1903.

[2] Liberty *Register,* December 20, 1889.

[3] In 1892 turnpike booster W.H.H. Williams was named President. Directors: H.J. Sarles, J.C. Lennon, John B. Kerr, T.H. Houlihon, C.M. Bonnell, J.W. Herron and W.H.H. Williams.

[4] The card consisted of a trotting race "free-for-all" for a purse of $25; $13 to first, $8 to second and $4 to third. Also instrumental in the smooth running of the races was the performance of the three judges; Dan Freer of Ellenville, George Waldorf of Hurleyville and Chas. Stanton of Liberty — Mr. Stanton also acted as starter. The races were generally followed in the evening by a platform dance and refreshments.

[5] Liberty *Register*, August 28, 1891.

[6] This bridge location was also the scene of a freak "cyclone" [June 22, 1887] that "lifted the covered bridge ... clear from its eastern foundation" demolishing one end. The bridge was 116 feet long and had been built in 1869 at a cost of $1600.

[7] The Town of Neversink (1970) is "dry."

PARKSVILLE

[1] The first Jewish resort listing, a farmhouse operated by Charles Schuman, appeared in the 1907 "Summer Homes."

[2] The largest movement of passengers over the O. and W. lines occurred in 1913 — 2,245,000 paying passengers.

[3] By 1928 business was booming with the Sullivan County National Bank reporting a Monday deposit in August topping-out at $306,000.

[4] The committee was composed of: Charles Golembe, Morningside Hotel, Hurleyville; Joseph Holder, Young's Gap Hotel, near Liberty; Elmer Rosenburg, Lakeside Hotel, Lake Huntington; Hyman Merl, Hotel Ambassador, Fallsburgh and Moses Kove, of Monticello.

[5] In July, 1932, the O. and W. announced a 45% reduction in fares from New York City.

[6] Others were also thumping for promotional campaigns, namely the Max Schwartz Co. (now Steingart Associates) in South Fallsburgh, a pioneer advertising agency in Sullivan County, established in 1920 and the Fallsburgh Printing Co., also in South Fallsburgh, starting as a printing establishment in 1921 and later branching into advertising. The Cohen enterprise was an early advocate of direct mail promotion.

[7] Net income for September of $84,342 compared with $54,646 in September of 1931. Also a contributing factor was a 10% wage cut put into effect February 1st.

[8] It was estimated by engineers that by eliminating the grade between Roscoe and Parksville, from 10 to 12 or even more cars could be hauled per train.

[9] The first official release on this appeared on May 22, 1902; however, as far back as January 6, 1893, the press was releasing "all sorts of rumors" as to "the double tracking of the O. and W."

[10] There were fifteen in the official party headed by Pres. Thomas P. Fowler, who went to Hancock with two cars attached to the Sunday evening express, Mr. Fowler's car "Warwick" and the Pullman sleeper "Albemarle."

[11] New York Times, April 18, 1902.

[12] Completed and in use September 11, 1903.

[13] At the same time O'Hehir & Curran of Warwick received the contract for the section between Middletown and Cambell Hall in Orange County.

LIVINGSTON MANOR

[1] Dr. Edward Livingston came from a very distinguished family. In 1775 Chancellor Robert R. Livingston acquired five-sixteenths of the Hardenburgh Patent. He afterwards divided it among his brothers and sisters. Under the laws of primogeniture then prevailing, the eldest son entered into possession of his father's estate. Dr. Edward Livingston inherited the Sullivan County property from his father, John R. Livingston. Dr. Livingston came to Sullivan County in 1824, the owner of a 200 acre tract where the village of Livingston Manor now stands. In addition to his cultural pursuits, he enjoyed hunting and fishing with the Frenchman DeChandla for whom Shandelee Lake was named.

[2] The station officially became Livingston Manor on April 1, 1882, with a new depot completed in August of the same year.

[3] The first fishing club was started at Balsam Lake above the Beaverkill falls; later the Salmo Fonitnalis Club was started on the Deal Farm.

[4] Quantity of trout put in the streams by the O. and W. since 1878:

Year	Amount	Year	Amount
1878	20,000	1883	155,000
1879	74,000	1884	310,000
1880	85,000	1885	460,000
1881	96,000	1886	900,000
1882	120,000		

The National Express Co. assisted by carrying the cans free for the entire program.

[5] Some trout were in the stream below the factory which had probably come in after the acids had dissipated, proving how quickly acids are absorbed and how hard it is to be on the ground at the proper time to obtain legal evidence.

[6] The case was argued by Judge Clearwater and Charles L. Andrus for the N.Y.O.&W. and by Howard Chipp and Dean, King, Tracy and Smith for Livingston.

[7] At 7:30 it was foggy, obscuring the bulk of the locomotive until the gas driven speeder was on top of it. Dutcher yelled to his men to jump; he himself, grabbing for the bar used when a quick stop is necessary, missed and met almost instant death. Ironically, among the five other men was his brother Floyd, who was the first at his side.

[8] Hazel, site of a wood acid factory built in 1902, four miles north of the "Manor," was established as a depot and Post Office in June, 1903. It was originally known as Appley's Switch.

[9] Liberty Register, September 9, 1887.
Attendance by Post:

Post	Location	Count
Waterbury Post	Wurtsboro	20
Ratcliff Post	Monticello	25
Morgans Post	Rockland (Roscoe)	40
Garrett Post	Liberty	35
Hammond Post	Fallsburgh	40
Purvis Post	Livingston Manor	35
Teller Post	Grahamsville	25
Bell Post	Fremont Center	20

[10] Inevitably, each excursionist had a copy of "Summer Homes" tucked under his arm for handy reference; and, if he didn't, he could find a hard cover copy hanging on a ring conveniently near the ticket window in the depot. Hard cover copies first appeared in 1898.

[11] In 1908 one other Jewish family resided in the "Manor" – the Sam Cohen family.

[12] Interview with Les Wood, EDITOR, Monticello Evening News.

[13] Liberty Register, July 5, 1923.

[14] Liberty Register, January 13, 1888.

[15] Two years later (May, 1890) this bar was abuzz with

exciting rumors of a narrow gauge railroad to be built from the "Manor" to Emmonsville. A Mr. Elias of Buffalo had purchased the H.G. Prindle tract, 4,000 acres, with intent of cutting and marketing.

ROSCOE

[1] Originally known as Westfield Flats, the Post Office had been officially changed to Roscoe in April, 1881 — the depot, however, bore the name Rockland.

[2] Ironically, the inn was reported leased in March of the same year to Daniel Kraesner of New York City for six months with an option to buy from George L. Treyz, the prosperous local lumber and wood acid producer.

[3] The first golf course opened in America was St. Andrews in Yonkers in 1888. One year later the Tuxedo Golf Course at Tuxedo Park was organized. In February, 1925, the Sullivan County Golf and Country Club was organized at Liberty and in 1932, Grossingers unveiled their new 9-hole championship golf course.
The June 7, 1901, Liberty *Register* reprinted a New York *Evening Post* (June 1) feature which noted Sullivan County with three "good nine-hole courses, one in the outskirts of Liberty, (a) course at the edge of White Lake and a third at Kiamesha."

ROSCOE WEST

[1] Stewart later died. Thomas Brehony, Lewis Norton and L.D. Cole survived with "grievous wounds."

[2] Consist of train: six loaded milk cars and a passenger coach.

[3] Riding No. 11 "deadhead" from Middletown to Cadosia was Lafayette Bennett, father of Oscar O. Bennett of Hancock. He leaped clear, just before the impact.

[4] When Engineer St. John saw No. 12 coming down the level stretch at full steam he yelled a warning to Trainman Frank E. Monroe and Fireman Tulley and all three jumped. St. John was catapulted into a field by a crashing milk car which saved his life. Tulley, struck by the edge of the tender was cut in two.
Frank Monroe, his foot trapped between the sand blower and locomotive hand rail and badly scalded, lived only seven minutes after being released.
Engineer O'Neal had evidently been struck in back by some great weight: "his head crushed to a thickness of only about two inches."
[O'Neal was injured in a similar accident at Red Hill switch about eight years previously.]
Fireman Reese, on the southbound with O'Neal, was found buried under a huge pile of coal — suffocated by inhalation of coal gas from the engine.

[5] An overheated wheel journal which can result in the severing of an axle.

[6] Fireman John W. Lawrence and Brakeman George A. Mills were fatally scalded by clouds of steam from ruptured steam lines. Fortunately, for the crew of No. 316, they had just left the caboose to attend to the hot-box.

[7] Recorded by the Walton *Reporter*.

[8] The wood was cut in four-foot lengths and seasoned for a year. Then it was piled into retorts which were sealed except for a vent in the back. A hot fire was built under them, and the smoke and gas that came from the vents was condensed into a liquor and distilled into wood alcohol. The residue was mixed with lime and when dried became acetate of lime, important in the production of smokeless powder. What remained was charcoal. It was the Keery Chemical Company that later used ovens instead of retorts. In these they could haul in a car of lumber, making the process a faster one. The whole process took about twenty-four hours to complete. Usually a factory was a settlement all of its own, consisting of the factory, a company store, a blacksmith shop, boardinghouses as well as barns for the teams.

[9] It was at Acidalia that the Treyz brothers got their start.

[10] Stations: Harvard, Shinhopple, Gregorytown, Colchester, Pepacton, Downsville, Shavertown, Andes, Kaufmans, Pleasant Valley, Union Grove, Arena, Halls Bridge, Dunraven, Margaretsville and Arkville where the line connected with the Ulster and Delaware.

[11] Through carloadings which neither originated nor terminated along the lines of the O. and W.

[12] Engineer, Clare Cowan; Conductor, Howard Little and Mail Clerk, Harry Odell.

[13] The last passenger train on the Scranton Division ran on September 5, 1930; Trainman, C. Ball; Conductor, J.J. Collins; Fireman, M. Bartosavage; Engineer, E. Brooks and Trainman, M.F. Joyce.

[14] The writer was of course an industry propagandist — there were curves aplenty — the worst being "dead man curve" between Preston Park and Starlight, later the scene of frequent disastrous derailments.

[15] Captained by Oliver H. Clark — the transfer boat "Hart" handled 50 to 100 loaded cars each day.

[16] Liberty *Register,* August 2, 1901.

[17] Originally a trestle and the scene of many bad wrecks and considered the most dangerous on the Scranton Div. It was filled-in in 1904.

[18] A low point in the grade at Hancock before the short run to Cadosia.

EPILOGUE

[1] Just being refurbished.

[2] Number 405 passed into history on April 20, 1948, when she was sold to Luria Brothers for scrapping.

[3] Operating income before other income and deductions and before fixed charges but after net rents payable.

[4] Peak in operating revenue of $14,127,867 was reached in 1921. Peak clear profit year – 1907.

[5] Investigators observed that scars on the ties were visible from Liberty to the scene of the derailment indicating presence of dragging running gear. Observations were made as to the disastrous results had the dragging element caught while crossing the Ferndale trestle.

O. & W. Right-of-Way just west of So. Fallsburg (1970)

Bibliography

Adams, Joey, with Henry Tobias. *The Borscht Belt.* New York: The Bobbs-Merill Company, Inc. 1966.

Allen, Richard Sanders. *Covered Bridges of the Northeast.* Brattleboro, Vermont: The Stephen Greene Press, 1957.

Anderson, Stott, *Ulster County's Old Timbered Crossings.* Privately printed, 1964.

Annual Reports of the Board of Railroad Commissioners, Albany, New York: James B. Lyon, 1884-1906.

Annual Reports of the New York, Ontario and Western Railway Company, 1880-1956.

_____. *The Story of Anthracite.* New York: Prepared and Published by the Hudson Coal Company,, 1932.

_____. *50 Years Working Together* (booklet) Anniversary publication of *Associated Co-operative Fire Insurance Co's of Sullivan and Adjoining Counties.* Woodridge, New York, 1963.

_____. *History of Valley of the Beaverkill* (pamphlet), Dedication of Beaverkill Church, November 25, 1883.

Beers, F.W. *County Atlas of Ulster, N.Y.* New York: Walker and Jewett, 1875.

_____. *County Atlas of Sullivan, N.Y.* New York: Walker and Jewett, 1875.

Best, Gerald M. *Minisink Valley Express, A History of the Port Jervis, Monticello & New York Railroad and its Predecessors.* Beverly Hills, California: Published by Gerald M. Best, Printed by El Camino Press, 1956.

Best, Gerald M. *History and Motive Power of the New York, Ontario & Western Railroad* (sic.) Bulletin #40, Railway and Locomotive Historical Society, 1936.

Birmingham, Stephen. *Our Crowd, The Great Jewish Families of New York.* New York: Harper & Row, 1967.

Booth, Malcolm A. *Roebling's Sixth Bridge, "Neversink."* Bulletin of the Orange County Community of Museums and Galleries. Reprinted from the Journal of the Rutgers University Library, XXX. New Brunswick, New Jersey: December 1966.

Booth, Malcolm A. *The Delaware and Hudson Canal, with special Emphasis on Deerpark, New York,* (a thesis) 1965.

Boroff, David. *Don't Call It The Borscht Belt, New York Times Magazine,* May 6, 1965.

Branning, Edwin Forest. *Picturesque Sullivan County.* New York: (privately printed), 190-?

Burbank, James W. *Cushetunk, the First White Settlement in the Upper Delaware River Valley.* Callicoon, New York: Sullivan County Democrat (reprint from), January and February, 1952.

Burbank, James W. *The Jersey Claim Line, Its Relation to Sullivan County,* (booklet) Narrowsburg, New York: The Delaware Publications, printers, February, 1951.

Burroughs, John, *In The Catskills,* Selections from the writings of John Borroughs, New York: Houghton Mifflin Company, 1911.

Busch, Noel F. "Trout Fisherman, Sportsman of the old school and eccentric in the grand style, E.R. Hewill calls himself "last of the gentlemen mechanics" *Life* (magazine) [194-?]

Carney, Reuben D. *Historical Sketch of the Reformed Church, Grahamsville, New York; Written and Read by Reuben D. Carney at the Dedicatorial Services for the Memorial Windows June 17, 1904.*

In The Catskills. Devoted to Boarding-Houses and Hotels of the Catskills, Shawangunks and Mountains of Sullivan County. May 28, 1932.

Child, Hamilton, (compiler and publisher). *Gazetteer and Business Directory of Sullivan County, N.Y. for 1872-3.* Syracuse, New York: Printed at the Journal Office, 1872.

Sullivan County *Civil War Centennial Commission* of the Sullivan County (N.Y.) Historical Society. *Brass Buttons and Leather Boots.* So. Fallsburg, New York: Steingart Associates, 1963.

Christman, Henry. *Tin Horns and Calico, An Episode in the Emergence of American Democracy.* New York: Henry Holt and Company, Inc., 1945.

Crumb, Frederick W. *Tom Quick, Early American.* Narrowsburg, New York: Delaware Valley Press, 1936.

Cuddeback, Dr. William L. *Deerpark – the Delaware and Hudson Canal; An Address before the Minisink Valley Historical Society.* Port Jervis, New York: February 22, 1928.

Curley, Edward F. *Old Monticello.* Monticello, New York: Printed by the *Republican Watchman,* 1930.

Cusator, Mrs. James. *Tanneries in the Town of Liberty,* (pamphlet), Liberty, New York: Liberty *Register* [reprint], May 15, 1952.

Davidson, Gabriel, *Our Jewish Farmers and the Story of the Jewish Agricultural Society,* New York: L.B. Fischer, 1943.

Decker, Amelia Stickney. *That Ancient Trail, The Old Mine Road.* Trenton, New Jersey: Petty Printing Company, 1942.

———. *A Century of Progress, History of the Delaware and Hudson Company,* 1823-1923. Albany, New York: J.B. Lyon Company, Printers, 1925.

———. *Delaware County New York, History of the Century, 1797-1897, Centennial Celebration, June 9 and 10, 1897,* Edited by David Murray L.L.D. Delhi, New York: William Clark, Publisher, 1898.

———. *The Upper Delaware Valley Vacation and Tourists Guide.* Narrowsburg, New York: Delaware Valley Press, 1939.

DeLisser, R. Lionel. *Picturesque Catskills, Greene County.* Northhampton, Mass.: Picturesque Publishing Co., 1894.

———. *Picturesque Ulster,* Kingston, New York: Styles and Bruyn, 1896.

———. Summer Resort *Directory, 1903, Brooklyn Daily Eagle.*

Duke, William E. "Silent Ghosts of the O. and W. Railway," *Middletown Times Herald RECORD,* May 18, 1960.

Eager, Samuel W. *An Outline History of Orange County.* Newburgh, New York: S.T. Callahan, 1846-7.

Edelson, Edward E. "The Rise and Fall of the O. & W., as seen by William F. Helmer," (book review) *Middletown Times Herald RECORD,* March 8, 1960.

———. *Beautiful ELLENVILLE* (pamphlet) Philadelphia, Penna: F.L. Maule, printer, [189-?]

Embler, William J. *Orange County Links in Sullivan County History,* (manuscript), Address before Sullivan County Historical Society, November 12, 1956.

Eno, Daniel M. *Looking Back,* Souvenir Book of the Wayne County Fair Centennial Celebration. 1962.

Fisk, Joel C. and William H.D. Blake. *A Condensed History of The 56th Regiment New York Veteran Volunteer Infantry, part of the "Tenth Legion" in the Civil War, 1861-1865* Newburgh, New York: Newburgh Journal, Printer, 1906.

———. *A Condensed History of the 143d Regiment, New York Volunteer Infantry of the Civil War, 1861-1865.* Newburgh, New York: Newburgh Journal, Printer, 1909.

Gerow, Joshua. *Alder Lake,* Liberty, New York: (privately printed booklet).

Goodrich, Phineas G. *History of Wayne County (Pa.).* Honesdale, Pennsylvania: Haines and Beardsley, 1880.

Gould, Jay, *History of Delaware County and Border Wars of New York,* Roxbury, New York: Keeny and Gould, Publishers, 1856.

Gridley, Inez George (compiler). *Papers of the Reverend J. Milton Harris.* Grahamsville, New York: Pastoral Press, 1967.

Gross, H.H. "Shawangunk Barrier" *Railroad Magazine,* September, 1946.

Haring, H.A. *Our Catskill Mountains,* New York: G.P. Putman & Sons, 1931.

Harlow, Alvin C. *Old Towpaths, the Story of the American Canal Era.* New York: D. Appleton and Company, 1926.

Harland, Marion. *Country Living For City People.* New York: American Bank Note Company, 1887.

Harris, Harold. *Treasure Tales of the Shawangunks and Catskills.* Published in Commemoration of the Ellenville Sesquicentennial by Harold Harris. Ellenville, New York: 1955.

Harris, Robert C. *Johnny Appleseed, source book.* Originally appeared in the *Old Fort News,* Vol. IX, Nos. 1-2, March-June 1945.

Hart, Moss. *Act One,* New York: Random House, Inc., 1959.

Headley, Russel. (editor) *The History of Orange County New York.* Middletown, New York: Van Deusen and Elms, Publisher, 1908.

Helmer, William F. *O. & W., the Long Life and Slow Death of the New York, Ontario & Western Railway.* Berkeley, California: Howell-North Press, 1959.

———. "E.L. Henry, An Historian's Artist," *Naho* (magazine) Vol. 1 No. 4, September, 1968.

Hick, Charles S. *The Town of Fremont, a History,* Callicoon, New York: *Sullivan County Democrat* [reprint], November 1951.

Hick, Charles S. *Landmarks in Town of Callicoon,* Early Roads and Turnpikes Used by Early Settlers Coming into the Town. *Sullivan County Record,* July 1, 1943.

———. *Early History in the Town of Callicoon,* Connecticut Yankees and Hudson Valley Dutch Came First. *Sullivan County Record,* February 17, 1944.

Hine, C.G. *The Old Mine Road [1909]* New Brunswick, New Jersey: Rutgers University Press, 1963.

Hope, Jack E. *The Catskill Tanning Industry—Its Rise and Fall.* The New York State *Conservationist.* (magazine), October-November 1960.

Hungerford, Edward. *Men of Erie, A Story of Human Effort.* New York: Random House, 1946.

Irvine, Charles and Charles E. Beach, *History of the Cochecton Bridge Co.* Honesdale, Pennsylvania: Thomas J. Ham, printer, 1883.

Keller, Allan. *The Next Drink is on Lackawack* (N.Y.) (all articles appear in the New York World-Telegram.)

———. "250 Families Uprooted So New York's Millions Can Get a Drink of Water." 1938

———. "60 Years Ago He Saw a Show – But Life Wasn't Blighted." 1938.

———. "A Tannery and 'Ghosts' Once Occupied the Site of New Water Supply." 1938.

———. "A Physician Recalls Tragedies of Career, But Has Some Chuckles." 1938.

———. "Old Inn In Path of New Dam." 1938.

———. "Vast Reservoir Soon to Cover Scenes of Gaiety." 1938.

Knapp, Frances J. *Frances J. Knapp's 103 Years, A Brief History of the Development of Sullivan County.* An address delivered before the May 1956 meeting of the Sullivan County Historical Society by William Heidt, Jr. Published by Sullivan County Historical Society, 1956.

LeRoy, Edwin D. *The Delaware and Hudson Canal, A History.* Honesdale, Pennsylvania: The Wayne County Historical Society, 1950.

The Liberty Herald, Liberty, New York: Historical Edition Supplement, July, 1903.

———. *Town of Liberty, Sesquicentennial.* Historical Summary-Program 150th Anniversary. Liberty, New York: 1957.

———. *Liberty, N.Y., indelible photographs.* (Photograph brochure), Liberty, New York: c. Fred Sprague, 1893.

———. *Liberty, N.Y.,* (Color-tinted photograph brochure). Issued by the Liberty Business Men's Association. Copyrighted, Photographed and for Sale only by Otto Hillig. Liberty, New York: 1917.

The Liberty Register, Liberty, New York. Mid-Summer Souvenir Edition, August, 1899.

The Liberty Gazette, Liberty, New York. Mid-Summer Souvenir Edition, August, 1899.

The Liberty Gazette, Liberty, New York: Celebration of Liberty's Centennial, Special Issue, June 12, 1907.

———. *The Indians: or Narratives of Massacres and Depredations on the Frontier, In Wawasink and its Vicinity, during The American Revolution.* By a Descendant of the Huguenots (Abraham G. Bevier) Rondout, New York: Bradbury and Wells, printers, 1846.

Lindsey, James. *The Fish Car—ADIRONDACK—An Era Passes.* The New York State *Conservationist* (magazine), Dec.-Jan. 1958-59.

Longstreth, T. Morris. *The Catskills.* New York: Century, 1918.

Mayham, Albert Champlin. *The Anti-Rent War, An Episode of the 40's.* Jefferson, New York: Frederick L. Frazee, Publisher, 1906.

McAndrew, M.J. *History of Hawley, Pennsylvania,* 100th Anniversary Celebration, August 14 to August 20, 1927. Special publication. 1927.

Meyers, Arthur N. *"Coxey" Bivens – Delaware Valley Cave Dweller.* (booklet) Reprinted from *New Folklore Quarterly,* September 1963.

Meyers, Arthur N. *Douglas...the Delaware Valley City, 1867-1878, Long Eddy, N.Y.* Narrowsburg, New York: The Delaware Valley Press, 1969.

Meyers, Arthur N. *Milanville, the Center of Cushetunk,* Milanville, Pennsylvania: W.C. Dillmuth, publisher, 1964.

Meyers, Arthur N. *Told Around the Pot Belly (stove)* Narrowsburg, New York: The Delaware Valley Press, 1969.

Meyers, Arthur N. *The Fabulous Thomas Family of Cushetunk in the Delaware Valley.* Narrowsburg, New York: The Delaware Valley Press, 1969.

Meyers, Arthur N. *...and They Called It Tusten.* Narrowsburg, New York: 1967.

———. *Monticello, N.Y. and Port Jervis, Monticello and New York RailRoad.* (Photograph brochure, sponsored by Port Jervis, Monticello and New York R.R. and Erie Ry.) Glens Falls Publishing Co. 1900.

———. *Mountain, Lake and Brook—Monticello, New York-Port Jervis, Monticello and New York RailRoad* (Promotional illustrated brochure sponsored by the Port

Jervis, Monticello & New York R.R. Co.) Glens Falls Publishing Co., May 1, 1899.

———. *Historical Journal.* Monticello (N.Y.) Sesquicentennial Publication, September 8 - 11, 1954.

The Republican Watchman, Monticello, New York. Historical Souvenir Edition, September 7-11, 1954.

Moore, E.B. *Timber Rafting on the Delaware. American Forests,* (magazine), November, 1941.

Morgan, David P. "He Sold Streamlining," *Trains* (magazine), July 1952.

Mott, Edward Harold. *Between the Ocean and the Lakes, The Story of Erie.* New York: John S. Collins, Publisher, 1899.

———. *Directory of the New York, Ontario and Western Railroad* (way) *from Cornwall to Sidney for the Year 1900.* Newburgh, New York: Breed Publishing Co., 1900.

———. *Directory of the New York, Ontario and Western Railroad* (way) *from Cornwall to Norwich, and Branches, for the Year 1890.* Newburgh, New York: Thompson and Breed, Publishers, 1890.

———. *Directory of the New York, Ontario and Western Railroad* (way) *from Cornwall to Norwich, for the Year 1898.* Newburgh, New York: Breed Publishing Co., 1898.

———. *Directory of Port Jervis, Monticello, Matamoras, Milford and the New York, Ontario and Western Railway from Port Jervis to Monticello, 1910-11.* Newburgh, New York: Breed Publishing Co., 1910.

"The Mighty O&W," *The Courier Magazine,* October 1953.

———. "N.Y.O.&W. Restyles Summer Passenger Train." *Railway Age,* (trade magazine), June 4, 1938.

Oakley, P.B. "The Old and Weary, N.Y., Ontario and Western R.R.," *Syracuse Herald American,* February 2, 1964.

———. "Obituary of an Old Woman" [The New York, Ontario and Western] *Trains* (magazine), July, 1957.

———. "The O. & W. Story" (an editorial) *Middletown Daily RECORD,* February 11, 1957.

Palen, Alice D. *Historical Reminiscences, Sullivan County in the Early Days. Things, People and Events of a Former Generation.* (All articles appear in the *Liberty Register.*)

——— i "Introduction," March 23, 1923.
——— ii "Early Days Around the County Seat," March 30, 1923.
——— iii "The Darbee House and the Darbess," April 6, 1923.
——— iv "Highways, Byways and Bridges," April 13, 1923.
——— v "Lakes and Little Rivers," May 4, 1923.
——— vi "Lakes and Little Rivers, continued," May 11, 1923.
——— viii "Country Life—Past and Present."
——— xi "The Strangers Within Our Gates," July 5, 1923.
  "Sullivan County in the American Revolution," July 26, 1923.
  "Revolutionary War Period," August 16, 1923.

———. *The PIONEER, A Commemorative Book, on the Occasion of the Dedication of the Livingston Manor Central School.* Livingston Manor, New York: Published by the Livingston Manor Central School Board of Education, May 19, 1939.

Plank, Will. *Banners and Bugles, A Record of Ulster County, New York and the Mid-Hudson Region in the Civil War.* Compiled with the cooperation of the Ulster County Board of Supervisors. Marlborough, New York: Centennial Press, 1963.

Quinlan, James Eldridge. *History of Sullivan County, Embracing An Account of its Geology, Climate, Aborigines, Early Settlement, Organization; The Formation of its Towns, with Biographical Sketches of Prominent Residents, Etc.Etc.* Published by G.M. Beebe and W.T. Morgans. Liberty, New York: W.T. Morgans & Co., Printers & Stereotypers, 1873.

Quinlan, James Eldridge. *Tom Quick the Indian Slayer and the Pioneers of Minisink and Wawarsink,* Liberty, New York: The Liberty Register Company, 1912.

———. *History of Rafting on the Delaware.* Read at Meeting of Minisink Valley Historical Society by Wm. Heidt, Jr, assisted by Charles T. Curtis. Port Jervis, New York: Gazette Book Print, 1922.

Raynor, D. Nelson and R.B. Coler *Where The Rivers Meet, 1957.* Golden Jubilee, Port Jervis (N.Y.) 1907-1957.

Reynolds, George B. *Memories of Long Ago, History of Events in the Town of Neversink.* (booklet, privately printed) 1936.

Richards, Mark V. (compiler) *The Sesquicentennial of the Battle of Minisink. A Story of the Commemoration Held on the Battlefield at Minisink Ford, Sullivan County, N.Y., July 22, 1929.* Monticello, New York: Published by the Monticello *Republican Watchman,* 1929.

———. *Town of Rockland,* Sesquicentennial History and Program, Livingston Manor, New York: Livingston Manor *Times* Publication, 1959.

Rockwell, Rev. Charles, *The Catskill Mountains and the Region Around,* New York: Taintor Brothers & Co., 1867.

Ross, Donald G. and Lee DeNike, *Shawangunks To The Catskills,* Brief overview of the Delaware and Hudson Canal, The New York State *Conservationist.* (magazine), October-November, 1968.

———. *Route 97 Dedication, (souvenier program).* Narrowsburg, New York: Delaware Valley Press, August 30, 1939.

Sanderson, Dorothy Hurlbut. *The Delaware and Hudson Canalway, Carrying Coals To Rondout.* Ellenville, New York: The Rondout Valley Publishing Co. Inc., 1965.

Sanderson, Dorothy Hurlbut. *Ellenville Days and Ways.* Ellenville, New York: The Rondout Valley Publishing Co. Inc., 1968.

Sandberg, Sara. *Mama Made Minks.* New York: Doubleday and Co. Inc., 1964.

———. "The New Line to Scranton." *The Coal Trade Journal.* (weekly trade newspaper), July 2, 1890.

Schrabisch, Max. *Archaeology of Delaware River Valley, Between Hancock and Dingman's Ferry, in Wayne and Pike Counties Vol. 1.* Harrisburg, Pennsylvania: Publications of the Pennsylvania Historical Commission, 1930.

Schwadron, Robert "The O. & W., a railroad Remembered," *Middletown Times Herald RECORD,* March 25, 1964.

Scriber, Adelbert M. *Sullivan County As A.M. Scriber Knew It.* (pamphlet) [194-?]

Scribner, Daniel. *Middletown to Cadosia, the Building of the O. and W. in Sullivan County.* (Unpublished manuscript in possession of Daniel Scribner, Wurtsboro, N.Y.)

Shank, William H. *Historic Bridges of Pennsylvania,* York, Pennsylvania: Buchart-Horn, Publisher, December 1966.

Shaughnessy, Jim. *Delaware and Hudson.* Berkeley, California: Howell-North Books, 1967.

Sherwood, Warren G. *Poems from the Platt Binnewater, 1940-1947.* Compiled by Historian of Lloyd Township, Mabel E.L. Lent, Grahamsville, New York: Pastoral Press, 1967.

Shultis, Neva. *From Sunset to Cocks Crow, Woodstock Folklore.* Woodstock Historical Society, Woodstock, New York: 1957.

Skinner, Jennie L. *A Historical Sketch of Narrowsburg, N.Y. and Vicinity.* Narrowsburg, New York: Delaware Valley Press, 1932.

Smith, Philip H. *Legends of the Shawangunk (shon-gum) and its Environs.* Syracuse, New York: Syracuse University Press, 1965.

Smith, Richard, *A Tour of Four Great Rivers, The Hudson, Mohawk, Susquehanna and Delaware in 1769* (A Journal) New York: Charles Scribner's Sons, 1906.

———. *Something To Cherish,* Service Record Book of Men and Women of Monticello, New York and Community, Sponsored by the American Legion Post No. 73, Monticello, N.Y.[194-?]

Steinman, D.B. *The Builders of the Bridge, The Story of John Roebling and His Son.* New York: Harcourt Brace and Company, 1945.

———. *Summer Homes.* O. & W. Resort Region Guidebook issued yearly 1878 to 1950 (exception 1919?) under a variety of headings generally referred to as *Summer Homes.* 1878–*Summer Homes on the Midland,* 1884–*Summer Homes Among the Mountains,* 1890–*Summer Homes Along the New York, Ontario and Western Railway,* 1892–*Summer Homes,* 1932–*Vacation Guide,* 1948–*The Shortline Guide to Vacationing* (A bus publication issued as well as the regular O. and W. publication).

———. *Winter Homes.* O. & W. Winter Season Resort Guidebook issued 1897 - 1906.

Sylvester, Nathaniel Bartlett, *History of Ulster County, New York.* Philadelphia: Everts and Peck, 1880.

———. *Synfleur's 75 Years, 1889-1964.* (booklet) Monticello, New York: Synfleur Scientific Laboratories, Inc. 1964.

Taub, Harold Jaediker. *Waldorf-in-the-Catskills, the Grossinger Legend.* New York: Sterling Publishing Co., Inc., 1952.

Terwilliger, Katharine T. *Before Today's Headlines* (All articles by the Town of Wawarsing historian appear in the *Ellenville Journal.)* January 23, 1969.

———. Part i "Where the Canal Went Through Ellenville." March 6, 1969.

———. Part ii "Where the Canal Went Through Ellenville." March 13, 1969.

———. Part iii "Where the Canal Went Through Ellenville." March 20, 1969.

———. Part iv "Where the Canal Went Through Ellenville." March 27, 1969.

Tyler, Alsup Vail, *Damascus Manor, An Early History of the Upper Delaware Valley.* Narrowsburg, New York: The Delaware Valley News, 1936.

Summer *Vacation Guide,* Season of 1908, *New York American.*

VanZandt, Roland. *The Catskill Mountain House, the birth, glory, and death of the great Hudson Valley hotel which symbolized the American Romantic Era.* New Brunswick, New Jersey: Rutgers University Press, 1966.

Wakefield, Manville B. *Coal Boats To Tidewater, The Story of the Delaware and Hudson Canal.* So. Fallsburg, New York: Steingart Associates, 1965.

———. *The Reformed Church Presents Grandfather's Woodbourne 11,* (pamphlet), Brief history of Woodbourne, privately printed, March 7, 1949.

———. *Illustrated Wayne County, 1900* Honesdale, Pennsylvania: Benjamin Franklin Haines, Publisher, 1900.

Wood, Leslie C. *Holt T'Other Way,* Monticello, New York: (privately printed), 1952.

Wood, Leslie C. *Rafting on the Delaware River,* Livingston Manor, New York: Livingston Manor Times Publishing Co. [193-?]

Wright, Monroe H. *Along the Neversink in the Seventies, No. 1* (pamphlet) Liberty, New York: Liberty *Register* [reprint], March 2, 1933.

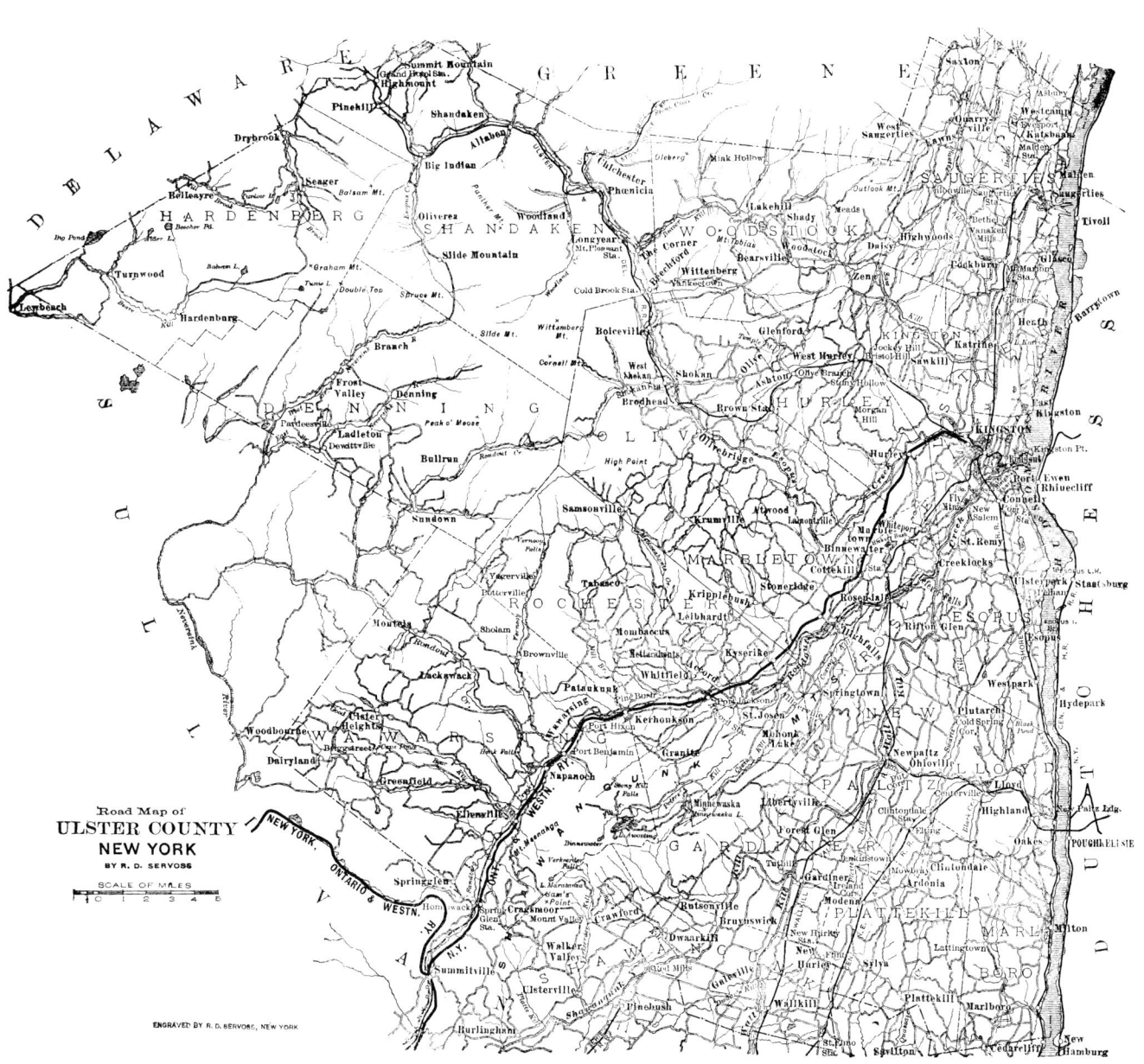

Ulster County

Index

— A —

Acidalia, 353, 355*
Acid industry, 355
Adams, George, 80
Adgate, George H. Jr., 78
"Adirondack," 320*
Ahrenholz, Gus, 382*
Albert House, 133
Aldrich, M., 222*
Allen, John, 82, 84
Allen, Walter, 365
Alligerville, 65
Alpine House, 289
Ambassador Hotel, 144, 145*, 190
"American Road", 1
Anapel, Adam, 154*
Anderman, Aaron, 85
Anderson, J.C., 55
Andover Iron Co., 156
Angel, Carrie Flagler, 140
Anti-semitism, 29, 81, 82
Armstrong, Charles, 353
Armstrong Hotel, 148*
Armstrong, Josephine 304, 305*
Attorney, C.W., 105
Atwell, Eli, 82, 84
Auto bus line, 39

— B —

Baldwin House, 331
Banks Hotel, 343
Banks, Oley, 47
Barnum, Charles, 55
Barryville, 109
Bassett, Henry W., 335
Beaverkill, 319-323
Beaverkill House, 338* 340*
Beaverkill State Campsite, 323
Beaver Lake Lodge, 331
Beauty Maple House, 135*
Becks Department Store, 274
Beck Hotel, 269
Beiling, George, 272
Bellinger, Charles, 39
Belmore Hotel, 134*
Bennett Hotel, 43, 42*
Bennett, Oscar O., 88, 374
Berkowitz, Charles, 204*
Berlinger, N.S., 39
Bethel, 109, 277
Billings Hotel, 121*
Billings, Judson, 69
Biltmore Hotel, 93*
Black Appel Inn, 189*
Bloom Brothers, 144
Bloomingburg, 29, 32, 42, 51, 60, 82, 167
    Coaching Day, 40*
    Tunnel (Highview), 44*
Blizzards,
    1893, 310
    1899, 313
    1914, 312*, 316
Blondin, Wilfred, 156
Blue Mountain, 1
Blue Mountain House, 144
Bluestone, 2, 355*
Boardinghouse Keepers' Assoc., 55
Board of Trade, White Lake, 135
Bonnell, Grover C., 238
Boyce, Charles, 88
Breezy Hill Hotel, 301
Brickman House, 104*
Bridgeville, 3, 60
Brock, Bill, 90, 93, 170
Brookdale Chemical Co., 353

*Indicates photo reference

Brophy's Mad House, 161, 165*
Brophy's Mountain View Farm, 165*
Brophy, Mrs. M., 161
Browns Hotel, 189*
Browns Pond, 170
Brown, George R., 234
Brown, Joe E., 287
Bryers, G.E., 157*
Buckley Acid Factory, 356*
Buckley Hotel, 223* 230
Bullis, Reilly, 48
Bullock Diner, 187*
Bunger's Spring Lake Farm, 195*
Bunner, A.F., 282
Burless, George, 352*
Burnham, Emphaim Lyon, 128
Burnside Hotel, 24
Burnt Hill, 156
Business Men's Assoc.,
    Liberty, 61
    Monticello, 61
Butler Hotel, 59
Butternut Grove House, 157, 345

— C —

Cadosia, 367
Cadosia Acid Factory, 355
Cadosia trestle, 315*
Callicoon, 6, 39
Callicoon Center, 190
Callicoon Depot, 105
Campbell Hall, 27
Campbell Inn, 340*
Capitol Coach Lines, 36*, 42
Capitol Hotel, 188*
Carillot, Maurice, 187
Carley House, 99*
Carley, R.G., 100
Carlisle, Fred, 127
Carpenter, D.G., 35, 82
Carpenter, George H., 249
Carmody, Attorney General, 82
Case, F.B., 48
Cathcart, Joe, 102
Centennial Arch, 233*
Centerville House, 86*, 91*
Central House, 362*
Century Hotel, 13*
"Chenango", 318*
Chestnut Woods, 1
Chiloway, 353
Civil Rights Law, 82
Clarendon Inn, 59
Clark, Edward, 318*
Clark, John T., 193
Clark's Waldorf House, 160*
Clay Hotel, 331
Cleary, Congressman William E., 67
Clements, John, 193
Clements House, 230*
Clements Lake Farmhouse, 193-199, 196*
Close, George, 318*
Coal Trust, 64
Cochecton, 1, 3, 9
Cocheton and Great Bend Turnpike, 3
Cochran Boarding House, 335
Colcord, Samuel, 105, 113
Collins, D.F., 43
Columbia House, 166*
Columbo, Russ, 287
Commodore Hotel, 289
Concord Hotel, 115*, 116
Conductor's Clambake, 328
Conklin, Edmond H., 80
Conkling, Art, 318*

Connecticut Company, 1, 2
Consolidations, 374
Consumptives, 241-242
Continental Trust Co., 105
Cooks Falls, 345, 355
Cooks Falls Suspension Bridge, 348*
Copper ore, 1
Corin, Marcus, 43
Cornell Steamboat Co., 65
Cotter, Frank, 246
Couch, Chester, 103
Covered bridges,
    Bridgeville, 7*
    Cochecton, 5*
    Cooks Falls, 348*
    Neversink, 299*
Coykendall people, 64, 65
Cragsmoor, 67
Craig-e-clare, 331
Craig, W.P., 246
"Crawford", 258*
Crawford House, 157
Crawford, Leander, 29
Criterion, 289
Cross, Benjamin, 47, 48
Cross, Ora H., 157
Crystal Spring House, 289
Cuddeback, Abraham, 13*
"Curio", 151*
Curley's Hotel, 121*
Currey, Andrew B., 154*
Currey, Gabriel F., 154*
Cushetunk Settlement, 1

— D —

"Dago Flyer", 66
Davis, Charles, 78
Davis, Walt, 374
DeBear, Harry J., 61
DeBruce, 190, 331
DeBruce Hatchery, 320
DeHoyes, Luis, 128
Delaney, John J., 67
Delaware and Eastern Railroad, 357
Delaware and Hudson Canal, 5, 7*, 50*, 53, 64, 65
Delaware and Northern Railroad, 357
Delaware Aqueduct, 6
Delaware Company, 1
Delaware Company Charter, 1
Delaware Hotel, 358*
Delaware House, 9*
Delaware River, 2, 3, 6
Delaware River Bridge, 369*, 374
Delaware Valley, 1, 2
Delaware Valley and Kingston Railroad Co., 64
Delaware Water Gap, 1
Delhi, 39
Denman, Michael, 55
Denman, Smith, 365
Denman, W.V., 298
Dennien and Murphy, 55
Dennistons, 24
Denniston, Charles, 103
Depew, Myron D., 149*
Depression, 304
Dick, Mrs. L., 27
Dickson, Thomas, 371*
Dierfelter, Ward, 157
Dieselization, 381*
Dieter, D.W., 226
Dill, Charles, 122*
Dittmar, Valentine, 9
Diver, DeForest, 18*, 21*
Divine Corners, 179
Dix, Gov. John A., 60

Dodge, Augustus, 353
Dohrmann, John, 231*
Donovan, Mahlon, 152*
Dorrance House, 53, 55
Dorrance House, 55*
Double tracking, 313, 314*, 315*, 317
Dougherty, Les, 327*
Doughty, Oscar, 156
Downing, A.J., 156*
Draper, C.A., 76
Dress Code, 135
Driving Park Assoc., 133
Drucker, Jack, 191*
DuBois General Store, 333*
Dunham, John, 69
DuNord Hotel, 230, 231*
Durland's Livery, 81
Dutcher Family, 324

— E —

Eagle Hotel, 269, 270*, 271*
Earlington Hotel, 306*
East Branch, 357
Echo Cottage, 153
Echo Lake, 101*, 170
Echo Lake Farm House, 165
Edd Ost's Hotel, 103
Edgemere House, 296*
Edgewood, 330*
Eisenberg, Frank, 207
Eisenstein, Izzy, 187
Eldred, 109
Ellenville, 29, 39, 63, 64, 66-67
Ellenville and Kingston Railroad, 65-67
Elk Brook, 355*
Elmore House, 165, 167*
Elmore, Williard, 165
Elmore, W. Ray, 165
Elm Shade, 144
Empire Hotel Corp., 82
Engelmann, Joseph, 133
Erie Hotel, 8*
Erie Railroad, 8*, 9*
Esopus, 1
Esther Manor, 135*
Eureka, 156
Evans, Bill, 60
Evans Hotel, 183, 186*
Evans Store, 43
Everard House, 8*, 9*
Exchange Hotel, 121*, 131
Excursion trains, 329-330

— F —

Fahrenz, Peter, 9
Fairs, 133
Fallsburgh, 6, 90
Fallsburgh Lake, 170
Fallsburgh Lumber, Feed and Coal Co., 144
Fallsburgh Station, 99
Fallsburgh and Monticello Electric Railroad Co., 105, 108*
Faubel House, 339*
Feldman's Hotel, 28*, 34*
Ferncliff, 230
Fern Cliff House, 209*, 232*
Ferndale, 72, 82
Ferndale Trestle, 192*, 207-208, 209*, 211
Ferndale Villa, 193, 199, 207
Fern Hotel, 274*
Fernwood, 353
Field and Hanson, 251

411

Finch, Ray, 352*
Finch's Restaurant, 154*
Finnegan's General Store, 362*
Fires,
  Bloomingburg, 40*, 42
  Callicoon, 8*
  Cohen, Max, Boarding House, 172
  Fishs Eddy, 362*
  High Grove House, 172
  Hotel fires, 172-175
  Hurleyville, 172
  Jeffersonville, 269-272
  Leona House, 172
  Liberty, 249-254, 252-253*
  Liberty House Fire, 239, 239
  Loomis, 243, 244
  Monticello, 131
  National Hotel, 172
  New Liberty House, 237*
  Parksville, 310
  Republican Watchman, 128
  Roscoe, 339*, 335-343
  Shindler's Prairie House, 175
  White Sulphur Springs, 267
Fire Prevention Week, 89
Fire regulations, 177
Fischer Hotel, 151*
Fishing, 320*
Fish, Charles, 382*
Fish, Max, 204*
Fish's Eddy, 361
Fish's Eddy House, 362*
Flagler, 141*, 142*, 145*
Flagler Hotel, 101, 140-144
Flagler, Nicholas, 140
Flagstone, 2, 4*
Fleisher, Asias, 140
Floods,
  Callicoon, 14*
  Cochecton, 12*
  Grahamsville, 157-159
  Livingston Manor, 325*
Flurer, Emma, 85
Flurer, Dr. William F., 74*, 79*, 84*, 85
Forest City and State Line Railroad, 367
Forestine, 109
Forsgate, Charles, 75
Fouquet, Lewis D., 215
Fox, John, 49
Francisco, V.A., 345
Freer, George, 326*
Freer's Neversink Orchestra, 298
French and Indian War, 1
Fullers Boardinghouse, 157*
Fuller, Bruce W., 157
Fulton Hotel, 284*
Furst Hotel, 144, 144*

— G —

Gadwood, William, 170
Galbraith, John, 150
Gardner, Mrs. Augustus P., 229
Garner, George W., 128
Garrick, Theatre Co., 251
Gaudinier, Mrs. E., 29
Gelberg, Louis, 304, 305*
Gerow, Ben, 42, 190
Gerow, Joshua, 199
Gerson, John, 80
Gilbert, Bradford Lee, 215, 218*, 342*
Gilbert, George, 80
Gillett, Herman, 80
"Glass House," 256*
Glass Hotel, 143*, 144, 145*
Glen Wild, 80

Glenwood, 53, 54*
Gluck's Hillside Hotel, 112*
Godfrey, Charles, 32
Godfrey House, 32
Goff's Mountain View House, 289
Gold, Ben, 80
Gold, Jacob, 80
Goldstein, Barney, 81
Goldstein, Jake, 81
Goldstein, Nathan, 81
Goldstein, Phillip, 135*
Gonsalus, Emanuel, 1
Goodman, Simon, 330*
Gordon, "Waxey," 191
Goubelman Building, 272
Grade Crossing Act of 1926
Graeff and Gardner, 259
Grahamsville, 1, 97, 99
Grahamsville House, 154*
Grand Hotel, 301
Grand Trunk Railroad, 109
Grand View Heights, 195*
Grand View Hotel, 172
Greco, Philip, 43
Gridley, Inez G., 154*
Gregory, Charles R., 167
Green Building, 250*
Greenfield, 67
Greenfield House, 81
Green's Clothing Store, 254
Greer, George L., 167
Grey's Casino, 276*
Griffin, Morton C., 39
Grooville, 331
Grossinger, Selig and Malke, 193
Grossinger's, 202
Grove Hotel, 282
Guildersleeve House, 222*
Guimond, L.F., 133
"Guinea Express," 66
Gumaer House, 57*, 59
Gumaer, Samuel, 57*
Guntlow, August, 150*

— H —

Haas, Philip, 60
Hack, C.L., 172
"Hairpull," 387*
Halcyon House, 289, 291*
Half Holiday Mountain Express, 213
Halley, John, 132*
Hall House, 223*
Hall, Joseph, 154*
Hallock and Angle, 61
Halran House, 131
Hamilton, Stephan, 132*
Hammond, Stoddard, 353
Hancock, 39, 367
Hancock and Pennsylvania Railroad, 367
Hancock House, 367
Hanfield and Rutherford, 107
Hankins, 2
Hanlon, Joe, 102
Hanoffee's Garage, 262*
Hanoffee, Martin, 267
Harden House, 101
Harding, Fred, 53
Harding House, 50*, 53
Hart, 368
Hart, Moss, 144, 145*
Hartman, Don, 144
Hartwood, 119
Hartwood Depot, 122*
Hasbrouck, 147
Hasbrouck Building, 251
Hasbrouck, Gus, 147

Hatch's Feed Store, 103
Hawk Mountain, 365, 366*
Hawk Mountain Control Tower, 365*
Hawk Mountain Tunnel, 364*, 366*
Hawley, Simon, 48
Hayden, Charles O., 222*
Hector, Solomon, 82
Heifech Hardware, 267
"Hell Hole," 9
Herlihy, Dan, 66
Herman, Henry, 69
Herron Cottage, 298*
High View, 29*, 30, 35*, 44*, 52, 79, 83
High View Tunnel, 9, 15, 45, 389*
Hill Crest Farm, 195*
Hillig Castle, 256*
Hillig-Hoiriis Flight, 256*
Hillside Greenhouse Co., 209*
Hindley, George, saloon, 121*
Hirsh, Lewis, 207*
Hirst, Bob, 374
Hoffman House, 133, 282
Hoffman's Mountain View House, 101*
Holcomb Factory, 355
Holder, Joseph, 305*
Hollenback, Mayor Edward, 137
Holmes and Martin, 272
Holmes, Wright, 147
Hommel, Charles, 147
Hope, Edward, 174*
Hornbeck Farm House, 173*
Hornbeck, Grover, 159*
Horseshoe Lake Farm, 289
Horton, 353
Horton's Switch Wreck, 349
Hotelmen's Protective Assoc. of Monticello, 151
"Hotel Row," 144
Houlihan, Thomas H., 238
Houser, William, 72
Howath, Lorraine, 102
Howes, Ben, 80
Huckleberry Train, 63
Huguenot, 125
Hugenots, 1
Hurleyville Creamery, 168*
Hurleyville Sentinel, 81

— I —

Ice industry, 4*, 170
Ideal House, 111
Idlewile, 78
Ihlefeldt, Gus, 373*
Irvington, 144

— J —

Jackson, Seth, 68
Jackson & Co., J.M., 65, 66
Jacobs, Merle, 373*
Jannuzz, Michael, 108
Jeffersonian Dinner (1921), 142
Jeffersonville, 2, 39, 89, 105
Jeffersonville Brewery, 272*
Jeffersonville Coronet Band, 273*
Jeffersonville House, 268*, 269, 272*
Jeffersonville and Monticello Turnpike, 6
Jeffersonville Transportation Co., 39
Johnston, R.H., 61
Jones Hotel, 357
Junction House, 368*

— K —

Kantor's Pharmacy, 207*, 211
Kaplowitz, Morris, 135*
Katrina Falls, 205
Katzmer, M., 207*
Kauneonga Lake, 191
Kay, Danny, 331*
Kemble, Dr. Urban T., 159
Kenmore, The, 285*
Kenny Brothers, 2
Kenoza Lake Hotel, 274*, 275*
Kensington, The, 284*
Kent's Barber Shop, 121*
Kent, Charles, 88
Kerhonkson, 67
Keyes, Harry, 4*
Kiamesha Country Club, 114*
Kiamesha Ideal Hotel, 115*, 117
Kiamesha Lake, 112*
Kiamesha Lake Casino, 110*
Kiamesha Mansion, 112*
Kilcoin Hotel, 289
Killian's Tranfer, 259
Kilman, Louis, 187
King Brothers, 353
King Eugene F., 355*
Kingston, 1, 63, 65, 66, 69
Kinne, D.B., 282
Kinne, LaRue, 122*
Kinne, W.C., 282
Kirk, John, 45
Klein's Hillside, 301
Knapp's Columbia Farms Hotel, 165
Knapp, Maxwell, 177
Knickerbocker Ice Co., 170
Knife Factory (Grahamsville) 157*
Knoll, The, 149*
Kortright, B.D., 157
Kraach, Charles, 9
Kraach's Hotel, 9
Kraach's Pavillion, 10*
Kuchalane, 82, 100
Kuhler, Otto, 377
Kutsher Country Club, 134*

— L —

Labach Farm House, 173*
Lackawack, 67, 156
Lackawack House, 67, 68, 71*
Lackawaxen, 64
Laidlaw, L.G., 170
Lake House, 282
Lake Huntington, 8*, 9, 10*
Lake Huntington Pond Hotel, 9
Lake Ophelia, 193, 200*, 201
Lakeside Hotel, 42*
Lakeside House, 278
Lakeside Inn, 144, 204*
Lake View Cottage 282
Lake Wood Farm, 335
Lancashire, Frederick William, 229*
Lapidus, Morris, 117
Laurels, The, 134*
Laurel House, 282
Lawrence Hotel, 183, 188*
Lawrence House, 262*, 263*
Lechtman, Fannie and Julius, 331
Lechtig Building, 272
LeFever, Dan, 154*
Lefever's Hotel, 156
Lehigh and Eastern Railroad, 367

412

Lenape Hotel, 223*
Lennon House, 220*, 239
Leona Hotel, 263*, 267
LeRoy, Gardner, 42
LeRoy, Garrett, 187
LeRoy House, 185*, 187
LeRoy Hotel, 100*, 190*
LeRoy, N.M., 180
Leslie, Frank, 133
Levine, Meyer, 85
Levitt, 144
Levitt Hotel, 143*
Lew Beach, 331
Lewis' Grove, 281*
"Liberty" 256*
Liberty, 1, 6, 39
   Baptist Church, 220*, 251
   Board of Trustees, 39
   Brass Coronet Band, 63, 224*
   Coaching Day Parade, 197, 231*
   Depot, 215
   Driving Park Assoc., 206*, 207
   Music Hall, 249
   Town Board, 42
   Trestle, 257*, 316, 381*, 387*
Liberty and Jeffersonville Trolley, 245
Liberty and Jeffersonville Electric Railroad Co., 246
Liberty and White Lake Turnpike, 109, 277
Liberty Falls (Ferndale), 76, 193
Liberty Highway, 58*, 61, 388*
Liberty Highway Assoc., 61
Liberty House, 212*, 230, 234, 237
Liberty House (Old), 235*
Liberty Reading Room, 228
Liberty Register, 81, 82
Linden Manor, 245*
Lindhardt, Frank, 306*
Little Beaverkill, 300*
Little Britian, 24
Littlejohn, John, 9
"Little Worlds Fair," 152*, 154*, 155*, 156
Livingston, Dr. Edward, 319
Livingston Manor, 6, 39, 90
Livingston Manor Depot, 322*
Livingston Manor Lumber Co., 220*
Loch Sheldrake, 81, 161
Loch Sheldrake House, 187*
Lohman, Herman C., 238
Lockwood, J.C., 27
Long Eddy, 2
Loomis, Dr. Alfred, 240
Loomis Sanitarium, 228, 242-244
Loomis Sanitarium Administration Building, 241*
"Lord High Admiral" [See Daniel Skinner] 3
Lord's Pond, 5
Lorriliard, Pierre, 229*
Low, Henry, 133*
Low, Judge Henry R., 16
Lupton, Merton, 372*
Luzerne Chemical Co., 354*
Luzon Depot, 164*
Luzon and Lock Sheldrake Hotelmen's Assoc., 179
Lyceum, 133
Lyon, Ephraim, 131*

     — M —

Maccabee Hall, 362*
Mackhackemeck, 2
Machson, Gussie, 132*
Madison, H., 102
Mahoney, J.J., 102
Mamakating, 1, 51, 60
Mamakating Depot, 53*
Mamakating Valley, 53, 63
Mance Pharmacy, 254
Manion, John, 238
Manny, Anthony, 2
Manny and Ross, 2
Manor House, 325*
Mansion House, 131, 132*, 205, 228, 230*, 273*, 275, 282, 282*
Maples, The, 357
Mapledoram, Blake, 109
Maple Grove, 185*
Maple Grove Casino, 185*
Maple Grove House and Casino, 180
Maple Grove House, 205, 294*, 295
Maple Lawn Villa, 53
Marion's Cottage, 187
Martin's Pines, 357
"Mary Powell", 329-330
Mass, George B, 10*
Masten Lake, 51, 54*
Matzinger, J.L., 47, 101
Mayfield Yard, 374, 375*
McCormack House, 101*
McCormack, Tom, 238
McCune, Frank, 53, 55*
McEwan, A.T., 29
McKee's Pond, 5
McMullen, Fred J., 95
McNickle, Robert, 128
Meadow Brook, 24
Mead's, 319
Mecca, 222*, 228
Meinhold's Waldorf House, 173*
Meola and Meola, 39
Merriman Dam, 67
Merritt Construction Company, 60
Merritt House, 150*
Merwin's, 319
Messiter, Alfred, 234
Messiter House, 222*
Messiter, U.S., 221, 238
Metro-Goldwyn Mayer, 144
Michaels, Mortimer, 85
Middletown, 27, 39, 72, 375*
Midland Transit Corp. 39
Milk Dealers (1905), 169*
Milk Industry, 165-169
Miller, Thomas B., 69
Milliken Building, 133
Mingle, R.B., 246
Mintz, Joe, 101
Mitchell, Lamont, 125*
Mitchell's Station, 100
Mohawk Stages, 36*
Mongaup Falls, 205
Mongaup Farm House, 195*
Monika Lodge, 104*
Monitor, 228, 250*
Monster Mardi Gras, 289
Montela, 67, 156
Monte-Valle House, 78, 81*
Monticello, 39, 63, 68, 97
Monticello and Fallsburgh Turnpike, 97, 105
Monticello and Kiamesha Stage, 122*
Monticello and Middletown Traction Co., 109
Monticello and Middletown Railroad, 108*
Monticello Academy, 129*
Monticello Amusement Park, 135, 136*
Monticello, Fallsburgh and White Lake Trolley, 107
Monticello House, 127, 130, 131
Monticello Inn, 127, 131, 132*
Moodna Trestle, 24
Morgan, J. Pierpont, 243
Morgenstern, Phillip, 140
Morningside Hotel, 176*
Moroney, J.J., 376*, 382*
Morrison, J.V., 15
Morsston, 6, 319
Morsston House, 327*
Morton, Charles, 230*
Mott, Mayor Emil, 135
Moulin Rouge Night Club, 144
Mountaineer, 49*, 377, 378*, 379*, 380*
Mountain Bus Co., 39, 133
Mountaindale, 78
Mountaindale Hotel, 78
Mountain Lake Hotel, 345, 351*
Mountain Spring, 123*
Mountain Spring House, 150*
Mountain Top House, 149*
Mountain View, Summerhome of J.J. Trowbridge, 111
Mountain View Farm House, 161
Mount Hope and Lamberland Turnpike, 6, 13*
Mount Meenahga, 69*, 70*
Mount Pleasant House, 29, 298, 298*, 299
Mullen, Martin, 170
Mulligan, James, 45
Munson, Dr. J.A., 149
Murder Incorporated, 187
Murderer's Creek, 24
Murdocks Boardinghouse, 319
Murphy, G.W., 238
Murray, Peter, 125
Music Hall, 250*

     — N —

Napanoch, 67
Narrowsburg Hotel, 13*
Nemerson, Hotel, 106*
Nevele Hotel, 72*
Neversink, 29, 97
Neversink and Liberty Turnpike Co., 295
Neversink Driving Park, 298
Neversink Falls, 99, 109
Neversink Hotel, 296*
Neversink River, 3, 139, 295
Neversink River Trestle, 95*
Neversink Valley Railroad, 153, 295
Neversink Reservoir, 299
New Brighton, 301
Newburgh, 24
Newburgh-Cochecton Turnpike, 2, 3, 5, 53, 59, 60
New Concord, 115*
New Empire, 284*
Newkirk, Chauncey, 57*
Newkirk, Mrs. Harry, 72*
New Liberty House, 235*, 236*
New Prospect House, 80*
Newton, Jean, 135, 137
New York and Erie Railroad, 6
New York City, 2
New York City Board of Water Supply, 67
New York Maxwell Motors, 61
New York State Conservation Dept., 87
New York Railway, 93
New York 143rd Volunteer Infantry Regiment Reunion, 238
Nichol's Boardinghouse, 193
Nichol's Farm, 193
North White Lake, 191
Norton's Casino, 289, 293*
Norwich, 95
Nuelle, J.H., 102, 121
Nutshell Hotel, 10*

     — O —

Oakland Valley, 119
Olcott House, 56*, 59
Olcott, George H., 59
Old Falls, 99
Old Mine Road, 1, 2, 53, 59
O'Neill, Andy, 75
O'Neill, Hotel, 172, 174*
Ontario, Carbondale and Scranton Railroad, 367
Orange and East Branch Turnpike, 139
Orange County, 42
Orchard Grove House, 275
Orrs Mills, 24
Orrs Mills Trestle, 20*
Osborne, Henry, 78
Overlook, 183
Overlook Hotel, 32
Overlook House, 186*
Overlook Place, 32*

     — P —

Pahquarry-on-the-Delaware, 1
Palatine Hotel, 124*, 125
Palen, Rufus, 139
Palen Tannery, 138*, 139, 140
Palm, Hotel, 127, 130*, 133
Paramount Hotel, 301
Paramount Pictures, 144
Park House, 82
Parkston, 331
Parksville, 6
Parmalee, William S., 238
"Parthenia", 226
Peakville, 356*
Pelton, Sheriff Geo., 111
Perlwyn Lodge, 307
Philadelphia, 2
Phillipsport, 67
Pierce, C.W., 157
Pierce, J.O., 146*
Pike Pond, 274*
Pike Pond Hotel, 275*
Pines, The, 359*
Pines Hotel, 104*
Pinney House, 193, 201, 202
Pleasant Lake, 105, 111
Pollack's Fallsburg Country Club, 142*, 144
Pond Eddy, 2
Pony Express Bus Line, 89
Porter, Granville, 275
Porter, Sylvester E., 154*, 157
Porter, Theron, 154*
Porter, William M. (Mrs.), 153
Port Jervis, 2, 51, 68, 97
Port Jervis, Monticello, and New York Railroad, 119
Potts, William, 365
Powell, Val, 66
Poyntelle, 374
Prairie House, 176*
President Hotel, 293*
Preston Park, 374*
Prohibition, 187
Prospect House, 277, 279*, 282
Prospect Inn, 301
Public Service Comm., 39, 102
Pullman, George, 85
Purple Swan Coach, 37*

413

– Q –

Quinlan, James, 9

– R –

Rafting, 2*, 3*, 8*, 13*
Raleigh Hotel, 107*
Rampe, Norman, 239
Ramsey House, 282
Ratner House, 107*
Red Apple Rest., 189*
Red Hill, 75, 76*, 78, 85*
Regatta Day
    (1898), 276*
    (1913), 114
Republican Watchman, 121*
Revonah Hill, 216*
Revonah Mountain House, 232*
Rexford, Melvin A., 183
Reynolds, George, 156, 156*
Reynolds, John, 156
Rialto Theater, 133
Richardson, Henry Hobson, 215
Righter, Irving, 107
Riley, Andrew, 76
Riverside Hotel, 15*
Riverside House, 295, 296*
Riverview, 144
Robertsonville, 261
Robinson, Charles, 376*, 382*
Rock Hill, 53, 54*
Rockland House, 342*
Rock Spring Lodge, 289
Rock Tavern, 24
Rockwell Construction Co., 60
Rockwell, George W., 238
Rockwell, Hotel, 122*, 126, 127,* 131, 137*
Roebling Suspension Bridge, 7*
Rogers, Joseph, 39
Romero, Cesaer, 229*
Rondout Creek, 1, 159*
Rondout Reservoir, 159
Rondout Valley, 2
Rondout Valley Railroad Co., 63
Roosa Building, 251
Roosa, M.J., 183
Roosa Hotel, 183
Roosa House, 186*
Roosevelt, Franklin D., 142
Roscoe, 9
Roscoe Depot, 338*
Rose, Eliphalet S., 4*
Rosen, Hotel, 74*, 85*
Roth, M., 101
Route 4 – 60
Route 17 – 60
Roxy Hotel, 189*
Royal House, 80*
Royce, Ben, 72
Royce, Solomon, 132*
Russell Brook, 353*
Russell House, 99*
Ryan's Hotel, 100*, 103

– S –

Sage, Walter, 187, 191*
Sam's Point, 67
Sandburg, 78, 82
Sand's Creek Trestle, 369*, 374
Savoy Hotel, 117*
Saxony Hotel, 143*, 144, 145*
Scaley, Casey, 68
Scanlon, William, 95
Schaefer, John, 220*
Schary, Dore, 144
Schenk's Paramount Hotel, 106*

Schrader, Fred, 227*
"Scoopers", 333
"Scoot", 69
Scott, Warren L., 221
Scranton and Forest City Railroad, 367
Seaside Place, 53
Seaside, Supply Store, 50*
Seeholzer, William, 27
Seeholzer's Restaurant, 25*
Seigel, Henry W., 293
Seiken House, 190
Seligman, Joseph, 29
Seresky, Herman, 133
Shady Side Grove, 55
Shandelee, 331
Sharp Electric Equipment Co., 221
Sha-wan-ga Lodge, 35, 35*, 82
Shawangunk Mountains, 9, 35
Shawangunk Mountain House, 32
Shawangunk Tunnel, see High-/View
Sheffer, Ronnie and Co., 246
Sherman House, 345
Sherwood, Hotel, 325*
Sherwood Island Park, 328, 329*
Sherwood Mill, 333
Sherwood Stables, 251
Sheils, John, 67
Sheils, James, 68
Sheils, Tom, 68
Shindler Prairie House, 35
Shupp's Lock Sheldrake House, 180*
Six Lake House, 53
Skinner, Daniel, 2
Skinner, Joseph, 1
Sky Farm, 297*
Skywinsky, Rosa, 80
Smith, Alfred, 67
Smith, Anson and Martha, 152*
Smith Farm, 82
Smith Hill Cut, 170
Smith , Howard, 72
Smith, M.A., 105
Smith, Moe, 187
Smith, "Peck", 152*
Smith, S.N., 154*
Snow Plowing, 254, 259
Somers, W.H., 27
Sprague, Sam, 87, 88
Spring Brook, 353
Spring Brook House, 298
Spring Glen, 67
Spring Street Tannery, 131*
Standard Oil Company Pipeline, 12*
Stanton, Charles, 99, 269, 278
Starlight, 374
State Highway Comm., 60
State Prison, 151
State Railroad Commissioners, 63, 64
Steigerts, Sam, 207*
Steiglitz, Morris, 187, 190
Steingartz, Isaac, 144
Steinman, Michael, 330*
Stephens, Bennett & Co., 9
Stevens Concert Co., 201
Stevensville, 39, 105, 277
Stevensville Lake Hotel, 289
St. Josephs, 119
Stoessel, Edward A., 102
Stone Ridge, 66
Strong, Austin, 147
Strong, Starr and Co., 128
Stucco Construction, 142
"Sugar Wreck", 327*

Sullivan County Agricultural Society, 133
Sullivan County Chamber of Commerce, 61
Sullivan County Club, 51, 54*
Sullivan County Coaching Day Assoc., 228, 231*
Sullivan County Community College, 190*
Sullivan County Express, 90
Sullivan County Fair, 133
Sullivan County Historical Society, 3
Sullivan County Hotelmen's Assoc., 55
Sullivan County Limited, 224
"Summer Homes", 17*, 181*-183*
Summit Level, 5
Summitville, 6, 51, 63, 65, 68, 69, 72, 75, 78
Sunny Glade Boarding House, 282
Sussman, I., 80
Swamp Mill Pond, 4*
Swan, Alden S., 289
Swan Lake, 187
Swan Lake Board of Trade, 151
Swan Lake Hotel, 289, 292*, 293
Swan Lake Mills, 289
Swannanoa, 218, 227*, 228
Swan's Casino, 289
Sweeney, Alfred L., 244
Sycamore House, 157
Sylvan Grove House, 286*
Sylvan View House, 345
Synfleur Scientific Laboratories, 128
Syreen House (Pleasant Valley Farm), 222*

– T –

Takamine, Dr. J., 122*
Tally-Ho Stageline, 99, 197, 277
Tammany Hall, 67
Tanning, 56, 129, 361
Tanneries
    Palen, 138, 139, 140
    Spring Street, 141*
    Woodbourne, 147
Temperance Hotel, 12*
Tennanah Lake House, 341*
Terwilliger, Elias, 43
Terwilliger House, 43, 70*
Thomas, Moses, 1
Thompson, Howard P., 118*
Thompson, L.G., 100
Thompsonville, 97, 99
Tidewater, 64
Torre, Joseph, 72
Transportation Corporation Law-Section 26, 39
Transville, 301
Travis, Charles W., 161
Treyz Brothers, 355
Treyz Company Store, 325*
Treyz, G.I., 353*, 354*
Treyz, George, General Store, 351*
Tripp, Marvin, 45
Tripps, 319
Trojan Lake Lodge, 330*
Trout Brook, 356*
Trout Fishing, 319-323
Tunnel Hill, 95*
Tusten Depot, 6
Tuttle, Sidney, 275
Tuxedo Park, 51
Tyler, U.S., 361

– U –

Ulster-Orange Branch Turnpike, 6
Ulster Heights, 67

– V –

Valley Junction, 63
Valquette, J.D. 170
Van Barriger, Paul P., 78, 80
Vandermark, Chester, 327*
Van Keuren Store, 296*
Van Orden, John J., 282
Van Steinberg, B., 105
Van Wert House, 282
Vaughn, Elmer "Shorty", 72
Vaux, Calvert, 156*
Victoria, Hotel, 133
Victoria Mansion, 186*, 187
Von Isakovics, Mrs. M. Upshur, 128
Von Unruh Sanitorium Inc., 244

– W –

Wadler, Hotel, 103*
Waldemere, The, 330*
Waldorf, John, 100
Waldorf, Hotel, 165
Wallkill Valley Railroad, 27
Walnut Mountain House, 205, 270*
Warde, Frederick, 287
"Wardesden", 283*
Warner, J.F., 228
Wawanda, Hotel, 218, 220*, 221-226, 225*
Wayside Inn, 13*, 53, 71*
Weaver's, 319
Weber, Edward, 376*
Wedemeyer, A.J.D., 216*, 249
Weiss, Jack, 307
Wells, Melvin, 234
Welworth Hotel, 103*
West, George W., 374
Westbrookville, 125
Westfield Flats, 9
West Shore House, 282, 283*, 287*
Wheat, Major Salmon, 3, 5*
"White Bridge", 259
White Bridge Crossing, 257*, 259*
White Company, 61
White House, 11*
White House Curve, 326*
White Lake, 39
White Lake Railway Co., 278
White Lake "Season", 287
White Lake Spring House, 282
White Lake Stage, 280*, 290*
White Lake Tally-Ho, 278* 280*
White Roe Lodge, 331*
White Sulphur Spring, 267*
White Sulphur Springs, 29, 260* 240
White Sulphur Springs House, 255*, 261, 264*, 265*, 266*
Whiting, Mel, 373*, 374
Whitman, Paul, 287
Williams, W.H.H., 295
Willowemoc, 319-323
Wilson, Andrew, 88
Winarick, Arthur, 115*, 117
Windsor Hotel, 106*
Winokur, Henry, 42
"Winter Homes", 242, 243, 243*

Winterton, 27*, 191
Winterton Depot, 27
Winter, W.W., 27
Wolff, Pete, 341*
Wolf Pond, 5
Wolf, William, 69
Women's Christian Temperance Union, 135
Wood, Howard, 172
Wood, J.F., 336
Woodbourne, 81, 97
Woodbourne House, 101, 147, 148*
Woodcrest Villa. 149*
Woodland Manor, 245*
Woodridge, 88
Woolsey House, 331*
Worden, Joseph H., 161
Wright and Curry, 153
Wright, Daniel, 157
Wurts, Maurice, 5
Wurtsboro, 3, 5, 50*, 51, 53, 55, 60
W.X. Tower, 48*

— Y —

Yankee Lake, 5
Yaugh House Springs, 52*
Ye Clarendon Inn, 57*
Ye Lancashire Inn, 218, 228, 229*, 250*
Yendes Inn, 230*
Ye Olde Inn, 57*
York, Jesse, 88
Young, George, 221
Young, J.C., 221
Young Farm (William), 305*
Young's Gap, 300*, 310-313, 311*, 312*, 313*, 375
Young's Gap Hotel, 301, 305*

Abandoned handball court just south of Woodbourne.

Summitville

At one time the tempo of activity at this vital New York, Ontario and Western Railway junction point prompted the designation "Grand Central." Understandably so, with its transfer and switching activities to the Port Jervis-Monticello line, and the valley line to Ellenville and Kingston, plus its normal mainline service. Here the Kingston branch is occupied by water-taking locomotive 249, while a southbound mainline train unloads headend express.